MW00575492

Drama in the Music of Franz Schubert

Drama in the Music of Franz Schubert

edited by
Joe Davies and James William Sobaskie

THE BOYDELL PRESS

First published 2019
The Boydell Press, Woodbridge

ISBN 978 1 78327 365 2

The Boydell Press is an imprint of Boydell & Brewer Ltd
PO Box 9, Woodbridge, Suffolk IP12 3DF, UK
and of Boydell & Brewer Inc.
668 Mt Hope Avenue, Rochester, NY 14620–2731, USA
website: www.boydellandbrewer.com

A CIP catalogue record for this book is available
from the British Library

The publisher has no responsibility for the continued existence or accuracy of URLs
for external or third-party internet websites referred to in this book, and does not
guarantee that any content on such websites is, or will remain, accurate or appropriate

This publication is printed on acid-free paper

For Susan Wollenberg
with affection, admiration, and gratitude

Contents

List of Figures

List of Tables

List of Contributors

Brian Black is Associate Professor of Musicology at the University of Lethbridge in Alberta, Canada. He earned his Bachelor of Music and PhD from McGill University where he worked with William E. Caplin. He also is an Associate of the Royal College of Music and a Licentiate of the Guildhall School of Music and Drama in London. He has published articles in *Schubert durch die Brille*, *Intersections*, and *Intégral*, has contributed chapters to *Rethinking Schubert* (Oxford, 2016) and *Formal Functions in Perspective: Essays on Musical Form from Haydn to Adorno* (New York, 2015), and has given papers at the annual meetings of the American Musicological Society, the Society for Music Theory, and the Canadian University Music Society.

Lorraine Byrne Bodley is Professor of Musicology at Maynooth University. She has published fourteen books including: *Goethe and Zelter: Musical Dialogues* (Farnham, 2009), *The Unknown Schubert* (Aldershot, 2008), and *Schubert's Goethe Settings* (Aldershot, 2003). Recent publications include *Schubert's Late Music: History, Theory, Style* (Cambridge, 2016), and *Rethinking Schubert* (Oxford, 2016), both co-edited with Julian Horton, and a special Schubert edition of *Nineteenth-Century music Review* co-edited with James Sobaskie. She is currently writing a new biography of Schubert commissioned by Yale University Press. Recent awards include a DMus in Musicology, a higher doctorate on published work from the National University of Ireland (2012); two DAAD Senior Academic Awards (2010 and 2014), and a Gerda-Henkel Foundation Scholarship (2014). In 2015 she was elected President of the Society for Musicology in Ireland (2015–2021) and Member of The Royal Irish Academy. In 2016 she was awarded a personal chair in musicology at Maynooth University.

Joe Davies is College Lecturer in Music at Lady Margaret Hall, University of Oxford. His research interests are in the aesthetics and cultural history of eighteenth- and nineteenth-century music, with particular emphasis on Franz Schubert and women composers. His recently completed DPhil (which was supported by an Arts and Humanities Research Council scholarship) offers a hermeneutic framework for interpreting the expressive worlds of Schubert's late instrumental works, focusing on notions of the gothic, the sublime, and the grotesque. In 2014, under the auspices of the annual Oxford Lieder Festival, he co-organized the international conference 'Schubert as Dramatist' on which this volume is based. He is currently developing a monograph on Schubert and the gothic, and preparing an edited volume of essays focused on the music of Clara Schumann.

Xavier Hascher is Professor of Musicology at the University of Strasbourg. He is the author of a number of publications on Schubert's music, among which are *Schubert: la forme sonate et son évolution* (Bern, 1996) and *Symbole et fantasme dans l'Adagio du Quintette à cordes de Schubert* (Paris, 2005). He has edited *Le style instrumental de Schubert* (Paris, 2007) as well as the journal *Cahiers Franz Schubert* (1992–2000), and also contributed to the volumes *The Cambridge Companion to Schubert* (ed. Christopher Gibbs, Cambridge, 1997), *Schubert-Lexicon* (ed. Ernst Hilmar and Margret Jestremski, Graz, 1997), *Schubert-Jahrbuch 1998* (ed. Dietrich Berke et al., Kassel, 2001), and *Schubert und das Biedermeier* (ed. Michael Kube et al., Kassel, 2002). His most recent publications are chapters for *Schubert's Late Music: History, Theory, Style* (ed. Lorraine Byrne Bodley and Julian Horton, Cambridge, 2016) and *Rethinking Schubert* (ed. Lorraine Byrne Bodley and Julian Horton, Oxford, 2016).

Marjorie Hirsch is Professor of Music and Chair of the Department of Music at Williams College in Williamstown, Massachusetts. Her first book, *Schubert's Dramatic Lieder* (Cambridge, 1993), examines dramatic textual and musical elements in Schubert's solo songs, while her second book, *Romantic Lieder and the Search for Lost Paradise* (Cambridge, 2007), explores manifestations of the archetypal myth of lost paradise in songs by Schubert, Schumann, Brahms, and Wolf. Hirsch's writings appear in *The Journal of Musicology*, *The Journal of Musicological Research*, *The Journal of the American Musicological Society*, *Nineteenth-Century Music Review*, *The Unknown Schubert* (Aldershot, 2008), *Schubert's Late Music: History, Theory and Style* (Cambridge, 2016), and *The Oxford Handbook of Faust in Music* (Oxford, forthcoming).

Anne Hyland is Lecturer in Music Analysis at the University of Manchester and Critical Forum Editor for *Music Analysis*. Her research aims to develop a historicist approach to the analysis of nineteenth-century musical form, and focuses in particular on Schubert's instrumental music. Her work has appeared in *Music Analysis* (2009 – awarded the 25th Anniversary Prize of the journal), *Music Theory Spectrum* (2016), *Rethinking Schubert* (Oxford, 2016), *Schubert's Late Music: History, Theory Style* (Cambridge, 2016), and *The String Quartet: from the Private to the Public Sphere* (Turnhout, 2016). She is the recipient of a British Academy/Leverhulme Trust Research Award for a project investigating an alternative history of the String Quartet in Schubert's Vienna. She is currently writing a monograph on Schubert's String Quartets.

Christine Martin joined the editorial board of the *Neue Schubert-Ausgabe* (*NSA*) in 2006 and has held a teaching appointment at Tübingen University since 2007. Born in Wiesbaden in 1961, she studied musicology, German literature, and Romance languages in Frankfurt am Main, Heidelberg, and Turin, taking her master's degree with a dissertation on parody technique in Handel's *Jephtha* in 1987. After working at the German Historical Institute in Rome (1988), she was a research associate at the central headquarters of the *Répertoire International des Sources Musicales* (RISM) in Frankfurt am Main (1989–98). In 2000 she took her doctorate with a dissertation on Vicente Martín y Soler's opera *Una cosa rara* and its historical impact in Mozart's Vienna. Dr Martin's published work includes critical editions of Schubert's *Fierabras, Operneinlagen, Rosamunde* (prepared with Walther Dürr) and *Claudine von Villa Bella* (prepared with Dieter Martin) for the *NSA*, as well as articles on Schubert in the *Schubert-Jahrbuch* and *Schubert: Perspektiven*.

Clive McClelland is Associate Professor of Music at the University of Leeds, where he delivers teaching in harmony, counterpoint and analysis. He is chorus master of Leeds Baroque, and is Chairman of the Schubert Institute UK. His recent book *Ombra: Supernatural Music in the Eighteenth Century* has become established as the standard text on the subject, with a companion volume *Tempesta: Storm Music in the Eighteenth Century* published in 2017. Other publications include 'Death and the Composer: The Context of Schubert's Supernatural Lieder', in *Schubert the Progressive: History, Performance Practice and Analysis* (ed. Brian Newbould, Aldershot, 2003); 'Shadows of the Evening: New Light on Elgar's "Dark Saying"' for the *Musical Times*; and '*Ombra* and *Tempesta*' in *The Oxford Handbook of Topic Theory*. He has also published on Waxman's *Bride of Frankenstein* score in the *Journal of Film Music* and on Spohr's *Faust* in *The Oxford Handbook of Faust in Music*.

James William Sobaskie is Associate Professor of Music at Mississippi State University and serves as Book Reviews Editor of *Nineteenth-Century Music Review*. With Susan Youens he guest-edited Volume 5/2 (2008) of the journal, a special issue entitled *Schubert Familiar and Unfamiliar: New Perspectives*, and with Lorraine Byrne Bodley, he guest-edited Volume 13/1 (2016), entitled *Schubert Familiar and Unfamiliar: Continuing Conversations*. A member of the Comité Scientifique for *Oeuvres complètes de Gabriel Fauré*, his critical edition of Fauré's last two compositions, the *Trio pour piano, violon et violoncelle*, Op. 120, and the *Quatuor à cordes*, Op. 121, inaugurated the monument in 2010. Dr Sobaskie's publications include essays on the music of Franz Schubert, Fryderyk Chopin, and Gabriel Fauré, as well as the theories of Heinrich Schenker and Arnold Schoenberg. He is currently completing a book entitled *The Music of Gabriel Fauré: Style, Structure and the Art of Allusion*.

Lauri Suurpää is Professor of Music Theory at the Sibelius Academy, University of the Arts Helsinki. His main research interests are in analysis of tonal music. His publications have typically combined Schenkerian analysis with other approaches, such as programmatic aspects, narrativity, form, musico-poetic associations in vocal music, eighteenth-century rhetoric, and Romantic aesthetics. He is currently a member of the editorial boards of four international scholarly journals and the Editorial Committee of the *Jean Sibelius Works*, the critical edition of Sibelius's complete works. His publications include *Death in Winterreise: Musico-Poetic Associations in Schubert's Song Cycle* (Bloomington, 2014), *Music and Drama in Six*

Beethoven Overtures: Interaction between Programmatic Tensions and Tonal Structure (Helsinki, 1997), and numerous journal articles and book chapters. He is currently working on a monograph entitled *Haydn in the Concert Hall and in the Chamber: Public and Private Modes of Musical Discourse in the London Symphonies and Late String Quartets.*

Laura Tunbridge is Professor of Music at the University of Oxford. She gained her PhD from Princeton in 2002 and then lectured at the Universities of Reading and Manchester, before being appointed at Oxford in 2014. She has been a Visiting Fellow at Columbia University in New York and at the Max Planck Institute in Berlin, as well as a recipient of grants from the Arts and Humanities Research Council and the Leverhulme Trust. Her publications include the monographs *Schumann's Late Style* (Cambridge, 2007), *The Song Cycle* (Cambridge, 2011), and *Singing in the Age of Anxiety: Lieder Performances in New York and London between the World Wars* (Chicago, 2018), and articles in *Journal of the American Musicological Society, Representations, 19th-Century Music, 20th-Century Music,* and *Cambridge Opera Journal.* She was the editor of the *Journal of the Royal Musical Association* and co-founder of the Oxford Song Network, and is a Director-at-large of the International Musicological Society.

Susan Wollenberg was until October 2016 Professor of Music at the University of Oxford, and Fellow and Tutor in Music of Lady Margaret Hall (where she is now an Emeritus Fellow), as well as Lecturer at Brasenose College. Among her publications have been contributions on Schubert to a variety of journals and symposia, including *Schubert Studies* (ed. Brian Newbould, Aldershot, 1998), *Schubert durch die Brille* (Journal of the International Schubert Institute, 2002 and 2003), and *Le style instrumental de Schubert: Sources, analyse, évolution* (ed. Xavier Hascher, Paris, 2007). Her monograph *Schubert's Fingerprints: Studies in the Instrumental Works* was published in 2011. She co-edited, with Aisling Kenny, *Women and the Nineteenth-Century Lied* (Farnham, 2015).

Susan Youens, who received her PhD from Harvard University in 1976, is the J. W. Van Gorkom Professor of Music at the University of Notre Dame. She is the author of eight books on German song, including *Schubert, Müller, and Die schöne Müllerin* (Cambridge, 1997), *Hugo Wolf and his Mörike Songs* (Cambridge, 2000), *Schubert's Late Lieder* (Cambridge, 2002), and *Heinrich Heine and the Lied* (Cambridge, 2007), as well as over sixty scholarly articles and chapters. She is the recipient of four fellowships from the National Endowment for the Humanities, as well as additional fellowships from the Guggenheim Foundation, the Institute for Advanced Study at Princeton, and the National Humanities Center, and has lectured widely on the music of Schubert, Hugo Wolf, and other song composers.

Acknowledgements

The inspiration for this anthology arose at the international conference 'Schubert as Dramatist', held at the Faculty of Music, University of Oxford on 24 October 2014, under the auspices of the Oxford Lieder Festival. We offer sincere thanks to the Festival's Artistic Director, Sholto Kynoch, for his support of the conference project, and to the Oxford Faculty of Music for sponsoring the event.

Many of the book's chapters have been developed from papers read on that occasion, while others were solicited to complement them. Together they provide a nuanced view of drama in Schubert's oeuvre. With the warm spirit of collegiality that exists among many Schubertians today, the commissioning process was both straightforward and rewarding. One of the distinguishing features of the volume is its scholarly diversity: our contributors represent no fewer than seven countries and include musicologists, theorists, and analysts. It is a pleasure to renew our thanks to our authors for their cooperation and commitment to the task of bringing to light a hitherto underexplored aspect of Schubert's music. We are especially grateful to Laura Tunbridge for her eloquent response to the results of our collegial endeavour in the volume's Introduction.

It is an honour to thank Michael Middeke and Megan Milan of Boydell & Brewer for their support, patience, and encouragement throughout the duration of the project. We express our kindest sentiments to the external reader, who offered valuable advice regarding the refinement of the book, together with affirmation that our premises were both firm and insightful; and to our copyeditor, Henry Bertram, for his meticulous reading of the manuscript. We are pleased also to acknowledge the following individuals and institutions: Karl Ulz of the Wienbibliothek im Rathaus for his assistance with our enquiries pertaining to the digital reproduction of the manuscript of 'Adelwold und Emma' featured on the volume's front cover, Helmut Selzer of the Wien Museum for his help with obtaining copies of the Schubert portraits, and Katharina Malecki of Bärenreiter Verlag for granting us permission to base many of the book's music examples on scores from the Bärenreiter catalogue. Further thanks are extended to Rohais Landon and Nick Bingham of Boydell & Brewer for their invaluable guidance in bringing the book to completion.

Our dedication of this volume to Susan Wollenberg represents a timely opportunity to celebrate the significant contribution over four decades of an eminent and widely admired Schubertian. In Professor Wollenberg's scholarship we find an influential approach that combines rigorous analytical investigation with an intrinsically poetic manner of illuminating the stylistic and aesthetic qualities of Schubert's music. Yet it is personal kindness and professional generosity that may distinguish her most, as well as explaining why she has become emblematic of the Schubertian community. In dedicating our book to Susan, we offer a collective expression of heartfelt gratitude and admiration.

Joe Davies

In addition to our collegial acknowledgement of Susan Wollenberg's contribution to Schubert studies, I owe a further, entirely personal debt of gratitude. For Susan's selfless intellectual guidance over the years, and for her kind-hearted encouragement in general, I shall be forever grateful. It is thus a privilege to offer this dedication through the lens of friendship.

My co-editor, James Sobaskie, deserves special mention here. His creativity and efficiency, together with his enthusiasm for the dramatic innovations of Schubert's music, have been crucial driving forces in bringing the volume to fruition. I am truly appreciative of the collaborative connection we have established in the service of Schubertian hermeneutics.

Warm thanks are due to Professor Laura Tunbridge for her helpful responses to research enquiries throughout the book's gestation; the final product has benefitted in no small measure from her sustained input. It is a pleasure to acknowledge the kindness and support of Professor Lorraine Byrne Bodley, while expressing gratitude for all that she has done to enrich our understanding of Schubert's music and cultural milieu. I am honoured also to have been on the receiving end of Professor Susan Youens's insights and generous words of encouragement on innumerable occasions over the last few years.

Beyond Schubert studies, friends and colleagues at the University of Oxford have been an invaluable source of scholarly inspiration. In particular, I am indebted to Dr Gascia Ouzounian, with whom I share teaching duties at Lady Margaret Hall, for her infectious levels of collegiality and keen interest in my research projects. Dr Benjamin Skipp has similarly provided good cheer at all stages in the preparation of the book.

In closing, I offer heartfelt thanks to my family and Min Sern Teh for their unwavering support of my scholarly endeavours.

James William Sobaskie

I thank my co-editor, Joe Davies, for his energy, enthusiasm, and cooperation during the development and refinement of *Drama in the Music of Franz Schubert*, much of which was conducted electronically between Oxford and Starkville. Like all creative endeavours, this has been a learning experience, and I am glad to have had such an imaginative and stimulating collaborator.

My colleagues at the Mississippi State University Department of Music have offered encouragement throughout the development of this project, and indeed, ever since I came to campus in 2008. In particular, my music theory colleague, Rosângela

Yazbec Sebba, and my department head, Barry Kopetz, have supported my research in numerous ways, for which I am grateful.

I thank the administration of Mississippi State University, especially the Dean of its College of Education, Richard Blackbourn, for granting me a sabbatical in the spring of 2018. It is through such sponsorship of innovation that Mississippi State has gained and sustained its reputation as a university of very high research activity, as well as asserted itself as a leader in the fields of education and music, and I have benefitted greatly from the institution's commitment to creativity.

I am honoured to collaborate with Susan Youens once more within *Drama in the Music of Franz Schubert*, following our cooperation on special issues of *Nineteenth-Century Music Review* in 2008 and 2016. Susan's advocacy of what she calls 'scholarly conversation' has profoundly influenced the character of Schubert studies, as has her generous collegiality, and all of us are in her debt.

Finally, I extend cordial and sincere gratitude to four friends – Brian Black, Lorraine Byrne Bodley, Xavier Hascher, and Susan Wollenberg – with whom I have had the good fortune to collaborate on numerous projects over the years, including this one. May there be many more!

Preface

Joe Davies and James William Sobaskie

Constraints and Misconceptions

As Lorraine Byrne Bodley suggests in the first chapter of our volume, Franz Schubert was thought a failure in the field of dramatic music throughout much of the twentieth century.[1] This perception stemmed in part from the lack of critical acclaim for certain of his large-scale stage works, as well as ignorance of other projects that were never performed nor closely studied. For instance, the melodrama *Die Zauberharfe* (D. 644) and the Singspiel *Die Zwillingsbrüder* (D. 647) were briefly staged in Vienna during 1820, but they attracted little attention and enjoyed no revivals during the composer's lifetime.[2] Regrettably, the more substantial operas *Alfonso und Estrella* (D. 732; 1822)[3] and *Fierabras* (D. 796;

---

[1] Consider the following observation, published in 1982, which exemplifies a belief once commonly held: 'Neither influence nor historical importance can be claimed for Schubert's operas. [...] Of the seventeen projects on which he embarked, seven were never finished and one survives incomplete. Four of the remainder are light pieces in a single act, but three – *Des Teufels Lustschloss* (1813–14), *Alfonso und Estrella* (1821–22) and *Fierrabras* (1823) – are among the most ambitious of Romantic operas. As works of art they are total failures. Like Haydn, but to an even greater degree, Schubert had no innate gift for the theatre. He was either unaware of this or thought it of no importance, for he never attempted to gain practical experience; and he compounded the deficiency by accepting librettos from personal friends with even less flair for drama or literature. [...] A glance at the three big operas shows that, except in quality of musical invention, Schubert scarcely developed at all. *Fierrabras* is as disproportionately misshapen and as dramatically preposterous as *Des Teufels Lustschloss* [*sic*], the first opera he completed'; see Winton Dean, section X, 'German Opera', in *The New Oxford History of Music, Vol. 8: The Age of Beethoven, 1790–1830*, ed. Gerald Abraham (Oxford: Oxford University Press, 1982), pp. 515–17.

[2] For discussions of Schubert's operatic projects, see Elizabeth Norman McKay, 'Schubert as a Composer of Operas', and Peter Branscombe, 'Schubert and the Melodrama', both in *Schubert Studies: Problems of Style and Chronology*, ed. Eva Badura-Skoda and Peter Branscombe (Cambridge: Cambridge University Press, 1982), pp. 85–104 and 105–41, respectively.

[3] On *Alfonso und Estrella*, see Thomas A. Denny, 'Schubert's Operas: "The Judgment of History?"', in *The Cambridge Companion to Schubert*, ed. Christopher H. Gibbs (Cambridge: Cambridge University Press, 1997), pp. 230–33.

1823)[4] were never produced, while several other promising theatrical endeavours, including *Adrast* (D. 137; 1817),[5] *Claudine von Villa Bella* (D. 239; 1815),[6] and *Der Graf von Gleichen* (D. 918; 1827),[7] as well as the sacred oratorio *Lazarus* (D. 689; 1820),[8] remained incomplete at his death. Without positive critical reception of these works, and no demonstrable evidence of their influence on later composers, the opinion arose that Schubert lacked the capacity for dramatic music.

Many factors seem to have conspired to limit Schubert's success in the venerable vocal domain. Italian and French opera remained dominant in early nineteenth-century Vienna, and new, home-grown works were hard-pressed to compete. The unique achievements of Mozart's *Die Entführung aus dem Serail* (K. 384; 1782) and *Die Zauberflöte* (K. 620; 1791) were difficult to duplicate and had not yet led to a strong, clearly defined German tradition, while the implications of Carl Maria von Weber's *Der Freischutz* (Op. 77; 1821) had not yet been fully realized. There was limited local financial support for opera at the time, and, quite understandably, benefactors hesitated to take chances on unproven artists. Certainly the implications of the newly emerging Romantic aesthetic for dramatic music were not quite clear. And of course, Schubert needed to earn a living and could not focus solely on opera.[9] While this survey surely represents an over-simplification of the composer's creative circumstances, it appears that the time just was not right for Schubert to contribute to traditionally recognized dramatic genres.

Other misconceptions arose during the twentieth century. For instance, it was commonly held that Schubert was suited to smaller forms because of his miraculous melodic gifts.[10] His Lieder – profoundly innovative, strikingly personal, extraordinarily numerous, and exceptionally popular – offered immediate

[4]   See Christine Martin's chapter, 'Pioneering German Musical Drama: Sung and Spoken Word in Schubert's *Fierabras*', in this volume.

[5]   On *Adrast*, see Elizabeth Norman McKay, 'Schubert and Classical Opera: The Promise of *Adrast*', in *Der vergessene Schubert: Franz Schubert auf der Bühne*, ed. Erich Wolfgang Partsch and Oskar Pausch (Vienna: Böhlau Verlag, 1997), pp. 61–76.

[6]   See Lorraine Byrne Bodley's chapter, 'Opera that Vanished: Goethe, Schubert, and *Claudine von Villa Bella*', in this volume.

[7]   See Lisa Feurzeig, 'Elusive Intimacy in Schubert's Final Opera: *Der Graf von Gleichen*', in *Rethinking Schubert*, ed. Lorraine Byrne Bodley and Julian Horton (Cambridge: Cambridge University Press, 2016), pp. 333–54.

[8]   For more on *Lazarus*, see Leo Black, *Franz Schubert: Music and Belief* (Woodbridge: Boydell Press, 2003), pp. 82–91.

[9]   See John Gingerich, *Schubert's Beethoven Project* (Cambridge: Cambridge University Press, 2014).

[10] For a survey of some of the myths surrounding Schubert's abilities as a 'natural' composer, see Christopher Gibbs, '"Poor Schubert": Images and Legends of the Composer', in *The Cambridge Companion to Schubert*, ed. Christopher Gibbs (Cambridge: Cambridge University Press, 1997), pp. 36–55.

and convincing proof. Reinforcing that view was the contention that Schubert could not handle larger forms.[11] Within instrumental genres, his penchant for lyrical, otherworldly themes, notably in sonata structures, was seen to negate the teleological trajectory of his music, emphasizing instead moments of stasis and retention. Connected to such elements is the opinion that the composer's 'heavenly lengths', to borrow Schumann's evocative description of Schubert's generous instrumental essays, were too repetitive and lacking in structural cohesion.[12] As is widely acknowledged, until late in the twentieth century, the general assumption was that Beethoven's motivic and structural methods represented the benchmark against which to measure the work of his contemporaries.[13] In such comparisons, Schubert's instrumental music often was found wanting: the distinct compositional principles and procedures underpinning the 'heavenly length' of his larger instrumental works were overlooked.[14]

[11]   Consider Henry Heathcote Statham's assertion that: 'The materials for exquisite musical structures are there, but the will or the power to combine them into an effective whole is wanting; and even those of his longer compositions which are quite balanced and symmetrical in form almost always affect one as too long, owing to their loosely-knit structure and want of *verve* and finish of detail. [...]'; see Statham, *My Thoughts on Music and Musicians* (London: Chapman & Hall, 1892), pp. 328–9, quoted in Suzannah Clark, *Analyzing Schubert* (Cambridge: Cambridge University Press, 2011), p. 43. Such criticism persisted into the twentieth century: 'Indeed a certain flabbiness, manifesting itself in lack of ambition or of definite purpose, as in other ways, is one of Schubert's chief weaknesses'. See Arthur Hutchings, *Schubert*, 1st edn (London: J. M. Dent, 1945) and rev. edn (London: J. M Dent, 1973). Fortunately this opinion began to change near the end of the century; see Thomas A. Denny, 'Too Long? Too Loose? And Too Light? Critical Thoughts about Schubert's Mature Finales', *Studies in Music* 23 (1989), pp. 25–52.
[12]   For a reappraisal of Schumann's familiar epithet, see Scott Burnham, 'The "Heavenly Length" of Schubert's Music', *Ideas* 6/1 (1999).
[13]   On Beethoven's approach to formal and motivic economy, see Scott Burnham, *Beethoven Hero* (Princeton: Princeton University Press, 1995).
[14]   Curious – and fortunately now anachronistic – condescension appears in some mid-twentieth-century writing on Schubert's instrumental music, as the following excerpt shows: 'Schubert's piano writing, even at its best, is less varied in texture than Beethoven's and he accepted the sonata form with far less intellectual curiosity. He handles it in his own inimitable way and often, as in the first movement of the B flat Sonata, shows wonderful imagination in presenting a theme against a completely new harmonic background. But his general effects are usually less cumulative than Beethoven's, and it is the individual beauties rather than the whole design that remain in the memory. Schubert made no attempt to curb his exuberant lyricism and frequently allowed single episodes to form themselves into completes designs of their own, regardless of the effect on the general plan of the work'. See Phillip Radcliffe's account in section VIII, 'Piano Music', in *The New Oxford History*

In the last few decades, however, scholars have begun to recognize that Schubert pursued a unique approach to large-scale structure, premised on different principles from those expressed in Beethoven's music.[15] Arising from this gradual shift in scholarly perspective is, on the one hand, an assertion that preconceptions have obscured the dramatic aspects of Schubert's oeuvre, and on the other, a suggestion that the composer developed distinctive ways of incorporating drama within genres other than those traditionally regarded as dramatic, such as opera, oratorio, passion, and cantata. In particular, it seems clear that Schubert's vocal and instrumental music incorporates much more drama than previously recognized; his dramatic innovations were sensed yet not defined nor explained – awaiting appropriate contextualization. Such insights have contributed significantly to the enhanced view of Schubert's music that has inspired the chapters of the present volume.

Evolving Images

While the emergence of new images of Franz Schubert and his music may be associated with the founding of the Neue Schubert-Ausgabe in 1965, and might be linked to the gradual increase in research that occurred thereafter, particularly with respect to sources, there is no doubt that scholarly interest in the composer has greatly accelerated in recent decades, leading to fundamental changes in our understanding of his artistic persona and compositional approach.[16] These continue to evolve today and will do so for the foreseeable future as new research discoveries emerge. Several contributions have been especially consequential, particularly for those fascinated with the drama evident in Schubert's music.

At the forefront of developments in Schubert scholarship has been the recognition of extreme expressive concentration in the composer's Lieder. In this regard, Edward T. Cone's essays on Schubert's songs and instrumental music in the 1970s and 1980s set in motion a new scholarly trend, establishing frameworks for discussing issues of characterization, musical personae, and contextual processes.[17]

---

of Music, Vol. 8: The Age of Beethoven, 1790–1830, ed. Gerald Abraham (Oxford: Oxford University Press, 1982), p. 374.

[15] See Gordon Sly, 'Schubert's Innovations in Sonata Form: Compositional Logic and Structural Interpretation', Journal of Music Theory 45/1 (2001), pp. 119–50, especially pp. 130–34. See also Hans-Joachim Hinrichsen, Untersuchungen zur Entwicklung der Sonatenform in der Instrumentalmusik Franz Schuberts (Tutzing: Hans Schneider, 1994); and Xavier Hascher, Schubert, la forme sonate et son évolution (Bern: Peter Lang, 1996).

[16] For an overview see Lorraine Byrne Bodley and James William Sobaskie, 'Introduction, Schubert Familiar and Unfamiliar: Continuing Conversations', in Nineteenth-Century Music Review 13/1 (2016), pp. 3–9.

[17] See Edward T. Cone, 'Some Thoughts on "Erlkönig"', 'Persona, Protagonist, and Characters', and 'Text and Texture: Song and Performance', in The Composer's Voice (Berkeley:

Cone's close focus on the idiosyncratic details of Schubert's music, free of confining preconceptions, sketched an individuated approach to analysis whose influence may be detected throughout this book.

Since Cone's pioneering studies, scholarship on Schubertian song has been thoroughly transformed by the magisterial work of Susan Youens. In her monographs, as well as sixty-some articles and book chapters, Youens probes beneath the musical surfaces of Schubert's songs to uncover the psychology of the poetic texts and characters portrayed therein, prominently positioning his music within the history of human expression.[18] No less influential has been her demonstration that for a rewarding interpretation, each Lied should be perceived within the deepest and richest context possible. Her contribution to this volume illustrates both pursuits, confirming that her ever-expanding influence should not be underestimated.

Subsequent studies by Lisa Feurzeig,[19] Marjorie Hirsch,[20] Richard Kramer,[21] Lorraine Byrne Bodley,[22] and Lawrence Kramer[23] have further enhanced the critical discourse on the cultural history of Schubert's songs. Embedded within their scholarship is the proposition that Schubert cultivated a personalized form

---

University of California Press, 1974), pp. 1–19, 20–40, and 57–80, respectively; see also Cone, 'Schubert's Promissory Note: An Exercise in Musical Hermeneutics', *19th-Century Music* 5/3 (1982), pp. 233–41; and 'Schubert's Unfinished Business', *19th-Century Music* 7/3 (1984), pp. 222–32.

[18]   See Susan Youens, *Retracing a Winter's Journey: Schubert's Winterreise* (Ithaca, NY: Cornell University Press, 1991); *Franz Schubert: Die schöne Müllerin* (Cambridge: Cambridge University Press, 1992); *Schubert's Poets and the Making of Lieder* (Cambridge: Cambridge University Press, 1996); *Schubert, Müller, and Die schöne Müllerin* (Cambridge: Cambridge University Press, 1997); *Schubert's Late Lieder: Beyond the Song Cycle*s (Cambridge: Cambridge University Press, 2002).

[19]   See Lisa Feurzeig, *Schubert's Lieder and the Philosophy of Early German Romanticism* (Farnham: Ashgate, 2014).

[20]   See Marjorie Hirsch, 'Schubert's Greek Revival', in *Romantic Lieder and the Search for Lost Paradise* (Cambridge: Cambridge University Press, 2008), pp. 33–62.

[21]   See Richard Kramer, *Distant Cycles: Schubert and the Conceiving of Song* (Chicago: University of Chicago Press, 1994).

[22]   See Lorraine Byrne Bodley, *Schubert's Goethe Settings* (Aldershot: Ashgate, 2003); Byrne Bodley, 'In Pursuit of a Single Flame? On Schubert's Settings of Goethe's Poems', *Nineteenth-Century Music Review* 13/2 (2016), pp. 11–33; and Byrne Bodley, 'Challenging the Context: Reception and Transformation in Schubert's "Der Musensohn", D 764, Op. 91 No. 1', in *Rethinking Schubert*, ed. Lorraine Byrne Bodley and Julian Horton (New York: Oxford University Press, 2016), pp. 437–55.

[23]   Lawrence Kramer, *Franz Schubert: Sexuality, Subjectivity, Song* (Cambridge: Cambridge University Press, 1998).

of *intellectualism* imbued with profound psychological insight.[24] Perhaps more than any other, this component of Schubert's evolving image will drive forthcoming research, since it banishes any remnant of condescension that might yet remain while providing new avenues for enquiry.

Alongside these scholarly developments in song studies, our understanding of Schubert's instrumental music has been greatly enriched by Susan Wollenberg's work on his stylistic 'fingerprints'.[25] In her recent monograph, Wollenberg elucidates the ways in which Schubert took compositional inspiration from his predecessors, notably Mozart, while simultaneously crafting his own distinctive stylistic idiom based on such elements as 'violent' outbursts, 'poetic' transitions, and threefold constructions, together with his fondness for modal interchange, Neapolitan harmonies, and lyrical melody.[26] What emerges from Wollenberg's close investigations of these fingerprints is a compelling view that Schubert's instrumental style is influenced above all by the musical and poetic worlds of song.

Equally illuminating are Robert Hatten's semiotic readings of the topical and gestural universe of Schubert's Piano Sonatas in A minor, D. 784, G major, D. 894, and A major, D. 959.[27] Hatten's work has drawn attention to the multi-layered nature of Schubertian drama and its physicality, as well as more generally contributing fresh perspectives to the evolving image of Schubert's compositional and artistic approach.[28] His contextual approach, which recalls that of Cone, informs many studies within this volume.

---

[24] On Schubert's cultural milieu, see David Gramit, '"The Passion for Friendship": Music, Cultivation, and Identity in Schubert's Circle', in *The Cambridge Companion to Schubert*, ed. Christopher H. Gibbs (Cambridge: Cambridge University Press, 1997), pp. 56–71; see also Christopher H. Gibbs and Morten Solvik, eds, *Franz Schubert and His World* (Princeton, NJ: Princeton University Press 2014); and Raymond Erickson, ed., *Schubert's Vienna* (New Haven, CT: Yale University Press, 1997).

[25] See Susan Wollenberg, 'Schubert's Transitions', in *Schubert Studies*, ed. Brian Newbould (Aldershot: Ashgate, 1998), pp. 16–61; 'The C major String Quintet D 956: Schubert's "Dissonance" Quintet?', *Schubert durch die Brille* 28 (2002), pp. 45–55; '"Dort, wo du nicht bist, dort ist das Gluck": Reflections on Schubert's Second Themes', *Schubert durch die Brille* 30 (2003), pp. 91–100; 'Schubert's Poetic Transitions', in *Le style instrumental de Schubert: Sources, analyse, evolution*, ed. Xavier Hascher (Paris: Publications de la Sorbonne, 2007); pp. 261–77; and 'From Song to Instrumental Style: Some Schubert Fingerprints', in *Rethinking Schubert*, ed. Lorraine Byrne Bodley and Julian Horton (New York: Oxford University Press, 2016), pp. 61–76.

[26] See Susan Wollenberg, *Schubert's Fingerprints: Studies in the Instrumental Works* (Farnham: Ashgate, 2011).

[27] See Robert Hatten, *Interpreting Musical Gestures, Topics, and Tropes: Mozart, Beethoven, and Schubert* (Bloomington: Indiana University Press, 2004).

[28] See Robert Hatten, 'A Surfeit of Musics: What Goethe's Lyrics Concede When Set to Schubert's Music', *Nineteenth-Century Music Review* 5/2 (2008), pp. 7–18; 'Schubert's

In the field of music theory, scholars have offered fruitful reappraisals of the tonal and structural principles that govern Schubert's instrumental works, with recent contributions focusing on the juxtaposition of paratactic and hypotactic modes of planning,[29] chromatic elements,[30] hexatonic cycles,[31] and three-key expositions.[32] Besides attracting significant analytical and theoretical attention, Schubert's instrumental music also has prompted the development of innovative hermeneutic approaches to musical meaning and the representation of subjectivity in nineteenth-century culture. Prominent in this regard are the recent studies devoted to the Romantic 'wanderer' figure,[33] gender and sexuality,[34] and memory and nostalgia.[35] Collectively, these approaches offer a range of critical lenses through which to interpret the distinct features of Schubert's compositional style and cultural milieu.

Alchemy: Transformative Surfaces, Transfiguring Depths', in *Schubert's Late Music: History, Theory, Style*, ed. Lorraine Byrne Bodley and Julian Horton (Cambridge: Cambridge University Press, 2016), pp. 91–110.

[29]   See Su Yin Mak, 'Schubert's Sonata Forms and the Poetics of the Lyric', *Journal of Musicology* 23/2 (2006), pp. 263–306; and Anne Hyland, 'The "Tightened Bow": Analysing the Juxtaposition of Drama and Lyricism in Schubert's Paratactic Sonata-Form Movements', in *Irish Musical Studies, Vol. 11: Irish Musical Analysis*, ed. Gareth Cox and Julian Horton (Dublin: Four Courts Press, 2014), pp. 17–40.

[30]   See David Damschroder, *Harmony in Schubert* (Cambridge: Cambridge University Press, 2010); and James William Sobaskie, 'The "Problem" of Schubert's String Quintet', *Nineteenth-Century Music Review* 2/1 (2005), pp. 57–92.

[31]   Richard Cohn, 'As Wonderful as Star Clusters: Instruments for Gazing at Tonality in Schubert', *19th-Century Music* 22 (1999), pp. 213–32.

[32]   On approaches to form in Schubert's music, see Suzannah Clark, *Analyzing Schubert* (Cambridge: Cambridge University Press, 2011).

[33]   See Charles Fisk, *Returning Cycles: Contexts for the Interpretation of Schubert's Impromptus and Last Sonatas* (Berkeley: University of California Press, 2001).

[34]   See (among others) Maynard Solomon, 'Franz Schubert and the Peacocks of Benvenuto Cellini', *19th-Century Music* 13/3 (1989), pp. 193–206; and Susan McClary, 'Constructions of Subjectivity in Schubert's Music', in *Queering the Pitch: The New Gay and Lesbian Musicology*, ed. Philip Brett, Gary Thomas, and Elizabeth Wood (New York and London: Routledge, 1994), pp. 205–33.

[35]   On Schubertian memory and temporality, see the essays by Walter Frisch, John Daverio, John Gingerich, Charles Fisk, and Scott Burnham in the special issue 'Music and Culture' of *The Musical Quarterly* 84/4 (2000); and Benedict Taylor, 'Schubert and the Construction of Memory: The String Quartet in A Minor, D. 804 ("Rosamunde")', *Journal of the Royal Musical Association* 139/1 (2014), pp. 41–88.

Avenues and Contributions

Drama in the Music of Franz Schubert responds to the surge of scholarly activity surrounding the composer over the past two decades and opens up new avenues of intellectual enquiry centred on the dramatic innovations perceptible within his music. Our volume offers a timely re-evaluation of the reception history of Schubert's operatic works, presenting fresh perspectives on their musical content, while also uncovering previously unsuspected locations of drama in the vocal and instrumental music. In what follows we outline the volume's main areas of investigation, providing a brief overview that, together with Laura Tunbridge's more detailed Introduction, prepares readers for the ensuing chapters.

Our colleagues demonstrate that Schubert's operatic innovations reside in his novel reinterpretation and fusion of inherited traditions. Such is the case in *Claudine von Villa Bella*, a neglected work that, as Lorraine Byrne Bodley explains, can be viewed as an exercise in 'stylistic pluralism', its distinct blend of French and Italian models suggesting an endeavour to 'discover a blueprint for German opera'. Christine Martin explores the topic of theatrical hybridity in connection with *Fierabras*, focusing closely on Schubert's new ways of transitioning between song and spoken word within a musical language that incorporates references to the *parlante* style and techniques associated with melodrama. The result, Martin suggests, is a work that straddles the boundaries between opera and German music drama.

As the chapters in Part II illustrate, in Schubert's music, operatic gestures are not exclusive to the theatre, but also represent a prominent source of drama within his Lieder. Among the contributions that highlight this aspect of Schubertian dramaturgy are Marjorie Hirsch's discussion of the aria-like lyricism of 'Gretchen im Zwinger', D. 564, and Susan Wollenberg's identification of aria and recitative styles within the expressive landscape of 'Adelwold und Emma', D. 211. Continuing the theme of generic interplay, Susan Youens reveals that in 'Gruppe aus dem Tartarus', D. 583, Schubert not only draws upon operatic conventions but invokes a specific opera familiar to all of his listeners, Mozart's *Don Giovanni*, reflecting its damnation scene in both the surface and the structure.

Behind several of the chapters in this volume, particularly those in Part III, lies the view that, in contrast to late eighteenth-century compositional style, where dramatic action is often conveyed at the surface level through a swift succession of contrasting topics, Schubertian drama resides in curious places. Its locations range from passages of poetic introspection, such as those explored by Xavier Hascher in his reading of the A major Piano Sonata, D. 959, to strange moments of stylistic and harmonic disjuncture, as discussed by Joe Davies in connection with the slow movements of the String Quintet, D. 956 and D. 959. In all three cases, the drama reverberates beyond the boundaries of the music, drawing us into its internal worlds, and resisting straightforward notions of tension and reconciliation.

Another mode of drama in Schubert's music pertains to storytelling and the incorporation of characters and narrative in both texted and un-texted works. James William Sobaskie proposes that Schubert's Mass in A♭ major tells the story of a dramatic persona's gradual yet certain transformation from penitent to anticipant, portraying spiritual development within the context of the five movements of the Catholic Ordinary. By contrast, Sobaskie suggests that Schubert's settings of 'Ständchen ("Horch, Horch! die Lerch")' (1826) and 'Ständchen', from *Schwanengesang* (1828), contain convincing characters whose stories are intentionally left unresolved, enabling listeners to decide how they might end. Picking up on the notion of internal drama, Lauri Suurpää shows how, in the slow movements of D. 958 and D. 960, expectations elicited by one dramatic persona (a protagonist) are convincingly challenged by another (an antagonist) – the first of which, he suggests, portrays a narrative progression from struggle to victory, while the second implies movement from tragedy to transcendence. In these piano sonatas from Schubert's last year, as well as in his Mass and serenades, listeners are able to project themselves into the drama, vicariously experiencing the choices, paths, and possibilities of the characters they portray. The general concept of the *dramatic persona*, together with the more specific notions of protagonist and antagonist, appear to have illuminative potential in the analysis of music apart from the songs and operas, and may even lead to the identification of 'supporting characters' in Schubert's symphonies and chamber music.

Taken together, the chapters assembled here contribute to an enhanced understanding of the dramatic innovations in the music of Franz Schubert. More than two decades after the Schubert bicentenary, our collegial project builds on the flurry of research that has emerged in the years following that occasion and illuminates an area that is ripe for further analytical and critical exploration. In so doing, it invigorates all of us to contemplate how much more there is to learn about Schubert's music.

Introduction: Internal Dramas

Laura Tunbridge

What did drama mean for Schubert? What does drama in Schubert mean now? These two questions run in the background of this volume. Schubert has rarely been lauded as a dramatic composer, at least when using nineteenth-century criteria. It is clear from contemporary criticism that, in German-speaking lands, 'drama' was associated then almost exclusively with the theatre. Attempting to un- or recover an understanding of the dramatic in Schubert thus prompts consideration of the ways in which his music is heard these days. It also asks which musical genres are heard as dramatic: Schubert wrote in almost every genre available to him, and what might be thought of as dramatic needs to be adjusted according to whether he was dealing with the theatre, concert stage, church, salon, or home. That his operatic works are often judged to have failed 'dramatically' perhaps signals a problem of definition above all.[1]

In its entry on Schubert, *Grove Music Online* includes a section by Robert Winter on 'Dramatic music', said to be the arena that caused him most 'frustration':

> At first blush, the sense of drama evinced by songs like *Erlkönig*, not to mention his dazzling lyrical gift, would seem to have marked Schubert as an ideal composer of dramatic music. But like Haydn, Schubert lacked the instinct for long-range planning and cumulative dramatic development that came so naturally to a Mozart or a Verdi.[2]

Furthermore, circumstances were against him: the two principle Viennese theatres, the Burgtheater and Kärntnertortheater, were both in decline, there was a dearth of decent librettists, and the works of Rossini dominated operatic repertoire from 1816 onwards.[3] Yet Schubert began more than sixteen dramatic works between 1811 and 1827; over half were Singspiele and the rest ranged from grand opera (*Alfonso und Estrella* and *Fierabras*), to melodrama (*Die Zauberharfe*), and incidental music

---

[1]   David Schroeder, *Schubert the Dramatist: An Evaluation of his Failure as a Composer of Opera* (MA dissertation, University of Western Ontario, 1973).

[2]   Robert Winter et al., 'Schubert, Franz', *Grove Music Online. Oxford Music Online.* Oxford University Press, accessed 6 October 2017, http://www.oxfordmusiconline.com/grovemusic/view/10.1093/gmo/9781561592630.001.0001/omo-9781561592630-e-0000025109.

[3]   On Viennese operatic life prior to Rossini's arrival, see Michael Jahn, *Die Wiener Hofoper von 1794 bis 1810. Musik und Tanz im Burg- und Kärnthnerthortheater* (Vienna: Der Apfel, 2011).

(for Helmina von Chézy's *Rosamunde, Fürstin von Zypern*). Not even the completed compositions have attained a secure footing in the repertoire in their original form, although portions of some scores – notably *Rosamunde* – have enjoyed an afterlife in other, primarily instrumental genres.

The relative familiarity of Schubert's symphonic and chamber music today has changed the ways in which the composer's abilities as dramatist are evaluated. Drama is proposed to reside in the sense of tension or conflict produced as musical narratives unfold. Gone, then, are concerns about libretti or stagecraft. Instead, it is to those unexpected moments in instrumental works that scholars turn to explain how Schubert's music can intensify emotions or subvert expectations – in short how, even without words, it can tell stories and even surprise us.

Yet interrogating Schubert's theatrical works illuminates historical preconceptions: both those of the nineteenth century and those of today. As Lorraine Byrne Bodley explains in her chapter on Schubert's fragmentary setting of Goethe's Singspiel libretto *Claudine von Villa Bella* from 1815, so few of the composer's staged works were performed during his lifetime it was impossible for him to learn from practical experience what would succeed in the theatre. The music he produced for *Claudine* is of its time, bearing marks of the composer's youth, his tutelage with Salieri, and his willing compliance with the conventions of *opera buffa*. The same might be said of the later *Fierabras*; however, the craze for Rossini's operas in Vienna made acute anxieties over the need for a German school of operatic composition. Schubert had some sympathy with the desire for German opera; after experimenting with all-sung drama in *Alfonso und Estrella*, though, he returned to the closed-number pattern of French models for *Fierabras*. Christine Martin explores how Schubert nonetheless remained attracted to the idea of replacing the French practice of including spoken dialogue and his careful gradation between recitative and arioso. It is the passages of melodrama in *Fierabras* that, according to Martin, indicate Schubert's ability to provide affective musical illustration within a taut dramatic structure.

Mention of Rossini, *opéra comique*, and melodrama underlines the extent to which the dramatic world within which Schubert worked was not the German Romantic milieu with which his instrumental works and mature Lieder were associated.[4] Instead, John Warrack observes, his theatrical works 'fit comfortably within Viennese expectations' and 'derive much of their flavour from composers familiar to Schubert in local repertoire'.[5] In order to understand what Schubert

---

[4] A useful, detailed account of available early nineteenth-century musico-theatrical forms can be found in Thomas Betzwieser, *Sprechen und Singen: Ästhetik und Erscheinungsformen der Dialogoper* (Stuttgart and Weimar: J. B. Metzler, 2002). See also Peter Branscombe, 'Schubert and the Melodrama', in *Schubert Studies: Problems of Style and Chronology*, ed. Eva Badura-Skoda and Peter Branscombe (Cambridge: Cambridge University Press, 1982), pp. 105–41.

[5] See his *German Opera: From the Beginnings to Wagner* (Cambridge: Cambridge University Press, 2001), p. 298.

might have thought would work on stage, in other words, it is necessary to have a more historically sensitive understanding of his background, rather than considering it through the operas of later composers, most notably Wagner and Verdi.[6]

Comparisons of Schubert and Rossini are instructive. As Suzannah Clark observes, 'nineteenth-century attitudes towards Schubert's compositional process tended to align him with a Rossinian aesthetic model, emphasizing the effortlessness with which he composed'.[7] The notion that both men enjoyed a 'barely conscious creative process',[8] and their music's repetitive nature, served to contrast them with the serious, teleological work of Beethoven.[9] There is little purpose here in rehashing the historiographical arguments over the validity of pairing these composers.[10] It is, though, worth pausing over the consequences of extensive musical repetition for conceptions of drama. The Rossinian crescendo might use accelerating repetition as means to achieve a dramatic climax. In some of the later Lieder, repetition of motives can intensify emotional tension (consider the build-up of 'Die Stadt'). But for the most part repetition is used by Rossini and Schubert, particularly in their operas, for melodic pleasure.

According to Warrack, in Schubert's texted music, an emotional moment is depicted or related rather than enacted. It is lyric rather than dramatic. For Warrack, and many other commentators, this distinction explains why Schubert was more suited to Lieder than opera. Yet the kinds of deviation from convention for which Schubert's Lieder were criticized during the nineteenth century, according to Marjorie Hirsch, 'betray the influence of dramatic music'.[11] There is undoubtedly drama within some of Schubert's 600-odd songs, it just needs to be thought of on different terms: within a rhetorical, rather than an exclusively theatrical,

---

[6]   The historiographical challenges of opera studies have long been debated: see, for example, James Webster in 'Viewpoint: To Understand Verdi and Wagner We Must Understand Mozart', *19th-Century Music* 11 (1987), pp. 175–93. Part of the problem is that aspects of Schubert's operas, such as the through-composed elements of *Alfonso und Estrella*, are seen as proto-Wagnerian: ironically, the historical view is habitually forwards rather than backwards.

[7]   Suzannah Clark, 'Rossini and Beethoven in the Reception of Schubert', in *The Invention of Beethoven and Rossini: Historiography, Analysis, Criticism*, ed. Nicholas Mathew and Benjamin Walton (Cambridge: Cambridge University Press, 2013), pp. 96–120, here, p. 98.

[8]   Clark, 'Rossini and Beethoven', p. 99.

[9]   See Emanuele Senici, 'Rossinian Repetitions', in *The Invention of Beethoven and Rossini: Historiography, Analysis, Criticism*, ed. Nicholas Mathew and Benjamin Walton (Cambridge: Cambridge University Press, 2013), pp. 236–62.

[10]   Recent contributions to this discussion include John Gingerich, *Schubert's Beethoven Project* (Cambridge: Cambridge University Press, 2014), and Kristina Muxfeldt, *Vanishing Sensibilities: Schubert, Beethoven, Schumann* (New York: Oxford University Press, 2012).

[11]   Marjorie Wing Hirsch, *Schubert's Dramatic Lieder* (Cambridge: Cambridge University Press, 1993), p. 2.

framework. In the last verse of Wilhelm Müller's 'Gefrörne Tränen', for example, the protagonist realizes he has been crying only as the frozen tears fall from his cheek; he then reproaches the tears for freezing as easily as morning dew, when he feels so burned up with passion inside. This use of apostrophe, direct address of something specific rather than a more general readership or audience, is marked in Schubert's 1823 setting of Müller's poem by a drop in register and dynamic; voice and piano, now in unison, eschew the lyricism of the first two verses for a grudging neighbour-note figure on the mediant as the tears are asked to explain themselves. According to Rufus Hallmark, such apostrophe is a potent means of devising with 'literary-rhetorical flair' a dramatic frame.[12] He concludes:

> apostrophe is one of the most potent means by which Müller in particular created the crux of a poem; some of his poems that lack apostrophe are deficient in drama because they forego the presence of the "other" that apostrophe implies – although Schubert still finds musical ways to heighten the poem's point.[13]

Drama, it seems, is other people. Hirsch similarly defines Schubert's dramatic Lieder as those that 'depict one or several personae, often identifiable by name, engaged in a particular course of action'. The drama resides in the personae experiencing 'a change of circumstance: simple or complex, physical or psychological, "something happens"'.[14]

The 'others' in Schubert's works, however, are not always physically present. Indeed, they might emerge from the music rather than the text. Hallmark contends that in *Winterreise* the wanderer may, 'through Schubert's music, invoke presences in the poem that the poet had not explicitly addressed'.[15] Those presences are often considered to manifest inwardly rather than outwardly, as James Sobaskie explores in his chapter on Schubert's Mass in A♭, which imagines an auditor who becomes a dramatic persona interacting with the liturgical setting.

Within Schubert's Lieder dramatic effect is sometimes also created through the invocation of other genres. Susan Wollenberg goes so far as to suggest that the ballad 'Adelwold und Emma' might be treated as an adaptation, akin to a book becoming a film. For some it might seem that, in the addition of (so much!) music to Friedrich Bertrand's poem, Schubert failed to observe that different media can accomplish similar effects through different means; while music might conjure up 'others' who comment on what is happening, illustrating all that happens in the text risks redundancy. This is to misunderstand, though, the aesthetics of the ballad as

[12] Rufus Hallmark, 'The Literary and Musical Apostrophe in *Winterreise*', *19th-Century Music* 35/1 (2011), pp. 3–33, here p. 30.
[13] Hallmark, 'The Literary and Musical Apostrophe in *Winterreise*', p. 32.
[14] Hirsch, *Schubert's Dramatic Lieder*, p. 2.
[15] Hallmark, 'The Literary and Musical Apostrophe in *Winterreise*', p. 21, n. 50.

a genre, which depend on a narrator – and by extension, the music's narration – to tell the story.[16]

Marjorie Hirsch's chapter focuses on Schubert's abandoned 'Gretchen im Zwinger', a Lied that seemed to strain towards aria. The tensions between (Italianate) opera and (Germanic) song may have been behind Schubert's decision not to pursue this particular work further, although there were, as Hirsch acknowledges, multiple other factors. Schubert had set scenes from Goethe's *Faust* before – very successfully so in 'Gretchen am Spinnrade' – but it was a text with its own, complex relationship to the stage and musical adaptation, as many composers before and since have found. *Faust*'s imaginary theatre allowed a flexible and fantastical dramaturgy that – as attested to by the extensive scholarly literature – tested the capabilities of read versus realized drama.[17]

Hirsch points out that after 1817 Schubert wrote few 'dramatic Lieder' and subsequently rarely drew on operatic conventions. This implies that his later works need to be understood according to a new dramaturgy; one that seems, from the following chapters, to derive from musical form. Sobaskie's chapter on Schubert's two famous serenades, 'Horch, horch, die Lerch!' and 'Ständchen' suggests that, in the Shakespeare setting, the composer was willing to liberate the text from its original comedic context. Once it 'no longer serves a theatrical function' the serenader's pleas instead motivate repetitions within the musical structure: the song's outcome is left to the listener's imagination. The appealing gestures of *Schwanengesang*'s 'Ständchen' are still more deeply internalized: the drama is psychological and has to be carefully drawn out in performance.[18]

Drama also exists in the unexpected and the otherworldly. Both Susan Youens and Clive McClelland invoke topical references to *ombra* and its stormy counterpart *tempesta* in Lieder from throughout Schubert's career, from 'Erlkönig' to 'Der Tod und das Mädchen', 'Gruppe aus dem Tartarus' and 'Am Meer'. *Tempesta* topics are devices, according to McClelland, by which to ratchet up the drama. They are not dramatic in themselves but raise tension and on occasion provide surprises. What is more, they have a long lineage: as McClelland points out, they extend far further back than the *Sturm und Drang* conventions of the late eighteenth century. They

---

[16] The cross-genre dramaturgy of one of Schubert's most famous ballads, 'Erlkönig', is discussed in Betzwieser, *Sprechen und Singen*, pp. 145–6.

[17] See, for example, Beate Agnes Schmidt, *Music in Goethe's 'Faust'* (Sinzig: Studio Verlag, 2006); Hedwig Meier, *Die Schaubühne als musikalische Anstalt: Studied zur Geschichte und Theorie der Schauspielmusik im 18. Und 19. Jahrhundert sowie zu ausgewälten 'Faust'-Kompositionen* (Bielefeld: Aisthesis Verlag, 1999); and Lorraine Byrne Bodley, ed., *Music in Goethe's Faust* (Woodbridge: Boydell and Brewer, 2017).

[18] The role of the performer in making Schubert's Lieder dramatic is discussed in Walther Dürr, 'Schubert and Johann Michael Vogl: A Reappraisal', *19th-Century Music* 3/2 (1979), pp. 126–40; see also Jennifer Ronyak, '"Serious Play," Performance, and the Lied: The Stägemann Schöne Müllerin Revisited', *19th-Century Music* 34/2 (2010), pp. 141–67.

thus also allow for a connection to be made between Schubert and composers such as Mozart and Gluck. Again, historical context proves all important in the definition and understanding of musical dramaturgy.

So too does genre. Anne Hyland argues for the importance of what she calls 'intra-generic dialogue' in the dramatic conception of Schubert's early chamber work, the Overture for String Quintet in C minor, D. 8. Invocations of orchestral climaxes (reminiscent of Cherubini) and singing styles (as in Schubert's early 'Hagars Klage'), not to mention the titular reference to a meta-theatrical genre, the overture, are taken to indicate that drama resides in the frictions between instrumental and vocal forms. Drama is not, though, simply a question of noisiness; of the quintet striving to sound louder and bigger than it is. It also resides in the formal parallels between Cherubini's overture for his opera *Faniska* and Schubert's piece. The Overture for String Quintet reveals the composer learning his trade, perhaps, but also, Hyland proposes, engaging with his precursors: the dramatic 'other' here is a musical model rather than the poetic presences noted by Hallmark.

The final chapters in the last section of this volume make it clear that dramatic exchanges of this kind are heard with some frequency in Schubert's solo instrumental works. Often they derive from moments of contrast and juxtaposition. It may be argued that narratives of musical form depend on a sense of alterity (consider the struggles between first and second subjects in sonata forms, even if Schubert famously problematizes those binaries) but then, if drama is defined in terms of conflict and resolution, it is a quality possessed by the majority of music within the Western classical tradition.

For Brian Black, drama exists when:

> the music projects the continuity of a coherent chain of events moving irresistibly to a final denouement, much like the unfolding of a well-crafted play. Its hold on the listener depends upon consistency in the music's plan and a progressive development of its material in which the implications of initial actions are realized later in the form.

According to this definition, the lyric has a place within the dramatic. Schubert's instrumental works – such as the C minor Impromptu on which Black focuses – can, then, be understood as implicitly dramatic. The two 'characters' at play are tonal: C minor and A♭ major, conveyed through contrasting themes. Variation enables an intensification towards resolution.

Xavier Hascher finds a similar build-up of tension through the phrase structure of the first movement of Schubert's Piano Sonata in A major, D. 959. Fermata and modulation present what appears to be a moment of reminiscence, something from outside of the sonata. It is telling that Hascher here invokes the writings of Sigmund Freud. Seemingly, in these later works of Schubert, drama has moved from external action to introspection. Poetry and the novel (as defined, again, by Goethe, that arch-bender of genres) become models for understanding the dramaturgy of Schubert's Sonata.

The slow movements of two more late piano sonatas, D. 958 and D. 960, are taken by Lauri Suurpää as vehicles through which to explore the relationship between emotion and persona in music. The trope that an instrument may comment on, support or undermine another, leading to situations where characters may exert direct control of the orchestra, according to Matt Baileyshea, is 'inherently dramatic'.[19] Baileyshea may be writing within a Wagnerian logic rather than a Schubertian one, but the influence of scholarship on narrative and voice can be felt within many of the interpretations put forward in this volume.[20] In the case of these slow movements, Suurpää proposes that the listener sympathizes with the thematic and tonal protagonist and their struggle to overcome their thematic and tonal antagonist.

Finally, Joe Davies attends to the strangeness of Schubert's music, to those moments that combine the *ombra* effects discussed by Youens and McClelland with the narrative structures explained by Sobaskie, Black, Hascher and Suurpää. The harmonic and gestural disjunctions Davies is attracted to in the late piano sonatas and chamber works return to a notion of drama as being inherently a phenomenon of the theatre. Here, though, it is the 'hermeneutical theatre' theorized by Richard Kramer.[21] Twenty-first-century interpreters, in other words, deal more readily in psychological drama than in the spectacle and occasional shabbiness of the stage. Schubert becomes a dramatist of the mind.

Listeners to Schubert today are less likely to experience his songs and chamber music within the sociable sphere of the concert hall than in the privacy of their own homes, or at least on their own headphones. This kind of solitary listening is perhaps one reason why definitions of Schubert's music as dramatic are so slippery, and often combined with notions of intimacy and interiority. An archetypal modern Schubertian is Colin Dexter's fictional detective, Inspector Morse. At the end of a long day, tumbler of whisky in hand, he could be brought to tears by hearing a Lieder recital on the radio; even his gruffer colleagues regret disturbing his listening sessions.[22] In the first episode of the sixth season of the television series, 'Dead on Time', the Adagio of the String Quintet serves, first, to soundtrack the last hours of

---

[19] Matt Baileyshea, 'The Struggle for Orchestral Control: Power, Dialogue, and the Role of the Orchestra in Wagner's Ring', *19th-Century Music* 31 (2007), pp. 3–27, here p. 4.

[20] Carolyn Abbate is crucial here, particularly her *Unsung Voices: Opera and Musical Narrative in the Nineteenth Century* (Princeton: Princeton University Press, 1996), which arguably was taken up by Schumann scholars before Schubert was considered; see, for instance, Nicholas Marston, '"Im Legendenton": Schumann's "Unsung Voice"', *19th-Century Music* 16 (1993), pp. 227–41.

[21] Richard Kramer, 'Against the Grain: The Sonata in G (D. 894) and a Hermeneutics of Late Style', in *Schubert's Late Music: History, Theory, Style*, ed. Lorraine Byrne Bodley and Julian Horton (Cambridge: Cambridge University Press, 2016), pp. 111–33.

[22] See the opening two chapters of the last novel in the series: Colin Dexter, *Inspector Morse: The Remorseful Day* (London: Macmillan, 1999).

the victim. Its tempestuous middle section is heard when Morse attends a concert with the victim's widow, an old flame. The camera hones in on each listener, as if it needs to burrow into their head to understand the mental machinations taking place within. The 'inner drama' of Schubert's music has few better illustrations: it is personal, even private; evident but evasive.[23] Recognizing the dramatic in Schubert is another way towards understanding the subtle and sophisticated ways in which his music draws interpreters in, to listen to a story or admire a view, and imagine what might happen next.

❧

[23]   Alternatively the use of the Adagio in this episode encapsulates modern-day Schubert hermeneutics: from late style to romantic frustration and, finally, subjective despair. Thanks to Sarah Walker for reminding me of this episode.

PART I

STAGE AND SACRED WORKS

1

Opera that Vanished: Goethe, Schubert, and *Claudine von Villa Bella**

Lorraine Byrne Bodley

For Susan Wollenberg, who reads our work
with a musician's ear and a scholar's mind for argument

Prologue: Reception History of Schubert's Operas

In the first scholarly study of Schubert's operas, written in the 1920s, Rudolfine
Krott raised the controversy between the lyrical and the dramatic, which has run as a
leitmotif through Schubertian literature.[1] In the absence of a historical performance

* I am grateful to many Schubertian friends for their engagement with this chapter:
Christine Martin in Tübingen, who knows the music intimately through editing the
orchestral edition of *Claudine* for the *Neue Schubert Ausgabe*, read this chapter with searching
insight and I am profoundly grateful to her for that. To Xavier Hascher I owe more than I
can say for his meticulous reading at a later stage; to Joe Davies and Jim Sobaskie who have
graciously given their time and shared their wisdom in bringing this Susan-fest together.

[1] Rudolfine Krott, *Die Singspiele Schuberts* (PhD dissertation, University of Vienna, 1921).
See Georg Göhler, 'Zwei Schubert-Opern', *Zeitschrift für Musik* 90 (1923), p. 306; Walter
Van Endert, *Schubert als Bühnenkomponist* (PhD dissertation, University of Leipzig, 1925);
Otto Erich Deutsch, 'Von zwei Opern, die Schubert nicht komponiert hat', *Moderne Welt*
Special Schubert edition, 'Der intime Schubert' (1925), p. 271; Karl Blessinger, 'Romantische
Elemente in den Opern Schuberts', in *Almanach der dt. Musikbücherei* (Regensburg: Bosse,
1924); Helmut Wolter, 'Schubert als Opernkomponist', *Der Auftakt* 8 (1928), pp. 241–4;
Alfred Orel, 'Schuberts Bühnenschaffen, *Der neue Pflug* 3 (1928), pp. 35–40; P. Stefan,
'Schubert und die Oper', *Neue Zürcher Zeitung*, 18 November 1928; Hugo Leichtentritt,
'Schubert's Early Operas', *The Musical Quarterly* 14 (1928), pp. 620–38; Hans Graeser,
'Schuberts musikdramatisches Werk', *Neue Zeitschrift für Musik* 114 (1953), pp. 653–7; A.
Hyatt King, 'Music for the Stage', in *Schubert: Music of the Masters*, ed. Gerald Abraham
(London: Lindsay Drommond Ltd, 1946), pp. 198–216; P. J. Revitt, *Franz Schubert's
Works for the Theatre* (PhD dissertation, University of Washington, 1949); Marcia Citron,
Schubert's Seven Complete Operas: A Musico-Dramatic Study (PhD dissertation, University
of North Carolina, 1971); Reinhard van Hoorickx, 'Les Opéras de Schubert', *Revue
Belge de Musicologie* 28–30 (1974–1976), pp. 238–59; Cornelia Kritsch, 'Franz Schubert

tradition, the usual solecisms for Schubert's 'failure on stage' have been repeated: the lyrical composer who was incapable of writing dramatic music,[2] coupled with the poor quality of his libretti.[3] Beyond the question of Schubert's musical reaction to the libretto and the already-loaded questions of text setting, the general principles of stage dramaturgy, performance practice, and history apply.[4] This criticism moves far beyond the lyrical and the dramatic and is rooted in negative prejudice, Schubert's lack of theatrical experience, fragmentary sources and, until recently, the lack of a proper performance edition.

Only on two occasions was Schubert granted the experience of watching his own operas in performance. He never benefitted from dissension at rehearsals that lead to the kind of solutions worked up in the theatre rather than imagined in the writing of a score.[5] Most successful operatic composers are very well aware of this process. When revising his opera *Le prophète*, Meyerbeer directly acknowledged 'the difference between an opera that comes from one's head, and the one that one sees in the theatre';[6] and when editing multiple versions of a Donizetti opera, Roger Parker acknowledges this practice of constant revision and conceded, 'The more one becomes aware of this type of activity, the more arbitrary it seems

---

und die Oper. Literarhistorische Überlegungen zu einem offenen Problem', *Jahrbuch des Wiener Goethe-Vereins* 84 (1980), pp. 133–43; Christian Pollack, 'Problemstellung zum dramatischen Schaffen Schuberts', *Schubert durch die Brille* 1 (1988), pp. 5–10.

[2]   See Edgar Istel, whose opinion exemplifies this debate: 'During most of his life he cherished an unrequited love for the stage, and wrote a number of dramatic works without achieving any noteworthy success. He was no man of the theatre and hence, unlike Mozart, was unable to gain genuine dramatic texts; yet, again and again, most powerfully in "Fierabras" and "Die Zauberharfe", two compositions which miscarried as dramatic units, there occasionally flashes forth a genuine stroke of drama, one which might justify great hopes', 'Schubert's Lyric Style', *The Musical Quarterly* 14 (1928), pp. 575–95, here p. 576.

[3]   Even contemporary reviews of *Rosamunde* and *Die Zauberharfe* often praise Schubert's music while berating the playwrights. See Otto Erich Deutsch, ed., *Schubert: Die Dokumente seines Lebens* (Kassel: Bärenreiter Verlag, 1964, reprinted 1980 and 1996) trans. Eric Blom as *Schubert: A Documentary Biography* (London: J. M. Dent & Sons, 1946), pp. 148 and 321. As early as 1974, Cunningham challenged this argument; see George Cunningham, *Franz Schubert als Theaterkomponist* (PhD dissertation, Freiburg, 1974).

[4]   For a discussion of opera during Schubert's compositional lifetime, see Michael Jahn, *Die Wiener Hofoper von 1810 bis 1836. Das Kärnthnerthortheater als Hofoper* (Vienna: Der Apfel, 2007).

[5]   See Christine Martin, 'Die Particell-Entwürfe zu Schuberts Fierabras und ihre Bedeutung für den Kompositionsprozess der Oper', *Schubert-Perspektiven* 8/1 (2008), pp. 1–16.

[6]   Alan Armstrong, 'Gilbert-Louis Duprez and Gustav Roger in the Composition of Meyerbeer's *Le Prophète*', *Cambridge Opera Journal* 8/2 (1996), pp. 147–65, here p. 164.

to choose one particular stage of a work to present as its "base text"'.[7] Most of Schubert's operatic scores are 'base texts', yet one only has to glance across at the four manuscripts of 'Erlkönig' D. 328 to see how willing Schubert was to fine-tune through performance,[8] and how song for him was a fluid rather than a fixed form. Such music of revision is rarely found in Schubert's operatic scores, and this lack of opportunity had a drastic and long-lasting effect on his reception history. The general public of his day did not have the opportunity to get to know Schubert's operas more intimately, as they did with his songs, male-voice settings, and liturgical works. In his lifetime only his melodrama, *Die Zwillingsbrüder* D. 647, and his one-act Singspiel, *Die Zauberharfe* D. 723, were staged – neither of which became habitués of the Viennese stage – and later efforts by Johann Herbeck, Franz Liszt, and Felix Mottl made the works available in abbreviated forms so that a historical performance tradition has never been properly established.[9] Although the past fifty years have witnessed performances and recordings of all his completed works and *Fierabras*, in particular, has enjoyed a modern-day revival,[10] the reception of Schubert's operas remains peripheral.

This lack of a proper performance tradition for Schubert's operas has not only led to misinterpretations and negative judgements, but has impeded serious musicological engagement with the subject. Although the first scholarly studies began to appear around the centenary of Schubert's death, it was really only after the *Schubertjahr* in 1978 that a more exact preoccupation with his theatrical works began.[11] In his

[7]   Roger Parker, 'A Donizetti Critical Edition in the Postmodern World', in *L'opera teatrale die Gaetano Donizetti*, ed. Francesco Bellotti (Bergamo: Comune di Bergamo-Assessorato allo Spettacolo, 1993), pp. 57–68, here p. 64.

[8]   Andrea Lindmayr-Brandl has traced this brilliantly in 'Schuberts Erlkönig: Entstehung, Werkgestalt und Dramatisierung des Werkkonzepts', in *Musikgeschichte als Verstehensgeschichte. Festschrift für Gernot Gruber zum 65. Geburtstag*, ed. Joachim Brügge et al. (Tutzing: Hans Schnieder Verlag, 2004), pp. 261–77.

[9]   As early as 1959, Brown argued the need to experience Schubert's operas in performance most notably in 'Schubert's Two Major Operas: A Consideration of the Possibility of Actual Stage Production', *Music Review* 20 (1959), pp. 104–18.

[10]   On the reception history of *Fierabras*, see the very detailed Appendix of concert and stage performances and reviews in Liane Speidel, *Franz Schubert – ein Opernkomponist?* (Vienna, Cologne, and Weimar: Böhlau Verlag, 2012), pp. 254–363.

[11]   See Elizabeth Norman McKay, 'Schubert as a Composer of Operas', in *Schubert Studies: Problems of Style and Chronology*, ed. Eva Badura-Skoda and Peter Branscombe (Cambridge: Cambridge University Press, 1982), pp. 85–104. Other significant sources released in the following decade include Christian Pollack, *Franz Schubert: Bühnenwerke: Kritische Gesamtausgabe der Texte* (Tutzing: Hans Schneider, 1988) or the photographic reproduction of the autograph draft of Schubert's final opera in Ernst Hilmar, ed., *Franz Schubert: Der Graf von Gleichen* (Tutzing: Hans Schneider, 1988), also Richard Kramer's extensive review of this publication in *19th-Century Music* 14 (1990), pp. 197–216.

analysis of *Fierabras* in 1985, Walter Thomas threw down the gauntlet, claiming a 'serious scholarly engagement with Schubert's stage works is still outstanding'.[12] While pioneering steps in rehabilitating Schubert as a composer of opera were taken by Elizabeth Norman McKay,[13] Till Gerrit Waidelich[14] and Thomas Denny[15] in the 1990s, and editors of the *Neue Schubert Ausgabe* have done stellar work in the recuperation of his operatic works,[16] even today there is not a single article on Schubert's operas in the *Cambridge Opera Journal*, a journal that specifically aims at multidisciplinary approaches, and only a sheaf of articles on *Fierabras* appear in *The Opera Quarterly*. A serious study of Schubert's operas, examined from an array of critical perspectives, is long overdue.

This neglect of Schubertian opera is not confined to the composer's reception history but reflects the marginalization of opera in musicology and theatre studies in general. It was only from the 1990s that opera studies really emerged as a discipline and even more recently that it has been taken seriously as a dramatic genre. The human psychologism of Kerman's approach in *Opera as Drama*[17] unwittingly mitigated against the study of most early Romantic opera,[18] and not one of the

---

[12]   Walter Thomas, 'Bild und Aktion in *Fierabras*. Ein Beitrag zu Schuberts musikalischer Dramaturgie', in *Franz Schubert. Jahre der Krise 1818–1823. Arnold Feil zum 60. Geburtstag am 2. Oktober 1985*, ed. Werner Aderhold et al. (Kassel: Bärenreiter, 1985), pp. 85–112.

[13]   Elizabeth Norman McKay, *Franz Schubert's Music for the Theatre* (Vienna: Hans Schneider, 1991).

[14]   Till Gerrit Waidelich, *Franz Schubert: Alfonso und Estrella. Eine frühe durchkomponierte deutsche Oper. Geschichte und Analyse* (Tutzing: Hans Schneider, 1991).

[15]   A significant article for the *Schubertjahr* was Thomas A. Denny, 'Schubert's Operas: "The Judgment of History?", in *The Cambridge Companion to Schubert*, ed. Christopher Gibbs (Cambridge: Cambridge University Press, 1997), pp. 224–40. See Thomas A. Denny, 'Archaic and Contemporary Aspects of Schubert's *Alfonso und Estrella*: Issues of Influence, Originality and Maturation* in *Eighteenth-Century Music in Theory and Practice – Essays in Honor of Alfred Mann* (Stuyvesant, NY: Pendragon Press, 1994), pp. 241–61, here pp. 244–50.

[16]   See, for example, the operatic editions and separately published critical commentaries [hereafter *Kritische Berichte*, or *KB*] for Franz Schubert, *Neue Ausgabe sämtlicher Werke* [hereafter *Neue Schubert-Ausgabe*, or *NSA*], Series II: *Bühnenwerke*, vols 1–18, especially vols 8a–c, *Fierabras*, ed. Thomas Denny (vol. 8a) and Christine Martin (vols 8b and 8c) (Kassel: Bärenreiter, 2005, 2007 and 2009 [*KB* 2011]); vol. 12, *Adrast*, ed. Mario Aschauer (Kassel: Bärenreiter, 2010 [*KB* 2011]); vol. 14, *Claudine von Villa Bella*, ed. Christine Martin and Dieter Martin (Kassel: Bärenreiter, 2011 [*KB* 2012]); vol. 17, *Der Graf von Gleichen*, ed. Manuela Jahrmärker (Kassel: Bärenreiter, 2006) and vol. 18, *Operneinlagen* (*zu Hérolds Zauberglöckchen*), ed. Christine Martin (Kassel: Bärenreiter, 2010 [*KB* 2010]).

[17]   Joseph Kerman, *Opera as Drama*, new and revised edn (Berkeley and Los Angeles: University of California Press, 1988), p. xiv.

[18]   Nicholas Till, 'Introduction: Opera Studies Today', in *The Cambridge Companion to Opera*, ed. Nicholas Till (Cambridge: Cambridge University Press, 2012), pp. 1–22, here p. 10.

twenty-four chapters of Nicholas Cook and Mark Everist's *Rethinking Music* of 1999 is devoted to opera,[19] though the book is a compendium of the wide range of disciplinary approaches undertaken by musicology. Against this backdrop it is unsurprising that Schubert's operas are neglected, and he is not alone in this regard. For many composers who are remembered today primarily for their instrumental music – Haydn, Mendelssohn or Dvořák – opera constituted a substantial part of their output. Mozart's singular reception as a master of both operatic and non-operatic genres was attributed to his deployment of the inherently dramatic and developmental structures of instrumental sonata form, which allowed opera to develop an eloquent dramatic language. The tenuous nature of this argument is immediately evident when applied to Haydn, a master of sonata form who, by our lights, was unsuccessful in opera.

In order to reframe Schubert's contribution to opera it is vital to recognize how it 'converses' with the conventions of genre and reconnect it with the context in which it is embedded. To show that Schubert had the savvy to use his compositional talent to striking dramatic effect, the remaining sections of this chapter will examine Schubert's setting of Goethe's libretto, *Claudine von Villa Bella*, whose distinct historical fingerprints presents the possibility of harnessing a reception study onto its slender musical shoulders. Both Goethe and Schubert drew judiciously on Italian and French models while furthering their aims of creating a national tradition. The resulting stylistic pluralism of a work as apparently innocent as *Claudine* bears testimony to their enormous endeavour to discover a blueprint for German opera and shows how musical and theatrical works are, to a significant extent, conceived and shaped according to the musical, theatrical and social systems for which they are created.[20]

A Capstone Libretto: Goethe's *Claudine von Villa Bella*

'Thematically, scenically, and atmospherically rich and varied, lyrical, humorous, and with a lucid plot that produces one *coup de théâtre* after another, Goethe's *Claudine* at the very least challenges the argument of Schubert's poor-quality libretti'.[21] Not only is it an exception among Schubert's dramatic works in terms of authorial authority, but also the poet's aspiration to create a German national opera sets him apart from Schubert's other librettists. Goethe's desire to elevate the Singspiel to an artistic level commensurate with the other arts in Germany, and with Italian *opera*

---

[19]   Nicholas Cook and Mark Everist, eds, *Rethinking Music* (Oxford: Oxford University Press, 1999).

[20]   Robert Donington, *Opera and its Symbols: The Unity of Words, Music and Staging* (New Haven, CT and London: Yale University Press, 1990).

[21]   Nicholas Boyle, *Goethe: The Poet and the Age, Vol. 1: The Poetry of Desire* (Oxford University Press, 1992), p. 214.

buffa, inspired him to produce several works in this form. Between the years 1773 and 1785 he produced seven ballad-opera libretti, all written for the Weimar court (see Table 1.1).

Goethe's libretto exists in two versions. This first version was completed on 4 June 1775[22] and published in Berlin by August Mylius in May 1776 with the subtitle, 'Ein Schauspiel mit Gesang' – a term Goethe coined to indicate the literary quality of the text.[23] The innovative text was greeted rather hesitantly by critics and composers.[24] One Altona journalist could not believe it to be Goethe's work except that his name stood on the title page and decided that it must be a satire on operettas.[25] One archly conservative critic found the whole thing too 'novelesque' and 'unnatural' and concluded that 'Nature has not fashioned Herr Goethe to be a musical poet'.[26] Only the critic and director, Johann Joachim Eschenburg (1743–1820) brought sympathetic insight to the libretto. He found it incomparably better than Goethe's earlier Singspiel, *Erwin und Elmire*, its songs light, musical and demanding 'a lively, indeed succinct composition, especially those which are constructed in the manner of the finales in Italian operettas'.[27] Unlike many of his fellow German critics, Eschenburg had first-hand experience with the genre he mentions, having produced Italian opera, and had based his libretto for *Robert und Kalliste* on Guglielmi's setting.[28]

---

[22]   See Goethe to Knebel, 4 June 1775, in *Weimarer Ausgabe: Goethes Werke,* ed. Gustav von Loeper, Erich Schmidt et al., 143 vols (Weimar: Herman Böhlau, 1887–1919) [hereafter *WA*], IV, vol. 2. pp. 265–6. For progress on the libretto, see Goethe to Johanna Falmer, 10 April 1775, *WA*, IV, vol, 2, p. 254, and Goethe to Knebel, 14 April 1775, *WA*, IV, vol. 2, pp. 254–5.

[23]   *Claudine von Villa Bella, Ein Schauspiel mit Gesang, 1774–75,* in *Münchner Ausgabe. J. W. von Goethe Sämtliche Werke nach Epochen seines Schaffens*, ed. Karl Richter et al. (Munich: Hanser, 1985–1998), 21 vols [hereafter *MA*], I, vol. 2, p. 78 and *Claudine von Villa Bella. Ein Singspiel*, *MA*, III, vol. 1, p. 360.

[24]   André, who directed Italian opera in Berlin, was one of the few composers to undertake a setting of Goethe's text but neither it nor Seckendorff's setting were ever performed. The first performance took place on 13 June 1780 at the Hofburgtheatre in Vienna with music by Ignaz van Beeke and Aloysia Weber as Goethe's first *Claudine*. A further performance at the Stuttgart Opera House took place in 1783 with music by C. G. Weber.

[25]   According to the publications *Beytrag zum Reichs-Postreuer* and *Neuer gelehrter Mercurius*, cited in Thomas Bauman, *North German Opera in the Age of Goethe* (Cambridge: Cambridge University Press, 2009), pp. 285–7 and 172 respectively.

[26]   *Auserlesene Bibliothek der neuesten deutschen Literatur* 10 (1776), pp. 2490–98; Bauman, p. 172.

[27]   *Allgemeine deutsche Bibliothek* 31/2 (1777), p. 495, Bauman, p. 172.

[28]   Pietro Alessandro Guglielmi (1728–1804), Italian opera composer best known for his dramma giocoso *La sposa fedele* (Venice, 1767) translated by Eschenburg as *Robert und Kalliste* (Berlin, 1777).

Table 1.1   Goethe's libretti

1766	*La sposa rapita*
Ballad-opera	
1773	*Jahrmarktfest zu Plundersweilen*
1773–5, revised 1787	*Erwin und Elmire*
1774, revised 1787	*Claudine von Villa Bella*
1777	*Lila*
1779	*Jery und Bätely*
1782/82	*Die Fischerin*
1784/85	*Scherz, List und Rache*
Operatic fragments	
1785/86	*Die ungleichen Hausgenossen*
1795/1800	*Der Zauberflöte Zweiter Teil*
1814	*Der Löwenstuhl*
1814/15	*Feradeddin und Kolaila*
Melodrama	
1776/77 (revised 1815)	*Proserpina*

The adverse reaction of critics can be explained by the innovative nature of Goethe's text, which is a capstone in opera historiography. *Opera buffa* audiences expected familiarity, not the novelty that Goethe presented. Both in its unconventional subject matter, demanding dramaturgical structures and Spanish setting, *Claudine* is wholly unprecedented in earlier German-language libretti. The only other North German opera to have a Spanish setting is Grossmann's adaptation of Beaumarchais's *Le barbier de Séville*, which in every other respect differs from Goethe's operatic tapestry.[29] It is also the only North German libretto with anything remotely approximating Bretzner's abduction scene in *Die Entführung aus dem Serail*; it is the first *Sturm und Drang* libretto in German opera;[30] while the long, impressive finale at the end of Act II is the first true finale in North German opera. Most North German composers had little or no practice in dealing with this or the other compositional problems Goethe posed here. Guidance was

[29]   Gustav Friedrich Grossmann (1746–1795), actor, theatre director of librettist, most famous for his adaption from Pierre-Augustin Caron de Beaumarchais's play, *Le barbier de Séville*, premiered in Friedrich Ludwig Benda's setting at the Theater am Rannstädter Tor, 7 May 1776.

[30]   Bauman, p. 169.

needed from Italian models, an evident influence in Ignaz van Beeke's setting premiered at the Hofburgtheater in Vienna on 13 June 1780 – thirty-five years before Schubert's setting.

Goethe's decision to revise *Claudine* a decade later was prompted by his direct experience of Italian opera in Italy and Göschen's publication of his collected works in 1788.[31] His correspondence with Charlotte von Stein shows how conscious he is of breaking new ground,[32] and in a letter to Herder on 6 February 1788 he records the pains he took in creating a better libretto for the composer:

> Here is Act Three of *Claudine*; I hope you get just half the pleasure for it that I feel from having finished it. Since I am better acquainted now with the requirements of lyric theatre, I have to accommodate the composer and actor by making some sacrifices. Cloth that is to be embroidered must have its threads set wide apart, and for a comic opera it must be absolutely woven like marli. But in this work, as in *Erwin*, I have also been concerned with the reader. In a word, I have done what I could.[33]

Johann Friedrich Reichardt, who had heard of the revised version beforehand and pestered Herder for copies, set to work with gusto when the libretto was published and in April 1789 showed up in Weimar with his new setting of *Claudine*.[34] He

---

[31]   Christine Martin and Dieter Martin trace the revisions in detail in the preface to their edition, *NSA*, II, vol. 14, pp. xiii–xviii. See also Jörg Kramer, *Deutschsprachiges Musiktheater im späten 18. Jahrhundert. Typologie, Dramaturgie und Antropologie einer populären Gattung*, 2 vols [Studien der deutschen Literatur, vols 149–150] (Tübingen: Niemeyer, 1998), vol. 1, pp. 496–507.

[32]   Goethe to Charlotte von Stein, 24 January 1786, *WA*, IV, vol. 7, p. 165. See also the Paralipomena [supplementary content] to the *Italienische Reise* [*Italian Journey*] which traces the poet's efforts to complete the libretto. See, for example, no. 29 and no. 30 where Goethe records, 'Einwirkung der Italiänische Oper' ('Influence of Italian Opera'), in *Erwin und Elmire. Claudine von Villa Bella*, *WA*, I, vol. 32, November 1787, pp. 463–4; and 25 January 1787, where Goethe records 'Schwere Rechenschaft Claudine' ('Serious Re-evaluation of Claudine'); *WA*, I, vol. 32, p. 473, and in January 1787 under the rubric of 'Poetische Arbeiten' ('Lyrical Works') he again registers 'Iphigenie fertig [Iphigenie complete]. Claudine'. See also Goethe's correspondence around this time: Goethe to Frau Schultheiss in Zürich, 8 September 1787, *WA*, I, vol. 32, pp. 465–6; Goethe to Kayser, 11 September 1787, *WA*, IV, vol. 8, p. 256; Goethe to Carl August, 8 December 1787, *WA*, IV, vol. 8, p. 305; Goethe to Charlotte von Stein, 19 January 1788, *Hamburger Ausgabe: Goethes Werke*, ed. Erich Trunz, 14 vols (Hamburg: Christian Wegner Verlag, 1948–60; re-released Munich: C. H. Beck: October 1981) [hereafter *HA*], vol. 2, p. 76.

[33]   Goethe to Herder, 6 February 1788. The letter is included in the *Italienische Reise*, *HA*, vol. 11, pp. 519–27. The term *marli* refers to an ornamented raised border of a plate.

[34]   In later years Engelbert Humperdinck also set Goethe's libretto, *Claudine von Villa Bella* EHWV 5 (1868–1872).

remained eleven days in Weimar, living at Goethe's home from 23 April to 5 May, and going through the score with him. Reichardt's setting received its premiere at the National Theatre in Charlottenburg, Berlin – and under the composer's direction – on 20 and 29 July 1789.[35] Despite Goethe's efforts, the court audience received the work coldly – a reaction duplicated at the public performances at the Theater am Gendarmenplatz in Berlin on 3 and 4 August 1789. The singers at these performances were incapable of finding the right style for the spoken metrical dialogue, and for the Weimar revival on 30 May 1795 Goethe's brother-in-law Christian August Vulpius – against the poet's wishes – turned it into prose.[36]

Nicholas Boyle attributes its lack of success to Goethe's 'assumption that Germany, particularly northern Protestant Germany possessed either a theatre to put on such works or audiences to enjoy them'.[37] The public for which Goethe wrote both versions of *Claudine* was a reading public,[38] which is characteristic of early Romantic opera. In the late eighteenth and early nineteenth centuries it was assumed that opera should convey the character of its primary creator (now invariably associated with the composer). Eighteenth-century Italian opera bills accordingly announce the librettist's name in large letters with the composer's name in smaller print. The title page of the manuscript of Eberwein's melodrama to Goethe's *Proserpina* observes this convention. The title page of Schubert's score, 'Claudine von Villa Bella. Singspiel in 3 Akten von Goethe. In Musik von Franz Schubert gesetzt',[39] acknowledges Goethe as its primary creator, a practice Schubert inherited from Salieri.

Two years after Schubert composed his setting of *Claudine* in 1815, the composer Carl Maria von Weber drew this distinction between Italian and the German approaches to music theatre: 'Whereas other nations [i.e. the Italians] concern

35   Rolf Pröpper, *Die Bühnenwerke Johann Friedrich Reichardts*, vol. 1 (Bonn: H. Bouvier, 1965), p. 83, n. 18. See Goethe's discussion of the performance with Reichardt on 15 June 1789, *HA*, vol. 2, p. 118 and on 20 June 1789, *WA*, IV, vol. 9, pp. 136–7. Subsequent productions of *Claudine von Villa Bella. Ein Singspiel* include a setting by Friedrich Ludwig Seidel, which was performed in a private theatre in Berlin; Eberwein completed his setting in February 1816, followed by the Polish composer, Johann Christoph Kienlen, who submitted his score to Goethe in December 1816. Kienlen's setting was performed in Potsdam on 30 April 1818 and was repeated in Berlin from 8 May to 24 June. An account of this production is given in Graf Brühl's letter to Goethe, *Berliner Ausgabe: J. W. von Goethe: Werke*, 22 vols, ed. Siegfried Seidel, 3rd edn (Berlin, Weimar: Aufbau-Verlag, 1970–81), vol. 4, p. 672.

36   See Goethe's letter to Schiller on 16 May 1795, *WA*, IV, vol. 10, pp. 258–9 and Goethe's letter to Reichardt on 21 December 1795, *WA*, IV, vol. 10, p. 351.

37   Nicholas Boyle, *Goethe: The Poet and the Age*, vol. 1, p. 494.

38   See Goethe, *Italienische Reise*, entry of 10 January 1788, *MA*, vol. 15, p. 565.

39   Gesellschaft der Musikfreunde, Vienna A207, vol. 1, Ir, reproduced in Christine Martin and Dieter Martin's edition, *NSA*, II, vol. 14, p. xxiii.

themselves with the sensual pleasure of isolated moments, [the German] demands a self-sufficient work of art, in which all the parts make up a beautiful unified whole'.[40] Weber's identification of a unified operatic work is derived from nineteenth-century aesthetic theory, which espoused deeper levels of coherence between the literary and musical texts. Herder, with whom Goethe corresponded about *Claudine*, believed that 'one ought to be able to regard the organic artistic work as the impression of a living human soul', a revelation of a unique artistic personality.[41] Goethe's desire for organicism in an operatic work is evident in the distinction he makes between works which are unified and those which are assembled. He attacked the use of the term 'composition' to describe Mozart's *Don Giovanni* since composition implied the mere putting together of 'individual parts of a machine' rather than 'an organic whole made alive and pervaded by a unified soul'.[42] In conversation with Eckermann, Goethe admits that he can only enjoy an opera 'when the text attains the same perfection as the music, so that both can keep pace with one another'.[43] His admission to Herder that *Claudine* was intended to be read as well as sung acknowledges this unity of form and admits the poet's desire to restore opera to its dramatic roots.[44] That this aesthetic aim cut across the audience's 'framework of expectations'[45] is evident from contemporary reviews such as that written in Berlin in 1783, where one writer claimed, 'A Singspiel must be seen and heard, not read: if it reads excellently, then it is surely a tragedy or a comedy embroidered with songs, and no true Singspiel'.[46]

Goethe's critic was right – *Claudine von Villa Bella* is 'no true Singspiel' and the eclectic nature of his libretto reveals his desire to develop contemporary music

[40]   Carl Maria von Weber, *Writings on Music*, ed. John Warrack, trans. Martin Cooper (Cambridge University Press, 1981), pp. 206–7. For further discussion, see Christine Martin, 'Pioneering German Musical Drama: Sung and Spoken Word in Schubert's *Fierabras*' in this volume.

[41]   Cited by Martha Woodhouse, *The Author, Art, and the Market: Reading the History of Aesthetics* (New York: Columbia University Press, 1994), p. 55.

[42]   Johann Peter Eckermann, *Gespräche mit Goethe* (Stuttgart: Reclam, 1994), 20 June 1831, p. 775.

[43]   Eckermann, *Gespräche*, 9 October 1828, p. 220.

[44]   Goethe to Herder, 6 February 1788. The letter is included in the *Italienische Reise*, *HA*, vol. 11, p. 519. See also Goethe's correspondence to Charlotte von Stein, 26 January 1788, *WA*, IV, vol. 8, p. 336 and Goethe's letters to Kayser on 20 January 1780, *HA*, vol. 1, p. 293; 20 June 1785, *HA*, vol. 1, pp. 477–8); 5 May 1786, p. 509; 23 January 1786, *HA*, vol. 1, pp. 499–500 and 14 August 1787, *WA*, IV, vol. 8, pp. 244–5.

[45]   Harold Powers, '"La solita forma" and "The Uses of Convention"', *Acta Musicologica* 59 (1987), pp. 65–90, here p. 45.

[46]   *Literatur-und-Theater-Zeitung* 6 (1783), pp. 349–50. The full review is printed in Bauman, pp. 219–20.

theatre.[47] Before his retirement from writing and producing German Ballad Opera, Hiller had begun to move towards Italianate ideas, a move which had earned the respect of Agricola, Germany's foremost singing master and staunch supporter of Italian opera. In 1773, the year in which Hiller retired and Goethe began writing Singspiele, Goethe took up this thread. Even in the first working of his libretto this is signalled through the title, which plays upon a household formula that is advantageous not only in terms of theatricality but as the social formation in comedy. Written as 'mere entertainment', *Claudine* communicates complex and even contradictory sets of social values and is profoundly political in the broadest sense of the term. One can imagine Goethe's libretto exquisitely realized as a court opera in Weimar where the artificial conventions of *opera buffa* can be perceived as a mirror of the social conventions of the society to which it played, its elaborate codes valorizing the codified rules and social hierarchies of courtly social etiquette. Both might be seen as indicative of the wider social imperative for the individual to learn to suppress personal inclinations for the greater good of the collective as reflected in the conflicts between love and duty, which Pedro displays at the beginning of the play, a trope that lay at the heart of almost all of the narratives of classical *opera seria*.

Still under the spell of Italian opera when revising the libretto in 1786–1788, Goethe switched the location to Sicily and his characters towards *opera buffa* types: Alonzo, the comic father, is characteristically cast in the role of a *buffo* bass, the mother, as with all roles for older women, does not appear, while the sets of lovers offer familiar pairings. But even here Goethe began to break with conventions. The title role, Claudine, at first appears to be a typical *opera buffa* figure: the heroine is beautiful and her passivity appears to an integral part of her relational identity: in the revised ensembles (No. 1 and No. 2) she engineers no action but is at the focal point of everything. But Goethe even breaks this convention as the drama reaches a climax in Act III when Claudine sets off to rescue Pedro. In comparison to *Erwin und Elmire*, where the characters represent the upper-middle class on the fringes of the court, all of the protagonists in *Claudine* belong to minor nobility, uncommon to Singspiele at the time.[48] Claudine is not the quasi-*seria* figure, which in *opera buffa* is also reserved for persons of gentle birth, but a more sentimental character: a *mezzo carattere*. The characters of Pedro, a court official, and Rugantino, a bandit, and Don Juan, are linked with the motif of inimical brothers, which was uncommon in Italian libretti, though it was a popular motif in Italian spoken comedy – a more common source for German opera at this time. In the history of music theatre, Goethe's revised version of *Claudine* is extremely significant through its presentation

[47] Goethe to Charlotte von Stein, 26 January 1786, *HA*, vol. 1, p. 503.

[48] See Nicholas Boyle, *Goethe: The Poet and the Age*, vol. 1, p. 215. Markus Waldura, 'Zur Genese von Goethes Libretti zu Reichardts Goethe Opern', in *Johann Friedrich Reichardt. Zwischen Aussprechung und Provokation – Goethes Lieder und Singspiele in Reichardts Vertonung* [Schriften des Handel-Hauses in Halle, vol. 19] (Halle: Handel Hause, 2003), p. 314. I am also grateful to Nicholas Boyle for his correspondence with me about this point.

of the romantic bandits, which was the precursor of an entire series of robber plays. In *Dichtung und Wahrheit* of 1816, the year after Schubert's setting was written, Goethe himself acknowledges how he coaxed this theme onto the musical stage.[49] In his revised version of *Claudine* the chorus also takes on a more structural role in advancing the plot and affirming the philosophy of the drama. The beginnings of a common division in grand opera into male and mixed choruses can also be traced, representing an ideological separation between the socially divisive action of male authority figures (represented by Rugantino and the bandits) and social cohesion or 'nature' in its social form (represented by the *villa bella*).

Goethe's main musical enrichment of *Claudine* is found in the introduction and finales, in which he moves away from North German practice towards the Italian tradition through his use of music to progress the dramatic action on stage. The incipit chorus has a performative function: it introduces Claudine's birthday celebrations and her relationship with Pedro. Characteristically set as a processional piece and ceremonial hymn, this introductory ensemble joins together two pieces, the second of which is a reworking of the introductory choral song of the first edition. Here the texture moves from solo to duet to trio, which is expanded by the ensemble into a full sentence. This revision moves closer to the typical form of *opera buffa*,[50] yet by linking the two opening songs the traditional introduction to the *opera buffa* is changed. The second of these pieces, the opening ensemble, 'Fröhlicher, seliger, herrlicher Tag' – in which the choir begins, the soloists enter one by one and the choir then answers with a refrain – resembles the closing divertissement of Hiller's operas, though the composer never used them as an opening piece. This bedrock of opposing styles is evident in Goethe's finale (No. 8) 'Deinem Willen nachzugeben', which is not entirely in the style of an Italian operatic finale where the juxtaposition of two soloists with a choir is rarely found. And yet through the skilled division of the bandits' chorus Goethe creates a dramatic conclusion where all the conventions of the Italian finale are fulfilled: lively, eventful action, division of the text between individual singers and the increasing number of voices used.

One of the most significant changes made was converting the consistently natural and lively prose dialogue into verse, which gives rise to the question as to whether Goethe perceived *Claudine* as a through-composed opera. As is typical of the admixture of genres woven into the matrix of his libretto, Goethe created a compromise through the use of iambic and occasionally trochaic recitative: a form that can be spoken, as in Hiller's Singspiele and French *opéra comique*, or treated as *secco* recitative. Goethe's strict use of metre and use of the term 'Singspiel' (to indicate recitative opera in the manner of Wieland's *Alceste*) signals that he wanted the dialogue set. This preference is confirmed in the *Italienische Reise*, his

[49]   Goethe, Paralipomena to *Dichtung und Wahrheit*, *WA*, I, vol. 29, p. 217.
[50]   See, for example, Mary Hunter, *The Culture of Opera Buffa in Mozart's Vienna: A Poetics of Entertainment* (Princeton: Princeton University Press, 1999) and Mary Hunter and James Webster, eds, *Opera Buffa in Mozart's Vienna* (Cambridge: Cambridge University Press, 1997).

correspondence with Kayser,[51] and his correspondence with Reichardt in 1789.[52] Writing to the music director Alois Anton Polzelli on 24 May 1814, a year before Schubert composed his setting, he conceded that 'in handling the dialogue of *Claudine* rhythmically it was my intention to give the composer an opportunity to treat it as recitative in Italian style'.[53] Like most of his predecessors, Schubert passed up this opportunity and composed only the musical numbers.

Italianisms in Schubert's *Claudine von Villa Bella*

Using the revised edition of Goethe's text published by Anton Strauß in Vienna in 1810, Schubert commenced work on Act I on 26 July 1815, one of the most prolific months of his compositional career. He was seventeen years old (see Table 1.2).

Schubert's setting of *Claudine* D. 239 belongs to a propitious period in his life when he was intensely engaged in setting Goethe's works. Although he completed the Singspiel the following month, the music for Acts II and III was – according to Heinrich Kreissle von Hellborn in 1861 – burnt into oblivion by Josef Hüttenbrenner's servants during the revolution in Vienna in 1848.[54] The Hüttenbrenner brothers' carelessness in preserving for posterity Acts II and III of Schubert's *Claudine von Villa Bella*, as well as the final two movements of Schubert's Symphony in B minor D. 759 which was also in their possession – coupled with Anselm Hüttenbrenner's setting of the very same libretto – opens up a grey area in Schubert scholarship which lies beyond the scope of this article.[55] There is no doubt, however, that the Singspiel was once complete: Anselm Hüttenbrenner mentions it in his biographical sketch, *Bruchstücke aus dem Leben des Liederkomponist Franz Schubert*, which he wrote for Liszt in 1854;[56] the two volumes of the score which are held in the Gesellschaft der Musikfreunde are in fair copy;[57] and Otto Biba's belief that the opera was performed privately in a house concert,[58] or given a theatrical

---

51   Goethe to Kayser, 18 October 1789, *WA*, IV, vol. 9, p. 157.

52   Goethe to Reichardt, 29 June 1789, *WA*, IV, vol. 9, p. 136.

53   Goethe to Polzelli, 24 May 1814, *WA*, IV, vol. 32, p. 288.

54   Kreissle von Hellborn, *Franz Schubert* (Vienna: Carl Gerold's Sohn, 1865), p. 70.

55   See Lorraine Byrne Bodley, *Franz Schubert: A Musical Wayfarer* (New Haven, CT: Yale University Press, forthcoming).

56   Otto Eric Deutsch, ed., *Schubert: Die Erinnerungen seiner Freunde* (Wiesbaden: Breitkopf & Härtel, 1957, reprinted 1983), p. 207.

57   *Gesellschaft der Musikfreunde*, MS A207, vols 1 and 2.

58   Otto Biba, 'Schubert's Position in Viennese Musical Life', *19th-Century Music* 3/2 (1979), pp. 106–13, here p. 112. See also Otto Biba, 'Public and Semi-Public Concerts: Outlines of a Typical "Biedermeier" Phenomenon in Viennese Music History', in *The Other Vienna: The Culture of Biedermeier Austria*, ed. Robert Pichl and Clifford A. Bernd in collaboration with Margarete Wagner (Vienna: Lehner, 2002), pp. 257–70.

Table 1.2   Schubert's compositional output in July 1815

2 July	'Lieb Minna' (D. 222)
5 July	'Salve Regina' (D. 223)
	'Wandrers Nachtlied I' (D. 224)
	'Der Fischer' (D. 225)
	'Erster Verlust' (D. 226)
7 July	'Idens Nachtgesang' (D. 227)
	'Von Ida' (D. 228)
	'Die Erscheinung' (D. 229)
	'Die Täuschung' (D. 230)
8 July	'Das Sehnen' (D. 231)
9 July	Completion of the Singspiel, *Fernando* (D. 220) commenced on 22 June
11 July	'Hymne an den Unendlichen' (D. 232)
12 July	Symphony No. 3 (first movement) begun on 24 May
15 July	'Geist der Liebe' (D. 223)
	'Der Abend' (D. 221)
	'Tischlied' (D. 224)
	Symphony No. 3 (second movement)
19 July	Completion of Symphony No. 3 (D. 200)
22 July	'Sehnsucht der Liebe' (D. 180), new version
24 July	'Abends unter der Linde' (D. 235)
	'Das Abendrot' (D. 236)
	'Abends unter der Linde II' (D. 237)
	'Die Mondnacht' (D. 238)
26 July	Singspiel, *Claudine von Villa Bella* (D. 239), Act I finished on 5 August
26 July	'Huldigung' (D. 240)
	'Alles um Liebe' (D. 241)

performance of the kind Wilhlem Böcking has described,[59] is supported by the existence of vocal parts – in a very rushed hand by Schubert – for Rugantino's tenor arietta, 'Liebliches Kind' (Act II, No. 9) and Claudine's soprano part for her duet with Pedro, 'Mich umfängt ein banger Schauer' (Act III, No. 10).[60] The

[59]   Deutsch, *Erinnerungen*, pp. 397–8 and 400.
[60]   Goethe Museum, Düsseldorf, Anton-und-Katharina-Kippenberg-Stiftung, *NW* 1860/1984.

absence of a programme or reports in diaries or letters does not cast doubt on Biba's perception of a private performance but is typical of salon records and corroborated by Schubert's friends' familiarity with the music and their numerous attempts to have the overture performed.[61]

Even if *Claudine* was intended for private performance, the linguistic credentials of the libretto are a measure of Schubert's calling as a composer of opera. Schubert was aware of the esteem in which Goethe was held by the Viennese public and may have wanted to curry favour with contemporary audiences. August Wilhelm Schlegel's Viennese lectures, *Vorlesungen über dramatische Kunst und Literatur* (1809–1811), his journal, the *Österreichischer Beobachter*, and the timely flood of publications of Goethe's works in Vienna after Metternich's censorship laws contributed enormously to the favourable reception of the poet in 1815. Given Goethe's popularity with Viennese audiences in 1815, this absence of a public performance in Schubert's lifetime is even more poignant when one realizes that Schubert was the composer who came closest to realizing Goethe's ambitions as a librettist. Had Schubert sent Goethe his setting of the Singspiel instead of his Lieder settings in 1815 – or turned up in Weimar, like Reichardt, with his score under his arm – it would have undoubtedly sparked the interest of the poet, who, during his time as Director of the Weimar Theatre (1791–1817), arranged for 131 Singspiele to be performed. Schubert's Singspiel is tailor-made for the Weimar court. With Acts II and III missing, the main attraction of the work is now confined to scholarly interest but enough survives to affirm new directions and counter criticism levelled at Schubert as a composer of opera.

In a letter to Kayser in the Autumn of 1784, Goethe reveals the motivation behind his textual revisions: 'um einen deutschen Componisten der italiänischen Manier näher zu bringen'.[62] That Schubert shared this aim is first alluded to on the title page where he at once acknowledges his debt to his teacher and declares his ambitions in his form. All of the Singspiele of 1815 bear the inscription 'Franz Schubert … Schüler des Hr. Salieri' which announce him as the consummate Italian-trained musician. Salieri's guidance as a gifted orchestrator of Italian operatic scores is immediately felt in the *Vivace* section of Schubert's overture where there is a real feeling of experience, a sure handling of orchestral forces

[61] See, for example, Ferdinand Schubert to his brother Franz, mid-October 1818 in Deutsch, *Dokumente* pp. 72–3. For a brief performance history, both in Schubert's day and posthumously, see Lorraine Byrne Bodley, 'Revisiting *Claudine*: Schubert's Goethe Singspiel', in *Goethe and Schubert: Across the Divide*, ed. Lorraine Byrne Bodley and Dan Farrelly (Dublin: Carysfort Press, 2003), pp. 161–93. The North-South performance in Ireland of *Claudine von Villa Bella* in 2003 is outlined in Lorraine Byrne Bodley, 'Goethe and Schubert: *Claudine von Villa Bella* – Conflict and Reconciliation', in *The Unknown Schubert*, ed. Barbara Reul and Lorraine Byrne Bodley (Aldershot: Ashgate, 2008), pp. 126–33.

[62] Elmar Bötcher, *Goethes Singspiele* Erwin und Elmire *und* Claudine von Villa Bella und die *opera buffa* (Marburg: N. G. Elwert, 1912), p. 31.

(bars 20–28).[63] Schubert's use of the orchestra to achieve remarkable musical fluidity and dramatic verisimilitude is also evident in the pellucid timbral contrasts of the overture (bars 50–67), his use of bass motifs to create a strong sense of drama (bars 42–45) and through the many examples of effective doubling in the woodwind (bars 107–113). His theatrical use can be heard in his treatment of silence as a dramatic event where he calls the audience to attention in the overture (bars 135–136).

Yet it is not merely experience in orchestration but the social and aesthetic conventions of *opera buffa* which Schubert inherited from Salieri, whose first opera at the Burgtheatre in 1770 rolled out what Gustav Zeichmeister calls 'the Viennese triumphal procession of *opera buffa*'.[64] In order to understand the nature of Schubert's achievement, one must consider *Claudine*'s conservative frames as part of the poetics of *opera buffa*. As is characteristic of *opera buffa*, dynamic markings are characteristically complex and detailed, changing frequently to underscore both the declamation and meaning of the text. Details of articulation and texture are

Example 1.1   Schubert, *Claudine von Villa Bella*, D. 239, No. 5, Aria, 'Es erhebt sich eine Stimme', bars 1–19

63   For a contrary opinion, see Alfred Einstein who was one of the first to criticize it in *Schubert: A Musical Portrait* (Oxford: Oxford University Press, 1951), p. 90.

64   Gustav Zeichmeister, *Die Wiener Theater nächst der Burg und nächst dem Kärntnerthor von 1747 bis 1776* (Vienna: Böhlau, 1971), p. 345.

Note: Examples 1.1 and 1.2 are reproduced with permission from *Franz Schubert: Neue Ausgabe sämtlicher Werke – Serie II: Bühnenwerke, Band 14*, Vorgelegt von Christine Martin und Dieter Martin – BA 5568 © Bärenreiter-Verlag Karl Vötterle GmbH & Co. KG, Kassel.

also carefully and pleasurably variegated, drawing attention to the sonorous surface and to the text rather than to the underlying structure (see Example 1.1).

So too the relatively restricted harmonic vocabulary of Schubert's music renders it easily apprehensible and immediately effective; cadential phrases in various places of the musical structure are almost always repeated and, as is characteristic of an *opera buffa* aria, there are many repetitions (see Example 1.2).

The clarity of melodic line (bars 2–9) – direct, accessible tunes, carefully wrought phrases (bars 19–29) – and clear forms of Pedro's aria makes the music immediately memorable. Schubert's Viennese Classical style celebrates the emotional restraint and elegance of Goethe's revised *Claudine* and communicates a realism and naturalness in opera which resonates with the spirit of the time.

The poetics of *opera buffa* are also subtly present in Schubert's ensembles. The *introduzione* begins typically with a series of 'independent statements' with Alonzo's lines restated by Lucina and answered by Pedro. The Edenic good cheer of the ensemble, No. 2, is also characteristically defined in pastoral terms with clear articulation of sections which typically involve thematic contrast between paragraphs.[65] Its ternary structure, steady rhythm and uncomplicated harmony are all characteristic of four-part homophonic writing in this repertoire. A vestige of this tradition is evident in Rugantino's mercurial *Räuberlied*, where Schubert exploits rhetorical aspects of form – tonal, thematic and textual structures – to create a solid feeling of masculine virility (See Example 1.3) and Schubert's experience in writing for male voice choir (TTB) is already evident.

Schubert's dramatic power derives from a sparseness of means – particularly of harmonic density, with the result that the smallest shifts arrive with great effect – and the composer's ability to capture the stilted braggadocio of Rugantino's lines.

This imprint of *opera buffa* is also evident in Schubert's entrance arias, which eschew elaborate virtuosity and speech-like declamation patterns in favour of smooth lines in more or less regular phrases. Lucinde's and Claudine's *ariette cantabile* (No. 3 and No. 6) emphasize their song-likeness in strophic form, with accompaniments whose more or less constant rhythm is significantly faster that the rhythm of declamation in the voice, thus drawing attention to the 'singing quality' (No. 3, bars 1–20 and No. 6, bars 1–18). But even light-hearted ariettas are a yardstick to measure character, such as Lucinda's unrhymed song (No. 6) which complains in quasi-classical metres of the disturbance Cupid is bringing into their household. Such naturalness of expression combined with emotional truth also hold sway in Claudine's and Pedro's arias (No. 4 and No. 5), neither of which have showy theatrical bravura material to sing. Instead, Schubert demands expressive nuances rather than displays of technical virtuosity, where touching cantabile lines float

---

[65] For literature on pastoral expression, see Edmund Goehring, *Three Modes of Perception in Mozart: The Philosophical, Pastoral, and Comic* (Cambridge University Press, 2004) and Raymond Monelle, *Opera seria as Drama: The Musical Dramas of Hasse and Metastasio* (PhD dissertation, University of Edinburgh, 1968).

Example 1.2   Schubert, *Claudine von Villa Bella*, D. 239, No. 5, Aria, 'Es erhebt sich eine Stimme', bars 19–42

Example 1.2 (continued)

above rhythmically active and carefully orchestrated accompaniments (bars 39–65). The most vocally challenging aria is Claudine's lyric aria (No. 4), a simple rondo in triple time, where the directness of her feelings is effectively communicated and expressed in a dramatic crux (where she realizes her love for Pedro) characterized by a return of Section A (*più moto*; bars 46–65) and the accompanying return of the tonic. The expressive mode in Pedro's *aria di bravura* (No. 5) is also lyrical (bars 19–42), and his triple-metre description of the call of duty (bars 42–59) is calculated to engage the listeners' sympathy as much as their admiration.

As Salieri had shown a penchant for mixing established characteristics of specific operatic genres, this pushing against the boundaries of established conventions is already a hallmark of Schubert's operatic style and mirrors the dialectic in Goethe's

Example 1.3   Schubert, *Claudine von Villa Bella*, D. 239, No. 7, Räuberlied, 'Mit Mädchen sich vertragen', bars 1–29

Example 1.3 (continued)

Source: Lorraine Byrne Bodley, *Claudine von Villa Bella. Goethe's Singspiel set by Franz Schubert*, Piano Reduction by Lorraine Byrne Bodley (Dublin: Carysfort Press, 2002), pp. 97–100. Reproduced with kind permission of Carysfort Press.

libretto.[66] It is chiselled into the ensemble 'Fröhlicher, seliger herrlicher Tag' (No. 2), which has been compared to Mozart's 'Giovani liete' from *Figaro*, though its graceful solo for a child (bars 29–40) is a typical Singspiel ensemble setting with

---

[66]   For a detailed discussion of the range of stylistic influences that fed into Schubert's operatic style, including French reminiscence motifs, Gluck's reform opera, the tone of the Viennese Singspiel and Mozartian *opera buffa*, see Mary Wischusen, *The Stage Works of Franz Schubert: Background and Stylistic Influences* (PhD dissertation, University of Rutgers, 1983).

alternating choral and solo episodes. This concentration of styles is again evident in the closing choral numbers. Rugantino's *Räuberlied* with choir, 'Mit Mädchen sich vertragen' (No. 7), is scored as *Wechselgesang* following French-German practice, while the influence of *opera buffa* in Goethe's rousing finale 'Deinem Willen nachzugeben' (No. 8), is redeemed in the intensity of Schubert's music, the double choir edging up the dramatic tension, underscored by rising dynamics which give way to an epilogue of hammered triplets in the strings (bars 154–189). Here in this concluding scene, the fast pacing of Schubert's ensemble finale adds excitement and verve to the comic situation: its mock heroic style announces in musical terms that Rugantino and his bandits are no more a threat to the social and moral order than their counterparts in Gilbert and Sullivan's *Pirates of Penzance.*

Light-hearted though this romance is, Goethe's *Claudine* has Mozartian depths. As Nicholas Boyle identifies, the figure of Claudine who 'symbolically dies, only to be resurrected as an ideal with the power of unifying contraries, is an anticipation of other figures in later and far more earnest works of Goethe's'.[67] Schubert's identification with this kind of idealized female figure is evident in many works composed in the years following his mother's death. Equally poignant is his identification with the play's central conflict: Rugantino's struggle with the conventions of society. Rugantino is not simply a wanderer: he is the artist in the play whose manifesto could be Schubert's own: 'a song and its accompaniment are the greatest friends of humanity, they will protect me as I walk through the moonlit fields. There is no animal, no wild human that dares to insult the singer who has given himself entirely to the gods, to inspiration' (Act II, Scene 13, lines 795–800). The task of performers today is to present such lines in a way that is immediate, with real intensity and truth of expression. In a North-South production of *Claudine* in Ireland in 2003,[68] the cast struck up an extraordinary sympathy for Rugantino's character, which deals with common issues of love, lust, resistance and the conflicts we encounter in the reality our everyday lives. By the standards of *Faust* and *Iphigenie*, the pantheon of archetypal characters in *Claudine* may, on first reading, seem glib; however, the dramatic personae of Schubert's Singspiel elicit a certain kind of personal involvement and constitute

---

[67]   Boyle, *Goethe: The Poet and the Age*, vol. 1, p. 215.

[68]   The performance of Lorraine Byrne Bodley's edition and piano reduction of Schubert/ Goethe Singspiel, *Claudine von Villa Bella,* performed by young professional singers from north and south of the Irish border, conducted by Colman Pearce, Charles Pearson (piano), took place in the Katherine Brennan Hall, Royal Irish Academy of Music, Dublin on 5 April 2003 as part of the international conference *Schubert and Goethe in Perspective and Performance,* which was held at Trinity College Dublin, 4–5 April 2003. The North American premiere took place at the University of Regina, 5 December 2004.

communal points of reference.[69] Although Goethe's libretto and Schubert's setting captures the *Zeitgeist* of early-German romantic opera, at the same time it evolves in rhythms linked to the rhythms of a larger historical and cultural evolution. Our challenge as interpreters today is to rid Schubert's Singspiel of any vestiges of respectability and to release the huge emotional charge that lies beyond the beauty of its classical sobriety.

Epilogue

In conclusion, to place Goethe's libretto and Schubert's Singspiel together in the same 'hermeneutical theatre'[70] is to unravel how these works speak to each other and to understand something of the ambition inscribed beneath the placid appearance of Schubert's score. Both artists are working towards a national opera, both coupling Italian and German traditions, yet to read *Claudine* as a lambent mark in the unfolding of early German opera would risk exaggerating its significance. What it does offer us is something of the historical premise of Goethe's and Schubert's contribution to early German opera, and a rare glimpse into the mind of an operatic composer at seventeen. Goethe's lapidary libretto has its own story to tell: a text 'embroidered with its threads set wide apart' which sets the stage that Schubert sought. The resulting work, *Claudine von Villa Bella*, D. 239, sings across the boundaries of genre and affirms a precocious understanding of music theatre. Until relatively recently writers on Schubert's operas have not taken seriously how skilfully he used the languages of the repertoire: the more virtuosically he manipulates and combines conventional devices in *Claudine*, the more 'natural' his depiction of humanity seems to be. The work serves as a touchstone that illustrates how the reception history of a work is often determined by conditions other than the purely musical and the dramatic, and tells us more about changing cultural values than the work itself. That Schubert did not write *laissez-faire*, impresarial opera suggests that we should revisit it and explore the genre's shifting nexus of meanings.

[69]   An account of the rehearsal process and production is outlined in Lorraine Byrne Bodley, 'Goethe and Schubert: Claudine von Villa Bella – Conflict and Reconciliation', in *The Unknown Schubert*, ed. Barbara Reul and Lorraine Byrne Bodley, pp. 126–33.

[70]   I am referring to Lawrence Kramer's idea of a 'hermeneutical window' in *Music as Cultural Practice* (Berkeley: University of California Press, 1990) and also Richard Kramer's imaginative metaphor of a 'hermeneutical theatre' when comparing Schubert's G major sonata and 'Schwestergruß' D. 762 in 'Against the Grain: The Sonata in G (D. 894) and a Hermeneutics of Late Style', in *Schubert's Late Music: History, Theory, Style*, ed. Lorraine Byrne Bodley and Julian Horton (Cambridge: Cambridge University Press, 2016), p. 129.

2

Pioneering German Musical Drama: Sung and Spoken Word in Schubert's *Fierabras*

Christine Martin

Introduction

In the early decades of the nineteenth century, Italian works dominated operatic stages throughout Europe, but in the eyes of many German observers, they swerved from true drama and served only as a vehicle for vocal virtuosity. The confrontation between Italian and German conceptions of opera came to a head in December 1821 when the Italian impresario Domenico Barbaja leased the Viennese court theatres and produced mostly Italian operas, namely those of Gioacchino Rossini, gaining unprecedented success.[1]

Ignaz von Mosel (1772–1844), deputy director of the Viennese court theatres from 1820, insisted in his 'Essay on the Aesthetics of Dramatic Musical Composition' of 1813 that, above all, dramatic music should involve the 'heightened declamation and the powerful, vital, warm expression of the emotions that are to be found in poetry'.[2] For Mosel, music was not to hold up the action, nor distract listeners by means of empty showmanship.[3] In an earlier essay, 'On Sung Drama' (1807), the likeminded poet and playwright Heinrich Joseph von Collin (1771–1811) demanded the complete fusion of music and poetry, promoting the idea of a musical drama that could surpass other forms of theatre: 'if opera grants us everything that drama does and surpasses the latter in delight, shall we complain about a catastrophe from which we will gain a lot? I am convinced that the dramatic art will necessarily arrive at this point and thus be brought to the highest degree of perfection'.[4]

---

[1]   See Elizabeth Norman McKay, *Franz Schubert's Music for the Theatre* (Tutzing: Schneider, 1991), pp. 45–6.

[2]   Ignaz von Mosel, *Versuch einer Aesthetik des dramatischen Tonsatzes* (Vienna: Strauß, 1813), pp. 30–31: 'Sie soll daher … bloss eine erhöhte Declamation, ein kräftiger, lebhafter, warmer Ausdruck der Gefühle seyn, welche in dem Gedichte vorkommen'.

[3]   One of Mosel's central tenets was that one should never interrupt or delay the plotline, and moreover, to sustain and revive it through music: 'Nirgends soll die Handlung durch die Musik unterbrochen, aufgehalten oder kälter gemacht, sondern von derselben […] unterstützt und belebt werden'. See Mosel, *Versuch einer Aesthetik*, p. 57.

[4]   Heinrich Joseph von Collin, *Über das gesungene Drama*, first published in: *Morgenblatt für gebildete Stände* 1807, No. 121 (21 May 1807), p. 481, later in: *Heinrich J. von Collin's*

Schubert, who had begun to establish himself as a composer of stage music in 1820,[5] certainly followed the lively debate between the supporters of emergent German Romanticism and those of Italian opera.[6] While, under the wings of his teacher Antonio Salieri, he had modelled his early stage works on French and Italian comic opera,[7] the young composer now joined the 'German school' and soon adopted the idea of an all-sung drama for his opera *Alfonso and Estrella*, D. 732, of 1822. But, disappointed by its rejection at the court theatre in 1823, he returned to the traditional model of French comic opera when he began work on his next opera *Fierabras*, D. 796.[8] This meant adhering to the practice of closed musical sections separated by spoken dialogue. But Schubert had not given up on the idea of a fully 'sung drama', where music and poetry merged. Meeting the challenge to integrate dialogue and action into musical sections, he heightened and broadened their dramatic potential to realize his own vision of musical drama, as this chapter will demonstrate.

---

sämmtliche Werke, vol. 5 (Vienna: Strauß, 1813), p. 85: 'Wenn aber die Oper uns alles gäbe, was uns das Schauspiel gewähret, und uns noch höheren, reicheren Genuß verschaffte: dürfen wir sodann über eine Catastrophe trauern, die uns reicher machen würde? Es ist meine Überzeugung, daß die dramatische Kunst [...] auf diesen Punct, als zum dem höchsten Ziele ihrer Vollkommenheit, nothwendig gelangen muß'. Collin may be best known to musicians as the author of the tragedy *Coriolan* (1804), for which Beethoven composed his Overture, Op. 62 (1807).

[5]   See also Maurice J. E. Brown, *Schubert and the Kärntnerthor Theater: Essays on Schubert* (London: Macmillan, 1966), pp. 127–38.

[6]   Schubert was acquainted with prominent representatives of the Viennese theatre scene, among them Moritz Count Dietrichstein, the director of the court theatres, and his deputy Ignaz von Mosel, who also was responsible for the boys of the Court Chapel Choir, and thus had sustained the young composer since childhood. Mosel recommended Schubert in his certificate of 16 January 1821 as 'one of the most hopeful of our young composers, from all of which opera in general and particularly the I. & R. Court Opera Theatre, [...] may promise themselves the most gratifying art-products'. See Otto Erich Deutsch, *Schubert: A Documentary Biography*, trans. Eric Blom (London: Dent, 1946), p. 159. In addition, Ferdinand Count Pálffy von Erdöd, the owner of the Theater an der Wien, commissioned Schubert's incidental music for Georg von Hofmann's *The Magic Harp*, D. 644, first performed on 19 August 1820, and Helmina von Chezy's *Rosamunde, Princess of Cyprus*, D. 797, premiered on 20 December 1823.

[7]   See Lorraine Byrne Bodley's chapter in this volume.

[8]   Kupelwieser's libretto bears the title 'Fierrabras', which was adopted by Schubert, whereas Otto Erich Deutsch chose the Spanish version of the name, 'Fierabras', for his *Schubert: Thematic Catalogue of All His Works in Chronological Order*, in collaboration with Donald R. Wakeling (New York: Norton, 1951). So did the second edition of Deutsch's catalogue in German language (Kassel: Bärenreiter, 1978) and Franz Schubert, *Neue Ausgabe sämtlicher Werke, Series II: Bühnenwerke, Vol. 8: Fierabras*, ed. Thomas A. Denny and Christine Martin (Kassel: Bärenreiter, 2005–2009).

The Problem of Spoken Dialogue in 'Musical Drama'

Von Collin's view of musical drama did not involve the spoken word but instead envisioned a return to the practice of ancient Greek tragedy, wherein it was thought that the entire text had been sung.[9] Mosel's ideas were derived from the French *tragédies lyriques* of Christoph Willibald Gluck, which he and many contemporaries considered masterpieces of musical drama,[10] and from which he wished to establish an equivalent genre in the German tradition. As Mosel observed: 'Spoken dialogue should be totally excluded from tragic and heroic opera and replaced by recitative, since music generates its own language which is generally used throughout the entire opera, and because the alternation of declamation and song would greatly impede the sublime feelings that opera aims to evoke, as well as the high degree of illusion, on which the effect of the operatic performance is based'.[11]

Mosel's ideas had a strong effect on the dramaturgical conception of Schubert's first full-length opera, *Alfonso and Estrella*. Schubert and his librettist Franz von Schober consciously omitted (or reduced[12]) the spoken dialogue and based its structure on a steady alternation between recitative and arias or duets. Although their approach embodied the aesthetic ideals advocated in Mosel's writings, *Alfonso and Estrella* was not accepted for production at the Viennese Kärntnertor-Theatre.[13] In the relatively few documents at our disposal regarding the respective negotiations, there is no evidence to explain why the opera was not commissioned for performance in Vienna or in Germany, where it was also submitted for consideration.[14] But the then-unusual design of an all-sung drama may have prevented theatres from producing *Alfonso and Estrella*.[15]

---

[9]   See Collin, *Über das gesungene Drama*, p. 86.

[10]   See Mosel, *Versuch einer Aesthetik*, pp. 3–6.

[11]   Mosel, *Versuch einer Aesthetik*, p. 21: 'Der gesprochene Dialog muss von der tragischen und heroischen Oper ganz ausgeschlossen bleiben und das Recitativ seine Stelle einnehmen, weil hier die Musik eine eigene, stets beybehaltene Sprache bildet und der Wechsel der Declamation und des Gesanges die erhabenen Gefühle, welche die Oper beabsichtet, den hohen Grad von Täuschung, auf den sie ihre Wirkung baut, zu sehr stören würde'.

[12]   As the manuscript of Schober's libretto is lost, the possibility that spoken dialogue existed in addition to recitative cannot be ruled out. Yet the number and length of the recitatives clearly suggest that the authors tried to put every relevant scene into verse, which meant setting it to music.

[13]   A reference to this rejection appears in Schubert letter to Josef von Spaun on 7 December 1822; see Deutsch, *Schubert: A Documentary Biography*, pp. 247–50.

[14]   See Till Gerrit Waidelich, *Franz Schubert. Alfonso und Estrella. Eine frühe durchkomponierte deutsche Oper. Geschichte und Analyse* (Tutzing: Schneider, 1991), pp. 29–34.

[15]   For example, the singer Anna Milder was afraid that *Alfonso and Estrella* might fail to meet the taste of the Berlin audience, writing to Schubert on 8 March 1825 that 'people

Significantly, when von Collin tried to put into practice his ideas on writing a libretto for Beethoven called *Bradamante*, the composer turned it down because it lacked spoken dialogue.[16] In addition, the failure of Carl Maria von Weber's through-composed opera *Euryanthe*, premiered on 25 October 1823 at the Kärntnertor-Theatre, shows that the lack of spoken dialogue in German opera was heavily criticized. Weber's accompanied recitatives were repeatedly disapproved in the press as being too long and incomprehensible: 'Mr von Weber's recitatives deviate in their form from those of the Italian and also German masters: they complicate the declamation and naturally lead to indistinct pronunciation'.[17] It was not easy for the audience to distinguish between the accompanied recitatives and the musical numbers. As one contemporaneous reviewer observed, 'not only are the recitatives unnecessarily long and contain too many words, they are also very dull and not much distinguished from the sung text'.[18]

Schubert also rejected Weber's *Euryanthe*, which he considered uneven and without melody.[19] This might be an indication that he at least preferred closed musical numbers and a symphonic development of subjects instead of the through-composed ensembles and finales in *Euryanthe*.[20] In 1823, while Weber was at work

---

here are accustomed to grand tragic opera or French comic opera'; see Deutsch, *Schubert: A Documentary Biography*, pp. 408–9.

[16]   See Dieter Martin, 'Beethovens "verhinderter" Librettist Heinrich Joseph von Collin. Zum Problem deutscher Operntexte in Wien nach 1800', in *Österreichische Oper oder Oper in Österreich? Die Libretto-Problematik*, ed. Pierre Béhar and Herbert Schneider (Hildesheim: Olms, 2005), pp. 133–56, here, p. 153.

[17]   *Allgemeine Theaterzeitung* (Vienna), No. 153 (23 December 1823), pp. 619–20, here p. 619: 'Herrn von Webers Recitative weichen ihrer Form nach von jenen der italienischen und auch der deutschen Meister ab, sie erschweren das Sprechen und machen ganz natürlich das Wort undeutlich'.

[18]   *Wiener Zeitschrift für Kunst, Literatur, Theater und Mode*, No. 134 (8 November 1823), pp. 1102–4, here p. 1103: 'Die Recitative sind nicht nur oft ohne Noth zu lang, und enthalten allzuviele Worte, sondern auch sehr eintönig und wenig vom Gesangtext unterschieden'.

[19]   See Otto Erich Deutsch, *Schubert. Die Erinnerungen seiner Freunde* (Leipzig: Breitkopf & Härtel, 1957), pp. 421–2.

[20]   See Frank Ziegler, '"wahr und genau aufgezeichnet" [–] Webers Wien-Besuche 1822/23 und die Rezeption seiner Bühnenwerke in der Kaiserstadt 1821–1829 im Spiegel zeitgenössischer Erinnerungen', *Weber-Studien* 8 (2007), pp. 433–27, here pp. 498–9. Julius Benedict, on 5 January and 23 March 1861 reported to Max Maria von Weber: 'Franz Schubert […] hatte eine entschiedene Antipathie gegen Euryanthe, und gegen Weber'sche Compositionen im Allgemeinen. Er meinte: das sei keine Musik – namentlich verwarf er alle seine Ensemblestücke, Finales, als form- und regellos. Von kunstreicher, legitimer Durchführung eines Motiv's sei gar nicht die Rede […]'.

at *Euryanthe*, Schubert made an about-face and relinquished the idea of an all-sung opera. Josef Kupelwieser, manager of the Kärntnertor-Theatre, developed a heroic-romantic libretto, *Fierabras*, which appealed to Schubert. Departing from Gluck's neoclassicism, Kupelwieser chose a subject set in the Middle Ages, rather than antiquity. The story of *Fierabras* draws on two separate sources, *Eginhard and Emma*, a play of Friedrich de la Motte-Fouqué,[21] and a collection of various chivalric stories entitled *The Book of Love*.[22] In Kupelwieser's libretto, Emma, the daughter of King Karl,[23] is secretly engaged with the young knight Eginhard, while Florinda, princess of the Moors, falls in love with the Frankish knight Roland. Florinda's brother Fierabras, a Moorish knight who also adores Emma, was suspected to have seduced Emma and became imprisoned by Karl. The father of Fierabras, in turn, took the Frankish emissary Roland and his escort hostage. The plot involves various rescue operations to obtain the release of the hostages, which were typical of nineteenth-century 'rescue operas'. Schubert's choice of libretto therefore implicitly suggests that he chose to model his work on the features of French post-revolutionary opera.

Schubert adopted this approach because Viennese audiences were accustomed to it. Thus, in *Fierabras*, there are large portions of spoken dialogue, mostly at the beginnings of new scenes, when the audience needs historical context or plot details. From the then-avant-garde perspective on opera aesthetics aiming at a through-composed musical drama, this might have been judged as regressive. But Schubert and his librettist were not alone in continuing the traditional features of the French comic opera.[24] While the latter (and the German Singspiel) usually tolerated an abrupt change between spoken words and song, Schubert and Kupelwieser pursued innovative ways of creating fluent transitions from spoken prose to musical numbers.[25] This solution, perhaps the most remarkable aspect of the opera, may be most readily observed in the ensemble, No. 4, of *Fierabras*, where several dialogues demonstrate different affects, behaviours and narrative perspectives of the individual characters.

[21]   Friedrich de la Motte-Fouqué, *Eginhard und Emma* (Nuremberg: Schrag, 1811).

[22]   Johann Gustav Büsching and Friedrich Heinrich von der Hagen, eds, *Buch der Liebe* (Berlin: Hitzig, 1809). See Denny, 'Foreword', in Schubert, *Neue Ausgabe sämtlicher Werke*, series II, vol. 8, pp. xi–xiv.

[23]   Karl is equivalent to the historical figure of Charlemagne; the use of this version of the name results from Fouqué's play *Eginhard and Emma* (see footnote 21), based on medieval legend, from which Kupelwieser's libretto drew inspiration.

[24]   So, for example, did the Viennese contemporaries Conradin Kreutzer in his opera *Libussa* (Vienna 1822) or Joseph Weigl in his numerous Singspiele.

[25]   This is suggested by the different versions of Kupelwieser's libretto; see Denny, 'Foreword', in Schubert, *Neue Ausgabe sämtlicher Werke*, series II, vol. 8, pp. xvi–xix.

The Imitation of 'Spoken' Dialogue: Types of Recitative and Arioso in the Ensemble, No. 4, of *Fierabras*

Five different types of recitative and arioso can be identified in the multi-sectional ensemble of Scenes 4–5 in Act I of *Fierabras*:

a. a recitative with orchestral accompaniment, sometimes using specific thematic material, which represents a second (pantomimic) level of the plot on or off stage;
b. a cavatina or brief arioso emerging directly from the recitative to express the internal emotions of a character;
c. a recitative with simple chordal accompaniment that supports dialogue between characters on stage;[26]
d. a 'narrative arioso' related to the melodrama and the ballad that tells the history behind the plot which occurred in the past or happens off-stage;
e. a '*parlante*' passage featuring orchestral melody above which the singers engage in dialogue in the manner of Italian opera.[27]

At the beginning of the scene, King Karl is returning to court with his entourage after a victory over the Moors. Before the musical number begins, the King charges some of his knights to negotiate peace agreements with the Moors as they divide the spoils of war ('wenn sie des Sieges Beute erst geteilet'). This is soberly ordered in spoken words. What follows the victorious battle is a series of rituals: the plunder is divided, the prisoners of war are brought in, and the military leader Roland requests a favour from the King. Kupelwieser emphasizes the entry of the orchestra, placing the caption 'Ensemble' at the point where the knights repeat the words: 'Let the warriors, Lord, divide the spoils' ('Die Beute lasst, o Herr, die Krieger teilen').

Schubert bridges the transition from speaking to singing with a short prelude. During the following recitative the musical theme of this prelude reappears with pauses, but without referring to the dialogue's topics. Rather, the orchestral accompaniment represents a second level of the plot, in which the entry of the war prisoners is taking place behind the scene (Type a). The melody of the latter chorus, 'The wage of the winner' ('Des Siegers Lohn'), which accompanies their presentation on stage, is developed from the same theme.

After the entrance of the prisoners, Karl demonstrates his victorious power as well as his mercy against the defeated Moors. Both the rhetorical pathos of the public speech and the emotional appeal to the prisoners provide the foundations for a dramatic aria. The King, however, maintains the manner of recitation, 'speaking' while singing a cavatina (Type b): irregular periods (3+2+2+5+2 bars) and emphasized

---

[26] See Mosel, *Versuch einer Aesthetik*, pp. 46–8.
[27] See Julian Budden, 'Parlante', in *The New Grove Dictionary of Opera*, ed. Stanley Sadie (London and New York: Macmillan, 1997), vol. 3, p. 885.

breaks portray traces of spoken word. After the first sentence Karl pauses dramatically for two crotchets and one quaver underlining his promise 'don't be afraid' ('doch bang' euch nicht') and affirming the same after a second break, subtly reduced to one crotchet and one quaver (see Example 2.1).[28] A minim, the longest duration of the phrase, underscores the key word 'nicht'. The melodic line imitates the inflection of the text very closely, for example by leaping down an octave at the end of the phrase (bars 53–54). The melodic shape also seems to mimic the speaker's gestures: The affirmation, 'don't be afraid' is depicted by an upward-leaping sixth. Similarly, Karl's promise to allow the prisoners to be free men within his territory ('doch wandle jeder frei in meinem Staat') is presented by three upward-leaping intervals culminating on the word 'free'. The orchestral accompaniment of this arioso is based on a theme of seven bars and then continued with the same thematic material: a prominent head-motif in the string parts (see Example 2.1, motif a) and a gentle cadence with suspended notes in the wind parts (see Example 2.1, motif b) represent the contrast between the King's power and mercy. A threefold repetition of this pattern, framed within a cycle of fifths, suggests formal closure, while concealing the fact that the metric structure is completely open and free. The grey area between speaking and singing is left only at the end of the cavatina, when the King, from bar 66, proceeds with a longer phrase consisting of regular four-bar periods.

After the King's speech (bar 115), focus is placed on Fierabras, the prince of the Moors. A dotted motif in the orchestral accompaniment draws attention to the proud prisoner,[29] who does not reply to the King's questions. Schubert sets this section mostly as 'unaccompanied' recitative – a recitative with chordal accompaniment in the string parts, in this case intensified by a tremolo (Type c). Only the reprise of the dotted motifs alludes to the pantomimic reactions of the prisoner Fierabras. While the tempo is generally Allegro vivace, the King's declamations are set in free metre.[30] What adds to the dramatic effect of the music is the variation in the length of rhetorical pauses: while some syllables are augmented to emphasize the gestures of the royal speaker – for example the imperious phrase 'What's your answer!' ('Sag an!') (bars 121–122), others are shortened, notably to depict the impatience of the King. The voice enters sometimes with a long, sometimes with a short off-beat to avoid any regular measuring of the melodic line (see Example 2.2).

Schubert's setting of Kupelwieser's verses displays sensitivity to the rhythm and inflections of the text. Given there were very few models of recitative in contemporary German opera, Schubert's approach represents a dramatic innovation. But his use

---

[28] The examples in this chapter are derived from Franz Schubert, *Fierabras, Klavierauszug*, by Hans Schellevis (Kassel: Bärenreiter, 2015), based on Schubert, *Neue Ausgabe sämtlicher Werke*, series II, vol. 8.

[29] George R. Cunningham, *Schubert als Theaterkomponist* (PhD dissertation, Freiburg, 1974), pp. 188–90, remarks that Schubert used this motif repeatedly to characterize Fierabras – a technique rarely applied in Schubert's stage works.

[30] This is affirmed by the 'a tempo' marking the beginning of Roland's narration (bar 140).

Example 2.1   Schubert, *Fierabras*, D. 796, No. 4, bars 45–58

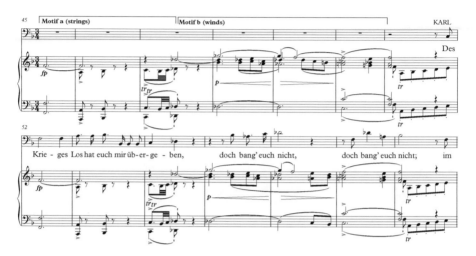

of recitative-like writing can be traced back to early songs including 'Verklärung' ('Transfiguration') D. 59; and, in ballads like 'Der Taucher' ('The Diver') D. 111 or the Ossian songs, there are large sections identified as 'recitative', which preceded the expressive recitatives in *Fierabras*.[31]

In the following section when Roland asks the King to pardon Fierabras by telling him the stirring story of their duel, the orchestra plays the leading part in this narrative arioso (Type d). At the beginning (bars 142–155) the string parts provide a harmonic backdrop, while the wind instruments occasionally interject with a suspended figure. In bar 149, this is transferred to the bass line and repeated several times. Roland's part presents a contrapuntally rising melodic line.[32] Both the chromatic ascent and the accelerated repetition of the bass figure illustrate the dramatic culmination in the hero's duel (see Example 2.3).

The change to triple metre in bar 157, together with a new pattern in the orchestral accompaniment, underscores the onset of the fight. Three times, a diatonically descending figure of semiquavers leads to weak half cadences consisting of three shortly plucked tutti chords, before a short transitional passage (bars 163–165) leads to D minor. Two statements of the pattern in D minor (bars 166–169) are followed, without transition, by three iterations in E♭ major (bars 170–175), the last one varied with a downward staggering figure (bar 174) showing Fierabras's fall on

---

[31]   Some songs, for example D. 126 'Scene from Goethe's Faust', even represent a dialogue between different characters. See Marjorie Wing Hirsch, *Schubert's Dramatic Lieder* (Cambridge: Cambridge University Press, 1993).

[32]   The reprise of this chromatically rising line (from bar 179) and the cadence in majestic D major, Roland's tribute to the defeated hero, links the end of the scene with its beginning.

the battlefield (see Example 2.4). Each thematic restatement, in conjunction with the chromatic shifts, serves to build unrelieved dramatic tension; the music remains tonally open for a further eight bars.

While the continuous sequence of harmonic or melodic patterns generates, like in songs, periodic phrases (of two or four bars), there remains a sense of unrestrained wandering. Schubert developed this kind of rhapsodic accompaniment in his song-like ballads, including 'Die Bürgschaft' ('The Guarantee') D. 246 or 'Der Taucher' ('The Diver') D. 111. Thus the narrative arioso resembles a declamatory song. The

Example 2.2   Schubert, *Fierabras*, D. 796, No. 4, bars 115–124

Example 2.3   Schubert, *Fierabras*, D. 796, No. 4, bars 144–151

Example 2.4   Schubert, *Fierabras*, D. 796, No. 4, bars 170–176

difference between the emphatic arioso and the regular accompanied recitative is felt clearly, when King Karl interrupts Roland's report (bar 192) bringing him back to reality.

The following scene (Act I, Scene 5) at the end of No. 4, involving the whole ensemble of soloists and the choir, is clearly dominated by music rather than text. When Princess Emma and her ladies-in-waiting appear to honour the King, the orchestra plays a rondo alternating between two musical sections (A+B). For Karl, the king and a basso, it was not appropriate to sing along with the virgins. The melody of section A is presented by the horns and cellos, while the King addresses the virgins in a '*parlante*' (Type e), a technique Schubert adapted from Italian opera to integrate a part of the plot into a musical section which traditionally would have stopped any action on stage.

Every solo part of this large ensemble is a 'speaking' song; the protagonists continually participate in the plot and dialogue even while they are singing. Various types of declamation in free metre serve the imitation of 'spoken' dialogue in recitative and arioso passages, while formal closure is provided through thematic elaboration and the periodic structure of the orchestral accompaniment.[33]

The Combination of Music and Spoken Word: Melodrama

Whereas in recitative and arioso spoken dialogue was imitated while singing, in the final section of the ensemble, No. 4, spoken word is embedded within the musical setting in the form of a melodrama.[34] When the virgins enter, Fierabras recognizes

---

[33]   Schubert inherited his technique of elaboration from the classical era, namely from Mozart's or Cherubini's operas. Specific thematic material is only applied within the same movement. He rarely adopted 'reminiscence motifs' recurring throughout the opera (see footnote 29).

[34]   The melodrama was a play or a dramatic scene, 'using short passages of music in alternation with or accompanying the spoken word to heighten its dramatic effect'. It was very prominent on the German opera stage in the early nineteenth century. See Anne Dhu Shapiro, 'Melodrama', in *The New Grove Dictionary of Opera*, ed. Stanley Sadie (London and New York: Macmillan, 1992), vol. 3, pp. 324–7.

Emma, the woman with whom he fell in love four years ago in Rome. Taken aback by her unexpected appearance, he is unable to restrain his feelings:

Fierabras: Ha!
Roland: What happens!
Fierabras: It's her!
Roland: The princess! Yes, the daughter of our king.
Fierabras: And my love!
Roland: Be quiet, madman!
Fierabras: Gods!

Kupelwieser's stage direction instructs that his monologue should be spoken 'rapidly and under musical accompaniment' ('schnell aufeinander und unter Musik zu sprechen').[35] Schubert directs it to be performed while the chorus of the virgins is fading out. The fact that Fierabras is speaking and not singing reflects his state of helplessness: far away from his social status as a prince, humiliated by being a war prisoner, and overcome with emotion at meeting Emma, he is unable to continue in the conventional manner of singing.[36]

The melodrama not only enabled Schubert to combine music with spoken text, but also allowed for the simultaneous representation of action and the protagonist's emotional reaction. Schubert had a gift for illustrating single words and affects of a spoken text with expressive musical gestures. At the same time, by means of thematic elaboration and development, he carefully structured his musical commentary, which at first sight seems to be exclusively related to the unforeseen events of the plotline. One such example can be observed in Act II, Scene 12, at the beginning of the ensemble (No. 15).

Here we encounter the Frankish knights imprisoned in a tower and frightened by an outside noise, represented by a sudden tremolo in the strings. Two of the knights report to the others what they see in the darkness. Their abrupt phrases and excited questions only partly reveal what is happening in front of the tower. A theme built on rising and falling staccato quavers (see Example 2.5, theme a) symbolizes, in conjunction with the mysterious movement off-stage, the observer's sense of insecurity. Theme a is heard twice, but does not break away from the tonic of A minor. Only with the third utterance, enriched by a canonic stretto, does the melodic line lead eventually to the dominant. The knight's cries, which occurred before only every fourth bar, now occur in rapid succession (bars 15–17). After a

---

[35]   Madeleine Häusler, 'Das Melodram als Mittel der Durchkomposition in Schuberts "Fierabras"', *Schubert-Jahrbuch* (1998), pp. 25–33, here p. 26, assumes it would have been Schubert's idea; she missed Kupelwieser's hint in the first version of his libretto, where it is given only after the dialogue between Fierabras and Roland and headed 'At the same time chorus' ('Zugleich Chor').

[36]   See Häusler, *Das Melodram als Mittel der Durchkomposition*, pp. 26–7.

short break, theme a starts again with a new ascending variation on the upbeat (see Example 2.5, theme a′): this is quite mechanically repeated for twelve bars and sustained by a timpani tremolo, a large crescendo from *pianissimo* to *fortissimo* and the successive entry of every wind part.

Hearing a stranger approaching their prison, the knight's tension is immediately conveyed to the audience by means of harmonic stagnation. The tonic A minor is reached only for the short event of Florinda's surprising entry. As soon as she appears on stage, the spoken report is changed into sung recitation. Florinda initially resumes the diatonic rise and harmonic development of the former section, telling anew how she forced her way into the tower to rescue her beloved Roland. The latter is enlarged and leads to the dominant of the dominant (B♯ major) to show her individual passion and fear. Shouting 'my Roland', she arrives at the knight's prison, represented by a return to the tonic, A minor. The suspended notes within her melody, like those of the orchestral accompaniment, are reminiscent of theme a within the melodrama.

Schubert is not by chance returning to the thematic material of the melodrama. This is revealed by the reprise of theme a with Roland's entry, combined with a varied repetition of Florinda's cadence (compare bars 50–56 and 73–77). The second recapitulation of former events, now from Roland's perspective, leads to the recognition of his beloved. Eventually at the beginning of the finale arioso 'At the graveside' ('Am Rand des Grabes') Roland takes over the head motif, which is itself a variant of theme a′ in an augmented form (see Example 2.6). Therefore, all the musical sections of this scene are linked through the same thematic invention and its elaboration.

Whereas the melodramatic scene of No. 15 belongs to a broader sequence, the melodrama of the second act's finale (No. 17) stands apart from its surroundings. In this scene Florinda observes Roland's attempt to escape the Moors, who are besieging the tower. The *teichoscopia* allowed the libretto to integrate a report of the events happening off-stage. Florinda is emotionally overwhelmed by the rapid change of events. There is no time to reflect. In a breathless dialogue with the orchestra, she expresses her thoughts and feelings without mediation.[37]

Schubert continuously invents new orchestral figuration to convey the unexpected plot turns outside the tower. They are loosely related to each other via similar rhythmic patterns or a particular manner of articulation. The same means of development, augmentation and diminution of thematic material found in No. 15 are applied, so as to reflect the tempo and sustain the tension of the plotline. Repetitions and sequences give the impression of a periodic structure, but cadences are consequently avoided. On the contrary, the harmonic progression, involving

[37]   Unlike Roland's narration of his fight with Fierabras there is no temporal distance between Florinda's observation and the events happening. Thus, she is not able to give a detailed and rhetorical framed account like he did. 'Narrative control' and 'complete story' are important criteria to distinguish between the ballad and the dramatic scene. See Hirsch, *Schubert's Dramatic Lieder*, pp. 88–91.

Example 2.5   Schubert, *Fierabras*, D. 796, No. 15, bars 7–20

Example 2.6   Schubert, *Fierabras*, D. 796, No. 15, bars 87–90

unexpected shifts and dissonances, remains permanently open – thus reflecting the plot's state of suspense: for instance, the pitch E♭ initially (bar 90) seems to be a tonic note, but during the first twenty bars of the melodrama it rapidly becomes the third of C♭ major (bar 94), the fifth of A♭ minor (bar 98), the key note of E♭ minor (bar 100) and again the third, now of C♭ minor (bar 103). At bar 106, the movement modulates to B♭ major, before shifting chromatically to B♯ minor in bar 110. The following middle section turns to the brighter sharp keys, temporarily reaching E minor (bar 122) and A minor (bar 138) with medial cadences, then subsequently returning to the dark E♭ minor of the beginning. The glimpse of E♭ major represents only the triumph of the hostile fanfares (bar 185).

Only occasionally does the reprise of a smooth cadence stop the rhapsodic wandering, establishing a weak connection between the different scenes of the movement. This calm motif is installed right at the beginning of the scene and sustains Florinda's prayer 'Guard him, ye eternal powers' ('Schützt ihn, ihr ewigen Mächte', bars 95–98 and 101–104). There is a strong contrast between this cadence played by the winds and the turbulent quavers and tremolos of the string parts. It accompanies every invocation of the Gods and is consequently lacking in the second part of the melodrama, when the enemies will gain ground and defeat Roland.[38] Here, the whole musical context is dissolved into a sequence of *fortissimo* chords, tremolos and mutilated motifs (see Example 2.7) until the hostile fanfares outside meet the horrified cry of the Frankish knights inside the tower (bars 185–190).

The observation of the events off-stage and the emotional expression in this scene are closely intertwined; the time structure of the plot leaves no room to sing an aria. Again the specific means of the melodrama enable both to be presented simultaneously and serve an exciting display of the drama on stage.

Opera as Drama

Melodrama was one of the latest techniques employed by the emerging German music theatre in the first half of the nineteenth century. Melodramatic scenes became omnipresent on Viennese stages, most notably in the adaptations of French operas, incidental music of the Romantic drama, and in the Singspiel, namely those by Joseph Weigl.[39] Schubert himself incorporated them in his earlier stage works, namely in *The Magic Harp* D. 644. Contemporary reports testify what enormous effect the expressive art of declamation at that time took on audiences.[40] The natural distance between the spectators and the events off-stage was compensated for when they saw and shared empathetically the emotional reaction of the narrating

Example 2.7   Schubert, *Fierabras*, D. 796, No. 17, bars 166–169

38   See Christiane Plank, *Die melodramatische Szene in der Oper des 19. Jahrhunderts; eine musikalische Ausdrucksform* (Munich: Utz, 2005), pp. 77–80.

39   See Peter Branscombe, 'Schubert and the Melodrama', in *Schubert Studies: Problems of Style and Chronology*, ed. Eva Badura-Skoda and Peter Branscombe (Cambridge: Cambridge University Press, 1982), pp. 105–41.

40   Tobias Lund, *Enthusiasm, Contemplation and Romantic Longing: Reconsidering Schubert's Sectional Songs in the Light of Historical Context* (Lund: Department of Arts and Cultural Sciences Lund University, 2009), pp. 80–87. The declamation of ballads and other poems was very popular around 1820 and took place even in such concerts as Eduard Jaëll's academy on

character. Yet it was also possible to create a tension out of narrative structures, like the ballad or the retrospective, which normally slowed the plot. The audience, listening to the melodrama, forgot that the events told on stage just happened in the (fictive) past.

In the dramaturgical conception of *Fierabras*, melodrama plays a key role. Schubert and Kupelwieser trusted in the immediacy of its dramatic impact and in the simultaneous representation of action and affect. They integrated as many as six different melodramatic scenes within their opera (see nos 4, 8, 15, 16, 17, 21), among them three at the peak of the drama at the end of the second act.

However, the frequent application of melodramatic scenes particularly reveals the partial replacement of the aria or any other solo scenes in *Fierabras*. It can be assumed, that Schubert, by avoiding large arias or scenes for his protagonists, wanted to symbolize the social and political restriction they experience in *Fierabras*: The verse 'Not even a glance is allowed to show what the soul knows' ('Und kein Blick darf zeigen, was die Seele weiß') from No. 6 seems to be an oppressing device for the behaviour of any character except the rulers.[41]

Nonetheless, the fact that the protagonists during the entire opera are more often 'speaking' and acting rather than reflecting on their feelings through song results primarily from dramaturgical considerations. The main objective of Schubert's and Kupelwieser's efforts was to prevent music at any rate from delaying the plotline. Schubert seemed to follow most willingly Collin's recommendation to use free recitative instead of arias: 'If a sensation is too fleeting, if a passion is too full of different affects to be expressed with an aria, it shall fade away, it shall spend itself in free recitative'.[42] Schubert wanted his singers to represent a drama like actors on the theatrical stages.[43] By integrating the dramatic dialogue largely into the musical fabric and using the latest techniques like the ballad, the melodrama or the Italian

---

4 March 1819 where 'Schäfer's Klagelied' ('Sheperd's complaint') D. 121 was performed. See Deutsch, *Schubert: A Documentary Biography*, pp. 114–15.

[41]   They only dare to show their feelings in special circumstances, for instance 'at the graveside' (like Florinda and Roland in No. 15), to hide their emotions 'deeply inside the breast' like *Fierabras* in his arioso or to leave carefully encrypted messages like Eginhard in his serenade (both in No. 6).

[42]   See Collin, *Über das gesungene Drama*, p. 87: 'Ist eine Empfindung zu flüchtig, eine Leidenschaft am mannigfaltigen Wechsel der Empfindungen zu reich, um in einer Arie festgehalten, abgerollt zu werden, so verfliege, verstürme sie im freyen Recitative'.

[43]   Collin sees the singer's status upgraded, if they become actors: 'If the only purpose of music will be the true and delightful expression of feeling, leaving behind any superfluous artificial deviation, the singer will rise to be an actor'. See Collin, *Über das gesungene Drama*, p. 86: 'Kommt es dahin, daß die Musik nur in dem wahren und schönen Ausdrucke der Empfindung, als ihrem Elemente, lebet, fällt alles, was nicht dahin strebt, als überflüssiger Auswuchs hinweg, so wird der Sänger […] sich unvermerkt zum Schauspieler erheben'. See also Mosel, *Versuch einer Aesthetik*, p. 57.

parlante, Schubert created impressive and multifaceted scenes. Considering the different intonations and dramatic contexts of his 'speaking' characters, he developed diverse and highly expressive ways of musical declamation – an outstanding feat on the theatrical stage of his time. Therefore, *Fierabras* impresses with its enormous speed and dramatic tension within the plotline and with declamatory song similar to a spoken text in drama. But the expressive qualities and means of music itself, however, are often pushed into the background. Both in the recitatives as well as in the melodrama the orchestral accompaniment mainly illustrates the text and sustains the rhetorical gestures of a dramatic declamation. Moreover, many of the musical pieces independent of the text are supposed to be incidental music including marches, serenades, hymns or battle music.[44] Whereas von Collin envisioned that poetry and music should form a whole, Schubert created a hybrid genre between opera and drama. Though he broadened the framework of the *opéra comique* he went only half way towards a real 'musical' drama, adhering to the aesthetics of the older model.[45] But surely Schubert was one of the first composers to adapt the Romantic avant-garde's vision, 'that the first and most important purpose of dramatic music is its fusion with the text and plot of the drama'.[46]

[44]   Incidental music to the melodramatic scene offered the opportunity to be divided into an external plotline (e.g. an event taking place with musical accompaniment) and the internal monologue of a single character. See Plank, *Die melodramatische Szene*, pp. 56–71.

[45]   Unfortunately, *Fierabras* never reached the stage in Schubert's lifetime and thus did not exert any influence on the development of German opera. Since Kupelwieser was fired in November 1823, the stage production of *Fierabras* at the Kärtnertor-Theatre was turned down. See Schubert, *Neue Ausgabe sämtlicher Werke*, series II, vol. 8, p. xi.

[46]   Mosel, *Versuch einer Ästhetik*, p. 59: 'daß das erste und notwendigste Bedingnis der dramatischen Musik ihre innigste Vereinigung mit dem Texte und der Handlung sei'.

3

The Dramatic Monologue of Schubert's Mass in A♭ Major*

James William Sobaskie

Introduction

Franz Schubert fussed over his fifth Mass. Starting the score in November 1819, he considered it complete three years later.[1] A letter sent to Josef von Spaun on 7 December 1822 testifies: 'My Mass is finished, and is to be produced before long. I still have my old notion of dedicating it to the emperor or empress, as I think it a success'.[2] Nevertheless, Schubert made substantial changes in 1826 and 1827.[3] While the Mass in A♭ major (D. 678) was the most expansive he had composed till then, its eight-year development is curious, given his reputation for quick work.[4]

---

* An earlier version of this chapter was read at the Conference in Honour of Susan Wollenberg, held in Lady Margaret Hall at the University of Oxford on 2 September 2016. I thank Lorraine Byrne Bodley, Xavier Hascher, and Susan Wollenberg for their encouragement on that occasion.

[1] Otto Eric Deutsch reports: 'The A♭ major Mass was begun in November 1819 and finished in September 1822 in a second version entitled "Missa solemnis"; it remained unpublished until 1875'; see Otto Eric Deutsch, *Schubert: A Documentary Biography*, trans. Eric Blom (London: Dent, 1946), p. 249. What Deutsch refers to as 'a second version' of the A♭ major Mass incorporates changes made to its Gloria and Sanctus four and five years later.

[2] Deutsch, *Schubert: A Documentary Biography*, p. 248.

[3] Schubert revised the Gloria and 'Osanna' in 1826 and 1827. See Robert Winter, 'Paper Studies and the Future of Schubert Research', in *Schubert Studies: Problems of Style and Chronology*, ed. Eva Badura-Skoda and Peter Branscombe (Cambridge: Cambridge University Press, 1982), pp. 238 and 242–3.

[4] Schubert's creativity, reflected in his comments and compositions, has been discussed since his own time, but also has given rise to myths and misconceptions that will not be resuscitated here. Nevertheless, the speed at which he *could* create at certain times remains genuinely amazing. For instance, Schubert's last Mass, D. 950, in E♭ major, was begun in June of 1828 and finished shortly before his death in November of that year, a span of just five months; see Deutsch, *Schubert: A Documentary Biography*, p. 742 and pp. 873–4. Incredibly, components of *Schwanengesang*, the whole of the String Quintet, and the last three piano sonatas were also completed during that same period. So the extended time taken for the A♭ major Mass surely is unusual for the composer.

Why would Schubert take such trouble?[5]

Sacred choral music flourished in nineteenth-century Vienna, fostered by the Catholic Church to gather and inspire its faithful. Initially, Schubert may have conceived the Mass in A♭ major as a contribution to his community's spiritual life.[6] Parts had been copied and plans had been made for its premiere at a Währing parish in 1824.[7] Even so, further refinement would come, perhaps prompted by other hopes and opportunities.

---

[5]   The present study proceeds from several sources beyond that of Deutsch, *Schubert: A Documentary Biography*, including: Robert Winter, 'Paper Studies and the Future of Schubert Research', in *Schubert Studies: Problems of Style and Chronology*, ed. Eva Badura-Skoda and Peter Branscombe (Cambridge: Cambridge University Press, 1982), pp. 209–76, especially pp. 238 and 242; Thomas A. Denny, 'The Years of Schubert's A♭ major Mass, First Version: Chronological and Biographical Issues, 1819–1822', *Acta Musicologica* 63/1 (1991), pp. 73–97; Glenn Stanley, 'Schubert's Religious and Choral Music: Toward a Statement of Faith', in *The Cambridge Companion to Schubert*, ed. Christopher H. Gibbs (Cambridge: Cambridge University Press, 1997), pp. 207–23, especially pp. 218–22; John Gingerich, '"To How Many Shameful Deeds must you Lend your Image": Schubert's Pattern of Telescoping and Excision in the Texts of His Latin Masses', *Current Musicology* 70 (2000): pp. 61–99, especially pp. 64–6 and 76–9; and Leo Black, *Franz Schubert: Music and Belief* (Woodbridge: Boydell Press, 2003), especially pp. 70–82 and 178–82.

[6]   Schubert left relatively few written statements regarding his own religious beliefs. In a letter to his father on 2 July 1825 Schubert wrote of the reception of his famous *Ave Maria* (D. 839): 'My new songs from Walter Scott's 'Lady of the Lake' especially had much success. They also wondered greatly at my piety, which I expressed in a hymn to the Holy Virgin and which, it appears, grips every soul and turns it to true devotion. I think this is due to the fact that I have never forced devotion in myself and never compose hymns or prayers of that kind unless it overcomes me unawares; but then it is usually the right and true devotion'; see Deutsch, *Schubert: A Documentary Biography*, pp. 434–5. If this assertion is sincere, Schubert's Mass in A♭ may offer considerable evidence of his personal faith.

[7]   Accounting records of Schubert's expenses kept by his friend Josef Hüttenbrenner suggest that the Mass in A♭ major was first copied in early 1823; see *Schubert: A Documentary Biography*, pp. 260–61 and 266–7. If, as Schubert averred on 7 December 1822, his Mass was 'to be produced before long', this suggests that payment may have been made for copies of a conducting score and performing parts. In a letter dated 3 July 1824, Schubert's brother Ferdinand told the composer that his friend Johann Rieder, a choirmaster in Währing, had plans to produce the Mass in A♭ major; see Deutsch, *Schubert: A Documentary Biography*, pp. 360–63. However, Deutsch asserts: 'The performances [of Schubert's Mass in A♭ major] in the churches of Vienna cannot be definitely established'; see Deutsch, *Schubert: A Documentary Biography*, p. 362. Glenn Stanley reports that 'Schubert's brother Ferdinand ... was dissatisfied with the first performance [of the Mass in A♭ major], at which he conducted a predominantly amateur ensemble in late 1822 or early 1823', but does not cite a source for this assertion; see Glenn Stanley, 'Schubert's Religious and Choral Music: Toward a Statement of Faith', p. 219.

Sacred choral music also served the Habsburg Empire as a reflection of power, and Schubert may have seen his Mass as a means of attracting imperial attention.[8] A warm reception surely would have brought new connections and commissions to the composer, then in his mid- to later twenties, demonstrating productive potential.[9] Indeed, both spiritual and temporal authorities would value its success.

Ultimately, Schubert's Mass in A♭ major served the composer as a professional credential.[10] Bolstering his application for the Court's Vice Chapel-Master post in 1826, it demonstrated that he could supply what was expected of the office-holder.[11] Nevertheless, a broader perspective reveals another potential source of motivation.

Schubert recognized that he belonged to an extraordinary creative culture centred in Vienna.[12] Emulating Haydn, Mozart, and Beethoven, his production was diverse as well as voluminous, and his confidence in himself and his art seems to have been braced by taking the long view. Moreover, Schubert seems to have realized that his music not only contributed to that culture, but also broke new

[8]   Leo Black observes that the Habsburg Empire used religion as a social instrument, of which Schubert must have been aware: 'It would scarcely have escaped his notice that the Catholic Church went hand in hand with the regime in keeping the populace in its place and thought to a minimum'; see Leo Black, *Franz Schubert: Music and Belief*, p. 20.

[9]   In 1826, Schubert gave the manuscript of his Mass in A♭ major to Franz Sales Kandler, apparently in the hope that Kandler would publish an article about it in one of the journals to which he contributed reviews, but when that did not occur, Schubert asked Kandler to send it to the music publishers Leidesdorf or Pennauer for their consideration; see Deutsch, *Schubert: A Documentary Biography*, pp. 535–6. It is not known if this ever happened.

[10]   Glenn Stanley opines: 'How naïve Schubert was to attach his final, vain hopes of an appointment at the Imperial Court to Mass No. 5 in A flat (D. 678), a *Missa solemnis* composed over the years 1819–22. For this purpose, it is much too subjective and passionately religious, thus rivalling – though utterly different in its modes of expression – and representing an artistic effort uncannily similar to the great work composed contemporaneously, Beethoven's *Missa solemnis*'; see Stanley, 'Schubert's Religious and Choral Music: Toward a Statement of Faith', pp. 218–19.

[11]   Schubert's pursuit of the Imperial Court's Vice-Kapellmeister's position is documented in letters within Deutsch, *Schubert: A Documentary Biography*, pp. 520–21, 575–8 and 599. Glenn Stanley explains: 'Josef Eybler, in 1827, denied Schubert's petition for a court performance of Mass No. 5 and thus blocked his [Schubert's] application for the position of *Vizekapellmeister*. This incident dashed his last hopes for a significant post, but also demonstrated his commitment to the genre independent of any professional considerations'; see Stanley, 'Schubert's Religious and Choral Music: Toward a Statement of Faith', p. 219.

[12]   Portraits of this remarkable creative environment appear in Raymond Erickson, ed., *Schubert's Vienna* (New Haven: Yale University Press, 1997), Christopher Gibbs and Morten Solvik, eds, *Franz Schubert and His World* (Princeton, NJ: Princeton University Press 2014), and David Wyn Jones, *Music in Vienna: 1700, 1800, 1900* (Woodbridge: Boydell Press, 2016).

ground.[13] Today it is both clear and certain that Schubert's Mass in A♭ major furthered the then still-evolving genre of the Viennese orchestral Mass, a species of sacred music exalted by Haydn and Mozart and esteemed outside Austria.[14] Indeed, it ranks with the very best of their contributions to that repertoire. Writing to the Mainz-based publisher Schott in February of 1828, he mentioned the Mass to stress his 'strivings after the highest in art', hoping to secure a contract that would circulate his music far and wide.[15] Schubert was both understandably and justifiably proud of this sacred setting, perhaps most of all for its innovation. That innovation is the subject of this chapter.

The Subsurface Narrative within Schubert's Mass

A subtextual dramatic monologue is perceptible within Schubert's Mass in A♭ major. At the very beginning, a dramatic persona emerges, reified by indices of presence and interiority.[16] Carefully conceived to appeal to Schubert's contemporaries, the implicit character initially manifests within the Kyrie via suggestive musical details. As the Mass's monologue unfolds, this dramatic persona seems to address

---

[13]   Schubert's oeuvre suggests that he was preoccupied with the notion of 'progress' and with developing a personal style that proceeded from those of composers he admired (Haydn, Mozart, and Beethoven), yet also was distinctive and non-duplicative. For a detailed examination and exposition of Schubert's musical style, see Susan Wollenberg, *Schubert's Fingerprints: Studies in the Instrumental Works* (Farnham: Ashgate: 2011).

[14]   For a broad view of the Viennese orchestral Mass tradition, see Daniel Heartz, *Haydn, Mozart and The Viennese School, 1740–1780* (New York: Norton, 1995). Glenn Stanley observes that Schubert's last two Masses stand apart from their predecessors: 'The decisive difference between these Masses and the first four lies in the most basic compositional challenge: taking a musically interpretive stance to the words. Now, finally, Schubert sometimes endeavoured to add meaning to the text by applying both the general technical advances that mark his mature style as well as the specific experience gained in composing the early Masses and the intervening dramatic music, both religious and secular'; see Stanley, 'Schubert's Religious and Choral Music: Toward a Statement of Faith', pp. 220–21.

[15]   See Deutsch, *Schubert: A Documentary Biography*, p. 740.

[16]   Edward T. Cone discusses Schubert's employment of musical personae in the chapters 'Some Thoughts on "Erlkönig"' and 'Persona, Protagonist, and Characters', in *The Composer's Voice* (Berkeley, Los Angeles and London: University of California Press, 1974), pp. 1–19 and 20–40. See also Chapter 12 in this volume, 'Virtual Protagonist and Musical Narration in the Slow Movements of Schubert's Piano Sonatas D. 958 and D. 960', where Lauri Suurpää explores the interactivity between two musical personae – a protagonist and an antagonist – in two of Schubert's last piano sonatas. The identification of implicit personae within Schubert's texted and non-texted music via various kinds of suggestive musical evidence appears to hold great promise for illuminating its inherent and often dynamic drama.

an apparently non-reified auditor, appropriating, exploiting and individuating the traditional Latin liturgical text. In turn, the persona's mien evolves, transforming from penitent, to adherent, to believer, to initiate, to anticipant over the course of the liturgical setting. The five parts of the Ordinary provide context and conventions, framing the monologue's narrative while facilitating portrayal of the persona's transformation. Intuited by amenable listeners, these two characters, one hypostatized and human, the other reflected and divine, portray the Christian experience in its most essential form. While responses of the divine auditor do not seem to be overtly articulated, perceptible changes in the dramatic persona encourage their inference. And while some listeners may equate the persona with Schubert himself, it actually represents a separate, individuated entity belonging to the Mass's dramatic content, a character with whom – ideally – listeners self-identify. Perhaps partly traceable to the Romantic aesthetic's premise of individuated expression, the incorporation of a subtextual dramatic monologue within a Mass setting could not have occurred any earlier in Vienna, or anywhere else for that matter. This expressive innovation – sensed but not explored until now – may account for the composer's attachment to his artistic achievement, as well as the affection of its audiences.

Devotion simulated in the Mass in A♭ major surely reflects profound introspection. Of course, what it reveals about Schubert's own piety remains a matter for each listener to consider.[17] What seems certain is that the Mass's subtextual dramatic monologue stimulates the imaginations of receptive listeners, encouraging subliminal identification with and empathy for its dramatic persona. By promoting self-investment, similar to that elicited by songs and plays, the monologue vivifies its listeners' experiences in unprecedented and transcendent ways. In turn, the Mass's ability to engage its listeners so intimately may explain its appeal, as well as the composer's dedication to its refinement. Let us examine evidence of the Mass's monologue. In focus will be musical and textual indices that suggest presence and interiority.

Kyrie

Schubert's Mass's Kyrie begins solely via breath, featuring a meandering phrase from solo bassoon in bars 1–4. Veiled by two clarinets, the bassoon's melody commands attention by displacing human voices, communicating reticence and vulnerability, as illustrated in Example 3.1.[18]

---

[17]   Glenn Stanley describes Schubert's Mass in A♭ major thusly: 'The master of the Lied and religious drama has come to terms with the Catholic liturgy by writing personal, subjective music for those parts of the text that spoke to his own religious convictions'; see Stanley, 'Schubert's Religious and Choral Music: Toward a Statement of Faith', p. 223.

[18]   The examples in this chapter are based with permission on Schubert, *Mass in A-flat major, D 678*, edited by Doris Finke-Hecklinger, BA 5623 and published by Bärenreiter-Verlag.

Example 3.1   Schubert, Mass in A♭ major, D. 678, Kyrie, bars 1–16, selective reduction with analysis

Initiating a *missa solemnis* involving as many as one hundred participants, the bassoon's high, thin and ambivalent line certainly is unexpected.[19] With substantial vocal and instrumental forces at the ready, plus plenty of precedent to use them at the start of a ceremonial work like this, Schubert's restraint with these resources dashes prior assumptions and derives new possibilities. The bassoon's entrance disarms and engages, manifesting a penitent persona.

Strings and organ respond warmly and generously to the modest woodwind strain, establishing exchange as an essential premise of the Mass via the principle of antiphony. Although bars 4–8 might be imagined to be a divine reply, they may be more convincingly interpreted as an internal response – the dramatic persona's *perception* of acknowledgement. Concluded by a half cadence in bar 8, the passage ends tentatively, yet replete with potential. By these instrumental means – which delay the choir's entry for eight full bars – the characters of the Mass's subtextual dramatic monologue come into being and begin to engage listeners.[20]

Example 3.1 shows that the substance of bars 9–16, which introduces the choir and also concludes with a half cadence, resembles that of bars 1–8. As the annotation suggests, the entire sixteen-bar span elaborates the dominant of A♭ – an E♭ major harmony. Bars 17–23 (not shown in Example 3.1) also derive from the opening music, expanding upon the dominant as well. Together, these three eight-bar segments delay confirmation of tonic A♭ until bar 24.[21] A 'precursive prolongation', this passage prompts increasing anticipation within listeners, enabling sympathetic experience of rising uncertainty similar to that felt before receipt of a response to a request.[22] In turn, the text 'Kyrie eleison' ('Lord have

19   While the term 'missa solemnis' is most often associated with Beethoven's Op. 123 (1823), the venerable genre of the 'solemn Mass' includes Bach's Mass in B minor (1749), Mozart's 'Coronation' Mass (1779) and Haydn's *Missa in Angustiis* (1798), as well as Schubert's Mass in A♭ major.

20   Glenn Stanley observes 'The orchestration and the motivic work in the introduction to the Kyrie of Mass No. 5 imbues the pastoral tone with a new richness that ushers the listener into a world of religious sentiment hitherto absent from the Masses'; see Stanley, 'Schubert's Religious and Choral Music: Toward a Statement of Faith', p. 219.

21   Example 3.3, further ahead in this chapter, portrays that 'arrival'.

22   The concept of 'precursive prolongation' represents an alternative to the notion of 'auxiliary cadence' within the context of Schenkerian tonal theory. Its fullest exposition may be found in James William Sobaskie, 'Precursive Prolongation in the *Preludes* of Chopin', *Journal of the Society for Musicology in Ireland* 3 (2007–2008), pp. 25–61. Precursive prolongations include melodic prefixes – appoggiaturas – and harmonic prefixes – secondary dominants – as well as more extended prefixial spans like this one, whose content is contextually dependent on a forthcoming harmonic element. Schubert appears to have found these forward-facing structures particularly useful, as the following suggest: James William Sobaskie, 'Tonal Implication and the Gestural Dialectic in Schubert's A Minor String Quartet', in *Schubert the Progressive*, ed. Brian Newbould (Aldershot: Ashgate, 2003), pp. 56–62; James William

mercy') acquires poignant sincerity, bearing an ingenuous plea with no hint of demand. The Mass's central dramatic persona, first embodied by bassoon, now 'speaks' through the entire ensemble.

Founded upon this prefixial harmonic structure, and exploiting the impatience it evokes, an instance of the 'rule of three' projects a palpable sense of 'striving' within the opening passage of the Kyrie.[23] Example 3.2 summarizes the span's sequence of melodic motions.

In physical terms, this passage corresponds to a protracted yet persistent approach toward an objective: an 'attempt' unfolds in bars 1–8, terminated by a half cadence, followed by another 'attempt' in bars 9–16, also thwarted via a half cadence, before one more 'attempt' in bars 17–24 finally leads to the 'achievement' of a contextual goal affirmed by an authentic cadence. Enhanced by registral and timbral shifts, these gestures press gradually yet determinedly within each eight-bar span, the last leading to tonal tangibility. As Example 3.2 reveals, the passage's core consists of step-related pitch classes unfolded by two constituent strands, one higher, one lower. Exploiting the perception of octave equivalence, they create the physical impression

Example 3.2   Schubert, Mass in A♭ major, D. 678, Kyrie, bars 1–24, threefold sequence of melodic motions

Sobaskie, 'The "Problem" of Schubert's String Quintet', *Nineteenth-Century Music Review* 2/1 (2005), pp. 84–6; and James William Sobaskie, 'Conversations Within and Between Two Early Lieder of Schubert', *Nineteenth-Century Music Review* 13/1 (2016), pp. 83–102.

[23] This threefold instance corresponds to what Susan Wollenberg calls a Schubertian 'fingerprint'; for more on this feature of the composer's style, see Chapter 3, 'Threefold Constructions', in her book *Schubert's Fingerprints: Studies in the Instrumental Works* (Farnham: Ashgate, 2011), pp. 191–212.

of reaching down and rising up. The lower strands, which appear in the second half of each of these three systems, move steadily and conjunctly, as if providing gentle, yet determined direction and support to the overall effort. Because the 'attempt, attempt, attempt → achievement' sequence is a familiar pattern, often associated with exertive endeavour,[24] the start of Schubert's Kyrie projects both corporeality and an expression of growing 'desire'. These qualities lend authenticity to the persona's plea for mercy. Engaged listeners empathize, subliminally sensing escalating 'effort' associated with the entreaty.

Another persona-reifying factor introduced at the start of the Kyrie is subtler, yet more far-reaching. The raised fifth scale degree – E♮ in the key of A♭ major – becomes a characteristic feature of the movement in its very first bar.[25] Communicating aspiration as well as apprehension – yearning with a tinge of anxiety – this chromatic inflection becomes a fundamental thematic element in the Kyrie through its frequency and prominence. Example 3.1 identifies several instances using solid rectangles. Each of these E♮s reaches out and up to the sixth degree, F, before the scalar alteration recedes and the diatonic dominant scale degree, E♭, returns to offer relaxation. The raised fifth scale degree's implications are confirmed via bars 23 and 31, where E♮s sung by the sopranos supply prominent passing tone dissonances. Both rising chromatic tones are projected by dynamics, with the second longer and more emphatic than the first, and together they lend pressing urgency to these instances of the term 'eleison' – which connoted 'please' in ancient Greek and came to represent 'mercy' in Latin. In turn, the Mass's implicit persona assumes an even more convincing presence, as Example 3.3 clarifies.

Dotted rectangles in bars 26 and 27 of Example 3.3 identify downward-resolving instances of the inflection that mitigate and relax. The raised fifth scale degree and its enharmonic equivalent, the lowered sixth scale degree, represent a 'problematic' element whose diatonic reconciliation is the objective of a contextual process that culminates near the Kyrie's end and underscores the plea for mercy borne by the text.[26] Communicative of fluctuation, perhaps the alternation between hope and doubt, the characteristic chromaticism has both structural and expressive implications that focus forward, even as it sustains compassion for the Mass's dramatic persona.

---

[24]   While not perfect analogues, consider the implications associated with the phrase used when transporting the injured or moving a heavy object – 'on three … one, two, *three!*' – and the phrase used to start a foot race – 'on your mark, get set, *go!*' In such instances, situational assessment and mental rehearsal during the initial stages enable a desired outcome.

[25]   See Edward T. Cone's 'Schubert's Promissory Note: An Exercise in Musical Hermeneutics', *19th-Century Music* 5/3 (1982), pp. 233–41, which traces how a prominent E♮5 in bar 12 of Schubert's *Moment musical* in A♭ major, Op. 94/6 (D. 750), elicits and sustains expectation until a contextually satisfying resolution F5 sounds in bar 47.

[26]   See James William Sobaskie, 'Contextual Drama in Bach', *Music Theory Online* 12/3 (2006): http://www.mtosmt.org/issues/mto.06.12.3/mto.06.12.3.sobaskie.html, for a discussion of contextual processes in two works of J. S. Bach.

Example 3.3   Schubert, Mass in A♭ major, D. 678, Kyrie, bars 19–33, voices with analysis

Presence and intention project more directly elsewhere within the Kyrie. For instance, the setting of its 'Christe eleison' text in bars 41–63, which unfolds in the dominant tonality of E♭, features solo voices and a sparsely accompanied, disjunct theme. Example 3.4 presents a reduced excerpt of a span near the passage's start.

In bar 46, syncopation transforms the word 'Christe' into a pressing interjection,[27] while chromaticism, dissonance, dynamics, timbre, texture, and agogic accentuation intensify its repetition at the start of bar 47.[28] The common-tone diminished seventh of bar 47, in particular, underscores the plea 'Christ have mercy', enabling the solo soprano to communicate the dramatic persona's interiority with persuasive insistence.

[27] See also the repetitions in bars 57 and 60 in the full score.
[28] See also the repetitions in bars 58 and 61 in the full score.

Example 3.4   Schubert, Mass in A♭ major, D. 678, Kyrie, bars 44–49,
                   selective reduction

The implicit presence of a dramatic persona within Schubert's Mass in A♭ major may be most readily perceived when the music departs from convention and challenges expectation, thus expressing an independent will. So when the thematic and tonal reprise of the 'Kyrie eleison' text and opening material in bar 68 does not lead directly to the movement's conclusion, the subtextual dramatic monologue of the Mass in A♭ major takes a serious turn, apparently deflected by intention. In bar 83, a modulation digresses from A♭ major to D♭, deferring closure. Following a retransition through the minor dominant in bars 92–100, a surprising reprise of the 'Christe eleison' text and musical material begins in bar 100, this time in the tonic A♭. Later, a third and final return of the 'Kyrie eleison' text and material, starting in bar 123, leads to the movement's conclusion. Example 3.5 illustrates the Kyrie's idiosyncratic textual sectionalization and its complementary tonal flow.

How does this unusual treatment of the prayer personalize the music? Listeners acquainted with Mass settings of Schubert's predecessors expect a Kyrie to be distinctly ternary, given its tripartite text and its traditional treatment. Yet this one features a five-part form. Surely the rondo-like design represents no accident, but a determined *decision* to diverge from convention. What might account for it? From an objective perspective, Schubert may have found that the movement's tonal and formal balance required internal expansion, given that convincing establishment of tonic A♭ is delayed until bar 24 – a span that represents almost fifteen per cent of the movement. However, from a more subjective perspective, the Kyrie's extension may be seen to simulate the interiority of the Mass's dramatic persona, perhaps reflecting recognition that the diffident opening of the prayer demanded a compensating reinforcement – a repetition motivated by internal impulse. But there is more.

The 'Christe II' section of the Kyrie, set in the tonic A♭, again features echoing solo voices at first, with the choir entering antiphonally near the end. Bar 122 brings the end of the second 'Christe' reprise and serves as a link to the third and

Example 3.5   Schubert, Mass in A♭ major, D. 678, Kyrie, sectionalization and
                   tonal flow

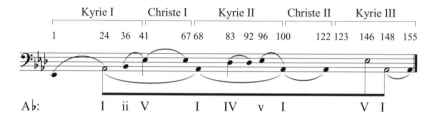

concluding 'Kyrie' section. In a subtle yet remarkable stroke, the returning 'Kyrie eleison' text and music features melodic material linked to the 'Christe eleison' in the 'Kyrie III' section, dramatically expressed by unaccompanied voices. As the brackets of bars 112–113 and bars 126–129 in Example 3.6 reveal, the choral altos of bars 126–129 articulate a distinctive melodic gesture, previously associated with the 'Christe eleison' text, while they sing the text 'Kyrie eleison'.

Surely this mixture of distinctive and previously separate musical materials adds to the Kyrie's structural cohesion. But the thematic combination also may be interpreted as a reflection of the dramatic persona's interiority: recognition of the oneness of the Lord and the Christ. A portrayal of personal insight that reifies the Mass's dramatic persona, this denouement also gives rise to the Kyrie's culminative conclusion.

The last section of the Kyrie introduces the decisive portion of the movement, coordinating the completion of its comprehensive contextual process with the conclusion of the penitent's prayer for mercy. As noted earlier, the raised fifth scale degree in the key of A♭ – E♮ – becomes a thematic element within the Kyrie via its frequency and prominence, a problematic detail calling for resolution. Instances where the chromatic pitch class E♮ rises directly to F within the tonality of A♭ major may be observed in bars 1, 5, 9, 13, 17, 23, 31, 68, 72, and 109–110. Instances where E♮, or its enharmonic equivalent F♭, fall back to diatonic E♭ may be observed in bars 26, 27–28, 64–65, 66–67, 98–100, 111–112, 114, and 129–130. These frequent chromatic passing tones prepare for the climactic span of Schubert's Kyrie, which is represented by the excerpt in Example 3.7.

As this passage reveals, the chromatic pitch F♭3 sounds for two full bars in the bass voice of bars 136 and 137. Instead of slipping down to E♭3, it skips up an augmented second to G3 in bar 138, 'missing its mark'. Contributing to a German augmented sixth sonority in bar 137 that does not resolve as might be expected, the bass's F♭3 communicates contextual instability and anxiety, symbolic of an unsuccessful effort. However, the alto of bars 138–139 appears to 'show the way'. What had been the bass's pitch, F♭3, then sounds three times in the tenor voice, in bars 140, 141–142, and 144, as the numbered rectangles show. If a melody can beseech, then this three-fold gestural sequence – a pivotal instance of the 'attempt, attempt, attempt → achievement' paradigm – surely does.

Example 3.6   Schubert, Mass in A♭ major, D. 678, Kyrie, bars 112–132, solo alto and soprano, choral altos and sopranos, with analysis

The F♭3's brief touch upon E♭3 in bar 143 seems to signal success and the advent of stability, an authentic 'breakthrough'. However, a contextually satisfying 'resolution' appears to require three more consolidating events here, including another instance of the 'attempt, attempt, attempt → achievement' paradigm that features a reach up to F3 in bar 144 by the tenor voices, a relaxation to E♭3 in the tenor voices of bar 146 over the dominant of A♭, and finally, a reiteration of E♭3 over the tonic harmony in the last two bars. At last, this sonorous coincidence seems to bring relief and optimism at the Kyrie's conclusion. And this quiet and spacious tranquility might be interpreted as a mix of repose and epiphany brought about by the perception of a deeply desired response.

Example 3.7   Schubert, Mass in A♭ major, D. 678, Kyrie, bars 135–155, voices
with analysis

Schubert's Kyrie enables auditors to experience the effects of anticipation and comfort associated with a sincerely posed and subsequently answered plea. Individuating the expression of its traditional text in a variety of ways, it establishes an implicit subtextual monologue that is articulated by a convincing dramatic persona, whose transformation has only just begun.

Gloria

The Kyrie's calm close brings relaxation and reassurance, but also prepares a startling surprise. A deep-drawn breath shared by every performer dominates the scant seconds of hushed ambience before the start of the subsequent Gloria. Symbolic of life itself, the always-audible communal inhalation is as much a part of the Mass as the sounds on either side. During its brief interval, *pianississimo* gives way to *fortississimo*, Andante con moto accelerates to Allegro maestoso e vivace, alla breve shifts to rolling triple metre, A♭ major cedes to E major, and restrained performing resources expand to include all available forces.[29] The extreme contrast between the end of the Kyrie and the beginning of the Gloria is anything but reserved or conventional, and surely is meant to astound. Indeed, the Gloria's ebullience, foreign to the decorum of sacred spaces, expresses vibrant presence and energetic intention, seeming at once impetuous and impassioned. Of course, the Gloria's key of E – whose tonic pitch class was essential to the Kyrie's contextual process – links the two movements by unexpectedly fulfilling the undercurrent of aspiration flowing throughout its predecessor. Through this astonishing juxtaposition, the Mass's dramatic persona may be understood to register reception of a divine response to the Kyrie's plea for mercy and manifest its transformation into an adherent.

Exhilaration becomes exuberance within the Gloria's initial passage, where seven-bar phrases, sung homophonically by the choir, rush forward, propelled by sweeping strings. Example 3.8 illustrates its rhythmic strategy, showing how two seven-bar phrases (equalling fourteen bars) are followed by phrases of four, six and four bars (also equalling fourteen bars) – which provide a transitional effect – after which four-bar phrases predominate.

Each of the Gloria's first two phrases seems just a little short, as though hurrying to get ahead. Near the end of the opening section, a fourteen-bar span (bars 15–28) provides for a transition to four-bar phrases. With these opening seven-bar phrases, the impact of the Gloria's opening becomes an impression of sustained momentum. And with this passage, the transformation of the Kyrie's penitent into an adherent would seem to be complete.

The opening passage's thrust brings listeners into the midst of the Gloria, where an idiosyncratic treatment of the traditional text may be interpreted to reflect the

---

[29]   The Kyrie's two oboes, two clarinets, two bassoons, two horns, voices, strings and organ are joined at the start of the Gloria by one flute, two trumpets, three trombones, and timpani.

Example 3.8   Schubert, Mass in A♭ major, D. 678, Gloria, bars 1–36, sopranos' and
                   basses' melodies

interiority of the Mass's dramatic persona. As Table 3.1 suggests, the Gloria falls into two principal parts, the first of which contains some repeated material (B′ represents a brief reprise), while the second divides into two subsections, plus a codetta.

In Section A of the Gloria, 'adoramus te' appears after 'glorificamus te', instead of right before as it does in the traditional Latin prayer. In Section C, 'Fili unigenite' ('only-begotten son'), and in Section D, both 'Filius Patris' and 'Tu solus Dominus' also appear later than normal. For listeners familiar with the 'telescoped text' of *missae breves*, such changes would be unlikely to attract much attention. Curiously, however, the phrases 'suscipe deprecationem nostram' ('receive our prayer') and 'Qui sedes ad dexteram Patris' ('You who sits at the right hand of the Father') from the traditional Latin Mass text are omitted altogether here. But through these omissions, the resulting phrases 'Domine Deus, Agnus Dei, qui tollis peccata mundi, miserere nobis' ('Lord God, Lamb of God, You who takes away the sins of the world, have mercy on us'), and 'Filius Patris, Agnus Dei, qui tollis peccata mundi, miserere nobis ('Son of the Father, Lamb of God, You who takes away the sins of the world, have mercy on us'), become separate, emphatic and personalized pleas for clemency directed toward the first two members of the Trinity. See bars 221–278 of the full score, where the first of these petitions is repeated before the

Table 3.1   Schubert, Mass in A♭ major, D. 678, Gloria, sectionalization and
text treatment

PART I

Section	Bars	Tempo	Metre	Text
A	1–112	*Allegro maestoso e vivace*	$\frac{3}{4}$	Gloria in excelsis Deo. et in terra pax hominibus bonae voluntatis. Laudamus te, benedicimus te, ~~adoramus te~~ glorificamus te, *adoramus te.* *Gloria in excelsis Deo.* *gloria Deo, gloria Deo, gloria Deo.*
B	113–149	*Andantino*	$\frac{2}{4}$	Gratias agimus tibi propter magnam gloriam tuam.
C	150–193	*Andantino*	$\frac{2}{4}$	Domine Deus, Rex caelestis, *gratias agimus.* Deus Pater omnipotens, *gratias agimus.* Domine ~~Fili unigenite,~~ Jesu Christe, *gratias agimus tibi.* *Fili unigenite, gratias agimus tibi.* *Domine Deus, Rex caelestis,* *Deus Pater omnipotens.*
B′	194–220	*Andantino*	$\frac{2}{4}$	*Gratias agimus tibi propter magnam gloriam tuam.*
D	221–332	*Allegro moderato*	$\frac{2}{2}$	Domine Deus, Agnus Dei, ~~Filius Patris,~~ qui tollis peccata mundi, miserere nobis. *Filius Patris, Agnus Dei,* qui tollis peccata mundi, ~~suscipe deprecationem nostram.~~ ~~Qui sedes ad dexteram Patris,~~ miserere nobis. Quoniam tu solus Sanctus, ~~Tu solus Dominus~~ Tu solus Altissimus, *Tu solus Dominus,* ~~Jesu Christe.~~

PART II

Section	Bars	Tempo	Metre	Text
Fugue, part 1	333–476	*Allegro moderato*	$\frac{2}{2}$	Cum Sancto Spiritu in gloria Dei Patris, amen,
Fugue, part 2	477–525	*Allegro moderato*	$\frac{2}{2}$	*Cum Sancto Spiritu in gloria Dei Patris, amen.*
Codetta	525–531	*Allegro moderato*	$\frac{2}{2}$	*Amen.*

Note: In the table, ~~strikethrough~~ isolates words of the Gloria's traditional text that have been omitted and/ or delayed, while *italicization* identifies words that have been repositioned and/or significantly repeated.

second ensues. Through these adjustments to the traditional text, the monologue within the Mass in A♭ major takes a determined and personalized turn, focusing on direct requests to the Father and the Son.

Equally telling are certain text repetitions. For instance, within section A, the reprise of 'Gloria in excelsis Deo' at the end of the section, which contributes to an embedded ternary subsection, revives the energy of the Gloria's opening. A three-fold 'Gloria Deo' brings the subsection to a close in bars 101–112. Most affecting are the textual repetitions expressive of gratitude.[30] 'Gratias agimus tibi propter magnam gloriam tuam' ('We give you thanks for your great glory') dominates the B and B′ sections of bars 113–149 and 194–200, while the Father and the Son are twice thanked within section C. Here too, departures from mere recitation of the traditional text signal agency and individuated intention.

These two persons of the Christian Trinity are praised in their oneness within a most dramatic passage that sets the text 'Quoniam tu solus Sanctus, Tu solus Altissimus, Tu solus Dominus' ('For You Alone are the Holy One, You Alone are Most High, You alone are the Lord'). Example 3.9 presents that climactic span. Beginning *pianissimo* and becoming *fortissimo*, the choral sopranos start at the bottom of their range on the pitch B3, reach B4 an octave above in bar 294, and culminate their two-octave ascent by attaining B5 in bar 301, supported in this dramatically rising expression of faith by the rest of the choir and orchestra.

Tonic E major arrives at the last syllable of 'Dominus' in bar 303, cadentially confirmed after an extended absence to provide a convincing signal of accomplishment. Repositioning of the traditional Latin Mass's 'Tu solus Dominus' and omission of 'Jesu Christe' in this context represents no heresy but an individuated expression of belief by the Mass's dramatic persona.

Yet the third person of the Trinity is by no means slighted in the Gloria of Schubert's Mass in A♭ major. No less than a third of the movement's span (bars 333–531) focuses solely on the text 'Cum Sancto Spiritu in gloria Dei Patris, Amen' ('With the Holy Spirit, in the Glory of God the Father, Amen'), which is set fugally. Example 3.10 illustrates its principal subject and the start of its tonal answer.

Running full tilt for a longer span than any of the Gloria's individual preceding sections, the fugue recaptures the eagerness of the movement's opening, powering a determinedly contrapuntal texture that communicates confidence and commitment. Reaching the dominant harmony in bar 476, after nearly 150 bars of imitative discourse, Schubert's Gloria could have closed with a coda ... but does not! As if taking yet another deep, renewing and communal breath in the minim's silence that completes bar 476, amid fading echoes of the preceding tutti chord, the fugue charges on for nearly fifty bars more, demonstrating that the inspired fervour of the Mass's dramatic persona knows no bounds. Like the surprising start of the movement, the extended end seems extreme, as if zealously propelled. And while this extra burst

---

[30]   Leo Black observes that 'Schubert dwells particularly on passages of praise and gratitude' within this Mass; see Black, *Franz Schubert: Music and Belief*, p. 75.

Example 3.9   Schubert, Mass in A♭ major, D. 678, Gloria, bars 287–303,
                   selective reduction

of vigour might be taken as evidence of external influence on the Mass's dramatic persona, in this context, could it not also at least partly reflect the persona's desire for *more* of that influence? Either way, extraordinarily determined and apparently inspired persistence portrays agency, both human and divine. And through this surge at the end of the Gloria, the subtextual narrative of the Mass in A♭ major leads to a new stage: the transformation of adherent to believer via a formal yet also quite personal expression of faith.

Credo

The Credo of Schubert's Mass in A♭ major, like its Kyrie, begins solely with winds (Example 3.11).

These sonorities convey ambient spatiality through their echoic effect, as well as timbral transformation via low brass blending into high brass and woodwinds. Functioning as a distinctive, harmonic-centred musical event, they return in bars 17–20, 183–186, 319–322, and 336–338, binding the Credo's broad ternary form via association.[31] Equally importantly, they embody and emblematize the movement's two-syllable title in the manner of a spoken or contemplated motto, as the implied text superimposed within Example 3.11 suggests.

Like the Gloria and Kyrie, this setting of the Credo text is idiosyncratic, interpretable as a personalized statement of belief by the Mass's dramatic persona, whose presence was established by the preceding movements. Table 3.2 portrays the Credo's sectionalization and its individuated treatment of the traditional Latin creed.

Within the A section, the omissions of 'Patrem omnipotentem' ('Father almighty') and 'Genitum, non factum, consubstantialem Patri' ('Begotten, not made, consubstantial with the Father') would seem to begin a new emphasis on the oneness of the Christian Trinity. Those omissions in the A′ section, including 'Et unam, sanctam, catholicam et apostolicam Ecclesiam' ('and one, holy, catholic and apostolic Church'[32] and 'Et expecto resurrectionem' ('And I expect the resurrection of the dead')[33] – long associated with doctrinal disagreements Schubert may have had

---

[31]   A compressed instance of the Credo's harmonic motive is heard in bar 130, just before the start of its contrasting centre section.

[32]   All of Schubert's Masses omit the phrase 'Et unam sanctam, catholicam et apostalicam Ecclesiam'.

[33]   Manuela Jahrmäker has suggested that Schubert's consistent omission of 'et unam sanctam catholicam ecclesiam' and 'et expecto resurrectionem' from his Masses reflects Schubert own 'private position'; see Manuela Jahrmäker, 'Von der liturgischen Funktion zum persönlichen Bekenntnis: Die Kirchenmusik', in *Schubert Handbuch*, ed. Walther Dürr and Andreas Krause (Kassel, Stuttgart, and Weimar: Bärenreiter and Metzler, 1997), p. 353. Given his participation in the free-thinking 'Unsinnsgesellschaft' ('Nonsense Society') in 1817 and 1818, as well as the cosmopolitan nature of Vienna during the composer's lifetime, it is logical

Example 3.10   Schubert, Mass in A♭ major, D. 678, Gloria, bars 333–340, bass and
                tenor entries

Cum San-cto Spi-ri-tu in glo-ri a De - i   Pa - tris, A - men, a - men,

Cum   San-cto Spi - ri- tu in

Example 3.11   Schubert, Mass in A♭ major, D. 678, Credo, bars 1–4, selective reduction
                with implied text

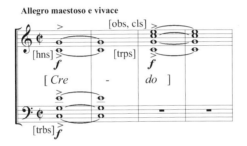

with Catholic belief – may be interpreted to represent those of the Mass's dramatic
persona, and potentially understood to reflect sentiments resonant with those held
by the composer's Viennese contemporaries.[34] That is, if Schubert sought, in the first
instance, to appeal to his community's own religious sensibilities and beliefs via his
Mass's dramatic persona, his adherence to the ancient text of the Credo could, quite
understandably, be somewhat less than orthodox.

Ultimately, repetition determines the ultimate expressive impact of the Credo,
as it does within the preceding movements. In the traditional Latin text of the

---

to assume that Schubert would decide for himself what he believed – intellectually – rather
than accept Catholic theology completely without question. In the context of his Mass in
A♭ major, his dramatic persona – a narratological device designed to secure his listeners'
engagement – could be seen as reflective of his contemporaries' beliefs, as well as his own.
For more on the 'Nonsense Society', see Rita Steblin, *Die Unsinnsgesellschaft: Franz Schubert,
Leopold Kupelwieser und ihr Freundeskreis* (Vienna: Böhlau, 1998).

34   See John Gingerich, '"To How Many Shameful Deeds must you Lend your Image":
Schubert's Pattern of Telescoping and Excision in the Texts of His Latin Masses', *Current
Musicology* 70, pp. 61–99.

Table 3.2   Schubert, Mass in A♭ major, D. 678, Credo, sectionalization and
text treatment

Section	Bars	Tempo	Metre	Text
A′	1–130	*Allegro maestoso e vivace*	𝟥/𝟤	Credo in unum Deum, ~~Patrem omnipotentem,~~ factorem caeli et terrae, visibilium omnium et invisibilium. *Credo, credo* ~~Et~~ in unum Dominum Jesum Christum, *Credo, credo in* Filium Dei unigenitum. *Credo,* Et ex Patre natum ante omnia sǽcula. *Credo* Deum de Deo, lumen de lumine, *Credo* Deum verum de Deo vero. ~~Genitum, non factum, consubstantialem Patri:~~ *Credo,* per quem omnia facta sunt. Qui propter nos homines et propter nostram salutem descendit de caelis. *Credo, per quem omnia facta sunt.* *Credo, credo, credo.*
B	131–182	*Grave*	𝟥/𝟤	Et incarnatus est de Spiritu Sancto Ex Maria Virgine, et homo factus est. Crucifixus etiam pro nobis: sub Pontio Pilato passus et sepultus est.
A′	183–433	*Allegro maestoso e vivace*	𝟥/𝟤	Et resurrexit tertia die, secundum Scripturas. Et ascendit in caelum, sedet ad dexteram Patris. Et iterum venturus est cum gloria, Judicare vivos, et mortuos, Cujus regni non erit finis. *Credo, credo* ~~Et~~ in Spiritum Sanctum, Dominum *Credo, credo* et vivificantem: *Credo, credo* qui ex Patre Filioque procedit. *Credo, credo* qui cum Patre, et Filio simul adoratur ~~et~~ conglorificatur: qui locutus est per prophetas. ~~Et unam, sanctam, catholicam et apostolicam Ecclesiam.~~ Confiteor unum baptisma in remissionem peccatorum. ~~Et expecto resurrectionem~~ <u>mortuorum,</u> Et vitam venturi saeculi. Amen.

Note: In the table, ~~strikethrough~~ isolates words of the Credo's traditional text that have been omitted and/or delayed, while *italicization* identifies words that have been repositioned and/or significantly repeated, and <u>underline</u> identifies a word whose presence quietly alludes to an absent tenet of faith.

Ordinary, the word 'Credo' appears just once, at the very beginning of the prayer.[35] However, within Schubert's setting, the word 'Credo' occurs no less than thirty times.[36] While the total of the term's instances may have its own implications, more striking is the sheer weight of emphasis placed on the assertion of faith itself: 'I believe!'

Similarly stressed is the word 'Amen' – 'So be it' – which appears just once within the text of the Latin Credo, at the very end of the prayer. Yet in Schubert's setting, 'Amen' occurs a total of twenty-seven times.[37] Again, while the total of the term's instances may have its own implications, most striking is the sheer weight of emphasis placed on the expression of the ancient affirmation: 'So be it'.

By nature, a monologue reflects interiority – a dramatic persona's state of mind – and thus is open to a variety of interpretations. Perhaps most easily and naturally, the Credo's many assertions of 'I believe', as well as its many affirmations of 'So be it', may be taken at face value and regarded as genuine indicatives of interiority – purely positive expressions of an adherent's faith. Of course, the extensive repetition of the words 'Credo' and 'Amen' also may be interpreted ironically, perhaps taken as suggestive of the dramatic persona's desire to self-convince, so this remains an open question for thoughtful listeners.[38] Yet within the Mass's dramatic monologue, where extremes seem to be indicative of interiority as well as heralds of change, these repetitions – at the very least – encourage an engaged listener's reflection and interpretation. And as with the preceding movements, the welcome conclusion of the Credo prompts contemplation of and anticipation for what comes next.

[35]   Following precedents established during the era of plainchant, Schubert's Mass in A♭ major incorporates a setting of the Nicene Creed, a formal statement of Christian belief that emerged from the First Council of Nicaea in the year 325 AD and remained standard for Catholic Masses through the nineteenth century. It contains more doctrinal detail than the shorter Apostles' Creed, which is shared by many Christian denominations today, complementing that familiar prayer.

[36]   See bars 5–6, 21–2, 33–4, 35–6, 41–2, 43, 49–50, 57–8, 65–6, 73–4, 99–100, 109–13, 117–21, 125–9, 251–2, 253–4, 255–6, 257–8, 259–60, 261–2, 263–4, 265–6, 275–6, 277–8, 279–80, 281–2, 283–4, 285–6, 287–8, and 289–90 of Schubert's Mass in A♭ major for instances of the word 'Credo'.

[37]   See bars 367–71, 375–81, 383–4, 385–6, 387–9, 390, 391, 392, 393, 394, 395–8, 399–400, 401–2, 403, 404, 405, 406, 407–9, 410, 411, 412, 413, 414, 415–20, 421–2, 429–31, and 432–3 of Schubert's Mass in A♭ major for instances of the word 'Amen'.

[38]   Noting Schubert's extensive repetition of the word 'Credo', Leo Black suggested that it was 'as if the congregation or even the composer himself were being exhorted to believe'; see Leo Black, *Franz Schubert: Music and Belief*, p. 77.

Sanctus

The beginning of the Mass's Sanctus elicits an enveloping and almost overwhelming perception of awe, as if the preceding Credo has opened a door to a new domain – the realm of the sublime.[39] Example 3.12 presents just the choral parts of the opening passage, plus its chromatic bass line.

Creating a wave-like impression of descending oscillation by means of a sequential chromatic pattern, the opening span of the Sanctus may be interpreted to simulate exposure to a profound mystery as well as temporary transcendence to a new spiritual plane.[40] Surprisingly, the choir enters a semitone higher than expected in bar 4, and apparently in minor, disrupting whatever sense of tonality had taken hold in the first two bars with an impression of a smooth ascent. Yet the pair of chords in bars 4–5, which suggests a half cadence, brings not stability but potentiality and continued flow. As Example 3.12 shows, while the opening passage is set in and framed by F major, the choir's utterances of 'Sanctus' ('Holy') move by descending thirds, alluding to the keys of F♯ minor, E♭ minor, and then C minor in short order, but confirming none. However, the subsequent setting of the words 'Dominus Deus Sabaoth' ('Lord God of Hosts') in bars 18–20 powerfully and convincingly confirms F major, thus re-establishing a sense of reality. Through these twenty bars, listeners experience engrossing wonder without worry, as if time itself stops, and in the context of the preceding three movements, may attribute these impressions to the transformation of the Mass's dramatic persona from believer to initiate.

The quiet yet expansive and energetic passage that follows in bars 21–29, which sets the text 'Pleni sunt caeli et terra gloria tua ('Heaven and earth are filled with Your Glory'), is almost exclusively diatonic, firmly elaborating F major. Framed by F major and C major harmonies, it represents an eight-bar expansion of the thrice-repeated cadential formula heard moments before. Ending with a suspense-building fermata, this second passage introduces a new opportunity for vicarious entry into the mind and being of the Mass's dramatic persona. The setting of 'Osanna in excelsis Deo' ('Hosanna in the highest to God!') that follows, whose initial bars appear in Example 3.13, enables identification with the character and the experience of elevated joy.

Startling changes of tempo, metre, rhythm, articulation, and mood in bar 30 introduce a twenty-nine bar passage that sounds almost angelic in its lightness and grace – indeed, almost transcendent in its freedom from guilt, worry and earthly cares. In retrospect, the profession of faith expressed within the preceding Credo

---

[39]   I thank Joe Davies for suggesting that this span may represent Schubert's portrayal of the sublime – a fleeting glimpse of heaven, as it were.

[40]   Leo Black puts it insightfully: 'Not surprisingly, it [the opening of the Sanctus of the Mass in A♭ major] has been felt as Schubert's attempt to communicate the ungraspable'; see Black, *Franz Schubert: Music and Belief*, p. 79.

Example 3.12   Schubert, Mass in A♭ major, D. 678, Sanctus, bars 1–20,
                    selective reduction

would seem to have opened a view to a new domain that holds both profound mystery and immediate joy.

The Benedictus section of Schubert's Sanctus offers contrast within the movement's compound ternary form. Set primarily in A♭ major and marked Andante con moto, its alla breve metric fabric features constant quavers that create an impression of continuous forward flow. While a sense that F major will return suffuses the Benedictus, sustaining an undercurrent of anticipation, expectation

Example 3.13   Schubert, Mass in A♭ major, D. 678, Sanctus, bars 30–36 ('Osanna'), selective reduction

within it is systematically manipulated to underscore the heraldic implications of the text 'Benedictus qui venit in nomine Domini'. As Example 3.14 suggests, a two-part contextual process involving the rising registral ceiling of the highest female voices directs attention ahead, spanning nearly the entire section.

Starting on the third of the tonic triad in A♭ major, the soprano soloist's highest pitch gradually rises to F5 in bar 9, seeming to encounter resistance in proceeding higher toward tonic A♭5. When the choral sopranos enter in bar 21, they too seem to be unable to progress further than the F5 in bars 25–26. However, when the soprano soloist re-enters in bar 29, she is able to 'push' beyond F5 to G5 in bar 34 … but reaches no higher. A second 'attempt' at breaching the registral ceiling ensues in bar 50, beginning with the soprano soloist as before, this time taking a new tack, ascending to G♭5 in bar 62. The choral sopranos 'touch' the goal pitch of A♭5 in bar 68, but the dissonant harmony that supports them there 'pulls' them back to G♭5 in the following bar, frustrating a satisfactory completion of the contextual process. The pitch G5 is regained in bar 98 by the soprano soloist, who, together with the choral sopranos, finally achieves A♭5 in the following bar, holding it for three more beyond that. The qualities of aspiration, endeavour, faith, perseverance and fulfilment, expressed here in musical terms by gradually rising soprano voices, colour the passage's text – 'Blessed is He Who comes in the name of the Lord' – which, in the context of the Mass, refers to the Second Coming of Christ. In turn, the setting

Example 3.14   Schubert, Mass in A♭ major, D. 678, Benedictus, contextual registral
               process in the soprano part

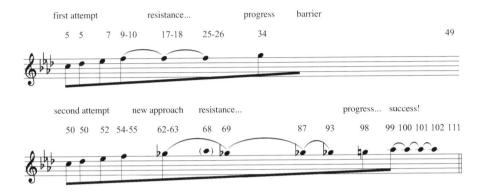

seems to imply internal recognition of qualities expected for the salvation promised
during the First Coming.

A reprise of the earlier 'Osanna' passage concludes the fourth movement of the
Mass, effectively confirming a positive shift in its comprehensive narrative. The
dramatic persona's transformation from penitent to adherent, believer and initiate
has been portrayed through the idiosyncratic interpretation of the Latin Mass's text,
often involving contrastive extremes and selective repetition. In the context of the
preceding movements, the Sanctus represents a culmination and a turning point.
However, one more stage of the Mass's dramatic monologue follows, an open-ended
phase expressive of watchful waiting in which its dramatic persona transforms from
initiate to anticipant.

Agnus Dei

Schubert's setting of the three-sentence text of the Agnus Dei – 'Agnus Dei,
qui tollis peccata mundi: miserere nobis; Agnus Dei, qui tollis peccata mundi:
miserere nobis; Agnus Dei, qui tollis peccata mundi: dona nobis pacem' – naturally
recalls the pleas for mercy of his Mass's Kyrie.[41] And like the opening movement,
it ends optimistically. But what dominates Schubert's Agnus Dei is an impression
of vigilant anticipation.

---

[41] 'Lamb of God, Who takes away the sins of the world, have mercy on us; Lamb of God,
Who takes away the sins of the world, have mercy on us; Lamb of God, Who takes away the
sins of the world, grant us peace'.

Example 3.15   Schubert, Mass in A♭ major, D. 678, Agnus Dei, tonal flux

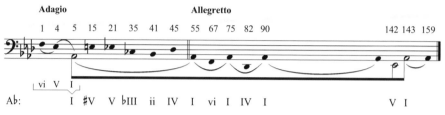

(Dona nobis pacem, Dona nobis pacem, Dona nobis pacem, Dona nobis pacem ...)

Example 3.15 illustrates that the Agnus Dei features a precursive prolongation in bars 1–5, that links its primary key (A♭ major) with that of the preceding Sanctus (F major).

The opening harmonic prefix vi → V → I, expressed within the instrumental introduction, delays A♭ major, generating immediate forward tonal flow while coordinating tonic confirmation with the entry of solo voices on the text 'Agnus Dei'. As Example 3.15 suggests, the first section of the composition, devoted to petitions for mercy, temporarily tonicizes five different degrees via authentic cadences, creating an impression of restless tonal peregrination in search of stasis during articulation of the text 'Agnus Dei, qui tollis peccata mundi: miserere nobis'. Tonic A♭ returns in bar 55, though temporarily displaced by brief allusions to the submediant and subdominant, otherwise holding sway until the end.

During this second span of over one hundred bars, the only words heard present a confident entreaty for peace: 'Dona nobis pacem'. Example 3.16 offers the first three statements, which serve as the thematic foundation for the remainder of the movement.

A brisk, light, and remarkably cheerful musical fabric, standing in stark contrast to the much more intense content of the preceding movements, brings Schubert's Mass in A♭ major to a close. As with the extensive repetition of selected text in the Gloria, Credo, and Sanctus, the continuous articulation of the request 'Dona nobis pacem' has a mantra-like effect in this final span that dominates the experience and memory of the entire movement, communicative of hopeful anticipation. Engaged listeners, in turn, experience this vicariously through the agency of the Mass's dramatic persona, who has transformed from initiate to anticipant.

The relative simplicity and brevity of the Agnus Dei movement may appear disproportionate, given the relative complexities and lengths of its predecessors. And its lack of a climactic conclusion or convincing apotheosis might seem to leave listeners wanting. But Schubert, perhaps sensing the impending evolution of the orchestral Mass from sacramental instrument to concert centrepiece, seems to have sought to close the extended experience thoughtfully and empathetically, depicting his Mass's dramatic persona in a buoyant, optimistic, and expectant state. Given the

Example 3.16   Schubert, Mass in A♭ major, D. 678, Agnus Dei, bars 55–66,
                    selective reduction

persona's spiritual journey within the Mass's five movements, Schubert's decision to conclude his masterpiece in this way makes perfect sense. Integrating the literary device of the dramatic monologue with the liturgical tradition of the Christian Mass, Schubert individuated his Mass in A♭ major from beginning to end.

A New Perspective on Schubert's Mass in A♭ Major

Some listeners assume that when a composer sets text, essential meaning lies at the surface of the music and consists of the semantic content of the words. Some assume that a composer's texted works must be significantly self-revelatory, reflecting personal experiences or beliefs that the artist felt compelled to share. Yet the ever-growing body of literature on Schubert's Lieder has demonstrated profound expressive depth and multiple layers of dramatic meaning in songs whose content and characters do not appear to harbour any autobiographical implications.[42]

---

[42]   For a small selection of recent literature that portrays unsuspected depth and drama in Schubert's music, see: Deborah Stein, 'The End of the Road in Schubert's *Winterreise*: The Contradiction of Coherence and Fragmentation', in *Rethinking Schubert*, ed. Lorraine Byrne Bodley and Julian Horton (Oxford: Oxford University Press, 2016), pp. 355–83; and Robert Hatten, 'Schubert's Alchemy: Transformative Surfaces, Transfiguring Depths', in *Schubert's Late Music: History, Theory, Style*, ed. Lorraine Byrne Bodley and Julian Horton (Cambridge: Cambridge University Press, 2016), pp. 91–110. In particular, consider the following exchange: Robert S. Hatten, 'A Surfeit of Musics: What Goethe's Lyrics Concede When

These discoveries, along with the preceding analysis, suggest a new perspective for interpreting Schubert's sacred works and prompt re-examination of the Romantic aesthetic relative to that repertoire.

The success of Schubert's Mass in A♭ major appears attributable to its ability to engage listeners' imaginations with a subliminally cultivated and gradually evolving dramatic persona whose ingenuous nature elicits self-identification and empathy, a character whose gradual transformation mirrors the theology expressed by the Latin Ordinary. While the sentiments portrayed therein could be linked to the Romantic artist's need for self-expression, it would seem that Schubert's fascination for artistic innovation, his pursuit of professional advancement, and even – quite possibly – a sincere wish to contribute to his community's devotional life, all deserve serious consideration. For Schubert, it seems, what vivified his secular music so effectively also could vivify the sacred. And while the dramatic persona of Schubert's Mass in A♭ major might appear to reflect the composer in some respects, it need not do so to function effectively within the context of this composition. Rather, the persona remains a dramatic device in the service of a narrative integrated within the Mass. Not only must we avoid imposing twenty-first century attitudes toward religion on this early nineteenth-century music, but we also must question the extent to which traditionally conceived Romantic subjectivity actually animates the content of this remarkable work. As this chapter has shown, Schubert's Mass may be heard in a novel way: from the standpoint of a dramatic persona. Thus, we may wish to reconsider long-held notions about the composer's rich repertoire of sacred music, which may hold much more drama than previously thought.

Indeed, Schubert's achievement as a composer, so often ascribed to his lyrical gifts, increasingly appears linked to his storytelling skills. If his instrumental music bears evidence of dialectical conflict and reconciliation,[43] musical problem-solving,[44]

Set to Schubert's Music', *Nineteenth-Century Music Review* 5/2 (2008), pp. 7–18; Lorraine Byrne Bodley, 'In Pursuit of a Single Flame? On Schubert's Settings of Goethe's Poems', *Nineteenth-Century Music Review* 13/2 (2016), pp. 11–33; Robert S. Hatten, 'Reflections Inspired by a Response', *Nineteenth-Century Music Review* 13/2 (2016), pp. 35–8. Finally, the articles in Graham Johnson's three-volume encyclopedia, *Franz Schubert: The Complete Songs* (New Haven and London: Yale University Press, 2014) offer excellent acquaintance with the composer's Lieder.

[43]   See James William Sobaskie, 'Tonal Implication and the Gestural Dialectic in Schubert's A Minor Quartet', in *Schubert the Progressive: History, Performance Practice, Analysis*, ed. Brian Newbould (Aldershot: Ashgate, 2003), pp. 53–79.

[44]   See James William Sobaskie, 'The "Problem" of Schubert's String Quintet', *Nineteenth-Century Music Review* 2/1 (2005), pp. 57–92, and 'Schubert's Self-Elegies', *Nineteenth-Century Music Review* 5/2 (2008), special issue, *Schubert Familiar and Unfamiliar: New Perspectives*, pp. 71–105.

and idiomatic contextual processes,[45] and if intertextual and extratextual relationships among his non-cyclic Lieder can have unsuspected dramatic implications,[46] then perhaps we might find evidence of other devices and structures within his oeuvre that have parallels within the domain of literature. Given how well and widely read Schubert was, surely there must be considerable drama to find within his legacy.[47]

※

[45]   See James William Sobaskie, 'A Balance Struck: Gesture, Form, and Drama in Schubert's E flat Major Piano Trio', in *Le style instrumental de Schubert: sources, analyse, evolution*, ed. Xavier Hascher (Paris: Publications de la Sorbonne, 2007), pp. 115–46, and 'Contextual Processes in Schubert's Late Sacred Choral Music', in *Rethinking Schubert*, ed. Lorraine Byrne Bodley and Julian Horton (Oxford: Oxford University Press, 2016), pp. 295–332.

[46]   See James William Sobaskie, 'Conversations Within and Between Two Early Lieder of Schubert', *Nineteenth-Century Music Review* 13/1 (2016), special issue, *Schubert Familiar and Unfamiliar: Continuing Conversations*, pp. 83–102, as well as Chapter 6, 'The Dramatic Strategy Within Two of Schubert's Serenades',in this volume.

[47]   David Gramit's *The Intellectual and Aesthetic Tenets of Franz Schubert's Circle* (PhD dissertation, Duke University, 1987) may have been among the first studies to focus on Schubert's intellectuality, but since then, the image of Schubert as an intellectual has gradually come to be more widely held. For context, see Christopher Gibbs, 'Introduction: The Elusive Schubert' and '"Poor Schubert": Images and Legends of the Composer', in *The Cambridge Companion to Schubert*, ed. Christopher H. Gibbs (Cambridge: Cambridge University Press, 1997), pp. 1–11 and 36–55; David Gramit, '"The Passion for Friendship": Music, Cultivation, and Identity in Schubert's Circle', in *The Cambridge Companion to Schubert*, ed. Christopher H. Gibbs (Cambridge: Cambridge University Press, 1997), pp. 56–71; and Rita Steblin, *Die Unsinnsgesellschaft: Franz Schubert, Leopold Kupelwieser und ihr Freundeskreis* (Vienna: Böhlau Verlag, 1998). Nevertheless, the work of Susan Youens may be most responsible for portraying Schubert as an intellectual; for instance, see: *Retracing a Winter's Journey: Schubert's Winterreise* (Ithaca, NY: Cornell University Press, 1991); *Franz Schubert: Die schöne Müllerin* (Cambridge University Press, 1992); *Schubert's Poets and the Making of Lieder* (Cambridge: Cambridge University Press, 1996); *Schubert, Müller, and Die schöne Müllerin* (Cambridge: Cambridge University Press, 1997); 'Schubert and his Poets: Issues and Conundrums', in *The Cambridge Companion to Schubert*, ed. Christopher H. Gibbs (Cambridge: Cambridge University Press, 1997), pp. 99–117; *Schubert's Late Lieder: Beyond the Song Cycle*s (Cambridge: Cambridge University Press, 2002); 'Swan Songs: Schubert's "Auf dem Wasser zu singen"', *Nineteenth-Century Music Review* 5/2 (2008). Most recently, two anthologies, *Rethinking Schubert*, ed. Lorraine Byrne Bodley and Julian Horton (Oxford: Oxford University Press, 2016) and *Schubert's Late Music: History, Theory, Style*, ed. Lorraine Byrne Bodley and Julian Horton (Cambridge: Cambridge University Press, 2016), demonstrate how the image of Schubert as an intellectual has become broadly and firmly established within musical analysis.

PART II

LIEDER

4

Schubert's Dramatic Lieder: Rehabilitating 'Adelwold und Emma', D. 211

Susan Wollenberg

Introduction: Genre and Reception

In the hierarchical framework that has formed around Schubert's production of Lieder, the longer dramatic settings traditionally have been somewhat undervalued.[1] Among these, 'Adelwold und Emma', D. 211 (1815), seems to have been particularly the victim of a classic vicious circle, neglected in performance and in scholarship – or despised by the critics when they have noticed it.[2] At this point we might invoke Schumann's well-known epithet of 'heavenly length'.[3] This feature of Schubert's work has tended to arouse a response at opposite ends of the spectrum – either admiration or opprobrium – among the composer's devotees and critics. And length is the feature that informs the total substance of Richard Capell's commentary on 'Adelwold und Emma' in his *Schubert's Songs*, his comment merely being consigned to a footnote apropos mention of 'some of the longest

[1] The majority of the dramatic ballads belong among his early Lieder (composed between 1811 and 1816). As Kristina Muxfeldt noted, 'numerous compositional models for Schubert's earliest songs have long been recognized and documented': Kristina Muxfeldt, 'Schubert's Songs: The Transformation of a Genre', in *The Cambridge Companion to Schubert*, ed. Christopher H. Gibbs (Cambridge: Cambridge University Press, 1997), p. 122. Marjorie Hirsch suggested that 'while Schubert was probably familiar with the dramatic songs of many composers, Zumsteeg's appear to have influenced him most', while also observing that Schubert's early songs 'are not slavish imitations': see Marjorie Wing Hirsch, *Schubert's Dramatic Lieder* (Cambridge: Cambridge University Press, 1993), pp. 70–71.

[2] The song's history is marked by a degree of obscurity: no performance is known from Schubert's lifetime, and the work was not published until 1894. Apropos the reception of Schubert's dramatic songs in general, Hirsch in her Introduction documented the 'discomfort' of nineteenth-century critics with Schubert's 'infusion of dramatic musical traits into traditional Lieder' (Hirsch, *Schubert's Dramatic Lieder*, p. 2).

[3] Fanny Raymond Ritter, ed., *Music and Musicians: Essays and Criticisms by Robert Schumann*, 4th edn (London: William Reeves, 1920), pp. 48–56, specifically p. 54; also printed in Robert Schumann, '"Schubert's Symphony in C" (1840)', in *Schumann on Music*, ed. Henry Pleasants (New York: Dover, 1965), pp. 163–8.

pieces' among the extended ballads, with Capell observing of D. 211 only that it is 'the longest of all … (26 pages)'.[4]

Length is used by Capell as a means of setting up a prejudice against these early ballads. He introduces them thus: '[Among the songs of 1815] there are the numerous extended compositions in various movements. They are usually less inviting than the little strophic songs'; although he goes on to admit that 'yet hardly one is without a beautiful page, whatever the inequalities of the whole'.[5] Capell's comments on other ballads of 1815 include (on 'Auf einen Kirchhof', D. 151): 'Schubert has adopted a quasi-dramatic form and the song fails through excess of exertion'.[6] Summing up the group of dramatic Lieder, he reiterates more forcefully the comparative stance he took at the start of the discussion: 'It might have been thought that years separated such music from the masterpieces of the period. These compositions show Schubert in the act of practising his pen in the intervals between the visits of his genius'.[7]

Marjorie Wing Hirsch's non-judgemental approach to the early ballads forms a welcome contrast to this.[8] Her schematic definition of the genre in her monograph, and her careful defence of the dramatic Lied, make a particularly valuable contribution to the literature. Although her discussion of individual settings includes relatively sparse commentary on 'Adelwold und Emma', importantly, in listing it among some dozen of Schubert's ballads that draw on similar sources from 'medieval lore', she reminds us that Schubert's taste in subject-matter here reflects 'the contemporary fascination with the Middle Ages'.[9]

Reviewing a selection of discs from the Hyperion *Schubert Complete Songs* on CD for *Nineteenth-Century Music Review* in 2008, I wrote of D. 211:

> The longest item and Schubert's longest-ever song is the chivalric ballad (more truly a miniature opera in monologue) *Adelwold und Emma* (Bertrand: CD 7, tracks 1–4), divided into four sections: "Hoch und ehern schier von Dauer", "Adelwolden bracht als Waise", "Gold, Gestein, und Seide nimmer", and finally "Dein ist Emma! Ewig dein!", totalling altogether 28' 05", finely sung by Martyn Hill, supported by Graham Johnson's sympathetic accompaniment, and disproving John Reed's remark (in his *Schubert Song Companion*) that performances of this work are "unlikely, to say the least".[10]

[4]   Richard Capell, *Schubert's Songs* (London: Ernest Benn, 1928), p. 90.
[5]   Capell, *Schubert's Songs*, p. 89.
[6]   Capell, *Schubert's Songs*, p. 89.
[7]   Capell, *Schubert's Songs*, p. 90.
[8]   See Hirsch, *Schubert's Dramatic Lieder*, Part II.
[9]   Hirsch, *Schubert's Dramatic Lieder*, p. 85.
[10] John Reed, *The Schubert Song Companion* (Manchester: Manchester University Press, 1985), p. 12. Graham Johnson's notes on 'Adelwold und Emma' in the Hyperion listener guide set a new level of discourse on the song. Johnson's commentary on D. 211 in his comprehensive study of the songs is probably the most extended available in print to date:

This fascinating and neglected piece, here given a fastidious, expressive and gripping performance, contains some lovely music.[11]

In the wake of that response to a first encounter with the setting, this chapter represents an opportunity to follow it up with a closer investigation of 'Adelwold und Emma', examining its dramatic and musical fabric in the spirit of rehabilitation it deserves in critical discourse as well as in performance. In this endeavour I explore particularly, on the one hand, the ways in which Schubert matches the poet's narrative and dialogic strategies in his musical structures and their content, and, on the other hand, how he endows his setting with a life of its own, rather as a film based on a book becomes a work in its own right once it has sprung from its source (which may itself have quasi-filmic qualities inherent in it). John Reed, devoting a mere couple of paragraphs to 'Adelwold und Emma', used a cinematic comparison (as well as the song's length) to its disadvantage: 'At 628 bars, *Adelwold und Emma* has the dubious distinction of being Schubert's longest song ... The naivety of the pictorialism ... fatally suggests to modern ears the days of the silent cinema'.[12]

On strictly generic grounds, my description of the song in the CD review as a 'miniature opera in monologue' should have been inflected to read 'quasi-opera', in line with Marjorie Hirsch's differentiation between dramatic scenes and dramatic ballads and in view of its featuring a narrator; though the added tag 'in monologue' made clear that this was not an exact equivalent to straightforward opera. Hirsch's fundamental distinction – whereby 'dramatic scenes' are genuinely more operatic, while 'dramatic ballads', as typified by the presence of a narrator, constitute a more indirectly operatic genre[13] – need not obscure the profoundly operatic nature of 'Adelwold und Emma'. For we find in it so many of the elements of opera, crossing over with the Lied.

Graham Johnson, *Franz Schubert: The Complete Songs*, 3 vols (New Haven and London: Yale University Press, 2014), vol. 1, pp. 64–8.

[11]   See my review of Franz Schubert, *Complete Songs* (Hyperion), Discs 7–12, in *Nineteenth-Century Music Review* 5/2 (2008), pp. 129–33. The inclusion of 'Adelwold und Emma' among the 'Early Ballads' in the Oxford Lieder Festival recital by Nicky Spence and Roger Vignoles (12 October 2014 at the Holywell Music Room, Oxford), gave evidence of the compelling effect the work could have on the concert platform.

[12]   Reed, *Schubert Song Companion*, p. 12. Johnson (*Franz Schubert: The Complete Songs*, vol. 1, p. 65) brings the comparison up to date with more favourable intentions, referring to the deployment of tricks of modern cinema in the work (he suggests that the latter term is more apt than 'song' for such a substantial setting); among the early ballads, Johnson elaborates on this cinematic quality particularly in connection with 'Der Taucher', D. 111 (*Franz Schubert: The Complete Songs*, vol. 3, p. 310).

[13]   Hirsch, *Schubert's Dramatic Lieder*, p. 11.

Analytical Approaches to 'Adelwold und Emma'

A particular concern in the sections on text and music that follow here is the evidence we can glean of Schubert's compositional control over his material in D. 211 (vital in sustaining its length successfully): to this purpose I will foreground the role of musical gesture and motif.[14] The idea that Schubert treated the dramatic ballad at this time as a vehicle for experiment with compositional techniques and effects is suggested in D. 211 partly by the variety of ways in which he handles aspects of form and expression, as if trying out the different possibilities.[15] These include devices that link adjacent sections within the song at their ends and beginnings; or that contribute to the portrayal of a character, or a moment in the plot, or trace a thread through the drama; also the handling of the combination of voice and piano.

An outline of Schubert's response to Bertrand's text is provided in Table 4.1 for reference in the discussion that follows.[16] Both text and musical score are so rich in motifs, references and connections, that in both Table 4.1 and the discussion based on it only a fraction of these can be highlighted here.

[14]   These elements intersect with the frames of 'topical' reference and intertextual relation to the work of other composers, as explored further in the sections below. For broader studies of these two aspects, see Robert S. Hatten, *Interpreting Musical Gestures, Topics, and Tropes: Mozart, Beethoven, Schubert* (Bloomington: University of Indiana Press, 2004); and Christopher A. Reynolds, *Motives for Allusion: Context and Content in Nineteenth-Century Music* (Cambridge, MA: Harvard University Press, 2003).

[15]   Elizabeth McKay divided the early ballads from the more ephemeral exercises Schubert may have designed for his 'Bildung circle': 'Many of these were written for particular meetings of the friends and were little more than exercises in songwriting, or unpolished occasional pieces, which Schubert never envisaged would be published. [...] Other songs of this period, which may or may not have begun as his offerings to the circle, are in a totally different category. Some were settings of dramatic scenes or ballads. Schubert had for several years been fascinated by, and experimented with, the dramatic song forms he had inherited from older composers'. Elizabeth Norman McKay, *Franz Schubert: A Biography* (Oxford: Oxford University Press, 1996), pp. 49–50.

[16]   For the full text of Schubert's 'Adelwold und Emma', together with an English translation by Richard Wigmore, see Graham Johnson, *Franz Schubert: The Complete Songs*, 3 vols (New Haven and London: Yale University Press, 2014), vol. 1, pp. 57–64. English translations of excerpts quoted in this chapter are drawn from this source with kind permission of Yale University Press.

Table 4.1   Outline of 'Adelwold und Emma', D. 211

Bar	Vs	Text incipit	Music	Type	Key
1	1	N: Hoch und ehern	1	recit.; chivalric	F →
18	2	N: **Aber** finstrer Kummer		pathos	d →
35	3	E: Vater! Rufe nicht K: Ich nicht rufen?	2 (b. 43)	b. 43: recit./aria	g → Bb → bb →
49	4	N: Emma hört's		empfindsam	f → bb
67	5	N: Heiter presst	3; 4 (b. 78); 5 (b. 83)	aria/Lied; recit.; sepulchral	Gb → ab
89	6	N: Zitternd folgte sie			ab
116	7	N: Unter'n Lämplein	6 (b. 126)	b. 126: recit.	→ Bb
132	8	K: Mein Geschlecht	7	aria: chivalric	Bb
148	9	K: Nie vergassen			
162	10	K: **Aber** Fluch!	8	sepulchral	g
180	11	N: Bleich, wie sie			
204	12	N: Adelwolden bracht	9	aria/Lied	Eb
218	13	N: **Aber** Emma			
237	14	N: Rosig auf zum Jüngling			Ab
254	15	N: Fest und fester	10 (b. 259)	b. 259: recit. →	bb → Bb
267	16	N: So das Fräulein	11	aria interjection	g → bb
273	17	N: **Doch** mit eins	12; 13 (b. 278)	recit.; aria (cf. 9)	g; G

Key to abbreviations: Vs: poetic verse; initials followed by colon preceding text incipits indicate characters speaking, as follows: A: Adelwold, E: Emma, K: Knight, together with N: Narrator; sections of the music are designated by numbers 1 to 28; within these 'Type' denotes genre (e.g. aria) or topic (e.g. sepulchral); keys are indicated by upper case major, lower case minor, and arrows modulatory (in transit).

Table 4.1 (continued)

Bar	Vs	Text incipit	Music	Type	Key
287	18	A: Leiten soll mich			→
303	19	A: Selig träumt'ich	14		D → B♭
341	20	N: Und schon			→ e →
384	21	E: Lindre, Vater	15	lament	a
395	22	N: Gold, Gestein	16	strophic Lied	a
	23	N: Ritter! ach			
411	24	N: Selbst dem Ritter	17; 18 (b. 423)	Lied fragment; recit. fragment	F → B♭ →
428	25	N: Hergeführt auf schwülen Winden	19 (b. 426)	catastrophe	g
433	26	N: Tosend gleich den Wogen			→ f (b.445)
450	27	K: Richter! ach	20 (b. 449)		f♯ →
463	28	N: Gleiten ab von tauben Ohren	21 (b. 468)	→ recit. fragment	B♭
479	29	N: Glut an Glut!			b♭ → B♭
498	30	N: Purpur kehrt	22; 23 (b. 503)	siciliano; recit.	E♭ → B♭
513	31	N: Starr zusammenschrickt	24	dramatic fragment	→ G
521	32	N: **Doch** den Zweifler	25	recit.	→ e
531	33	A: Deines Fluchs	26	chivalric/heroic	e
547	34	N: **Doch** mit unsichtbaren Ketten		→	→ C
559	35	N: Emma harrt	27	recit.	
569	36	K: Dein ist Emma!	28	strophic Lied	c → G♭
587	37	K: Nimm sie hin			B
	38	N: Fest umschlungen			

'Adelwold und Emma': Textual Considerations

Friedrich Anton Franz Bertrand emerges from the obscurity attributed to him by John Reed in his Master Musicians volume, where he is represented as an 'unknown versifier', at the opposite end of the spectrum from the 'most famous' (Goethe et al.).[17] Peter Clive is more informative (despite the caveat that 'very little is known about his life'): from Clive's dictionary entry on the 'poet and essayist' (giving his dates as 'b. 1757; d. after 1829') we learn that Bertrand studied law at Halle before 'working for some years at the tax office at Calbe an der Saale'; Clive outlines briefly the publication history of his writings.[18]

Bertrand's text has been regarded derisively by commentators on 'Adelwold und Emma', and it has been difficult for it to shake off the aura of incompetence this has created around it. It is unfortunate that Alfred Einstein, having described the early ballads as historically important and musically rich in 'surprising details of pictorial illustration', went on to say: 'This interest applies even to a "murder-story" like Hölty's "Nonne" ... or Bertrand's "Adelwold und Emma" [the latter is definitely not a murder story]', which now, he asserted, 'merely strike us as unintentionally funny'.[19] Bertrand bestowed on his narrator an elevated role in keeping with the ancient rules of rhetoric. Elaine Sisman, in her study of pathos, quotes Quintilian apropos the persuasive art of oratory: 'the prime essential for stirring the emotions of others is, in my opinion, first to feel those emotions oneself'.[20] Bertrand uses silence, too, to this effect. It is a remarkable moment when, overcome in evoking the morbid scene of the castle vaults, the narrator declares himself unable to continue. That Schubert evidently spent some trouble on editing Bertrand's text for his purposes suggests that he saw beyond its not entirely polished surface to the considerable dramatic possibilities it possessed.[21] In crafting his musical setting he responded to the invitation to be moved by its characters and their destinies.

The plot of 'Adelwold und Emma' (if approached from a negative stance) could seem to consist of a number of chivalric and romantic stereotypes stitched loosely together: love thwarted, honour in battle, rescue, repentance, love triumphant. But

[17] John Reed, *Schubert* [Master Musicians] (London: J. M. Dent, 1987), p. 34.
[18] Peter Clive, *Schubert and his World: A Biographical Dictionary* (Oxford: Clarendon Press, 1997), p. 14. Johnson, in his biographical note on Bertrand (*Franz Schubert: The Complete Songs*, vol. 1, pp. 300–301), explores in some detail the sources to which Schubert may have had access. Schubert also set Bertrand's ballad 'Minona' (D. 152), portraying its tale of revenge less effectively than his response to the very different plot of Bertrand's 'Adelwold und Emma'. Both Bertrand settings feature in volume 29 of the Naxos Deutsche Schubert-Lied-Edition.
[19] Alfred Einstein, *Schubert*, trans. David Ascoli (London: Panther Books, 1971 [1951]), p. 117.
[20] Elaine R. Sisman, 'Pathos and the *Pathétique*: Rhetorical Stance in Beethoven's C-minor Sonata, Op. 13', *Beethoven Forum* 3 (1994), pp. 81–105, specifically p. 87.
[21] For details of his emendations and omissions, see Johnson, *Franz Schubert: The Complete Songs*, vol. 1, pp. 65–8.

it can be read differently. Christopher Booker's study of plot types, suggesting that these are reducible to a small number of basic models, masks an infinity of nuances and twists that these and other possible models can be given.[22]

Bertrand's chivalric ballad certainly contains a number of universal – and powerful – literary themes. Adelwold, the humble figure growing up on the estate and falling in love with the landowner's daughter, resonates with latter-day parallels such as those in L. P. Hartley's *The Go-Between* or Ian McEwan's *Atonement*. The plot is full of elements which could well be featured in staged opera, and indeed have been through the ages: the castle setting (Bartók's *Bluebeard*);[23] and that castle going up in flames towards the end – perhaps the earliest example of operatic conflagration is Francesca Caccini's *Liberazione di Ruggiero* (1625). Other universal plot elements in D. 211 include the father's curse, Adelwold's exile and return, the rescue of the heroine from danger (the burning castle), the rescuer's identity revealed (as Adelwold), and the quasi-religious forgiveness reached at the conclusion of the drama.

What is involved in the poetic text here, above all, is the art of story, with its recourse to fundamental devices reminiscent of story-telling games, for example in the use of 'aber' ('but'), which, as Laura Tunbridge noted in her pre-concert talk on the work, serves as a recurrent linking figure between verses:[24] sometimes this is varied by the use of 'doch' to the same effect (the words are highlighted in bold in Table 4.1). This device could feature in the kind of game where each of the players invents a sentence or two, stopping abruptly on a cliff-hanger with 'but' or 'then', and the next person takes over the tale. Perhaps such dramatic ballads as Bertrand's could be associated not with being 'funny' (as Einstein thought) but with the kind of fun that is derivable from the evocation of shared story-telling experienced in a congenial and sociable context.

Throughout 'Adelwold und Emma', the poet's dramatic purpose is evident in his choice of tactics. Momentum is established instantly from the start by the immediacy with which we are plunged into the castle scene. The characters speak for themselves after the narrator's brief but intensely vivid opening gambit, whereby the scene is 'painted' for us (helped to come alive by the built-in sound effects and

---

[22]   Christopher Booker, *The Seven Basic Plots: Why We Tell Stories* (London and New York: Bloomsbury, 2004). Philip Pullman in his contribution to the Oxford Literary Festival (2004), speaking on the literary plot, declared that Booker's theory was nonsense: 'everyone knows there are eleven!'

[23]   Incidentally (apropos the seven doors of that castle) there can be something eerie about items being numbered – so the narrator in 'Adelwold und Emma' counts the seven lamps in the vaults, one for each of the Knight's dead sons.

[24]   Oxford Lieder Festival, 12 October 2014.

the accompanying symbolic references evoking danger and violence).[25] The Knight, and Emma, his daughter, are introduced in dramatic dialogue, thus speaking for themselves (Table 4.1, verses 2–5); they move on to enact their family history as they descend to the vaults, with Bertrand here presenting the crux on which the plot revolves: the Knight's grief over the loss of his seven sons in battle, and his hopes for the future, which rest on the acquisition of a suitable bridegroom for Emma (Table 4.1, verses 6–10).

It would be all too easy to assume on casual acquaintance with their story that the three speaking parts (besides the narrator) forming the cast of 'Adelwold und Emma' represent 'stock' characters; but the way they are presented by the poet lifts them above the level of wooden figures. It is striking that the elderly Knight (Emma's father) is the only one of the three who is not named (thereby drawing attention to the nobility of his status, which will be a crucial factor driving the plot). This is in contrast to Ritter Toggenburg, the knight of Toggenburg in Schubert's setting of Schiller (D. 397), whose name is invoked specifically in setting up the image of the character towards the start of the ballad that tells his story (verse 3, lines 5–6): 'Und des Toggenburgers Name / Schreckt den Muselmann'.[26] But it should not be thought that the anonymous knight in 'Adelwold und Emma' constitutes merely a cipher.

Bertrand shows a degree of insight into the human situation presented by the Knight and his daughter at the start, combined with a strong signal towards the unfolding of the drama that will follow. Thus Emma's utterance: 'Vater! – sieh dein Kind! – ach früh / War dein Beifall mein Bestreben!' (Verse 4, lines 3–4: 'Father, behold your child! Ah, since I was young / I have sought to win your approval') not only expresses the profound mental and emotional pressure inherent in the burden of responsibility carried by the survivor towards the bereaved parent (she herself as the bereaved sibling must carry a complex load of grief), but also bears significant implications for the direction the plot will take.

The dramatic intensity of those opening verses flows continuously into our first encounter with Adelwold, 'des Ritters Knappe', the 'knight's squire', lurking palely (to borrow a poetic adverb from Keats's ballad, 'La Belle Dame sans Merci',[27] originally written in 1819) and in terror (Table 4.1, verse 11). Adelwold's absorption of the sombre mood reigning previously is counterbalanced by the more restful pause now introduced by Bertrand for a portrayal of the would-be knight's life up to this

---

[25] Verse 1, conjuring a vision of bleakness mixed with grandeur (the lofty ancient edifice with its giant turrets, the snorting bears lying at the gate, 'awaiting their prey', and the eerie wind roaring 'like the sea').

[26] 'And the name of Toggenburg / Terrified the Mussulman'. The verse begins in heroic mode with mention of the 'great deeds' accomplished by the crusaders.

[27] Keats's lines, famously, are 'O what can ail thee knight-at-arms, Alone and palely loitering?'. Bertrand here gives: 'Bleich, wie sie, mit bangen Zagen / Lehnt des Ritters Knappe hier' ('Pale as the maiden, fearful and apprehensive, / The knight's squire lurks here').

point (Table 4.1, verses 12–16), offering welcome relief from the hectic atmosphere, while serving dramatic purpose in the longer term.

The narrator recounts Adelwold's 'back story' by a series of tableaux, with an effect comparable to the latter-day equivalent of leafing through and commenting on an old album of photographs from childhood (for example with lines like 'Froh umwand sie seine Lanze / Im Turnier mit einem Kranze', 'In the tournament she gaily / Crowned his lance with a wreath', verse 13). Johnson's comment: 'In the manner of a straightforward Loewe ballad, events concerning Adelwold's history over a number of years are quickly covered',[28] should not be taken to mean that this section of the text is perfunctory. In conveying vital information about the three protagonists, it simultaneously deepens our knowledge of the father and daughter and places Adelwold in relation to Emma, forming a basis for the drama that is to unfold. Significantly, it reveals the Knight's generous and affectionate treatment of the young orphan Adelwold, on whom he took pity (verse 12, line 2: 'mitleidsvoll', literally 'full of compassion'), bringing him to the castle and raising him among his own children.

Whereas Schiller's Ritter Toggenburg returns from his pilgrimage to find that his beloved has taken the veil (as a 'bride of heaven … wedded … to God'), Bertrand endows his 'Adelwold und Emma' with a *lieto fine*, the classic happy ending. But rather like Tamino in Mozart's *Die Zauberflöte*, though obviously in a very different context, Adelwold must first prove himself worthy. And in some respects like Pamina in *Die Zauberflöte*, Emma (left behind) has to suffer in consequence of the 'trial' or testing time that Adelwold must undergo. The 'happy ending' that is reached following Adelwold's return from his absence on pilgrimage, in a series of dramatic twists that sees the pair united with her father's blessing at last (neatly countering his earlier curse on anyone who would thwart his wishes for his daughter's future), is unique among the early ballads.[29] The concluding 'Dein ist Emma!' (verse 36) rings brightly with its intimations of the intense relief and joy at the reunion of Adelwold and Emma, amid the grateful and wholehearted bestowal of acceptance by her father.

The Musical Setting

Schubert's setting of Bertrand's 'Adelwold und Emma' helps its characters to 'spring to life', while the plot unfolds with a judiciously paced mixture of reflective and dramatic moods, against a scenic backdrop evoked musically – as Johnson observed – with filmic vividness.[30] The musical textures and topics at Schubert's disposal here

---

[28]   Johnson, *Franz Schubert: The Complete Songs*, vol. 1, p. 66. On Schubert's appropriately relaxed pacing here see 'The Musical Setting' in this chapter.

[29]   The curse was voiced by the Knight during the visit to the vaults ('Aber Fluch! …', 'But a curse! …') before he broke off in horror, dragging Emma out of the 'fearful place' ('… Zog er plötzlich sie … / Aus den schauervollen Orte': verse 10, lines 1–4).

[30]   See n. 12 above.

cover a dazzling range from quasi-orchestral effects to hymn-like chordal writing, and from forms of recitative to aria, as well as Lied (for an indication of the main types employed at various junctures see Table 4.1 above). True to the purest tradition of the genre, all this is achieved in metaphorical fashion by the combination of just one (flexible) voice with piano accompaniment.[31]

In view of the remarkable range and fluidity of Schubert's key structure in 'Adelwold und Emma', seen not only in the recitative sections but also in passages of more lyrical, aria-like writing, the outline in the final column of Table 4.1 indicates areas at the main sectional divisions, with a selection of the most dramatically significant stages passed through en route. The choice of key may convey associative and evocative use (for instance chivalric, or sepulchral) as well as reflecting Schubert's experimental approach to tonal moves and key schemes.[32] The music for the knight's recounting of his family history (described by Johnson as a 'proud B flat major polonaise': it displays from its start more tonal mobility than this might suggest)[33] responds to the couplet 'In des Grabes Dunkelheit / Sank die Reih' von Biederleuten' (verse 8, lines 4–5, conveying his ancestors' descent 'into the grave's darkness') by resolving the dominant seventh in bar 137 into the 'dark' key of Bb minor. It then proceeds by a circuitous route via Gb, reaching (via Schubert's favourite Neapolitan relation) a sombre F minor half cadence (bars 138–144: see Example 4.1); before the return to the major, Bb minor is again summoned portentously for the evocation of the 'last trump' which will wake all.

As with keys, so with topic and genre, a fluid surface is created by Schubert's moving in and out of these zones in response to the text. Table 4.1 gives some idea of the overlapping parameters this process creates. The sense of pacing with which such moves are accomplished is a sign of Schubert's being at ease in the compositional space he has created for his setting. He crafts transitions of appropriate length and

---

[31] The wide vocal range swings between differing registers for the various characters and moods: up to high Ab or Bb when Emma speaks under extreme pressure (as at bars 176–177 and 506–508), down to two octaves below that, for instance when the narrator describes feelingly the castle vaults (bars 93–97). Johnson (*Franz Schubert: The Complete Songs*, vol. 1, p. 68) proposes a multi-voice performance.

[32] In this regard, it is striking to find amid the hectic sequential fluctuation during the episode of the castle fire, a momentary shift to the Neapolitan minor – f to f♯ – associated with the late works (notably the Piano Duet Fantasy in F minor, D. 940): Table 4.1, verses 26–27. Clearly the major-minor pairings seen in Table 4.1, and the enharmonic move transforming and resolving flat tonic to sharp dominant note (Table 4.1, verses 35–36) resonate with the late style. On Schubert's characteristic treatment of keys, see particularly Elizabeth Norman McKay, *Schubert: The Piano and Dark Keys* (Tutzing: Hans Schneider, 2009); and Susan Wollenberg, *Schubert's Fingerprints: Studies in the Instrumental Works* (Farnham: Ashgate, 2011), esp. Chapter 2, "His Favourite Device": Schubert's Major-Minor Usage and its Nuances', pp. 15–46.

[33] Johnson, *Franz Schubert: The Complete Songs*, vol. 1, p. 66.

Example 4.1   Schubert, 'Adelwold und Emma', D. 211, bars 131–147

dramatic intensity where the text invites a linking process, or where he intends to dovetail musically across divisions in the verse structure. These interludes work at various levels: modulatory, motivic, referential, and affective. A particularly poignant example occurs at the close of verse 20 (bars 372–383), where the series of dramatic triplet octaves in the piano (sparked by the narrator's reference to the father's curse as Adelwold recalls its terrible effect), leads into a forceful cadential gesture in the prevailing key of E minor (bars 377–379); this is then echoed in new topical and harmonic guise, with the triplet quaver figure augmented to crotchets, and countering the *sforzandi* scattered through the preceding bars by the *piano* dynamic now governing the softer cadence towards A minor, the key of Emma's plaintive utterance at the start of verse 21 ('Lindre, Vater, meine Wunde!': 'Father, ease my pain!', bars 384–385).[34]

A further indication of Schubert's feeling 'at home' in the setting he constructs for 'Adelwold und Emma' (and of the care and attention he devoted to it)[35] is his insertion of a favourite fingerprint of his personal compositional style at various levels of the music: this is his use of palindrome. Thus the keys crossing over sections and sub-sections may form a palindromic set: see, for example, Table 4.1, bars 254–272. At a more compressed level, the curling ostinato figure that contributes to the sepulchral atmosphere in verses 5 through 10 (calling for orchestral scoring, as does so much of the music of this setting), matches the closed circle of Emma's existence, as she accompanies her father on their visit to the castle vaults.

The colourful palette of stylistic and topical references, into which Schubert dips in order to paint scenes, moods, and characters musically, gives the aural surface of the work an animated and exhilarating effect. In doing so, it draws attention to the crossover of the dramatic and the more intimate forms of utterance in Schubert's Lieder: between operatic and theatrical, on the one hand, and Lied and domestic sphere on the other. As already adumbrated, the topical allusions informing his setting draw on a variety of literary, historical and musical sources, including cultural environments (chivalric, together with martial and sepulchral topics), aesthetic/stylistic expressive modes (as with *empfindsam* vocabulary), and intimations of religiosity. This is a setting generously endowed with allusive traits.

---

[34] Emma's phrase here, repeated for pleading effect, recalls the pervasive triadic motif from the opening of the work (discussed further below) in one of its varied forms, introducing a dissonant passing-note on the third beat: the falling A minor triad the phrase outlines irresistibly brings to mind the song 'Schöne Welt, wo bist du', D. 677, with its yearning quality. The 'set-piece' that follows (the strophic Lied, 'Gold, Gestein und Seide', bars 395–410), prolongs the A minor tonal landscape, its pathos intensified by the singer's obsessive circling around the dominant note e" as if to emphasize Emma's bleak steadfastness, as, bereft of Adelwold, she vows to forgo worldly riches – the triadic motif is featured inverted here, as happens also in D. 677.

[35] The jacket illustration to this volume shows Schubert at work on the setting. On the compositional process, see Johnson, *Franz Schubert: The Complete Songs*, vol. 1, p. 65.

These references are not necessarily deployed in an obvious way, like labels stuck on to characters or scenes, but rather with a certain degree of subtlety. For example, when the narrator introduces Emma's direct speech (verse 4, line 1) with his words 'Emma hört's' ('Emma listens'), he already assumes the mantle of the expressive *empfindsam* mode that will characterize her utterance when it comes (see Example 4.2a). And when Adelwold first appears, described by the narrator as 'Pale as the maiden' (verse 11, line 1), the melody for that phrase of the text ('Bleich, wie sie': Example 4.2b) links him with her, echoing exactly, a semitone lower, that of the narrator's description of Emma earlier: this is then reproduced in a sequence exuding pathos,[36] with its descent by chromatic step. Schubert's quasi-operatic use of such devices creates structural cohesion over extended stretches of the music, in a complex, motivically interlocking network.

Within this network, motivic material is recreated inventively to suit the moment, as with the original three-note palindromic figure associated with Emma (marked 'x' on Example 4.2a), which is later intensified in five-note form as she pleads desperately with her father not to finish his terrible curse: 'O verwirf, verwirf mich nicht!' ('Do not, ah do not reject me!', verse 10, line 8: Example 4.2c). As marked on Example 4.2c, in Emma's heightened outburst, 'x' is combined with the triadic chivalric motif 'y' (see Example 4.3a) in its guise as 'y2' (see Example 4.3b), now stretched further on its repetition (marked 'y3' on Example 4.2c) to outline dramatically the diminished seventh that harmonizes it. These developmental processes are set in motion from the start, continuing to resonate with meaning throughout the work. The clean-cut, heroic, triadic fanfare motif ('y') evoking the castle setting in bars 1–5, appears in a series of new incarnations to match the shifts of expressive zone that follow, its tessitura first stretched to an octave to represent the giant towers described in bars 10–11 '(y1')'; then tracing the sinister diminished fifth ('y2') already inherent in 'y1', now accompanied with diminished-seventh harmony, at bars 13–15, where the roaring wind outside signals the troubled atmosphere within (see Examples 4.3a and 4.3b).

Echoes of Mozart operas (already suggested above in relation to plot and character) may be seen to form a particular set of referential elements in the work.[37] Emma's concern for her father and sense of filial duty are suggestive of Mozart's portrayal of Donna Anna's attachment to her late father in *Don Giovanni*. Specific passages in Schubert's score suggest a possible Mozartian source: in the interlude forming a transition between verses 1 and 2 and between the outer scene and the mood within (bars 17–19: see Example 4.4), the portentous D minor cadential bass in octaves sounds as if it could come from *Don Giovanni* (whose overall key it shares). The F minor pathos of 'Emma hört's' (Example 4.2a) shares its key and

---

[36] Sisman's exploration of pathos in its theatrical connotations (with the purpose of evoking feeling in the audience) is pertinent here: see Sisman, 'Pathos and the *Pathétique*'.

[37] These could derive from a common source rather than directly, though Schubert is known to have heard Mozart's operas in Vienna by 1812.

Example 4.2a   Schubert, 'Adelwold und Emma', D. 211, bars 45–59

Example 4.2b   Schubert, 'Adelwold und Emma', D. 211, bars 178–187

Example 4.2c   Schubert, 'Adelwold und Emma', D. 211, bars 174–177

Example 4.3a   Schubert, 'Adelwold und Emma', D. 211, bars 1–5

Example 4.3b   Schubert, 'Adelwold und Emma', D. 211, bars 10–15

mood with Alfonso's ironic, highly expressive aria in Act I of *Così fan tutte* (though non-ironically in Schubert's case), as well as with Barbarina's aria of loss at the start of Act IV in Mozart's *Le Nozze di Figaro*.[38] And the ending of 'Adelwold und Emma', with its plot satisfyingly resolved via restorative, peaceful words and music redolent of forgiveness, shares its elevated ethos to some extent with that of the Act IV finale of *Figaro*.[39]

Before concluding this chapter, I must signal the sheer beauty of the music that Schubert lavished on his 'Adelwold und Emma'. The measured, soothing narration of Adelwold's life up to the present, tracing the blossoming of his relationship with Emma ('backflash' would be too brusque a word for this section of the score, marked 'Mässig, erzählend'), is couched in an aria whose beauty is consonant with the pure and good character, and the nobility, associated with both Adelwold and Emma (Example 4.5).[40] Its key of E♭ (Masonic, three flats for the Trinity) resonates with music of lofty stature: Bach's 'St Anne' Prelude and Fugue, and Mozart's *Die Zauberflöte*, for instance. And the hymn-like quality it possesses shares some of its musical shaping with the Austrian Emperor's hymn, Haydn's 'Gott erhalte Franz den Kaiser'. Schubert's 'set-piece' in quasi-strophic form finds its cathartic equivalent in the even more stylized strophic song that embodies the final resolution of the drama: 'Dein ist Emma!' (verses 36–38), its joyousness producing an ornamental efflorescence in the written-out varied reprise of the music for the second and third verses (Example 4.6).[41]

[38]   To the child, the lost pin she was entrusted with looms large as a source of anguish. Additionally, elements of the rhythmic and melodic profile of Schubert's setting here are shared with Orfeo's famous lament for his Eurydice in Gluck's *Orfeo*.

[39]   Johnson interprets Schubert's response to the resolution of the plot at this point as indicating 'Schubert's hopes that the transfiguring power of his music could likewise change his own father, who doubted his musical future, into a loving supporter of his future career' (Johnson, *Franz Schubert: The Complete Songs*, vol. 1, p. 68). I would be inclined to see Schubert here as writing from a position enclosed temporarily and intensely within the world evoked by his musical setting, in tandem with Bertrand's text, rather than necessarily expressing purposely his own situation in life.

[40]   The promise of this is inherent in the name Adelwold *(adel* meaning 'noble'). In Emma's declaration (verse 15, lines 5–8): 'Was die Flitter, so mich zieren? / Was Bankete bei Turnieren? / Wappen, Land, Geschmuck und Gold / Lohnt ein Traum von Adelwold!' (a dream of Adelwold is worth all her banqueting, finery and heritage), his name is set with the heroic triadic motif in the chivalric key of B♭: Schubert stretches it lovingly (bars 265–266), recognizing the emotional impact for Emma of pronouncing the name (the narrator preparing the scene does likewise at bars 256–257, conveying Emma's longing for Adelwold; this extended treatment of names uttered becomes a recurrent motif).

[41]   Also belonging with these is the exquisite passage in tender siciliana style marking the return of colour to Emma's cheeks with Adelwold's kiss (verse 30, bars 498–502): this makes

Example 4.4   Schubert, 'Adelwold und Emma', D. 211, bars 15–20

Example 4.5   Schubert, 'Adelwold und Emma', D. 211, bars 204–212

Example 4.6   Schubert, 'Adelwold und Emma', D. 211, bars 587–598

Conclusion: Rehabilitating 'Adelwold und Emma'

Schubert's artistry in 'Adelwold und Emma', as discussed here, yields a coherent musical structure and authentic expressivity for this remarkable experiment in quasi-theatrical Lied. When freed from the critical straitjacket that traditionally focused negatively on its length, or that neglected the work because of its chronological and generic status (in belonging to the early ballads), his setting has the capacity to draw us powerfully into its world. It sustains this magnetic quality by the confident manipulation of the many diverse elements interwoven in its fabric, including motif and topic, texture and generic type, register, key, and harmony. The rich tapestry these form together makes D. 211 outstanding, in my view, among Schubert's early production of ballads, not so much for its exceptional length, but rather for the combination of its engagingly attractive yet deceptive simplicity of utterance at surface level, with, at the deeper level, its compositional strengths.

its effect all the more in relief against the backcloth of the tumultuous events preceding it (verses 25–29: the lightning strike, castle fire – Schubert grasps the melodramatic possibilities full-on).

5

Gretchen abbandonata: The Lied as Aria

Marjorie Hirsch

The Mystery of an Unfinished Song

'Gretchen im Zwinger' (D. 564), composed May 1817, is an incomplete, through-composed setting for solo voice and piano of Scene 18 from Goethe's *Faust, Part I*.[1] The scene takes place just after Gretchen learns the harsh consequences of another girl's seduction: impregnated, Bärbelchen has become the target of public denunciation and ridicule, and is required by law to do church penance. Newly aware of her own sinful pregnancy and fearful of abandonment by Faust, Gretchen has made her way to the outskirts of town to place flowers before a statue of the *Mater dolorosa* – the grief-stricken Virgin Mary gazing up at her son's crucifixion – which is set in a niche of the town wall. All alone in this remote spot, Gretchen beseeches the Holy Mother to grant her mercy, rescuing her 'from shame and death'.

A free adaptation of the medieval sequence *Stabat mater dolorosa*, Gretchen's *Zwinger* monologue comprises a total of eight verses: three 3-line verses, two 6-line verses, and three 4-line verses, with the last three lines of the monologue repeating the first three (see Figures 5.1 and 5.2). The autograph manuscript of Schubert's setting includes forty-three bars of music, cutting off just before verse 6. A new key signature appears at the end of the manuscript, suggesting that Schubert did not consider the setting finished and, at least at one point, expected to continue it.

What explains the fragmentary nature of this song? According to John Reed, 'the operatic quality of [Schubert's] unfinished *Faust* pieces suggests that he may have cherished an ambition to write an opera based on the drama; but he was not ready for that in 1817, and in the final (C major) cadences one can almost sense the feeling of uncertainty about what happens next'.[2] In a similar vein, Alfred Einstein speculates that Schubert quit 'after completing only forty-three bars – despite wonderful touches in each of these bars – because they struck him as being too lyrical, and because they

---

[1] Gretchen's *Zwinger* monologue appears in the *Urfaust* (1773/75), *Faust. Ein Fragment* (1790), and *Faust, Part I* (1808; lines 3587–3619). *Goethes Werke*, ed. Erich Trunz (Hamburg: Christian Wegner, 1948–1960), vol. 3, pp. 114–15. Schubert's setting, published by Diabelli in June 1838 under the title 'Gretchens Bitte', appears with a specious ending in Book 29 of the *Nachlaß*.

[2] John Reed, *The Schubert Song Companion* (Manchester: Manchester University Press, 1985), p. 252.

1	Ach neige, Du Schmerzenreiche, Dein Antlitz gnädig meiner Not!	You who are laden with sorrow, Incline your face graciously To my distress.
2	Das Schwert im Herzen, Mit tausend Schmerzen Blickst auf zu deines Sohnes Tod.	With the sword in your heart, And a thousand sorrows. You look up at your dying son.
3	Zum Vater blickst du, Und Seufzer schickst du Hinauf um sein' und deine Not.	You gaze up to the Father, And let a sigh rise up For His affliction and your own.
4	Wer fühlet, Wie wühlet Der Schmerz mir im Gebein? Was mein armes Herz hier banget, Was es zittert, was verlanget, Weißt nur du, nur du allein!	Who can feel How the pain Gnaws away in my bones? What my poor heart fears, What it dreads, what it craves, Only you can know!
5	Wohin ich immer gehe Wie weh, wie weh, wie wehe Wird mir im Busen hier! Ich bin, ach, kaum alleine, Ich wein', ich wein', ich weine, Das Herz zerbricht in mir.	Wherever I go, How it hurts, how it hurts, [how it hurts] Here in my breast! Alas, no sooner am I alone Than I weep, I weep, [I weep,] And my heart breaks within me.
6	*Die Scherben vor meinem Fenster* *Betaut' ich mit Thränen, ach!* *Als ich am frühen Morgen* *Dir diese Blumen brach*	*Ah, I sprinkled with dewy tears* *The broken pots at my window!* *When early this morning* *I plucked these flowers for you.*
7	*Schien hell in meine Kammer* *Die Sonne früh herauf,* *Saß ich in allem Jammer* *In meinem Bett schon auf.*	*When the early sun shone brightly* *Up into my room* *I, in all my misery,* *Was already sitting up in bed.*
8	*Hilf! rette mich von Schmach und Tod!* *Ach neige,* *Du Schmerzenreiche,* *Dein Antlitz gnädig meiner Not!*	*Help! Save me from shame and death!* *You who are laden with sorrow,* *Incline your face graciously* *To my distress!*

Figure 5.1   Goethe, *Faust, Part I* (1808), Scene 18 (Gretchen's *Zwinger* monologue)

Note: Translation by Richard Wigmore, drawn from Graham Johnson, *Franz Schubert: The Complete Songs*, 3 vols (New Haven and London: Yale University Press, 2014), vol. 1, pp. 799–800. English translations from this source are used with kind permission of Yale University Press.

1	Stabat mater dolorosa juxta Crucem lacrimosa, dum pendebat Filius.	At the Cross her station keeping, Stood the mournful Mother weeping, Close to her Son to the last.
2	Cuius animam gementem, contristatam et dolentem pertransivit gladius.	Through her heart, His sorrow sharing, All His bitter anguish bearing, Now at length the sword has passed.
3	O quam tristis et afflicta fuit illa benedicta mater Unigeniti!	Oh, how sad and sore distressed Was that Mother, highly blest, Of the sole-begotten One.
4	Quae moerebat et dolebat, pia Mater, dum videbat nati poenas inclyti.	Christ above in torment hangs, She beneath beholds the pangs Of her dying glorious Son.
5	Quis est homo qui non fleret, matrem Christi si videret in tanto supplicio?	Is there one who would not weep, Whelmed in miseries so deep, Christ's dear Mother to behold?
6	Quis non posset contristari, Christi Matrem contemplari dolentem cum Filio?	Can the human heart refrain From partaking in her pain, In that Mother's pain untold?
7	Pro peccatis suae gentis vidit Iesum in tormentis, et flagellis subditum.	For the sins of His own nation, She saw Jesus wracked with torment, All with scourges rent:
8	Vidit suum dulcem Natum moriendo desolatum, dum emisit spiritum.	She beheld her tender Child, Saw Him hang in desolation Till His spirit forth He sent.
9	Eia Mater, fons amoris, me sentire vim doloris fac, ut tecum lugeam.	O thou Mother! fount of love! Touch my spirit from above; Make my heart with thine accord:
10	Fac, ut ardeat cor meum, in amando Christum Deum, ut sibi complaceam.	Make me feel as thou hast felt; Make my soul to glow and melt With the love of Christ my Lord.
11	Sancta Mater, istud agas, crucifixi fige plagas cordi meo valide.	Holy Mother! pierce me through, In my heart each wound renew Of my Savior crucified:

Figure 5.2   Sequence: *Stabat mater dolorosa*

Note: Translation by Edward Caswall. *Lyra Catholica* (London: J. Burns, 1849), pp. 138–40.

12 Tui Nati vulnerati, tam dignati pro me pati, poenas mecum divide.	Let me share with thee His pain, Who for all my sins was slain, Who for me in torments died.
13 Fac me tecum pie flere, crucifixo condolere, donec ego vixero.	Let me mingle tears with thee, Mourning Him who mourned for me, All the days that I may live:
14 Juxta Crucem tecum stare, et me tibi sociare in planctu desidero.	By the Cross with thee to stay, There with thee to weep and pray, Is all I ask of thee to give.
15 Virgo virginum praeclara, mihi iam non sis amara, fac me tecum plangere.	Virgin of all virgins blest!, Listen to my fond request: Let me share thy grief divine;
16 Fac, ut portem Christi mortem, passionis fac consortem, et plagas recolere.	Let me, to my latest breath, In my body bear the death Of that dying Son of thine.
17 Fac me plagis vulnerari, fac me Cruce inebriari et cruore Filii.	Wounded with His every wound, Steep my soul till it hath swooned, In His very blood away.
18 Flammis ne urar succensus, per te, Virgo, sim defensus in die iudicii.	Be to me, O Virgin, nigh, Lest in flames I burn and die In His awful Judgment Day.
19 Christe, cum sit hinc exire, da per Matrem me venire ad palmam victoriae.	Christ, when Thou shalt call me hence, Be Thy Mother my defense, Be Thy Cross my victory;
20 Quando corpus morietur, fac, ut animae donetur paradisi gloria. Amen.	While my body here decays, May my soul Thy goodness praise, Safe in Paradise with Thee. Amen.

Figure 5.2 (continued)

reminded him too much of the theatre'.[3] Kenneth S. Whitton also hypothesizes that Schubert abandoned the song because of his desire to compose an opera,[4] while Graham Johnson observes that the song's 'psychological interest' is concentrated

[3]   Alfred Einstein, *Schubert*, trans. David Ascoli (London: Panther Books, 1971 [1951]), p. 168.
[4]   Kenneth S. Whitton, *Goethe and Schubert: The Unseen Bond* (Portland, OR: Amadeus Press, 1999), p. 227.

almost exclusively in the vocal line,[5] indicating that this may help to explain why Schubert left the work unfinished (a conjecture resting on the assumption that Schubert desired a more even balance of interest between voice and piano).

Richard Capell, on the other hand, states that the song was probably originally complete (a view shared by Reinhard van Hoorickx) but 'mutilated by chance',[6] adding that Schubert likely would have 'gone back to his opening strain in B-flat minor', given the repetition of the opening lines at the end. The notion that the song was once complete is reasonable, given that the music in the autograph manuscript stops at the end of a page (1 verso); there could have been one or more additional leaves. But no other documentary evidence supporting this theory survives. Both the autograph and a copy in the Witteczek-Spaun collection are fragments of forty-three bars, and, unlike Schubert's *Faust* settings 'Gretchen am Spinnrade' (D. 118) and 'Der König in Thule' (D. 367), the song was not published during his lifetime.[7] It thus makes sense to explore the possibility that Schubert abandoned his effort to set Gretchen's *Zwinger* monologue. Why might he have done so? Several writers' intuitions that the work's incompleteness has something to do with its operatic nature, and Schubert's ambitions as an opera composer are worth pondering. Is the setting's unfinished state a consequence of the music's aria-like lyricism? Did Schubert regard 'Gretchen im Zwinger' as a mere exercise in operatic writing? What other factors may have led him to lay it aside?

This chapter seeks to explain the work's incompleteness by examining the poetic text and musical setting through historical, analytical, and critical lenses. Late eighteenth- and early nineteenth-century genre distinctions between Lied and aria,

---

[5]   Johnson, *Franz Schubert: The Complete Songs*, vol. 1, p. 801.

[6]   Richard Capell, *Schubert's Songs* (London: Pan Books, 1973 [1957]), p. 133. See also Reinhard van Hoorickx, 'The Chronology of Schubert's Fragments and Sketches', in *Schubert Studies: Problems of Style and Chronology*, ed. Eva Badura-Skoda and Peter Branscombe (Cambridge: Cambridge University Press, 1982), pp. 297–325, esp. 313–14.

[7]   The autograph manuscript (Hs-6083), bearing the heading 'Gretchen' and the date 'May 1817', is housed in the Goethe Museum, Frankfurt am Main. The copy, bearing the title 'Gretchen im Zwinger', appears in volume 39, pp. 30–34, of the Witteczek-Spaun collection, housed in the Gesellschaft der Musikfreunde, Vienna. 'Gretchen am Spinnrade', composed 19 October 1814, was published as Op. 2 in April 1821. 'Der König in Thule', composed in early 1816, was published as Op. 5, No. 5 in July 1821. If Schubert did complete 'Gretchen im Zwinger', the manuscript could have been mutilated and the additional leaf or leaves lost, either before or after his death. If the former, the fact that the song was not published during his lifetime suggests he may have been dissatisfied with it and chose not to replace the missing material as necessary for publication. If the latter, the fact that it was not published during his lifetime may still indicate his dissatisfaction with the work. It is possible that Schubert himself mutilated the manuscript and discarded the additional leaf or leaves because he was not content with his setting of the final stanzas – a situation essentially equivalent to having never finished the song.

the structure and substance of Goethe's *Zwinger* monologue, aspects of Schubert's setting, and the creative context for D. 564 together suggest that if Schubert abandoned the work, he likely did so not because of its operatic nature but for a host of compositional and biographical reasons. The ensuing discussion illuminates the long-standing mystery surrounding the work's fragmentary state as well as the role of aria-like settings in Schubert's song oeuvre. In quasi-operatic songs such as 'Gretchen im Zwinger', aria-like lyricism signals the work's fundamentally dramatic conception; the lyrical outpouring itself represents an element of drama. Wrestling with how to set lyrico-dramatic texts such as the *Zwinger* monologue helped prepare Schubert to compose the works of his maturity.

Lied, Aria, and the *Zwinger* Monologue

Leon Plantinga, in his article 'Poetry and Music: Two Episodes in a Durable Relationship', notes that during the late eighteenth and early nineteenth centuries,

> [t]heorists of the Lied were unanimous in their zeal to establish a set of distinct contraries: the Lied as opposed to the aria; simplicity, sing-ableness, and folkishness as against artistic elaboration; German style versus Italian style; and, above all, an immediate dependence of musical form upon poetic form – as opposed to the use of a text as a sort of pretext for vocal extravagances.[8]

The Lied, according to writers such as Christian Gottfried Krause (1719–1770) and Heinrich Christoph Koch (1749–1816), has a strophic musical form, uniform expression, and little if any accompaniment.[9] It avoids excessive text repetition, decorative ornamentation, melismas, wide vocal ranges, large intervallic leaps, instrumental ritornelli, and variety of effects. As Koch indicates, the Lied is indeed a simple, natural song that anyone with healthy vocal cords can sing; no musical talent or training is necessary.[10] Long into the nineteenth century, the genre was

[8]   Leon Plantinga, 'Poetry and Music: Two Episodes in a Durable Relationship', in *Musical Humanism and Its Legacy: Essays in Honor of Claude V. Palisca*, ed. Nancy Kovaleff Baker and Barbara Russano Hanning (Stuyvesant, NY: Pendragon Press, 1992), pp. 321–53, here p. 345.
[9]   Christian Gottfried Krause, *Von der musikalischen Poesie* (Berlin: Johann Friedrich Voss, 1752); Heinrich Christoph Koch, *Musikalisches Lexikon* (Frankfurt am Main: August Hermann, 1802 [reprinted 1964; abridged 1807 as *Kurzgefasstes Handwörterbuch*]). See also Heinrich W. Schwab, *Sangbarkeit, Popularität und Kunstlied: Studien zu Lied und Liedästhetik der mittleren Goethezeit, 1770–1814* (Regensburg: Gustav Bosse, 1965) and Walter Wiora, *Das deutsche Lied: Zur Geschichte und Aesthetik einer musikalischen Gattung* (Wolfenbüttel and Zurich: Karl Heinrich Möseler, 1971).
[10]   'Lied. Mit diesem Namen bezeichnet man überhaupt jedes lyrische Gedicht von mehrern Strophen, welches zum Gesange bestimmt, und mit einer solchen Melodie verbunden ist, die

considered a form of *Hausmusik*, more suited for private music-making than public performance.[11]

The aria, by contrast, was associated with the dramatic stage and concert hall – public performance spaces that called for approaches to text-setting that the Lied avoided. If the Lied was unpretentious, the aria was elaborate. Music lexicographer Gustav Schilling (1805–1880), echoing Koch, describes the aria as 'a piece of music in which a person, through performed and fully developed lyrical song, brings some sentiment that is suitable for this mode of expression to a certain degree of saturation, or to a complete outpouring of the heart'.[12] Whereas a Lied can be sung by anyone, an aria requires 'a consummate and both artistically and especially technically trained singer'.[13]

As often noted, Goethe strenuously objected to Beethoven's and Spohr's through-composed song settings of Mignon's 'Kennst du das Land' because they muddied the traditional genre distinction. Beyond the 'identical distinguishing marks, occurring at the same point in each stanza', which signaled the need for a simple strophic setting, the enigmatic child character Mignon, Goethe insisted, 'can by her very nature sing a Lied, but not an aria'.[14] In discussing Goethe's objection, Plantinga remarks, '[I]f Mignon could not sing an aria, neither, presumably, could Gretchen'.[15] He is referring to Schubert's 'Gretchen am Spinnrade', a largely through-composed song whose vocal line soars into operatic realms, but the same point holds true for 'Gretchen im Zwinger'. Why, given Gretchen's simple nature

---

bey jeder Strophe wiederholt wird, und die zugleich die Eigenschaft hat, dass sie von jedem Menschen, der gesunde und nicht ganz unbiegsame Gesangorgane besitzt, ohne Rücksicht auf künstliche Ausbildung derselben, vorgetragen werden kann. Hieraus folgt, dass die Melodie eines Liedes weder einen so weiten Umfang der Töne, noch solche Singmanieren und Sylbendehnungen enthalten darf, wodurch sich bloss der künstliche und ausgebildete Gesang der Aria auszeichnet, sondern dass der Ausdruck der in dem Texte enthaltenen Empfindung durch einfache, aber desto treffendere Mittel erlangt werden muss'. Koch, *Musikalisches Lexikon*, pp. 901–2.

[11]   Edward F. Kravitt, 'The Lied in 19th-Century Concert Life', *Journal of the American Musicological Society* 18/2 (1965), pp. 207–18.

[12]   Gustav Schilling, *Encyclopädie der gesammten musikalischen Wissenschaften, oder Universal-Lexicon der Tonkunst* (Stuttgart: Köhler, 1837), p. 264: 'ein Tonstück, in welchem eine Person durch ausgeführten und völlig ausgebildeten lyrischen Gesang irgend eine, solcher Ausdrucksweise angemessene, Empfindung bis zu einem gewissen Grade der Sättigung, oder bis zur völligen Ausgießung des Herzens, zur sinnlichen Darstellung bringt'.

[13]   Gustav Schilling, *Musikalisch Dynamik oder die Lehre vom Vortrage in der Musik* (Kassel: Krieger, 1843), p. 333: 'einen vollkommen und sowohl allgemein künstlerisch als insbesondere technisch ausgebildeten Sänger'.

[14]   As cited in Plantinga, 'Poetry and Music', p. 346.

[15]   Plantinga, 'Poetry and Music', p. 348.

and lower social class, did Schubert compose a second Gretchen setting that suggests an aria-Lied hybrid?[16]

Foremost, the poetic structure precludes a strophic setting. Like other soliloquies in *Faust*, Gretchen's *Zwinger* monologue has an irregular form, comprising multiple verse patterns with different configurations of line length, metre, and rhyme. The opening 3-line verses feature lines of one, two, or four poetic feet in strict iambic metre with an *aab ccb ddb* rhyme scheme, the first two lines in each verse ending with an unstressed and the third with a stressed syllable. The subsequent 6-line stanzas include lines with one, three, or four poetic feet in iambic or trochaic metre and retain the previous pattern of rhymes and line endings. The first two 4-line verses have lines with three poetic feet in iambic metre (with a few anapests) and a loose, alternating line rhyme scheme and pattern of line endings. Given these differences in textual structure, a Lied-like strophic musical form is not an option.

As Richard Green has discussed, Goethe's conception of *Faust* was 'closely bound with thoughts of music'.[17] Part I of the drama includes many scenes and verses inspired by familiar sorts of music, including fanfares, choral pieces, accompanied and unaccompanied solo songs, duets, trios, and quartets, revealing Goethe's familiarity with operatic conventions of the late eighteenth and early nineteenth centuries.[18] Indeed, Green asserts, 'Virtually all the types of scenes found in the traditional Singspiel and German opera of the time are represented' (an all-encompassing aesthetic evoking Friedrich Schlegel's notion of Romantic poetry as described in Fragment 116 from the *Athenaeum Fragments* of 1798).[19] The irregular form of the *Zwinger* monologue, reflecting the flow of Gretchen's thoughts as she beholds the statue of the *Mater dolorosa*, suggests a through-composed aria arranged in multiple, contrasting sections – a musical form whose changing thematic material, textures, and tonal areas are well-suited to conveying dramatic development. Schubert's 'apprentice' operas from 1811–1816 include some through-composed arias. Kätchen's 'Gott! Höre meine Stimme' from the 1815 Singspiel *Der vierjährige*

---

[16]   For discussion of Schubert's mixed-genre Lieder, see Marjorie Wing Hirsch, *Schubert's Dramatic Lieder* (Cambridge: Cambridge University Press, 1993), pp. 95–135.

[17]   Richard D. Green, 'Music in Goethe's *Faust*: Its First Dramatic Setting', in *Our Faust?: Roots and Ramifications of a Modern German Myth*, ed. Reinhold Grimm and Jost Hermand (Madison, WI: The University of Wisconsin Press, 1987), pp. 47–64, here p. 48.

[18]   Green, 'Music in Goethe's *Faust*', p. 49.

[19]   Green, 'Music in Goethe's *Faust*', p. 52. 'Romantic poetry is a progressive universal poetry. Its mission is not merely to reunite all separate genres of poetry and to put poetry in touch with philosophy and rhetoric. It will, and should, now mingle and now amalgamate poetry and prose, genius and criticism, the poetry of art and the poetry of nature, render poetry living and social, and life and society poetic, poetize wit, fill and saturate the forms of art with solid cultural material of every kind, and inspire them with vibrations of humor'. Friedrich Schlegel, *Dialogue on Poetry and Literary Aphorisms*, trans. Ernst Behler and Roman Struc (University Park and London: The Pennsylvania State University Press, 1968), p. 140.

Posten, for example, comprises an 'Adagio con moto' opening prayer, an 'Allegretto' section, and finally an 'Allegro affetuoso'. In Gretchen's *Zwinger* monologue, however, the irregular poetic structure, calling for through-composition, eventually gives way to a cyclical impulse: the recurrence of the first three poetic lines at the end of the monologue suggests a musical *da capo*, or at least some repetition of the opening music.[20] By cycling back to the opening lines, Goethe intimates that the monologue represents the temporal expansion of a single moment, as characterizes *da capo* arias. Yet within the outer frame, the poetic material evolves both structurally and substantively, implying at least some degree of temporal progression and dramatic development. The *Zwinger* monologue thus combines features of traditional as well as more contemporary arias.

If the structure of the *Zwinger* monologue calls for an aria-like setting (whether in a through-composed or rounded musical form), so do its dramatic mode of presentation – according to Aristotle, the form of artistic imitation in which the poet creates an illusion of characters 'living and moving before us'[21] – and the particular scene portrayed. Alone at the town ramparts, Gretchen expresses anguish at the prospect of abandonment, a distressing circumstance often experienced by eighteenth- and nineteenth-century operatic heroines. Similar situations are encountered in other aria-like songs for voice and piano by Schubert, including 'Vedi quanto adoro' (D. 510), 'Amalia' (D. 195), and 'Iphigenia' (D. 573).[22] Schubert's contemporaneous operas also present dramatic heroines

---

[20]   Prince Anton Radziwill's (1775–1833) fully orchestrated, 177-bar setting of the *Zwinger* monologue, which, like the rest of his incidental music to *Faust*, he worked on in close collaboration with Goethe prior to the play's Berlin court premiere in 1820, features not only abundant, aria-like text repetitions but also a repetition of the opening music at the end. The *Zwinger* monologue settings for voice and piano of Bernhard Klein (1793–1832) and Karl Loewe (1796–1869) also repeat (with degrees of variation) some of their opening music at the recurrence of the first three textual lines. Bettina von Arnim (1785–1859), however, who likewise composed a setting for voice and piano, gives the repeated textual lines new music, resulting in an entirely through-composed song.

[21]   *Aristotle's Poetics*, trans. S. H. Butcher (New York: Hill and Wang, 1961), p. 53.

[22]   In 'Vedi quanto adoro', an 1816 setting of a text from Metastasio's opera libretto *Didone abbandonata* (Act II, Scene 4) of 1724, Queen Dido bitterly laments her lover Aeneas's departure, which she views as a betrayal of their love. Under Salieri's tutelage, Schubert composed a spirited, Italian operatic recitative and aria in quasi-ternary form. In 'Amalia', a through-composed, aria-like setting from 1815 of a text from Schiller's play *Die Räuber*, Amalia sits alone in a garden, yearning for her banished lover Karl. The song begins in a hymn-like manner, shifts into a dramatically rendered accompanied recitative as she remembers their burning passion and physical intimacy, then drastically alters course once again when she despairingly acknowledges that her lover is gone. 'Iphigenia', a through-composed, aria-like Mayrhofer setting composed in July 1817, portrays the title character wandering alone on the shores of Tauris, where she has been left by the goddess Diana. Iphigenia bemoans her

in states of actual or anticipated solitude, e.g., Luitgarde's aria 'Ihr unsichtbaren Geister' (Act III, No. 18) from the 1813–1814 Singspiel *Des Teufels Lustsschloss*, and Olivia's aria 'Einsam schleich' ich durch die Zimmer' (Act I, No. 4) from the 1815–1816 Singspiel *Die Freunde von Salamanka* (D. 326).

Like these works, 'Gretchen im Zwinger' reveals an identifiable character's emotional response at a particular moment within the drama, aligning with Schilling's definition of aria. An aria, he writes, is

> a song for a single voice, accompanied by one or more instruments, in which a specific sentiment or way of feeling conveys the particular emotional situation of the singer. The type and manner of this situation, which can be very different, then also in general determines the tone, the character of the performance, whether that be heroic or sentimental, cheerful and joyous or painful and so forth [translation mine].[23]

As with Schubert's quasi-operatic 'Gretchen am Spinnrade', 'Gretchen im Zwinger' portrays the solitary heroine's response to events at a particular point in her relationship with Faust. The fact that 'Gretchen im Zwinger' exists as individual song setting rather than a number within a *Faust* opera, or as incidental music for Goethe's play, does not negate this point; the larger dramatic context is implied. Gretchen's lyrical expression of emotion before the *Mater dolorosa* represents an element of the drama, as does her singing of a spinning song in 'Gretchen am Spinnrade' (including her momentary cessation of singing).

Fundamentally pious, Gretchen responds with grief to the calamity of her illicit pregnancy and complicity in her mother's death, and seeks understanding and compassion from the Virgin Mary – a divine figure regarded, since at least the fourteenth century, as a protector of humanity and benevolent intercessor at the time of Judgement. Beholding and addressing the *Mater dolorosa*, Gretchen assumes the position of the speaker in the *Stabat mater* sequence. The *Stabat mater*, whose thirteenth-century Latin text (of presumably Franciscan origin) comprises twenty 3-line verses in trochaic tetrameter, conveys its speaker's fervent desire to share the awful burden of Mary's suffering and be granted protection by her on Judgement Day.[24] Like the *Stabat mater*, Gretchen's monologue opens, as noted, with

---

isolation and expresses intense yearning for her Greek homeland. The song concludes with her passionate appeal to Diana for mercy, recalling Gretchen's supplication to the *Mater dolorosa* in 'Gretchen im Zwinger', which dates from just two months earlier.

[23] Schilling, *Musikalisch Dynamik*, pp. 332–3: 'ein, von einem oder mehreren Instrumenten begleiteter, Gesang für eine einzelne Stimme, in welchem sich ein bestimmter Gemüthszustand, eine Empfindungsweise, eine gewisse Gemüthssituation des Singenden ausspricht. Die Art und Weise dieser Situation, welche sehr verschieden seyn kann, bestimmt dann auch im Allgemeinen den Ton, den Charakter des Vortrags, ob derselbe ein heroischer oder sentimentaler, ein froher und freudiger oder ein schmerzlicher u. zu sehn hat'.

[24] The *Stabat Mater* text was adopted in the late fifteenth century as a sequence for the Mass of the Compassion of the Blessed Virgin Mary and sung to a plainchant melody (*Liber Usualis*

3-line verses in an *aab* rhyme scheme that dwell on Mary's emotional pain, given visual expression through the image of a sword piercing her heart.[25] Johnson has suggested that, in the first three verses of the *Zwinger* monologue, Gretchen seems to be reciting 'a formal prayer', which she knows by memory.[26] In the earlier 'Abend' scene of *Faust*, Gretchen, intuiting the presence of evil, absent-mindedly attempts to comfort herself by singing what is ostensibly an old folk ballad, 'Der König in Thule'. The *Zwinger* monologue opens with Gretchen similarly seeking to quell her agitation through a traditional song of devotion.

Gretchen may start by singing what is purportedly the *Stabat mater*, but from the outset, her monologue is intensely personal. Whereas the *Stabat mater* speaker does not express personal emotion until the ninth verse ('Eia Mater, fons amoris, / Me sentire vim doloris / Fac, ut tecum lugeam'), Gretchen does so in the first ('Ach neige, / Du Schmerzenreiche, / Dein Antlitz gnädig meiner Noth!'). These lines echo a verse in Friedrich Gottlieb Klopstock's (1724–1803) German paraphrase of the *Stabat mater* (1766). Klopstock's third verse opens with the line 'Liebend neiget er sein Antlitz', referring to Jesus Christ looking down upon his grieving mother; in Goethe's first verse, Gretchen begs Mary to look down upon *her*, another grieving mother (Figure 5.3).[27] In Gretchen's view, only Mary can understand the intensity of her suffering.

At 'Wer fühlet', the beginning of Goethe's verse 4, Gretchen's thoughts turn further inward, to the physical presence of her unborn child, destined, like Christ, to an early death, and to her tumultuous emotions – fear, grief, desire, and shame. Verse 5 expands upon Gretchen's anguish; the repeated mention of sorrow and weeping ('Wie weh, wie weh, wie wehe' and 'Ich wein', ich wein', ich weine') is presumably what prompts her subsequent recounting (in verses 6–7) of events from earlier that day (when her tears provided the only dew for the flowers she was picking). The reference to her broken heart at the end of verse 5 recalls the sword piercing Mary's body. Gretchen may begin by reciting a formal prayer, but, as in 'Gretchen am Spinnrade', her words increasingly suggest an interior monologue, or externalization of unspoken thoughts.

Poetic structure, dramatic mode of presentation, familiar operatic scenario, emotional response, word repetitions – all of these elements call for an aria-like setting of the *Zwinger* monologue. The evocation of Mary's grief is ultimately a vehicle for Gretchen to express her own.

1634v). The sequence was prohibited by the Council of Trent but restored by Pope Benedict XIII in 1727. The *Stabat Mater* also came into use as an Office hymn around that time.

[25]   As described in Luke 2:35.

[26]   Johnson, *Franz Schubert: The Complete Songs*, vol. 1, p. 802.

[27]   The rhetorical question in Goethe's fourth verse ('Wer fühlet / Wie wühlet / Der Schmerz mir im Gebein?') parallels rhetorical questions in Klopstock's text.

1	Jesus Christus schwebt am Kreuze!	Jesus Christ is hanging on the Cross!
	Blutig sank sein Haupt herunter,	His head, soaked with blood, sank down
	Blutig in des Todes Nacht.	into the night of death.
2	Bei des Mittlers Kreuze standen	At the Saviour's cross, filled with fear,
	Bang Maria und Johannes,	stood Mary and John,
	Seine Mutter, und sein Freund.	his mother and his friend.
	Durch der Mutter bange Seele,	Through the mother's fearful soul,
	Ach, durch ihre ganze Seele	through her entire soul
	Ach, drang ein Schwert.	a sword pierced.
3	Liebend neiget er sein Antlitz:	In love he inclines his face:
	Du bist dieses Sohnes Mutter!	you are the mother of this son!
	Und du dieser Mutter Sohn.	And you the son of this mother.

Figure 5.3   Friedrich Gottlieb Klopstock, *Stabat mater* ('Jesus Christus schwebt am Kreuze') (1766), verses 1–3

Note: Translation by Richard Wigmore. *Schubert Sacred Works*, vol. 1 (EMI Classics: CMS 7 64778 2), p. 29.

Schubert's 'Gretchen im Zwinger'

Given the textual association between the *Zwinger* monologue and the Latin *Stabat mater* as well as Klopstock's German paraphrase, one might expect Schubert to begin his setting of 'Gretchen im Zwinger' by alluding to one of the traditional *Stabat mater* melodies,[28] or perhaps to one of his two *Stabat mater* settings, which he had composed during the preceding two years. The first of these works, D. 175, composed April 1815, is a small-scale setting of the first four verses of the Latin *Stabat mater* text in G minor for SATB chorus, organ, and orchestra. The second, D. 383, completed February 1816, is a much larger, oratorio-like setting of Klopstock's German paraphrase in F minor for STB soloists, SATB chorus, organ, and orchestra. Both the entirety of D. 175 and the second number of D. 383, a soprano aria, present the image of Mary gazing up at Jesus's crucifixion, as do the opening verses of Gretchen's monologue. But while Schubert may have been inspired to set the *Zwinger* monologue in part by his close familiarity with the Latin and German *Stabat mater* texts, he makes no explicit reference to traditional

---

[28]   *Liber Usualis* (Ed. No. 801, Tournai: Desclee, 1934), 1634, and *Hymns Ancient and Modern*, revised edn (London: William Clowes & Son, 1950), p. 143, as cited in Frederick W. Sternfeld, *Goethe and Music: A List of Parodies and Goethe's Relationship to Music: A List of References* (New York: Da Capo, 1979), p. 84.

Stabat mater melodies or either of his *Stabat mater* settings in 'Gretchen im Zwinger'. Rather, the song opens in B♭ minor, 4/4 metre, and 'Sehr langsam' tempo with, as Johnson has noted, a striking musical reference to a recently-composed Lied: the Mayrhofer setting 'Auf der Donau' (D. 553); Schubert had written this somber meditation on mortality and the impermanence of human creations in April 1817, just one month before 'Gretchen im Zwinger'.[29]

In bar 1 of 'Gretchen im Zwinger', the piano plays an arch-shaped, semiquaver motif, as Example 5.1 illustrates. This motif also suffuses the opening section of 'Auf der Donau', sounding there twenty times, as Example 5.2 shows. In 'Auf der Donau', it illustrates the undulating motion of the water beneath the speaker's boat – waves that, 'like time itself, threaten destruction'. In 'Gretchen im Zwinger', this 'destruction' motif launches the first section of the song (bars 2–6) in the key of B♭ minor: the final three descending notes of the piano motif (D♭, C, B♭), played in dotted rhythm, are echoed by the voice, initiating the vocal melody. Like a submerged thought rising to consciousness, the motif, migrating from piano to voice, might be understood to represent Gretchen's growing awareness of impending death, both her own and that of her unborn child. Accentuated diminished-seventh harmonies (see bars 1, 2, 4, 5) lend additional force to her expression of anguish.

During the opening two verses, echoes continue to infuse the music, binding voice and piano accompaniment. In bar 5, at the cadence in D♭ major, the piano echoes both itself and the end of the vocal phrase of the preceding bar. In the setting of verse 2 (bars 7–10), which features a new melody and accompaniment pattern, an inner line of the piano and the voice echo one another with upward leaps followed by descending stepwise motion – a gesture harking back to the destruction motif of bar 1. The alternating hand pattern in the piano creates a sense of agitation while the upward leaps and descending motion suggest yearning and resignation. At the textual reference to Mary gazing at the crucifixion, the music darkens, shifting to the parallel key of D♭ minor (bar 9), a tonal area that is confirmed with a three-bar piano interlude.

After this point, however, there is little motivic connection between piano and voice; beginning with verse 3, the voice draws the listener's attention while the piano mostly serves a supportive role, providing the rhythmic and harmonic foundation. Through an enharmonic reinterpretation of the pitch D♭, verse 3 (bars 13–17) shifts from D♭ minor to A major. The lyricism of the vocal line, the voice's octave leap (bars 14–15), the broken chord patterns of the piano, and repetition of the textual line 'Und Seufzer schickst du' enhance the aria-like quality of this musical section. In bars 17–18, when the piano echoes the voice's cadential gesture, it adds a decorative turn. To be sure, the aria-like quality is not that of Italian bel canto opera. Far from elaborate or showy, Schubert's vocal lyricism is closely attuned to the meaning of the text – to Gretchen's simple character and the humble sincerity of her prayer – reflecting Schubert's sympathy with the operatic reform principles

---

29   Johnson, *Franz Schubert: The Complete Songs*, vol. 1, pp. 801–2.

Example 5.1   Schubert, 'Gretchen im Zwinger', D. 564, bars 1–43

Note: Example 5.1 is based with permission on Franz Schubert, *Neue Ausgabe sämtlicher Werke*, series IV, vol. 11, ed. Walther Dürr (Kassel: Bärenreiter, 1999), p. 230.

Example 5.1 (continued)

Example 5.2   Schubert, 'Auf der Donau', D. 553, bars 1–24

Note: Example 5.2 is based with permission on Franz Schubert, *Neue Ausgabe sämtlicher Werke* series IV, vol. 1, ed. Walther Dürr (Kassel: Bärenreiter, 1970), p. 148.

of Christoph Willibald Gluck (1714–1787). The limited text repetition serves as a means of emotional expression, and the words are readily understood.

Verse 4 begins in A minor (bar 18), where verse 3 had left off. The voice dips into a strikingly low register for the lines 'Wer fühlet, / Wie wühlet / Der Schmerz mir im gebein?', capturing the inward turn of Gretchen's thoughts. In this verse, the piano provides thin harmonic support with repeated semiquaver chords conveying agitation, followed by a consistent, broken chord pattern. The accented octaves in bars 21–22 and the chromatic single notes in bars 27–28 stand out, but otherwise the piano plays a subsidiary role. Once again, Schubert includes some aria-like text repetition ('weißt nur du, nur du allein'), filling out sequential musical phrases. The section ends in A major, with Gretchen asserting that only Mary can understand her suffering. Through the use of parallel keys for verses 3 and 4, Schubert thus links the images of the grieving Holy Mother and grieving Gretchen.

Verse 5 opens in a new tempo (Etwas geschwind), new metre (alla breve), and new key (F♯ minor). Gretchen is now thoroughly absorbed by her troubles; Mary has receded into the background. As noted, Goethe's text includes aria-like word repetitions, and Schubert enhances the impression by repeating several lines, whether to fill out a melody or emphasize poetic content. Here again, the piano is subordinate to the voice, primarily providing rhythmic energy and harmonic intensification through rapid ascending modulations: the key shifts from F♯ minor to G major, to A major, to B minor, and finally to C major, where the music remains for five bars. As in the setting of the first four verses (during which, as described, the key shifts from B♭ minor to D♭ major, D♭ minor, A major, A minor, and A major), the harmonic modulations serve as an important means of dramatization. The combination of rising modulations and an accelerando, recalling the final pages of 'Gretchen am Spinnrade', suggests that, once again, Gretchen is becoming increasingly overwrought.[30] But whereas in the spinning wheel song Schubert cycles back to the mood of the opening by repeating the initial lines and their musical setting (thus deflating Gretchen's erotic fantasy), here the music stops just before the new key signature of four flats. Opening with a musical prayer, the Zwinger setting ends abruptly partway through an interior monologue.

Resolving the Mystery

Why might Schubert have abandoned the setting, and why here? The fact that 'Gretchen im Zwinger' evokes music for the stage is likely irrelevant. There is no documentary evidence that Schubert planned to compose either a *Faust* opera or incidental music to Goethe's play. While in the mid-1810s Schubert did aspire to write a through-composed Romantic opera, Reed's suggestion that he abandoned 'Gretchen im Zwinger' because, in 1817, he did not yet feel ready to compose such a work, is purely speculative. Schubert had, in any case, already completed four *Faust* settings: the solo songs 'Gretchen am Spinnrade', 'Szene aus Faust', and 'Der König in Thule' and the choral piece 'Christ ist erstanden'. Moreover, 'dramatic songs' for voice and piano, in which the vocalist, to quote Schilling, assumes 'the rights of a stage singer', were a familiar and increasingly accepted phenomenon in the first decades of the nineteenth century.[31] Many of Schubert's predecessors in song composition incorporated stylistic and structural conventions of operatic writing into works for voice and piano: Mozart, Beethoven, Zelter, Reichardt, Spohr, and Zumsteeg had all written dramatic song settings, including of texts from *Faust,* before Schubert produced a significant number of his own, largely during the years 1814–1817. Mozart's 'Als Luise die Briefe ihres ungetreuen Liebhabers verbrannte', Beethoven's 'Adelaide', Zelter's 'Margarethe', Reichardt's

[30]   Johnson, *Franz Schubert: The Complete Songs*, vol. 1, p. 802.
[31]   Schilling, *Musikalische Dynamik*, p. 255. As quoted in Walther Dürr, 'Schubert and Johann Michael Vogl: A Reappraisal', *19th-Century Music* 3/2 (1979), p. 133.

'Monolog der Iphigenia', and Zumsteeg's 'Hagars Klage' are but a few such works.[32] Moreover, Schubert continued to compose dramatic songs after writing 'Gretchen im Zwinger'.

Rather than the operatic quality of the *Zwinger* monologue, a number of other factors likely would have played a role in Schubert's decision to abandon his setting. For one, he may have been unsure how to deal with the monologue's conflicting structural impulses and their musical implications. As described, the monologue presents an evolution of material – the initial *Stabat mater*-like verses, the inward turn of Gretchen's thoughts, and her drift into memory – followed, in verse 8, by a renewed appeal to the Virgin Mary. Schubert could have hesitated at the return of focus to Mary. During the monologue, as Gretchen becomes increasingly consumed by her own emotional pain, the town ramparts and statue of the *Mater dolorosa* recede into the background, just as Gretchen's room and spinning wheel recede during her flights of memory and fantasy in Scene 15 of *Faust*. In the spinning wheel monologue (and even more so in Schubert's setting of it), the refrain-like recurrences of the lament-like first verse suggest that Gretchen is slipping in and out of consciousness of the present. In the *Zwinger* monologue, the single recurrence of the prayer-like opening lines after Gretchen's thoughts have turned inward has a rather different effect and was perhaps motivated by musical convention as much as dramatic necessity. The monologue initially suggests a through-composed aria but then seems to switch gears in calling for a more traditional, rounded musical structure; progression is subsumed within a larger sense of stasis. Given the evolution of poetic material, and the significant musical changes that take place over the forty-three completed bars – the wandering harmonic modulations; the striking alterations of texture, vocal register, rhythm, tempo, metre, and dynamics; the shift in the relationship between voice and piano from equal partners to foreground/ background – Schubert may have hesitated to return to the opening poetic lines and their original musical setting at the end, as did Radziwill, Klein, and Loewe.[33]

Significantly, 'Gretchen im Zwinger' was composed in 1817 during a lull in Schubert's operatic composition. Having worked on seven operas – six of them Singspiele – he was eager to produce a through-composed stage work, a desire that would be realized with the 'grand heroic-romantic opera' *Alfonso und Estrella* of 1821–1822, and taken a step further with *Fierabras* of 1823.[34] Schubert's interest in through-composition on a large scale was matched on a smaller scale by his growing interest in exploring different aria forms, often freely structured in accordance with the action of the text, an inclination also most fully realized with *Alfonso und*

---

[32]   For an overview of dramatic songs before Schubert, see Hirsch, *Schubert's Dramatic Lieder*, pp. 17–27 and 63–71.

[33]   See footnote 20.

[34]   For more on *Fierabras*, see Christine Martin's essay in this volume.

Estrella.[35] During the later 1810s, number operas, and arias with conventional forms, had diminishing appeal to him, which may shed light on the fragmentary state of 'Gretchen im Zwinger', whose text hints at a 'da capo' musical structure.

Another plausible explanation for the work's incompleteness concerns a temporal shift within the monologue. The precise point in the text at which Schubert stopped composing – the beginning of verse 6 – marks a significant transitional moment. At this juncture, the monologue shifts abruptly from Gretchen's expression of present emotional pain to her recollection of events and emotions experienced early that morning, i.e., crying as she picked flowers to bring to the *Mater dolorosa*, and feeling numb with sorrow as she sat on her bed. Like the final repetition of lines 1–3, the sudden intrusion of autobiographical memory, and specifically of recent experiences that add little to the present emotional drama, may have struck Schubert as problematic: the monologue has already contained references to weeping and flowers, and the image of Gretchen sitting on her bed is dramatically static. Whereas Gretchen's spinning wheel monologue involves fluid transitions among present, past, and future, supporting a continuous musical flow, the *Zwinger* monologue's abrupt shift to past tense after the line 'Das Herz zerbricht in mir' seems awkward, posing a compositional challenge. In early songs, such as the 1814 Matthisson setting 'Erinnerungen' (D. 98) and 1814 Goethe setting 'Schäfers Klagelied' (D. 121), Schubert would often convey a poetic speaker's lapse into memory by introducing recitative, or at least a more declamatory vocal style than that of the preceding verses. By 1817, he may have regarded such a strategy as too heavy-handed. The lack of a good solution may have prompted him to turn to other projects.

Additional factors may also have played a direct or indirect role. Schubert may have been dissatisfied with what he had written, perhaps because, as Johnson observes, after the first several verses, the piano part has little intrinsic interest; it provides harmonic and rhythmic support for the vocal line but contains almost no motivic material, secondary melodic lines, or text-painting, and has no evident symbolic import. In this respect, the setting differs strikingly from 'Gretchen am Spinnrade', and Schubert may have thought the *Zwinger* monologue setting compared unfavourably with that masterful earlier song.

In the spring and summer of 1817, Schubert was also greatly absorbed by the composition of piano sonatas, composing a half dozen such works.[36] The Piano

---

[35]   George R. Cunningham, *Franz Schubert als Theaterkomponist* (PhD dissertation, Albert-Ludwigs-Universität zu Freiburg im Breisgau, 1974), p. 174.

[36]   Sonata in A minor (D. 537; March 1817), Sonata in A flat major (D. 557; May 1817); Sonata in E minor (D. 566; June 1817); Sonata in D flat major (D. 567, 1st version of D. 568; June 1817), Sonata in E flat major (D. 568; June 1817), Sonata in F sharp minor (D. 571, fragment of 1st movement, possibly intended to be combined with Andante, D. 604, and a scherzo and unfinished finale, D. 570; July 1817), Sonata in B major (D. 575; August 1817). On Schubert's early piano sonatas, see Eva Badura-Skoda, 'The Piano Works of Schubert', in *Nineteenth-Century Piano Music*, ed. R. Larry Todd (New York: Schirmer Books, 1990),

Sonata in A flat major (D. 557) dates from the same month as 'Gretchen im Zwinger'.[37] This compositional activity could have distracted him from tackling the challenges involved in satisfactorily completing the *Zwinger* monologue. Schubert's introduction in February or March 1817 to the court opera singer Johann Michael Vogl (whom he hoped would sing his Lieder), his increasingly close working relationship and friendship with the poet Johann Baptist Mayrhofer (who supplied him with texts for many dramatic songs), and his shared living quarters with the debauched Franz von Schober (which led to a significant reduction in his compositional production) may similarly have kept him from completing this final *Faust* setting. Perhaps too Schubert was frustrated that Goethe had returned unopened the packet of Schubert's Goethe songs upon receiving it the previous year (Schubert faced similar disappointment in spring 1817 when the Leipzig publisher Breitkopf und Härtel returned without comment the manuscript of his 'Erlkönig', having first sent it to a Franz Schubert in Dresden, who quickly dissociated himself from it).

To venture another possibility, the song's incompleteness could involve the final dissolution of Schubert's love relationship with Therese Grob, his 'beloved singer, whom he had hoped to marry in 1816',[38] and any hope of financial stability. In 1817, when Schubert gave up on his prior plan of becoming a teacher and moved in with Schober, Therese and her family may well have reached the conclusion that he did not intend to marry her.[39] Many scholars believe that Therese, the first soprano soloist in the 1814 premiere of his Mass in F major (D. 105), inspired Schubert to compose 'Gretchen am Spinnrade' shortly afterwards.[40] That three years

---

pp. 102–20; and Brian Newbould, *Schubert: The Music and the Man* (Berkeley: University of California Press, 1997), pp. 99–106.

[37]   Some writers have wondered whether Schubert intended to write a fourth movement to D. 557 because the second and third movements are both in the key of the dominant.

[38]   Rita Steblin, 'Schubert: The Nonsense Society Revisited', in *Franz Schubert and His World*, ed. Christopher H. Gibbs and Morten Solvik (Princeton: Princeton University Press, 2014), p. 31. See also James Sobaskie, 'Conversations Within and Between Two Early Lieder of Schubert', *Nineteenth-Century Music Review* 13/1 (2016), special issue, *Schubert Familiar and Unfamiliar: Continuing Conversations*, pp. 83–102.

[39]   The new marriage law ('Ehe-Consens Gesetz') enacted by Metternich's regime in 1815 required certain citizens to offer proof that they could support a family, i.e., provide evidence of profession and income, before they would be granted permission to marry. In April 1816 Schubert sought the job of music master in Laibach, perhaps with the ultimate aim of satisfying the marriage law, but on September 7, 1816, he learned that his application had been rejected. Therese Grob married Johann Bergmann, a master baker, in 1820. See Rita Steblin, 'Franz Schubert und das Ehe-Consens Gesetz von 1815', *Schubert durch die Brille* 9 (1992), pp. 32–42.

[40]   The autograph manuscript of 'Gretchen am Spinnrade' is dated 19 October 1814. According to Rita Steblin, the first performance of Schubert's Mass in F major was 25

later Schubert's abandonment of a conventional career, Therese, and the prospect of marriage may have had something to do with his concurrent abandonment of Gretchen and her *Zwinger* monologue is an intriguing thought.

In sum, at some point, Schubert presumably intended to complete this aria-like Lied (and perhaps did so) as suggested by the appearance of a new key signature at the end of the manuscript. James Sobaskie has also noted that the vocal line's 'gradually-rising registral ceiling initiated at the start – a contextual musical process – seems not to have reached a satisfactory apex in what the composer left us'.[41] That ceiling rises from a high F in bar 2, to G♭ in bar 9 (respelled as F♯ in bar 15), to G in bars 31, 37, and 41. Sobaskie surmises that Schubert may well have intended that the voice would rise to A♭ in the following section (which Schubert initiates with the new key signature of four flats), and perhaps yet higher to A and finally B♭ in the remaining unset stanzas, 'reaching a "money note" of sorts near the end'.[42] If Schubert did not actually complete the song, it was probably due to both compositional and biographical factors. Foremost is likely the difficulty he faced in figuring out how to satisfactorily meet the compositional challenges posed by Goethe's *Zwinger* monologue, particularly given that listeners might be inclined to compare the setting with Schubert's masterful 'Gretchen am Spinnrade'. Schubert may also have been distracted by other compositional projects. The emotional pain he surely experienced in forsaking the prospect of marriage with Therèse Grob is unlikely the primary reason that 'Gretchen im Zwinger' is incomplete, but it may have further disinclined him to finishing it.

***

Schubert's interest in composing song settings of dramatic monologues and dialogues, such as the aria-like 'Gretchen im Zwinger', reached a peak in 1817, when he produced as many as eight such works, most with texts by Mayrhofer: 'Fahrt zum Hades' (D. 526), 'Philoktet' (D. 540), 'Memnon' (D. 541), 'Orest auf Tauris' (D. 548), 'Der entsühnte Orest' (D. 699), 'Gretchen im Zwinger' (D. 564), 'Iphigenia' (D. 573), 'Der Kampf' (D. 594). But then he fairly abruptly stopped composing dramatic songs, only occasionally thereafter overtly drawing on operatic convention (for example, in the settings 'Epistel: Musikalischer Schwank' of 1822 and 'Il traditor deluso', published with both Italian and German texts, of 1827). Why did he abandon this compositional activity? The dramatic song settings may well have served their purpose, helping to 'pave the way to a grand Romantic opera', to tweak what Schubert, in 1824, would say about chamber works paving the way to a grand symphony. But their purpose lay not merely

---

September 1814. Steblin, 'Schubert's Beloved Singer Therese Grob: New Documentary Research', *Schubert durch die Brille* 28 (2002), pp. 62–4.

[41]   Thanks to James Sobaskie for this insightful observation.

[42]   James Sobaskie, personal communication.

in preparing him to compose opera. Apart from their own estimable aesthetic worth — for they include many gems — the quasi-operatic song settings of the 1810s helped ready him to compose his mature Lieder of the 1820s, above all the two Müller cycles and Heine settings, with their ingenious and unique fusions of dramatic, narrative, and lyrical elements. Aria-like songs such as 'Gretchen im Zwinger', 'Iphigenia', and 'Fahrt zum Hades', in which operatic lyricism blossoms within an implied dramatic context, paved the way towards complex works like 'Die junge Nonne', 'Suleika II', and 'Der Wegweiser', where dramatic development and lyrical expression are virtually indistinguishable, taking place within the mind of the (usually anonymous) Lied persona.

6

The Dramatic Strategy Within Two of Schubert's Serenades*

James William Sobaskie

Introduction

Franz Schubert's 'Ständchen ("Horch, Horch! die Lerch")' (D. 899; 1826) and 'Ständchen', from *Schwanengesang* (D. 957; 1828), rank among the composer's most beloved Lieder. Contrasting in mood – one exuberant, one ruminative – these songs reflect just some of the tremendous diversity of his oeuvre.[1] The first draws upon text adapted from William Shakespeare's late play *Cymbeline* and depicts an outdoor scene wherein an ebullient swain cajoles a silent lady nearby, enthusiastically coaxing her to arise and enjoy the beauty of nature. It expresses an active monologue, one in which the central character pursues a courtship goal. The second sets poetry by Schubert's contemporary, Ludwig Rellstab, and it portrays a more serious situation in which the primary persona, whose words betray both distance and desire, discloses yearning too intimate and insecure to be expressed directly. Ultimately revealed to be a rehearsed entreaty to the persona's beloved, rather than an in-person petition, it remains an interior monologue, articulated in isolation indoors by the song's main agent. Nevertheless, the two songs have much in common.[2]

---

* An earlier version of this chapter was read at the international conference, 'Schubert as Dramatist', a part of The Schubert Project 2014, organized by Joe Davies and Sholto Kynoch under the auspices of the annual Oxford Lieder Festival and held at the University of Oxford Faculty of Music on 24 October 2014. I thank Susan Wollenberg for her welcome words at that occasion and her insightful suggestions for this expansion.

[1] For introductions to these serenades, see Graham Johnson, *Franz Schubert: The Complete Songs*, vol. 3 (New Haven: Yale University Press, 2014), pp. 241–4 and pp. 20–24, respectively.

[2] Besides the two serenades discussed in this chapter, Schubert wrote one more, his 'Ständchen', D. 920 (1827), which features a light-hearted text by Franz Grillparzer that was initially set for solo alto and mens' chorus (TTBB) and then re-arranged upon request for solo alto and womens' chorus (SSAA). Described by Graham Johnson as a 'delicious *pièce d'occasion*', it was composed on commission as a birthday gift for Louise Gosmar, future spouse of Schubert's friend Leopold von Sonnleithner; see Graham Johnson, *Franz Schubert: The Complete Songs*, vol. 3, pp. 245–8, for more on this serenade. While the dramatic strategy

Both are serenades – love songs in which a dramatic persona addresses an object of affection.[3] In each instance, the latter never responds directly to the former's fervent words, yet is reflected in them. Neither Lied is 'serene', as the genre's name would imply, and neither seems the least bit casual or disinterested. Indeed, 'Ständchen ("Horch, Horch! die Lerch")' and 'Ständchen' present instances of interpersonal persuasion within which a central character hopes to gain a positive response from an apparently reticent companion. In these Lieder, drama resides within the portrayal of persuasion.

Both songs communicate dramatic implications of their poetic texts via contextual processes derived from the same persuasive plan.[4] These consist of purposefully positioned musical elements that direct attention ahead.[5] Eliciting

---

described in this chapter does not appear to unfold within that five-or-so-minute piece, Schubert's convivial composition charms in its own way.

[3]   Traditionally, a vocal serenade was a song sung in early evening to honour a lady, usually to the accompaniment of a stringed instrument, perhaps a lute in Shakespeare's day. On the surface, its poetry and eloquence were intended to charm and to entertain. However, a serenade's fundamental purpose was to persuade. Although the practice of serenading dates at least to the Renaissance, if not much earlier, Schubert's 'Ständchen', from *Schwanengesang* (1828), one of the Lieder examined here, is, in Graham Johnson's view 'probably the most famous serenade in the world'; see Graham Johnson, *Franz Schubert: The Complete Songs*, vol. 3, p. 20. Perhaps the only real rival to Schubert's 'Ständchen' as a classic examplar of the genre is Don Giovanni's serenade from the second act of Mozart's dramatic masterpiece. Sung outside Donna Elvira's house while Leporello – disguised as his master – tries to lead the lady away, 'Deh vieni alla finestra' features Don Giovanni, accompanying himself on mandolin, engaged in an earnest effort to seduce Donna Elvira's maid. I thank Susan Wollenberg for reminding me of this famous operatic serenade.

[4]   Edward T. Cone's classic article, 'Schubert's Promissory Note: An Exercise in Musical Hermeneutics, *19th-Century Music* 5/3 (1982), pp. 233–41, represents the first comprehensive and in-depth study of a contextual process within the music of Franz Schubert (1797–1828). Cone demonstrated how a prominent E♮5 in the twelfth bar of Schubert's *Moment musical* in A♭ major, an inflected fifth scale degree expressed within a V/vi harmony, was deflected downward from its apparent goal, F5, thus becoming 'a troubling element of which one expects to hear more' (p. 236) – what Cone called a 'promissory note'. Cone traced the distinctive tone's numerous returns, whose upward aspirations were consistently frustrated, until bar 47, when an F5 sounds prominently and persuasively, thus redeeming the 'promissory note'.

[5]   I have discussed contextual musical processes in a variety of Schubert's instrumental, choral and vocal music; see: 'Tonal Implication and the Gestural Dialectic in Schubert's A Minor Quartet', in *Schubert the Progressive: History, Performance Practice, Analysis*, ed. Brian Newbould (Aldershot: Ashgate, 2003), pp. 53–79; 'The "Problem" of Schubert's String Quintet', *Nineteenth-Century Music Review* 2/1 (2005), pp. 57–92; 'A Balance Struck: Gesture, Form, and Drama in Schubert's E flat Major Piano Trio', in *Le style instrumental de*

expectations and producing a perception of growing momentum that culminates in a climactic musical arrival, they underscore and vivify each text's unique dramatic narrative. Understanding these contextual processes involves identification of their shared strategy's functional phases, analysis of their expressive elements, assessment of their musical effects, and interpretation of the expressive messages they convey.

The Five Phases of Schubert's Dramatic Strategy

More specifically, 'Ständchen ("Horch, Horch! die Lerch")' and 'Ständchen' feature the same dramatic strategy: an ordered series of five phases that portrays persuasion. Figure 6.1 offers a simple representation of this sequence, which here unfolds left to right.

First, an approach phase initiates engagement while introducing instability, drawing upon rhythmic, melodic, and harmonic means to produce anticipation. Next, an appeal phase ensues, animated by ascending vocal gestures that reach out and up but seem to stop short of their goals. At a crucial and climactic moment within a breakthrough phase, a registral apex occurs, shattering apparent prior contextual resistance with what seems to be just the right pitch. Then, a settling phase featuring descending gestures signals an approaching conclusion.[6] Yet even as the music nears its end and a closure phase arrives, tension lingers, sustained by unmet expectations, which makes a fully satisfying end elusive. Both contextual processes unfold on their own planes within the two songs, complementing their

Schubert: sources, analyse, évolution, ed. Xavier Hascher (Paris: Publications de la Sorbonne, 2007), pp. 115–46; 'Schubert's Self-Elegies', *Nineteenth-Century Music Review* 5/2 (2008), special issue, *Schubert Familiar and Unfamiliar: New Perspectives*, pp. 71–105; 'Contextual Processes in Schubert's Late Sacred Choral Music', in *Rethinking Schubert*, ed. Lorraine Byrne Bodley and Julian Horton (Oxford: Oxford University Press, 2015), pp. 295–332; 'Conversations Within and Between Two Early Lieder of Schubert', *Nineteenth-Century Music Review* 13/1 (2016), special issue, *Schubert Familiar and Unfamiliar: Continuing Conversations*, pp. 83–102.

[6] The persuasive strategy highlighted here may recall Classical rhetoric, whose six phases included the *exordium, narratio, divisio, confirmatio, confutation,* and *peroratio*. Yet it bears an even more striking similarity to the five stages of dramatic structure later described by Gustav Freytag in *Die Technik des Dramas* (Leipzig: Hirzel, 1863), which include *exposition, rising action, climax, falling action,* and *denouement*, a sequence often graphically represented as a pyramid. Schubert's strategy differs from Freytag's in that the two songs considered here have no real denouement – they end with welcome tonal closure yet leave dramatic questions unresolved. Nevertheless, for many of today's readers and listeners, the persuasive sequence may recall contemporary marketing strategies in which a salesperson gains the attention of a potential customer, appeals to their conscious and unconscious needs, gains assent, moves to close the deal, and concludes the exchange.

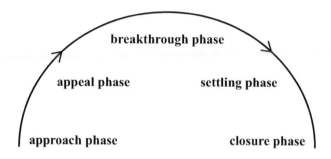

Figure 6.1   Schubert's persuasive strategy within 'Ständchen ("Horch, Horch! die Lerch")' and 'Ständchen'

texts in a manner similar to the way that body language reinforces speech. Each song involves two characters, one vocal, one silent, and is dramatic in its own way, portraying an intriguing approach, a struggling advance, perceived achievement, subsequent accommodation, and a partially satisfying resolution. Let us observe how each unfolds.

A Shakespearean Serenade Reimagined

Schubert's 'Ständchen ("Horch, Horch! die Lerch")' incorporates verses derived from William Shakespeare's late romance *Cymbeline*.[7] Figure 6.2 presents the Lied's seventeenth-century source alongside the song's German text, which includes Schubert's repetitions.

In *Cymbeline*, the words at the left of Figure 6.2 are heard at dawn outside the door of King Cymbeline's daughter Imogen, sung by a minstrel in the service of the brutish suitor Cloten, who had been told that music in the morning might win the lady's heart. Cloying and cheeky, the air provides comedic diversion as Imogen avoids Cloten's coarse advances by remaining still in her bedroom as the minstrel sings.

While the German text of Schubert's song retains Shakespeare's poetic metaphors and bucolic theme, and remains rather close to the Bard's metrics and rhyme scheme, its verses no longer serve a theatrical function. That is, in this reimagined setting, the song is not sung for comedic and ironic effect by a minstrel

---

[7]   This text comes from Act II, Scene 3, of Shakespeare's *Cymbeline*, which was first produced in April of 1611 and published in the *First Folio* of 1623. For more on this song, see Graham Johnson's discussion in *Franz Schubert: The Complete Songs*, vol. 3, pp. 241–4, where it is described as 'a masterpiece of economy and delight' (p. 243).

Hark! hark! the lark at heaven's gate sings,	Horch, horch! die Lerch im Ätherblau;
And Phoebus 'gins arise,	und Phöbus, neu erweckt,
His steeds to water at those springs	tränkt seine Rosse mit dem Tau,
On chalic'd flowers that lies;	der Blumen kelche deckt,
	der Blumen kelche deckt;
And winking Mary-buds begin	der Ringelblume Knospe schleußt
To ope their golden eyes:	die goldnen Äuglein auf;
With every thing that pretty is,	mit allem, was da reizend ist,
My lady sweet, arise:	du süße Maid steh auf,
	mit allem, was da reizend ist,
Arise, arise!	du süße Maid steh auf, steh auf, steh auf,
	du süße Maid steh auf, steh auf, steh auf,
	du süße Maid steh auf!

Figure 6.2   Shakespeare, *Cymbeline* (1611), Act II, Scene 3, 'Hark! hark! the lark';
German adaptation 'Horch, Horch! die Lerch' by August Wilhelm von
Schlegel, as set by Schubert

on behalf of an antagonist within a play set in ancient Britain. Instead, it belongs to
a more contemporary character with a personal agenda. In Schubert's setting, the
words acquire energetic enthusiasm and almost over-earnest eloquence that seems
both charming and disarming, as well as apparently quite sincere. Yet this music
subtly manipulates its listeners' expectations, imparting a vicarious experience of
interpersonal persuasion.

An Engaging Piano Introduction: The First Phase of Schubert's Strategy

The approach phase within the contextual process of 'Ständchen ("Horch, Horch!
die Lerch")' unfolds solely within the song's instrumental introduction, which
appears in Example 6.1.

The accompaniment projects a dancelike character at the outset, courtesy of
the passage's compound metre and numerous anacruses, its homophonic nature
somewhat suggestive of plucked and strummed strings. However, instability emerges
at once within the rhythmic domain. As Example 6.1 illustrates, the semiquavers
heard just before the second beats in the first two bars come 'early' and sound lower
in bar 3. Immediately reiterated, the gestures in the lower register seem to prod,
adding urgency as the phrase unfolds. Repetition of this rhythmic activity in the
second phrase augments the introduction's restlessness, its insistence serving to
herald what comes next. Though the dramatic persona of the serenade, embodied by
the singer, has not said a single word, his anxious state precedes him.

Other sources of tension in Schubert's introduction include what might be called
its 'nagging notes' – long-delayed melodic resolutions – that result from registral
differences among the elements that make up its strands. As the first arrow in

Example 6.1   Schubert, 'Ständchen ("Horch, Horch! die Lerch")', D. 889, bars 0–9,
                     with analysis

Note: The examples for Schubert's 'Ständchen ("Horch, Horch! De Lerch")', D. 889 are based on Franz Schubert: *Neue Ausgabe sämtlicher Werke – Serie IV: Lieder, Band 14, Teil a und b*, Vorgelegt von Walther Dürr – BA 5527 © Bärenreiter-Verlag Karl Vötterle GmbH & Co. KG, Kassel, pp. 18–19, which was used by permission. Cordial thanks are extended to Katharina Malecki of Bärenreiter-Verlag.

Example 6.1 suggests, the high F of bar 1 seems as if it is 'left hanging' until the first beat of bar 4, when E resolves it. Similarly, the high A of the fifth bar seems to remain unresolved until after the voice's entry, when G resolves it. Both tones tease, alluding to their resolutions as they increase anticipation. Listeners, in turn, experience impatience, empathizing with the serenade's central character. Certainly the antiphonal nature of the introduction – created by contrasting and conversing components – reinforces this anxious impetus.

Perhaps the most dynamic source of expectation appears to arise from the introduction's tonal structure. The Roman numeral harmonic analysis given below the systems in Example 6.1, shown with Arabic inversion figures, suggests that the dominant harmony controls the entire passage until cadential confirmation of tonic C major occurs in bar 8. Example 6.2 offers a representation of the passage that demonstrates its dwelling on the dominant.

Example 6.2   Schubert, 'Ständchen ("Horch, Horch! die Lerch")', D. 889, bars 0–8,
                   precursive prolongation

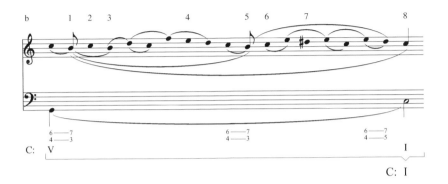

This dwelling on the dominant produces an extended harmonic prefix – a 'precursive prolongation' – that directs attention ahead toward the tonic's arrival.[8] Until bar 8, what appear to be C major sonorities within this span serve to sustain the composed-out dominant harmony and are subordinate to it, contributing to a perception of mounting suspense. The anticipation generated by these rhythmic, melodic and harmonic means simulates the interiority of the suitor prior to the start of his serenade, providing listeners with an opportunity to experience the apprehension and possibility he might sense in such a situation.

Yet anticipation arises via still other means. As the top brackets in Example 6.1 reveal, two instances of an anapestic pattern appear within the passage.[9] Reminiscent of the AAB design of Bar form, and corresponding to what Arnold Schoenberg described as a 'sentence', the anapestic pattern consists of two relatively

[8] See the following for more on the concept of 'precursive prolongation': James William Sobaskie, 'Tonal Implication and the Gestural Dialectic in Schubert's A Minor String Quartet', in *Schubert the Progressive*, ed. Brian Newbould (Aldershot: Ashgate, 2003), pp. 56–62; James William Sobaskie, 'The "Problem" of Schubert's String Quintet', *Nineteenth-Century Music Review* 2/1 (2005), pp. 84–6; and James William Sobaskie, 'Precursive Prolongation in the *Préludes* of Chopin', *Journal of the Society for Musicology in Ireland* 3 (2007–2008), pp. 25–61. Melodic prefixes like appoggiaturas, and harmonic prefixes like secondary dominants, represent brief precursive prolongations, but extended contrapuntal-harmonic passages, like the introduction to Schubert's 'Ständchen ("Horch, Horch! die Lerch")', represent more structurally significant instances. See also the beginning of the Kyrie to Schubert's Mass in Ab major, discussed in Chapter 3 of this volume.

[9] The anapest is a poetic unit that, depending on the language, consists of two short syllables followed by a long one, or two unaccented syllables followed by an accented one, a forward-leaning pattern traditionally represented as ˇˇ–.

similar events followed by a third that complements its predecessors and completes the unit.[10] Creating an impression that may be summarized as 'attempt, attempt, attempt → achievement', the initial instance establishes the anapestic pattern as a thematic premise within Schubert's Lied.[11] When the second instance begins to unfold, it focuses attention forward toward a reaffirmation of tonic C major.[12] Like the rhythmic, melodic and harmonic features identified earlier, these patterns engage the imagination, prompting curiosity and prediction. In turn, the resultant anticipation prepares for the next phase of Schubert's persuasive plan – a series of ascending vocal gestures.

Aspiring Vocal Gestures: The Second Phase of Schubert's Strategy

Musical material from the introduction returns as accompaniment for the singer's entry, as the last two bars of Example 6.1 hint. Thus, bars 8–18 continue to emphasize the rhythmic shift, dominant prolongation, and anapestic pattern, sustaining the introduction's anticipation as they support the now-entered voice. Example 6.3 presents the Lied's appealing vocal lines that make manifest its protagonist and correspond to the second phase of its contextual process.

As this excerpt shows, the voice starts with an emphatic reach from E to F in bars 8–9 on the words 'Horch, horch!', a melodic gesture that assumes the nature of an appeal as it articulates the text's own call to attention.[13] Set in the upper part of the singer's range, the rising step projects enthusiasm, encouraging prediction that the melody might rise even higher. Another ascending gesture of appeal appears in bars 12–13, expressed by the same two pitches in an equivalent metric location, reiterates an impression of aspiration. However, this repetition suggests that the voice

---

[10] Bar form, which may be traced to the Meistersingers of the Renaissance era, features two sets of words (*Stollen*) sung to the same melody (AA), which are known collectively as an *Aufgesang*, followed by a new and complementary set of words set to a new melody, which is known as an *Abgesang*. While the design originated in secular song, it appears in sacred hymns and instrumental music as well. Arnold Schoenberg's notion of musical sentence is discussed in his *Fundamentals of Musical Composition*, ed. Gerald Strang and Leonard Stein (New York: St. Martin's Press, 1967); see pp. 20–24 and pp. 58–63.

[11] This instance corresponds to what Susan Wollenberg calls a Schubertian 'fingerprint'; for more on this feature of the composer's style, see Chapter 3, 'Threefold Constructions', in her book *Schubert's Fingerprints: Studies in the Instrumental Works* (Farnham: Ashgate, 2011), pp. 191–212.

[12] See my other chapter in this volume, 'The Dramatic Monologue of Schubert's Mass in A♭ major, where the three-part 'attempt, attempt, attempt → achievement' sequence plays multiple roles in the Kyrie.

[13] To avoid confusion, specific pitch designations, such as E5 and F5, are not used in the current discussion, since the actual pitches sung by a tenor would sound an octave lower.

Example 6.3   Schubert, 'Ständchen ("Horch, Horch! die Lerch")', D. 889, bars 7–18, vocal melody with analysis

has met a 'barrier' of sorts at the pitch F – a registral ceiling – within this context.[14] Even so, placement of the possessive adjective 'seine' within this appealing gesture, a relatively weak word for such a prominent melodic tone, hints of the fragility of that contextually developed registral ceiling. And the anapestic pattern heard twice in the piano introduction, and twice again in the voice's accompaniment – the 'attempt, attempt, attempt → achievement' sequence – foreshadows the registral ceiling's eventual breach. Schubert's setting effectively brings us inside the mind of his central character.

A Breakthrough: The Third Phase of Schubert's Strategy

The trifold sequence of 'attempt, attempt, attempt → achievement, is expressed over a larger span in 'Ständchen ("Horch, Horch! die Lerch")'. As Example 6.3 (presented earlier) reveals, the first two rising vocal gestures stop at F, as if unable to progress higher. However, that contextual boundary finally gives way on the downbeat of bar 17, when the high G exceeds the apparent registral ceiling. The text sung there, 'der Blumen kelche deckt', repeats words heard earlier, so attention focuses on and is rewarded by the attainment of that pitch-related goal, which is the highest pitch ever to be heard in the Lied. The effect of its achievement is intuitive, suggestive of the main agent's internal realization – or hope – that the nearby beloved may have been moved by his rising appeals. As the remainder of the song unfolds, the high vocal G, once a goal, now becomes the point of origin for a set of descending closing gestures that aim for tonic C.

---

14   Blake Howe explores the notion of 'barrier' in his chapter, 'Bounded Finitude and Boundless Infinitude: Schubert's Contradictions at the "Final Barrier"', in *Schubert's Late Music: History, Theory, Style,* ed. Lorraine Byrne Bodley and Julian Horton (Cambridge: Cambridge University Press, 2016), pp. 357–82.

Example 6.4   Schubert, 'Ständchen ("Horch, Horch! die Lerch")', D. 889, bars 18–38,
                   vocal melody with analysis

Valedictory Gestures: The Fourth Phase of Schubert's Strategy

As Example 6.4 suggests, the concluding portion of Schubert's serenade begins with the voice in its lower register, proceeding through a region controlled by the flattened submediant (A♭ major) harmony.

The German augmented sixth of bar 23 heralds the return of the voice's high G in the following bar, as well as the first of several settling gestures that would seem to aim toward a satisfying cadence on the tonic pitch below. Brackets above the staves highlight the inherent stepwise motion perceptible within these closing gestures.

The first of these descending gestures falls short of its goal, stopping on E. The second interrupts its descent even earlier, stopping on F. Prior experiences of the anapestic pattern naturally leads listeners to expect that the third of these gestures should bring the expected concluding C. However, as Example 6.4 reveals, it does not. Instead, Schubert evokes even more anticipation by breaking his own contextually established pattern, thwarting expectations. The last gesture – and at five bars, the longest – does not disappoint, delivering the satisfying tonic C pitch in bar 38, where it is supported by the tonic harmony, as if achieved by extra effort.

An Imperfect Conclusion: The Closure Phase of Schubert's Strategy

'Ständchen ("Horch, Horch! die Lerch")' finishes with a return to the opening piano passage, whose ending offers relative repose on the tonic harmony (see bar 8 of Example 6.1). Yet must it, or even should it provide a stronger close? Perhaps not! Any more than this brief postlude would deprive listeners of the flight of fancy to which this Lied has led. Does the lady respond, and if so, how? What happens then? Listeners are left free to imagine how the scene plays out.

Schubert's Lied is sometimes sung with additional verses contributed by Friedrich Reil (1773–1843).[15] Yet a comparative audition of the two versions reveals that the latter soon wears out its welcome – Reil's extra verses dissipate desire to speculate by re-running the five phases of the Lied's contextual process twice more. Schubert's original version leaves listeners with a mixture of hope and uncertainty, encouraging them to speculate as to what might happen next within this musical vignette. And like so many of Schubert's works, both vocal and instrumental, it serves to stimulate the imagination, leaving the end of the experience less than explicit, but ultimately more rewarding. It falls to us to determine the dramatic outcome.

A Serious Serenade

Schubert's 'Ständchen', from *Schwanengesang*, also stimulates its listeners' imaginations, yet it does so in a very different way.[16] In striking contrast to the exuberance and extroversion of 'Ständchen ("Horch, Horch! die Lerch")', the Lied impresses us via its intimacy and its introversion. Although not immediately apparent, 'Ständchen' unfolds through words that are privately uttered by its dramatic persona. An interior monologue, its text suggests contemplative solitude within a remote rural locale, perhaps locating the character in an upper room near an open window.[17]

---

[15]   Diabelli published Schubert's 'Ständchen ("Horch, Horch! die Lerch")' in 1830 and released a second edition in 1832 with the extra verses by Friedrich Reil. Schubert's songs 'Das Lied im Grünen' (D. 917) and 'Glaube, Hoffnung und Liebe' (D. 954) set the poet's verses. For more on these matters, see Graham Johnson, *Franz Schubert: The Complete Songs*, vol. 2, pp. 632–3.

[16]   For a recent discussion of the influence of Schubert's 'Ständchen', see Laura Tunbridge, 'Singing against Late Style: The Problem of Performance History', in *Schubert's Late Music: History, Theory, Style*, ed. Lorraine Byrne Bodley and Julian Horton (Cambridge: Cambridge University Press, 2016), pp. 426–41.

[17]   Graham Johnson, noting that despite the extreme familiarity of 'Ständchen', 'this music is shot through with uncertainty and vulnerability, and it is this which makes it a quintessentially Schubertian creation'; see Graham Johnson, *Franz Schubert: The Complete Songs*, vol. 3, p. 21.

'Ständchen's' text appears with my translation in Figure 6.3. Softly beckoning songs sung aloft in the night, rustling moonlit treetops that promise to obscure intimate conversation, and knowing nightingales, whose sweet-sounding and silvery strains serve as sympathetic intermediaries for the yearning persona – all of these images communicate isolation and vulnerability. Indeed, despite the deep sincerity and passion emanating from this setting, it can be difficult to imagine someone actually singing it in the presence of a beloved, for the undercurrent of anxiety and uncertainty would seem to sabotage its service as a romantic overture. Instead, 'Ständchen' might be interpreted as an instance in which the serenade's agent is trying to persuade himself to persevere in courtship by expressing aloud his unfiltered thoughts and innermost desires, rehearsing his side of an imaginary exchange with his beloved.

An Evocative Introduction: The Approach Phase

As Example 6.5 illustrates, the serenade begins quietly. The song's accompaniment, marked staccato, evokes the centuries-old tradition of nocturnal serenading with a plucked stringed instrument, such as the lute or guitar, a social pursuit that still was popular in Schubert's own time.[18] Yet anyone aware of the practice's origins cannot help but be struck by Schubert's ironic intent. There is little that is serene or laudatory or courtly about the beginning of this Lied, whose delicately ambivalent minor mode and melancholy mood appear to contradict its name, and whose text surely betrays a disquieted soul. 'Ständchen' engages and intrigues, but initially through incongruity. Yet as in 'Ständchen ("Horch, Horch! die Lerch")', so, here too, persuasion is a premise underlying the song, and the five phases of its contextual process unfold similarly, albeit via means dictated by their more sober orientation. The instrumental introduction and the initial vocal phrases, which correspond to the approach phase of the Lied's contextual process, establish an unsettled premise from which the rest unfolds.

Tonal and metric expectations established in the opening bars soon face challenges, introducing instability associated with the approach phase of Schubert's contextual process. For instance, by the end of Example 6.5 (presented earlier), the key of D minor seems to have been locally and temporarily supplanted by F major, signalling a rising sense of hope. Yet tension emerges in the rhythmic domain as

---

[18]   Deutsch reports that Schubert wrote a 'Cantata for his Father's Name-Day' in 1813, to be sung for two tenors and a bass voice with guitar accompaniment, adding 'he is supposed to have played it', referring to the composer's guitar skills; see Otto Eric Deutsch, *Schubert: A Documentary Biography*, trans. Eric Blom (London: Dent, 1946), p. 38. The success of 'Ständchen' in arrangements for guitar and voice, as well as solo guitar, should encourage us to consider whether the medium's presence may be perceived in other contexts, even if serenading is not portrayed.

Leise flehen meine Lieder	Softly beckon my songs
durch die Nacht zu dir;	through the night to you;
in den stillen Hain hernieder,	in the quiet grove below,
Liebchen, komm zu mir!	Dearest, come to me.
Flüsternd schlanke Wipfel rauschen	Whispering slender treetops rustle
in des Mondes Licht;	in the moonlight;
des Verräters feindlich Lauschen	the hostile betrayers overhearing
fürchte, Holde, nicht.	fear, Darling, not.
Hörst die Nachtigallen schlagen?	Hear the nightingales' singing?
ach! sie flehen dich,	ah, they beckon to you,
mit der Töne süßen Klagen	with sweet-sounding plaints
Flehen sie für mich.	they beckon to you for me.
Sie verstehn des Busens Sehnen,	They understand the heart's yearning,
kennen Liebesschmerz,	knowing the pain of love,
rühren mit den Silbertönen	stirring with their silver tones
jedes weiche Herz.	each tender heart.
Laß auch dir die Brust bewegen,	Let them also stir within your breast,
Liebchen, höre mich!	Dearest, hear me!
Bebend harr' ich dir entgegen!	Trembling anxiously I await you!
Komm, beglücke mich!	Come, gladden me!

Figure 6.3   Schubert, *Schwanengesang*, D. 957, No. 4, 'Ständchen', text by
             Ludwig Rellstab, with translation

well. Polyrhythms on the downbeats of bars 5, 6, 11 and 12 – the first of which is boxed in Example 6.5 – add brief ripples of rhythmic wavering that slightly weaken the metric framework. In turn, agogic and tonic accents on the following notes in those same bars produce mild syncopations that challenge the primary pulse. Together, they communicate hints of internal distraction at odds with the affectionate sentiments being expressed, a basal level of unrest that soon will rise.

As in 'Ständchen ("Horch, Horch! die Lerch")', the approach phase of 'Ständchen' also prepares for coming appeals in the following passage by introducing two motivic elements, each of which appears within the first two phrases of the song. These include the pitch pair A and F, whose instances are marked by the upper set of brackets, and which assume the forms of a major third and a minor sixth. Also heard twice is the semitonal upper neighbour figure, A–Bb–A, which appears at the start of each phrase. Both of these motivic elements return at decisive points in 'Ständchen's unfolding musical argument.

Example 6.5   Schubert, *Schwanengesang*, D. 957, No. 4, 'Ständchen', bars 1–16, with analysis

Note: The examples for Schubert's 'Ständchen' from his *Schwanengesang*, D. 957, No. 4, are based on Franz Schubert: *Neue Ausgabe sämtlicher Werke – Serie IV: Lieder, Band 14, Teil a und b*, Vorgelegt von Walther Dürr – BA 5527 © Bärenreiter-Verlag Karl Vötterle GmbH & Co. KG, Kassel, pp. 118–120, which was used by permission. Cordial thanks are extended to Katharina Malecki of Bärenreiter-Verlag.

Example 6.6   Schubert, *Schwanengesang*, D. 957, No. 4, 'Ständchen', bars 17–28, vocal melody with analysis

Ascending Vocal Gestures: The Appeal Phase

The next phase of the song's persuasive strategy begins in bar 17. As Example 6.6 shows, the phrases beginning in bars 17 and 23 start with determined melodic ascents from A up to F that seem to aspire, over-reaching a readily-achievable goal (E), or perhaps aiming for but falling short of an even higher one (A) within the prevailing A major harmony.

Each rise articulates the now familiar A–F pitch pair, yet in both, the upper pitch F – dissonant in context because of the dominant harmony below – implies the presence of an apparent contextual barrier from which the voice is turned back. Twice in the second stanza, the appealing gestures of the voice seem to be unable to exceed it. Yet the pitch G heard near the end of the stanza – identified by an asterisk in Example 6.6 – does so, breaking the apparent registral barrier.[19] A dissonant tone, thanks to the dominant harmony that sounds below, the G nevertheless remains unresolved in the vocal part, though the piano offers compensation in bar 28. Its attainment seems qualified, as if complete success has been deferred – it may have exceeded the ceiling of F, but it does not satisfy. Two more stanzas, which correspond to 'Ständchen's' second verse, must unfold before the implications of its achievement become clear.

An Unexpected Realization: The Breakthrough Phase

Example 6.7 presents the final section of 'Ständchen'. Two new ascending gestures – appeals that seem more conservative yet more determined than those just heard, perhaps because of the lower-pitched chordal accompaniment and the echoing octaves in the pianist's right hand – unfold with increasing intensity. Sounding below, as the lower brackets show, are repeated instances of the upper neighbour

[19]   Coincidentally, the same pitches – F and G – serve, respectively, as temporary 'barrier' and eventual 'breakthrough' in 'Ständchen ("Horch, Horch! die Lerch")'.

Example 6.7   Schubert, *Schwanengesang*, D. 957, No. 4, 'Ständchen', bars 37–59,
                     with analysis

figure in the lowest register, which add momentum. Together, they bring a dramatic breakthrough in bar 33b on the self-revelatory word 'Bebend' ('trembling'). Supported by an applied dominant of the submediant minor, the high F♯ in bar 33b, lying *between* the F♮ heard in bars 11, 17, and 23 and the G heard in bar 27, represents a contextually determined goal, the culmination of the Lied's contextual melodic process. Yet it also represents a dramatic goal in its narrative – a point of reversal as well as a turning point. The song's central character, after having sketched a quiet scene, and invoked images of gentle nightingales, all while admitting grave doubt, recognizes that it is his deep and honest feeling, manifested by his physical reaction, which is his hope. And in this instance, the F♯ asserted so forcefully, becomes the crucial component that augments the song's tonal palette of scale degrees and enables D minor to become D major, reflective of doubt transformed into possibility.

Another Imperfect Conclusion: The Settling and Closure Phases

As Example 6.7 suggests, three vocal gestures in bars 37–44 lead to the lower F♯ on the final word. The first two are in D major, and the second of these starts higher than the first, sustaining the sense of hope brought by the earlier breakthrough. Yet the F♮s of bar 41, and the B♭s of bars 42 and 45 revive memory of D minor. Schubert's characteristic major/minor fluctuation thus communicates a quiet yet nagging uncertainty. As in 'Ständchen ("Horch, Horch! die Lerch")', the end of 'Ständchen' enables and indeed urges us to imagine the untold epilogue of this narrative, to speculate what happens next. But it doesn't resolve the drama. We decide.

Insights and Implications

Schubert's ability to portray persuasion in 'Ständchen ("Horch, Horch! die Lerch")' and 'Ständchen' proceeds from a profound understanding of human psychology, as well as a confident grasp of music's potential to engage, elicit expectation, and express. Indeed, the similar contextual processes in these two serenades reflect his awareness that the most convincing external influence involves strategic communication on multiple levels. Schubert's contextual processes, like those observed here, contribute significantly to the richness and vividness we admire so much in his art, and especially to its ability to move us. Surely they succeed if they prompt us to imagine how these two dramatic vignettes play out.

Of course, all of this has implications for performance. The unprecedented expressive depth of Schubert's Lieder obliges vocalists to be actors as well as singers if they aspire to present compelling performances. That depth also demands that interpreters plumb the depths of a song's drama if they hope to be faithful to the composer's intentions and avoid the banality of a cursory reading or rote recitation. In turn, it appears that proper preparation of a Schubertian song for public performance proceeds through five semi-simultaneous stages of development.

'Stage one' of faithful Schubertian song preparation begins with careful mastery of pitches, rhythms, words, pronunciations, and phrasing. 'Stage two' focuses on the development of effective ensemble with the partnering pianist. 'Stage three' entails expansive and reflective study of the Lied's historical and literary contexts, musical structure, and inherent aesthetic. 'Stage four' aims at apprehension of narrative, subtext, and innate idiosyncrasies. Perhaps most crucial of all, 'stage five' aspires to an insightful grasp of the unique and evolving interiority of the portrayed persona or personae. Each of these somewhat overlapping stages informs the next, so leaving anything out undermines a stirring performance. Of course that's a lot, to say the least. But rote learning – so superficial and shortchanging – just won't do. Schubert's 'Ständchen ("Horch, Horch! die Lerch")' and 'Ständchen' distil so much drama into about 1' 40" and around 4' 00", respectively, that any less preparation represents artistic injustice as well as opportunity lost.

7

'Durch Nacht und Wind': *Tempesta* as a Topic in Schubert's Lieder

Clive McClelland

> Wer reitet so spät durch Nacht und Wind?
> Es ist Der Vater mit seinem Kind.

Schubert's setting of these words is justly regarded as a milestone in the history of song writing. The depictions of the galloping horse, the terrifying storm, the resolute father, the frightened child, and the eerie Erlking combine to produce an evocation of the supernatural that is vivid and engaging. This is principally due to Schubert's employment of a style nowadays often referred to as *Sturm und Drang*, a phrase that seems all too fitting since the text of the song is by Goethe.[1] Yet this is a highly misleading label, as the musical style employed pre-dates the German literary movement by quite some time. The origins of the style really lie in the depiction of storms in Baroque opera, occurrences that were invariably instigated by an irate deity and therefore associated with the supernatural.

Theatrical Origins

Scenes involving gods, monsters, oracles, and magic were a staple in serious operas of the seventeenth and eighteenth centuries, and they provided composers with the opportunity to employ special musical devices. This was not just for pictorial effect though, as the evidence is clear that many composers in the latter half of the eighteenth century set out to generate feelings of awe and terror in their audiences. It was achieved by introducing discontinuous elements into the music. For the creeping horror of ghosts, incantations, oracles, and walking statues, different effects were used in combination such as a slow or moderate tempo, flat minor keys, tonal uncertainty, unusual harmonies (especially chromatic chords), fragmented or wide-leaping melodic lines, insistent repeated notes, tremolando, syncopated and dotted rhythms, sudden pauses or contrasts in texture or dynamics, and dark timbres with unusual instrumentation, especially trombones. These are the characteristics of

---

[1] For a detailed study of the song and its aesthetic context, see Christopher H. Gibbs, "'Komm geh mit mir": Schubert's Uncanny "Erlkönig"', *19th-Century Music* 19/2 (1995), pp. 115–35.

ombra, a term introduced by Hermann Abert in 1908 to describe the ghost scenes in operas by influential eighteenth-century Italian composer Niccoló Jommelli.[2] Such characteristics can be found in operas since Monteverdi, including examples by Cavalli, Purcell, Handel, Hasse, and Gluck, and reaching a peak in Mozart's *Don Giovanni*, where the statue of the murdered Commendatore bursts in and pronounces the Don's fate with chilling and awesome grandeur.

Closely allied to *ombra* is a more agitated style, involving a much faster tempo, rapid scale passages (often on strings), driving rhythmic figurations, strong accents, full textures, and robust instrumentation including prominent brass and timpani. Similar music was used for other frightening scenarios such as pursuit (especially by demons or furies, as in the damnation of *Don Giovanni*), madness, and rage (such as the Queen of the Night arias in *The Magic Flute*). These cases can be viewed as metaphorical extensions of the supernatural storm idea. *Sturm und Drang* is an inaccurate label for this kind of music, and many scholars have been uncomfortable with it for some time. In particular there has been a mythical association of the style with a supposed 'crisis' in Haydn's middle years that gave rise to his so-called *Sturm und Drang* symphonies for which there is absolutely no evidence. It is for this reason that I have sought to establish the adoption of the term *tempesta* for all manifestations of this more violent kind of music, because of its 'stormy' origins, and also to provide a suitable Italian-language counterpart to *ombra*, since the two styles are obviously related.

The use of these styles is more than merely representational in almost all cases. In combination with spectacular scenery and stage effects, the music evidently had a profound effect on audiences. The relationship between music and emotional response is a complex one, but a study by David Huron has shown that the reactions associated with what he terms 'awe' and 'frisson' derive from innate 'surprise' responses: 'awe' from the 'freeze' response in the face of unexpected danger, and 'frisson' from the more aggressive 'fight' reaction.[3] These terms map directly onto *ombra* and *tempesta*, and it is possible to equate musical devices with these physical responses. For example, repeated dotted or syncopated notes relate to irregular heartbeats, and pauses reflect the suspension of activity at the moment of shock. In the mid-eighteenth century, awe and terror were recognized as sources of the sublime, notably by Edmund Burke, so *ombra* and *tempesta* need to be regarded as musical manifestations of this phenomenon.[4] The same period also saw the emergence of

---

[2] Hermann Abert, *Niccolò Jommelli als Opernkomponist* (Halle: M. Niemeyer, 1908), pp. 120–21. For a detailed study of the subject, see Clive McClelland, *Ombra: Supernatural Music in the Eighteenth Century* (Lanham, MD: Lexington Books, 2012). See also Chapter 8 in this volume.

[3] See David Huron, *Sweet Anticipation: Music and the Psychology of Expectation* (Cambridge, MA: MIT Press, 2006), pp. 31–5.

[4] See Edmund Burke, *A Philosophical Enquiry into the Origins of Our Ideas of the Sublime and Beautiful* (London: J. Dodsley, 1757). Reprint ed. J. T. Boulton (London: Routledge

Gothic literature and art, with disturbing novels by the likes of Walpole, Lewis, and Radcliffe and later paintings by Fuseli, Loutherbourg, and Piranesi enjoying widespread popularity.[5] The 'sublime of terror' is therefore a more useful aesthetic for understanding frightening music than the German literary *Sturm und Drang*, especially as the latter seldom makes reference to the supernatural.

The use of both *ombra* and *tempesta* allowed composers to heighten the drama, and before long references to these styles begin to be made in sacred music (particularly depictions of portentous biblical events in oratorios) and even as topical references in instrumental music. For instance, *ombra* sometimes appears as a powerful opening gesture in slow introductions to symphonies (such as Mozart's Symphony No. 38 ['Prague'] or Schubert's Symphony No. 4 ['Tragische']), and *tempesta* is ubiquitous in allegro movements, especially in development sections. In such cases there is no direct supernatural reference, but the technique is employed for rhetorical and emotional effect. This is how the *tempesta* references in Haydn's so-called *Sturm und Drang* symphonies should be understood, and certainly not as expressions of some unspecified internal angst on his part.

'Erlkönig' is by no means Schubert's only supernatural composition. Much of his music (and not only his Lieder) exhibits his enduring fascination with the supernatural, a characteristic that sets him apart from his great hero Beethoven.[6] In many respects he is closer to the German composers writing supernatural operas in the early nineteenth century, such as E. T. A. Hoffmann, Spohr, Weber, and Marschner.[7] Here I will focus my attention on *tempesta*, since I have already examined Schubert's use of *ombra* as a topic in his songs elsewhere.[8]

---

and Kegan Paul, 1958). For the context of the 'sublime of terror', especially relating to Burke, see McClelland, *Ombra: Supernatural Music in the Eighteenth Century*, pp. 10–21, and Michela Garda, *Musica Sublima: Metamorfosi di un'Idea nell Settecento Musicale* (Milan: Ricordi, 1995).

5   For broader context, see Marjorie Hirsch, 'Schubert's Reconciliation of Gothic and Classical Influences', in *Schubert's Late Music: History, Theory, Style*, ed. Lorraine Byrne Bodley and Julian Horton (Cambridge: Cambridge University Press, 2016), pp. 149–70.

6   Several of Schubert's 'stormier' passages are considered in Hugh Macdonald, 'Schubert's Volcanic Temper', *Musical Times* 119/1629 (Schubert Anniversary Issue; 1978), pp. 949–52, where they are linked with certain traits of his personality. On Schubertian violence see also Susan Wollenberg, *Schubert's Fingerprints: Studies in the Instrumental Works* (Farnham: Ashgate, 2011), Chapter 6, 'Schubert's Violent Nature'.

7   For a table of early Romantic German operas on supernatural themes, see McClelland, *Ombra: Supernatural Music in the Eighteenth Century*, p. 216.

8   See Clive McClelland, 'Death and the Composer: The Context of Schubert's Supernatural Lieder', in *Schubert the Progressive: History, Performance Practice, Analysis*, ed. Brian Newbould (Aldershot: Ashgate, 2003), pp. 21–35.

The *Tempesta* Tradition

The features associated with *tempesta* gradually evolved from the late seventeenth century onwards, as composers sought to apply increasingly unsettling musical effects in theatrical storm scenes. Such effects then began to appear as metaphorical references in rage arias, mad scenes, conflicts, and pursuits in the early eighteenth century. Storms were also a popular subject for programmatic instrumental music, including several examples of *tempesta di mare* finales to concertos and symphonies. From here it is a short step to using the style as a topical reference in an abstract symphonic work.[9] It is important to remember that more than one of these defining characteristics would need to appear in combination to confirm the *tempesta* reference. Table 7.1 provides a summary of the musical characteristics that could be employed.

As a composer born right at the end of the eighteenth century, Schubert inherited this stylistic tradition. He certainly would have been influenced by major composers like Gluck, Mozart, and Haydn, who had frequent recourse to the *tempesta* style, and his teacher Salieri, whose operas *Armida* (1772) and *Les Danaïdes* (1784) end in supernaturally inspired chaos and conflagration. Storm scenes remained highly popular in opera in the early part of the nineteenth century, with Rossini seldom missing an opportunity for a lively storm depiction, and other composers providing several examples. These include the storms in Donizetti's *Enrico di Borgogna* (1818) and *Chiara e Serafina* (1822), Weber's *Silvana* (1810), *Der Freischütz* (1821), and *Oberon* (1826), Spohr's *Jessonda* (1823) and the dramatic damnation scene at the end of Marschner's *Der Vampyr* (1828). Schubert himself explored the territory in some of his stage works, including *Fernando* (1815), and *Die Zauberharfe* (1820). His *Alfonso und Estrella* (1822) contains a restless aria in Act III (No. 32, 'Wo find'ich nur den Ort'), in which stormy characteristics portray the inner turmoil of the usurper Mauregato, who fears retribution is at hand. As with 'Erlkönig', the principal key is G minor, and the orchestral accompanying figure to the main theme is built on an insistent alternation between bass and upper strings (the latter playing *tremolando*) that underpins a sinuous and chromatic melodic line. Neapolitan and diminished-seventh harmonies occur frequently, the latter most emphatically in a threefold repetition (ascending chromatically and with syncopations) at the moment when Mauregato is confronted by what he believes to be the ghostly figure of the usurped king Froila. There are also strong dynamic contrasts, ascending chromatic scales and prominent trombones. Crucially, the effects that Schubert employs serve to depict Mauregato's sense of rising panic while simultaneously working on the emotions of the audience. Schubert displays a mastery of the elements of *tempesta* writing in a dramatic context, elements that would also feature in his songs.

---

[9] See Clive McClelland, '*Ombra* and *Tempesta*', in *The Oxford Handbook of Topic Theory*, ed. Danuta Mirka (Oxford: Oxford University Press, 2014), pp. 279–300. See also McClelland, *Tempesta: Stormy Music in the Eighteenth Century* (Lanham, MD: Lexington Books, 2017).

Table 7.1   Characteristics of the *tempesta* style

General features	agitated, declamatory, stormy
Tempo	fast, or very fast notes in moderate tempi
Tonality	mainly flat minor keys, especially D minor and C minor, shifting, unusual modulations
Harmony	'surprise' progressions, bold, chromatic, frequently on the dominant
Melody	disjunct motion, often fragmented, with very wide leaps, sometimes augmented or diminished leaps
Bass	occasionally chromatic, sometimes augmented or diminished leaps, repeated notes (*Trommelbass*), pedals, ostinato
Figuration	rapid scale passages, tremolo effects, repeated notes, *tirades*
Rhythm	restless motion, driving forward, syncopation, irregular rhythms, sometimes pauses
Texture	full textures, but often lines doubled in octaves, sometimes imitative or sequential
Dynamics	mostly loud, strong accents, crescendo effects, double hairpins
Instrumentation	prominent string writing, full scoring often involving brass and timpani

Storm as Metaphor in Schubert's Lieder

A storm is seldom just a storm in Romantic poetry. It can stand for a range of emotions from heartache to rage, and frequently there are direct or indirect allusions to death and the supernatural. This variety of stormy references is reflected in Schubert's Lieder output, as illustrated in Table 7.2 (selected passages are identified below).

Flat minor keys feature prominently in this selection, suggesting that Schubert was influenced by the tradition of using such keys for fear and terror. 'Erlkönig' presents an unambiguous supernatural storm, involving galloping, heroism, and an evil spirit who ultimately brings about the tragic death of an innocent child. An integral part of the tonal plan for the song is the chromatic ascent from B♭ major, when the Erlking first appears, to D minor, just before the child's final utterance (marked triple *forte*). At this point, the dissonant G♭s in the vocal line and the descending diminished triad in the bass suggest a sudden shift towards B♭ minor, but this is denied by a further twist into G minor (Example 7.1).

The dramatic tension of this moment is highlighted by the heavily accented bass line driving towards the cadence (bars 128–130). In contrast, 'Rastlose Liebe' presents a storm as a metaphor for restless love. There is no supernatural allusion here, and although the tonality and right-hand semiquaver figuration are certainly restless, flat minor keys do not appear. In terms of a spectrum of supernatural

Table 7.2   A selection of storm references in Schubert's individual songs

Title	Keys	Harmony	Figuration	Dynamics
Erlkönig	g → c → B♭ → b → G → C → c♯ → d → g	chromaticism, extended Neapolitan at end	RH repeated triplet, LH triplet motif	sudden *f/p* contrasts, strong bass *sf*s
Rastlose Liebe	e → f♯ → b → G → a → c♯ → E	chromaticism	RH semiquaver ostinato	*sf*s
Schäfers Klagelied	c → a♭ → C♭	chromaticism	*tremolando*	*f* → *ff*
Am Meer	C → c → d	chromaticism	*tremolando*	crescendo/ diminuendo effect
Die jünge Nonne	f → D♭ → f♯ → f	chromaticism including diminished 7ths	RH *tremolando*, LH ascending arpeggio	*fp* (mainly *p*)
Kolmas Klage	c (d♭ → A♭ → c)	chromaticism, German 6th / diminished 7th	*tremolando*	*p* → *ffz*
Der Tod und das Mädchen	d → g → FV → dV	chromaticism including diminished 7ths	RH/LH repeated chords	crescendo effect, offbeat accents

Example 7.1   Schubert, 'Erlkönig', D. 328, bars 123–131

content within storm references in Schubert's songs, these two represent opposite ends. In between are several songs that evoke the supernatural in varying degrees. 'Schäfers Klagelied' contains a brief 'natural' storm from which the shepherd seeks shelter. The song begins in C minor, but at 'Regen, Sturm und Gewitter' there is a shift to Ab minor and then to Cb major, very flat keys, with the suggestion that it is more frightening than at first thought (Example 7.2).[10]

The loud dynamics and rapidly repeated semiquaver chords also contribute to the effect. Schubert's posthumous collection *Schwanengesang* contains a storm at sea in 'Am Meer', serving as a metaphor for the weeping beloved. At 'der Nebel stieg' there is a move from C major to C minor, then D minor, with rapid *tremolando* accompaniment and a change of modality towards flat minor keys suggesting approaching menace (Example 7.3).

The storm stands as a metaphor for passion in 'Die junge Nonne', but with supernatural associations, and ultimately religious salvation. The tempo is only moderate, and the triadic outlines of the melody and compound metre suggest heroic struggle. F minor is the home key, but there are interesting tonal excursions

10   Schubert's original key for this song was E minor, which would make some of the more extreme modulations less remote. His publisher would have wanted to him to make the vocal range more accessible to a wider public, but the eventual choice of C minor also might have been influenced by its supernatural associations.

Example 7.2   Schubert, 'Schäfers Klagelied', D. 121, bars 28–33

Example 7.3   Schubert, *Schwanengesang*, D. 957, No. 12, 'Am Meer', bars 12–17

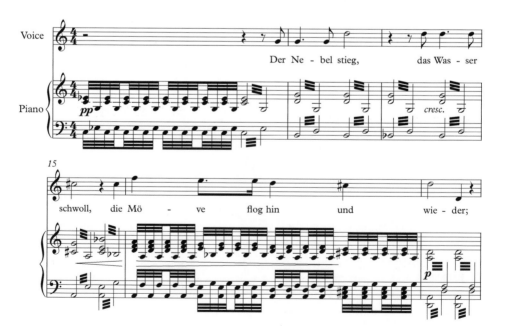

to the flattened submediant and the enharmonic equivalent of the Neapolitan. With 'Kolmas Klage', the storm signifies the heroine's distress at her separation from the beloved, and she expresses the German Romantic longing for death – *Todessehnsucht*. In the passage beginning 'Ihr Stürme, schweigt' there is a remarkable harmonic progression via chords of D♭ minor (a key so flat it lies beyond the boundaries of conventional theory!) and A♭ major, which is then treated as a pivotal German sixth to return home (Example 7.4).

'Der Tod und das Mädchen' presents *ombra* and *tempesta* in juxtaposition, with the two styles employed to characterize the protagonists. Death speaks in the *ombra* style, using the dactylic rhythm of the *verso sdrucciolo*, the Italian verse metre associated with funeral poetry, while the maiden's distress at her supernatural encounter is conveyed using several characteristics of storm imagery. The key is D minor and the tempo is *etwas geschwinder*, faster than the moderate introduction. The vocal line is angular, with agitated repeated notes in the accompaniment alternating between left and right hands. These features, together with the crescendo and three separate appearances of diminished seventh chords, serve to create a mounting sense of panic (Example 7.5).

Yet in the last few bars, Death's utterances are already anticipated, the descending stepwise motion in the voice and the accompaniment giving way to the slower dactylic rhythm. The maiden is already beginning to accept her fate, and the dramatic conflict approaches resolution.

All of these examples exhibit a strong tendency towards the use of flat minor keys, different kinds of active, unsettled figuration (especially *tremolando*), and highly expressive use of dynamic contrasts. They demonstrate Schubert's consistent response to the imagery presented in the text, while each preserves its own identity within the broad range of characteristics associated with the style.

Sinister Storms in *Winterreise*

Schubert's most extended treatment of weather imagery is to be found in his great song-cycle *Winterreise*, which is in many respects a supernatural work.[11] There are no monsters, ghosts or evil spirits, but there are harbingers of doom in the form of the will-o'-the-wisp in 'Irrlicht', and more than one appearance of ravens, birds of ill omen traditionally associated with death. Even the linden tree, normally a symbol associated with pleasant romantic encounters in German literature, appears more threatening here, inviting the traveller to find 'rest' entrapped in its branches. The wanderer is clearly journeying towards death (as was Schubert himself, of course), another expression of *Todessehnsucht*. Winter as a metaphor for the end of life is a common enough trope, and the idea is made explicit in the pivotal song

---

[11] See especially Lauri Suurpää, *Death in Winterreise: Poetic Associations in Schubert's Song Cycle* (Bloomington: Indiana University Press, 2014).

Example 7.4   Schubert, 'Kolmas Klage', D. 217, bars 34–51

Example 7.5   Schubert, 'Der Tod und das Mädchen', D. 531, bars 8–21

No. 20, 'Der Wegweiser', the signpost pointing along 'the road from which no-one has returned', with Schubert's setting employing an array of *ombra* devices. In this context the various occurrences of storms in the cycle take on a more sinister significance, and their main musical features are summarized in Table 7.3.

Again there is a clear emphasis on flat minor keys (although it is worth noting that Schubert originally conceived 'Rast' and 'Einsamkeit' in D minor, and 'Mut' in A minor).[12] The two most obviously stormy songs are 'Die Wetterfahne' and 'Der

---

[12]   For more on transpositions and the overall tonal plan, see Susan Youens, *Retracing a Winter's Journey: Schubert's Winterreise* (London and Ithaca, NY: Cornell University Press, 1991), pp. 95–104, and David P. Schroeder, 'Schubert's "Einsamkeit" and Haslinger's "Weiterreise"' in *Music & Letters* 71/3 (1990), pp. 352–60.

Table 7.3 Storm references in Schubert's *Winterreise*, D. 911

Title	Keys	Harmony	Figuration	Dynamics
Die Wetterfahne	a → e → d → a	chromaticism	ascending / descending arpeggios, trills, pauses	*f*/*p* contrasts
Der Lindenbaum	E → e → E	chromaticism, alternating V/VI	agitated RH triplets	*f*/*p* contrasts
Rückblick	g	chromaticism	rapid LH / RH alternation	crescendo/diminuendo effects, *sf*'s
Rast	c	chromaticism, German 6th	descending arpeggios, wide leaps	sudden *f*
Frühlingstraum	e → d → g → a	augmented 6ths, Neapolitan	rocking octaves, LH *tremolando*	sudden *f* *ff* arpeggio at end
Einsamkeit	b → dV → chromatic → cV	chromaticism	agitated motion, repeated triplets	crescendo effect
Der stürmische Morgen	d	chromaticism, extended diminished 7ths	angular line, displaced accents, fast arpeggios	*f* → *ff*
Mut	g	minor / major shifts	angular line, accents, fanfares	sustained *f*

stürmische Morgen', and both have extended passages that are unharmonized.[13] After the trudging footsteps alluded to in the first song, 'Gute Nacht', the stormy introduction to 'Die Wetterfahne' is a startling moment in the cycle. The stormy musical language reinforces the idea of the weathervane twisting in the wind as a symbol of the former sweetheart's fickleness, and also reflects the anger and resentment of the traveller as he departs. There is a marked emphasis on the arpeggio figuration in the piano, punctuated by trills and pauses and occasional appoggiaturas, all of which combine to create increased instability (Example 7.6).

The stormy weather that appears in 'Der stürmische Morgen' becomes a reflection of the wanderer's inner turmoil, if not deteriorating mental stability. Here the storm effects again include an angular melodic line in octaves, but now with diminished seventh chords either spread out or as block chords in almost every bar. The displaced accents in bars 14–15 go against the normal accentuation of the text and disrupt the line, and the repeated semiquaver chords marked *ffz* in the piano in bars 16–17 are full of rage and terror (Example 7.7).

Example 7.6   Schubert, *Winterreise*, D. 911, No. 2, 'Die Wetterfahne', bars 0–9

---

[13]   Susan Youens highlights the supernatural significance of unharmonized melodic lines and also observes that both these songs are preceded by 'nocturnal' pieces ('Gute Nacht' and 'Im Dorfe' respectively) which make the contrast all the more violent; see Susan Youens, *Retracing a Winter's Journey*, pp. 105 and 252.

Other songs contain passing references to storms, prompted by the differing emotional states of the wanderer. 'Rückblick' presents the storm as a metaphor for his anger at rejection, with rapid right hand and left hand alternation in the piano, rocking octaves and strong dynamic effects. It is anger rather than pain which is expressed in 'Rast', with a sudden outburst at 'der Sturm half fort mich wehen', containing wide vocal leaps and a German sixth chord. The storm is seen as a metaphor for an obstacle that must be overcome in 'Mut'. There is a kind of grim heroism here (including fanfare references), but it is a false display of resolve.[14] Once more there are angular lines in octaves and strong accents.

In 'Einsamkeit' the traveller declares that stormy emotions are preferable to loneliness and despair, expressed with a rapidly modulating passage and repeated semiquaver triplets (Example 7.8).

Beginning on the dominant of D minor, the harmonies here pass quickly towards B minor (the home key of the song), but the tonic is not achieved, the G major chord at the start of bar 29 being heard as an interrupted progression to VI. The chord now acts as a dominant of C minor (the key of the Neapolitan in B minor), but it is not confirmed by a tonic chord in root position. As the storm abruptly halts and the wanderer contemplates his misery, the dominant pedal is prolonged (now suggesting C major, but still Neapolitan), before its seventh is re-spelled as an E♯ at the end of bar 32, thus creating a German sixth in B minor and a return to the home key. Needless to say, this kind of tonal instability adds to the unsettling effect created by the rapid chord repetitions and big crescendo.

'Frühlingstraum' is essentially a scenic song, the dramatic narrative unfolding over three contrasting sections which are subsequently repeated to create an ABCABC pattern (see Example 7.9).[15] It is one of the few songs of the cycle in a major key, opening with a sentimental lilting melody for the dream of Spring, with hints at birdsong given by trills. The image of course is illusory, and the traveller awakens to be confronted by harsh reality. The music brings this home with more stormy references that depict both the external weather and the traveller's internal turmoil.

Beginning in E minor (not firmly established, as the detached chords are in first inversion), the music in Example 7.9 passes rapidly through D minor and G minor before finishing in A minor. Each phrase is punctuated with a sudden stab of pain using inverted augmented sixth chords and rocking octaves in the right hand, with the final phrase employing a Neapolitan over a *tremolando* bass, and ending with a rising *fortissimo* arpeggio in octaves. The third section presents a further contrast in mood, one which evokes a sense of regret. This succession of dramatic cameos

---

[14]   Youens refers to the 'tempest' key of B♭, used not only here but also in the second half of 'Der Stürmische Morgen', where it stands as the flattened submediant; see Youens, *Retracing a Winter's Journey*, p. 287.

[15]   Youens refers to this song as a 'study in contrast and disjunctions'; see Youens, *Retracing a Winter's Journey*, p. 171.

Example 7.7   Schubert, *Winterreise*, D. 911, No. 18, 'Der stürmische Morgen', bars 13–19

encapsulates the emotional narrative of the entire cycle, moving from love through loss to resignation.

On the surface, 'Der Lindenbaum' is a song of fond reminiscence, interrupted by the storm as a reminder of bitter reality. The gentle breeze rustling through the leaves evoked by the opening triplet figure against static harmony is suggestive of a lullaby, but rather like the brook in the final song of *Die schöne Müllerin*, and the figure of Death in 'Der Tod und das Mädchen', there is a sinister undertone that the peaceful sleep being offered is really death. The tree is therefore a supernatural entity, addressing the traveller directly and attempting to lure him to his doom.[16]

[16]   In rhetorical terms this is an example of *prosopopeia*, where inanimate objects become personified. For a discussion of this and its relationship to *apostrophe*, see Rufus Hallmark,

Example 7.8   Schubert, *Winterreise*, D. 911, No. 12, 'Einsamkeit', bars 28–34

The contrasting stormy section is not just a rude awakening, but a panic attack induced by the realization of a brush with death narrowly avoided (Example 7.10).

The entire passage is built on an alternation between dominant and submediant harmonies in the tonic minor (essentially a prolongation of the dominant), and never settles tonally. The triplet figuration from the opening now takes on a restless ferocity.

***

In considering all of these examples as a group, it is clear that, while Schubert adopts a consistent approach to depicting storms in his songs, there are layers of meaning to be uncovered. We can be sure that his aim was to go beyond naïve word-painting in making use of the dramatic devices of *ombra* and *tempesta*, particularly in *Winterreise*. This was recognized by at least one early reviewer, who praised Schubert's songwriting for going beyond mere pictorialism so that audiences perceived 'higher things in these impressions'.[17] Composers of supernatural operas evidently wanted

---

'The Literary and Musical Rhetoric of Apostrophe in *Winterreise*', *19th-Century Music* 35/1 (2011), pp. 3–33.

[17]   Otto Erich Deutsch, *Schubert: A Documentary Biography*, trans. Eric Blom (London: J. M. Dent, 1946), pp. 758–9.

Example 7.9   Schubert, *Winterreise*, D. 911, No. 11, 'Frühlingstraum', bars 14–26

Example 7.10   Schubert, *Winterreise*, D. 911, No. 5, 'Der Lindenbaum', bars 45–58

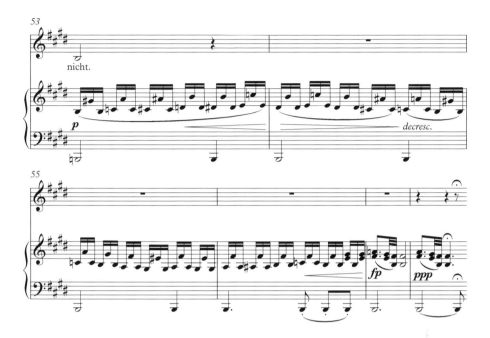

to instil feelings of awe and terror in their audiences, and in the case of Schubert's song cycle *Winterreise* we have the oft-quoted report of Schubert's friend Joseph Spaun that confirms his intention:[18]

> For some time Schubert appeared very upset and melancholy. When I asked him what was troubling him, he would say only, "Soon you will hear and understand". One day he said to me, "Come over to Schober's today, and I will sing you a cycle of horrifying [*schauerlicher*] songs" … We were utterly dumbfounded by the mournful, gloomy tone of these songs …

This account takes on a greater significance when understood in the context of the supernatural references made in this cycle. Schubert himself was very soon to take 'the road from which no-one has returned', and it is impossible to listen to these songs without recalling that.

When Schubert looks to make stormy allusions in his song settings, it is clear that the choices of key, and the inclusion of disruptions to harmony, line, rhythm, texture, and dynamics are all influenced by a long tradition of music written for theatrical storms. The supernatural association added to the frisson audiences could experience when confronted with such discontinuities in the music. Directly

[18]   Otto Erich Deutsch, ed., *Schubert: Memoirs by his Friends*, trans. Rosamund Ley and John Nowell (London: Adam and Charles Black, 1958), pp. 137–8.

influenced by masters of dramatic *tempesta* writing like Gluck, Mozart and Salieri, as well as a host of early Romantic opera composers, Schubert takes this collection of disturbing signifiers and brings them into the more intimate setting of the salon. The absence of actors, staging and special effects presented him with the challenge of creating the drama in the minds of his audience. He understood that stimulating the imagination was the most effective way of engaging the listener, and that the more powerfully this was done, the stronger would be the emotional response. *Tempesta* undoubtedly serves to bring his selected text to life, setting the scene, conveying turmoil and terror, and building the narrative tension, while allowing his audience to participate emotionally in the unfolding drama.

8

Reentering Mozart's Hell: Schubert's 'Gruppe aus dem Tartarus', D. 583

Susan Youens

'Vielfach sind zum Hades die Pfade', heißt ein
Altes Liedchen …

— from 'Erinna an Sappho' by Eduard Mörike[1]

The Backdrop to Schubert's Song

In September 1817, Schubert returned to a poem he had attempted to set a year and a half earlier: Friedrich Schiller's 'Gruppe aus dem Tartarus', or 'Group from Tartarus'. Only one page of the earlier version from March 1816 (D. 396) remains, and one can see why it did not please its creator, its trajectory unclear and the parallel fifths in the bass (Example 8.1) a bit shocking – but maybe in Hell, one can break the rules.[2]

By the next year, however, he was *ready* for Schiller's challenges. 1817 is a 'hinge year' in Schubert's life, a year of astonishing musical growth, impelled in part by his engagement with the poetry of his friend Johann Baptist Mayrhofer (1787–1836), as well as that of Goethe, Schiller, and Matthias Claudius. Any year that sees the creation of the Goethe songs 'Auf dem See', D. 543 and 'Ganymed', D. 544; the immortal 'Die Forelle', D. 550; 'Der Tod und das Mädchen', D. 531,

---

[1] "Many are the paths to Hades", goes the old song'. See Eduard Mörike, *Gedichte* (Stuttgart and Tübingen: J. G. Cotta, 1867, 4th augmented edition), pp. 154–6.

[2] Franz Schubert, *Neue Ausgabe sämtlicher Werke*, Series IV, vol. 2, part b, ed. Walther Dürr (Kassel and Basel: Bärenreiter Verlag, 1975), pp. 271–2. While we are glad he revisited the text the next year for a quite different conception (and eliminated the parallel fifths), we can already see and hear him playing fruitfully with the conventions of 'Hell music' in this preliminary version: the tritone distance from C to G♭ we travel between bar 1 and bar 6, the descending scalewise tritone in the vocal line and piano for bars 9–13 (A♭–D), his signature Neapolitan harmony in bar 4, and the accordion-like relationship between the two hands in the accompaniment to create Schiller's muffled noise. These fourteen bars constitute an ambitious fragment.

Example 8.1   Schubert, first version of 'Gruppe aus dem Tartarus', D. 396 (1816),
                   bars 1–13

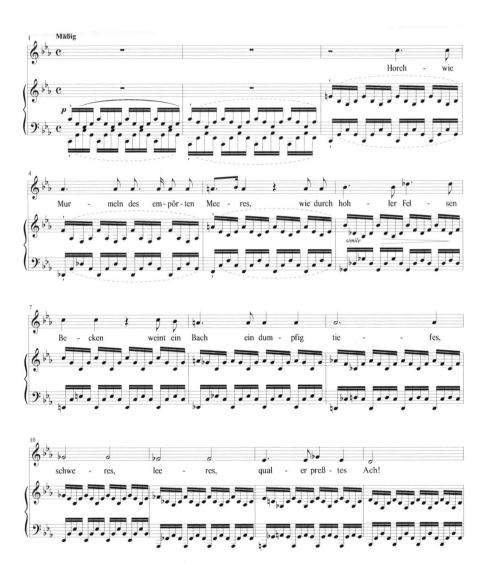

Note: The examples from 'Gruppe aus dem Tartarus' are reproduced with gratitude from
Franz Schubert, *Neue Ausgabe sämtlicher Werke*, Series IV, vol. 2a, ed. Walther Dürr (Kassel
and Basel: Bärenreiter-Verlag, 1975), pp. 13–19.

and much more is golden, whatever his personal difficulties at the time.[3] Schubert had known Schiller's poem since at least 1813, when he set the second stanza for male-voice trio as an exercise for his teacher Antonio Salieri (D. 65), but even such an astonishingly fertile teenage imagination needed a few more years to ripen before he could meet this poem with equivalent musical powers.

For much of my life, I have been interested in speculating about what brings a composer to a particular poem at that time and at that place, and why he (in this instance) treated the poem as he did. Always, the reasons are multiple. There are inevitably what one might call proximal influences, people and events cheek-by-jowl with the composer and steering him in certain directions. Beginning in autumn 1816, Schubert had decided not to work any longer at his father's school, where he had taught since 1814, and had moved in with his friend Franz von Schober as a guest in the wealthier student's lodgings, where he devoted himself to composition. The famous statement to Ferdinand Hiller (1811–1885) in 1827, 'I compose every morning, and when one piece is done, I begin another', was already a rule of thumb in the composer's late teens.[4] In February or March of 1817, Schober introduced Schubert to an older singer the composer had long admired, the patrician baritone Johann Michael Vogl (1768–1840), and a famous collaboration began. Vogl was well known for his roles in Christoph Willibald Gluck's operas on mythological subjects, and Schubert's *Antiken-Lieder*, or 'songs of antiquity', especially those with dramatic properties, suited him superbly; Vogl's personal love of classical literature – his favourite writer was Marcus Aurelius – would have made an impression on Schubert, who heard him in 1813 as Orestes in Gluck's *Iphigénie en Tauride* and was bowled over by the experience.[5] And there was another friendly force impelling Schubert towards the glory that was Greece and the grandeur that was Rome: the friendship with Mayrhofer, who Brahms called 'the most serious' ('ernsthafteste') of all Schubert's circle.[6] Mayrhofer was a leader in the *Bildungs-Kreis* or 'self-cultivation' circle of Schubert's friends, who met to

[3]   Elizabeth Norman McKay, in *Franz Schubert: A Biography* (Oxford: Clarendon Press, 1996), p. 65, points out that Schubert's response to such disappointments as the failed application to be a music master in Laibach, with marriage to Therese Grob therefore out of the question, was a renewed burst of creativity.

[4]   See Otto Erich Deutsch, *Schubert – Die Erinnerungen seiner Freunde*, 4th edn (Leipzig: Breitkopf & Härtel, 1957), pp. 324–5.

[5]   See Otto Erich Deutsch, *Schubert – Die Dokumente seines Lebens* (Kassel and Basel: Bärenreiter, 1964), p. 26, for the information that Theodor Körner and Schubert attended a performance of *Iphigenie auf Tauris* and that Schubert was enthralled by Vogl's performance, and p. 51 for information about Vogl and his great cultivation.

[6]   Max Kalbeck, *Johannes Brahms* (Vienna and Leipzig, 1904), vol. 1, p. 230. The quotation comes from a letter written in 1887: 'The true successor to Beethoven is not Mendelssohn, whose artistic cultivation was quite incomparable, also not Schumann, but Schubert. It is unbelievable, the music he put in his songs. No composer understands proper declamation

discuss literature and ideas and even brought out yearbooks in 1817 and 1818;[7] it was this erudite, pathologically depressed older man who fostered Schubert's turn to *Antiken-Lieder*, perhaps explaining to the young genius he loved the backdrop to Goethe's and Schiller's classicizing poems. It had been his family's wish that he enter the priesthood at St Florian's, but a psychologically scarred Mayrhofer left the novitiate with a permanent anti-clerical bent and thereafter took his cue from Plato and the Stoics; he and Schiller shared certain radical political ideals concerning the nexus of freedom, duty, and virtue, as did Schubert in his youth.[8] Given this backdrop, it is no wonder that Schubert went to classical Hell four times in the space of a year and a half: March 1816 saw the first setting of 'Gruppe aus dem Tartarus'; six months later, in September 1816, he set Johann Georg Jacobi's 'Lied des Orpheus (als er in die Hölle ging)', D. 474; in January 1817, he made something magnificent out of Mayrhofer's 'Fahrt zum Hades', 'Journey to Hades', and nine months after that, he would once again tackle Schiller's 'Gruppe'.

I wish I could have eavesdropped on the discussions at the *Bildungs-Kreis*. We know that Schiller was important to them, especially when his model of aesthetic activity independent of and nobler than mundane work replaced their earlier pursuit of action, *Tätigkeit*, in the world: Schubert's thirty-three Schiller songs between 1811 and 1817 are a testament to his high position in their universe. I wonder whether any of the young men read Joseph Schreyvogel's 1810 book, *Friedrich Schiller: Eine Biografie und Anleitung zum Verständnis seiner Schriften (Friedrich Schiller: A Biography and Guide to Understanding his Writings)*, an attempt by a friend to explain Schiller to the Viennese.[9] The Viennese-born Schreyvogel had come to know Schiller in Jena from 1794 to 1797 and had worked with the great dramatist on his periodical *Thalia* before becoming the director of Vienna's Burgtheater. Schreyvogel argues at some length against the prevalent notion that Schiller was anti-religious, this in the wake of the famous 1788 dust-

as he did … Of his friends, Mayrhofer was the most serious, and Schubert is surely not to be reproached for setting all sorts of mythological poems [by Mayrhofer] to music'.

[7] See David Gramit, *The Intellectual and Aesthetic Tenets of Franz Schubert's Circle* (PhD dissertation, Duke University, 1987), pp. 50–52; Gramit observes that the Dioscurii of Goethe and Schiller were the most admired literary models for the circle.

[8] For more on Mayrhofer, see Ilija Dürhammer, *Schuberts literarische Heimat: Dichtung und Literaturrezeption der Schubert-Freunde* (Vienna: Böhlau, 1999), pp. 91–7, pp. 221–34, and Susan Youens, *Schubert's Poets and the Making of Lieder* (Cambridge: Cambridge University Press, 1996), pp. 151–227.

[9] Joseph Schreyvogel, *Friedrich Schiller: Eine Biografie und Anleitung zum Verständnis seiner Schriften* (Bremen: Europäischer Hochschulverlag, 2010) (reprint of *Biographie Schiller's und Anleitung zur Critic seiner Werke* [Vienna and Leipzig: Cath. Gräffer and Heinrich Gräff, 1810], pp. 20–21. There is no mention of this work that I have been able to find in the extant Schubert documentation, but the possibility of someone in the *Bildungs-Kreis* finding and reading it still exists.

up about Schiller's 'blasphemy' in 'Die Götter Griechenlands', 'The Greek Gods' (Schubert would set a brief extract from this long poem to utterly haunting music in November 1819). 'When the gods were more human, human beings were more divine', Schiller wrote in the initial version of this work, which tended to confirm already existing speculation about his non-belief; his assertion that state-sanctioned monotheism represented a gigantic step backward in the history of human imagination aroused a firestorm of criticism.[10] Friedrich Leopold zu Stolberg-Stolberg, the poet of Schubert's 'Auf dem Wasser zu singen', waxed wroth about this poem, thereby incurring Gottfried August Bürger's capsule damnation of him for 'feeble-mindedness' ('Schwachsinnigkeit'); the literal-minded pious poet did not understand that for Schiller, gods are metaphors at best, political tools of enslavement at worst.[11] The gods of ancient Greece were to him as imaginary as the gods of newer religions but less dishonest and despotic in their instrumentality. For him, virtue was all, and the pathway from naïve virtue led through coerced virtue (religion) to the ultimate goal of virtue born of ennobled reason and free will.[12] In his tiny dialogue-poem 'Mein Glaube' ('My Belief') of 1796, Schiller taunted a reading public that had demonstrated an unhealthy interest in his views ever since the controversy: 'Which religion do I practice? None of all of these / That you suggest to me! "And why no religion?" It's my religion'.[13] 'Portrayals of Heaven and Hell', he wrote, 'are in the end only portrayals from the imagination, riddles without resolution, visions of terror and enticements from beyond'.[14] For a

---

[10]   Friedrich Schiller, lines 191–192, 'Da die Götter menschlicher noch waren, / Waren Menschen göttlicher' in the original version of 'Die Götter Griechenlands'; see *Schillers Werke*, vol. 1 (Weimar: Hermann Böhlaus Nachfolger, 1992), p. 195.

[11]   Jeffrey High, in 'Friedrich Schiller, Secular Virtue, and "The Gods of Ancient Greece" (1788)', in *Enlightenment and Secularism: Essays on the Mobilization of Reason*, ed. Christopher Nadon (Lanham, MD: Lexington Books, 2013), pp. 317–18, discusses Friedrich von Stolberg's accusations of blasphemy.

[12]   Schiller was already writing about virtue in 1779, with his 'Die Tugend in ihren Folgen'; see Friedrich Schiller, *Sämtliche Werke: Philosophische Schriften* (Berlin: Aufbau-Verlag, 2005), pp. 32–9. He would wrestle with this question of what constitutes virtue his entire life, including in dramas such as *Wilhelm Tell*.

[13]   Schiller's epigram 'Mein Glaube' from the *Musenalmanach für das Jahr 1797* in *Schillers Werke*, vol. 1, p. 296. 'Welche Religion ich bekenne? Keine von allen, / Die du mir nennst! "Und warum keine?" Aus Religion'. In his childhood and youth, he was, like his family, pious in Pietist fashion, but underwent a metaphysical crisis towards the end of the 1770s. Cordula Burtscher traces the stages of his disillusionment in *Glaube und Furcht: Religion und Religionskritik bei Schiller* (Würzburg: Königshausen & Neumann, 2014); see in particular, 'Wer glaubt, der fürchtet: Schillers Kritik religiöser Angstvisionen in den 1780er Jahren', pp. 99–123.

[14]   *Schillers Werke*, vol. 20 (Weimar: Hermann Böhlaus Nachfolger, 1963), , p. 91. 'Gemälde von Himmel und Hölle … – und doch sind es nur Gemälde der Phantasie, Räthsel ohne Auflösung, Schreckbilder und Lockungen aus der Ferne'.

Schubert already tending to anti-clericalism and differences with his pious father's religious strictures, Schiller's merger of punitive ancient Greek terror and punitive Christian terror in 'Gruppe aus dem Tartarus' might well have appealed on those grounds alone.

Schiller's Poem

The genesis of this poem (see Figure 8.1), written in 1780 when Schiller was only twenty-one years old, was entangled with the creation of his first drama, *Die Räuber*, (*The Robbers*), which made 'Schiller' a name to reckon with from that day forward. Extremes of expression mark both works.[15]

Schiller probably took his cue from Book VI of the *Aeneid*, as the Sibyl leads Aeneas into the Underworld that he might search for his father Anchises. Along the way to the Elysian Fields, he passes by Tartarus, ablaze with flame and horrific noise; the Sibyl explains that the tortured souls within are those who tried to rival the gods.[16] Aeneas goes on a much longer journey, one crowded with incident and with names, whereas Schiller compresses one small slice of the Roman account into two quatrains and a sestet.

In this poem, we are in Tartarus from start to finish, and there are no individuals except the readers of this work, which terrifies in short order. Schiller makes the reader into, first, an observer, someone enjoined by the unnamed speaker to 'Hark', 'Listen' (an imperative with *teeth*). By the end, each of us sees through the eyes of an amorphous conglomerate of souls; we become one of them, and that is not a comforting experience. In early Greek concepts of the soul, the psyche leaves the body at the moment of death and begins its afterlife, in which it appears as an *eidolon*, a shadow- or spirit-image of the person.[17] The *eidola* of 'Gruppe' are in

[15]   Schiller was capable of ironizing his own creative process at this period when he was so fascinated by patriarchal violence in *The Robbers*. First, he was 'stampfend und tobend'; then, delighted with his creations, he would 'schwelgen und leiden' along with them; and, finally, would draw back to a cooler distance to assess the effects of his 'tiefe Erfahrung des radikalien-Bösen'. See Emil Staiger, *Friedrich Schiller* (Zurich: Atlantis Verlag, 1967), p. 120.

[16]   See Virgil, *Aeneid Book VI: A New Verse Translation*, trans. Seamus Heaney (New York: Farrar, Straus and Giroux, 2016), pp. 56–9. 'Aeneas suddenly looks back and sees / A broad-based fortress under a cliff to the left, / Set behind three rings of wall, encircled / By a hurtling torrent, a surge and rush of flame, / Rock-rumbling, thunder-flowing Phlegethon, the fiery / Bourne of Tartarus. A gate rears up in front, / Flanked by pillars of solid adamant, so massive / No human force, nor even the sky-gods' squadrons / Could dislodge them'.

[17]   See Jan Bremmer, *The Early Greek Concept of the Soul* (Princeton, NJ: Princeton University Press, 1983), especially Chapter 3, 'The Soul of the Dead', pp. 70–124; Christiane Sourvinou-Inwood, 'To Die and Enter the House of Hades: Homer, Before and After' in *Mirrors of Mortality: Studies in the Social History of Death* (London: Palgrave Macmillan,

Gruppe aus dem Tartarus	Group from Tartarus
Horch – wie Murmeln des empörten Meeres,	Hark – like the murmuring of the angry sea,
Wie durch hohler Felsen Becken weint ein Bach,	Like a brook weeping through hollow, rocky
Stöhnt dort dumpfigtief ein schweres, leeres	gullies, you can hear over there, deeply muffled,
Qualerpreßtes Ach!	a heavy toneless groan, extracted with torment!
Schmerz verzerret	Pain contorts
Ihr Gesicht, Verzweiflung sperret	their faces, despair opens
Ihren Rachen fluchend auf.	their jaws with curses.
Hohl sind ihre Augen, ihre Blicke	Hollow are their eyes: their gaze
Spähen bang nach des Cocytus Brücke,	Peers anxiously back at Cocytus's bridge,
Folgen thränend seinem Trauerlauf.	Following tearfully its sad course.
Fragen sich einander ängstlich leise,	They ask one another softly, fearfully,
Ob noch nicht Vollendung sei!	whether the end is nigh!
Ewigkeit schwingt über ihnen Kreise,	Eternity whirls above them in circles,
Bricht die Sense des Saturns entzwei.	breaking Saturn's scythe in two.

Figure 8.1   Friedrich Schiller, 'Gruppe aus dem Tartarus' (1780), text with translation

Source: Friedrich Schiller, 'Gruppe aus dem Tartarus' ('Group from Tartarus'), in *Schillers Werke*, vol. 1, ed. Julius Petersen and Friedrich Beißner (Weimar: Hermann Böhlaus Nachfolger, 1992), p. 109, translation mine.

the worst of all possible places: Tartarus, the lowest realm of Hades and a place of eternal torment; it was, according to Hesiod, encircled by a great bronze wall and contained an abyss where one could fall for a year and not reach the bottom.[18] The anguished shades look back at the bridge over the Cocytus River, 'the river of wailing', one of five rivers encircling Hades and here, the unsuccessful last chance to escape eternal punishment. In his *Paradise Lost*, Milton invokes 'Cocytus, named of lamentation loud, / Heard on the rueful stream', and we hear that 'lamentation

---

1981), pp. 15–39; and Lars Albinus, *The House of Hades: Studies in Ancient Greek Eschatology* (Langelandsgade: Aarhus University Press, 2000), especially the discussion of 'psyche' in pp. 43–56.

[18] Hesiod, *Theogony. Works and Days. Shield*, 2nd edn, trans. Apostolos N. Athanassakis (Baltimore and London: The Johns Hopkins University Press, 2004), p. 29. 'Tartaros is fenced with bronze and round its gullet / drifts night in triple array, while above it grow / the roots of the earth and of the barren sea ... There, in proper order, lie the sources and the limits / of the black earth and of mist-wrapped Tartaros, / of the barren sea, too, and of the starry sky – / grim and dank and loathed even by the gods – / this chasm is so great that, once past the gates, / one does not reach the bottom in a full year's course, / but is tossed about by stormy gales; / even the gods shudder at this eerie place'.

loud' in Schiller's words and Schubert's song, in which suffering is turned into sound.[19] At the end, Schiller sets Eternity in dizzying motion overhead, then leaves us with the final image of Saturn's scythe broken by a stronger power. Now, not even the Gods have power to stop the torments of Tartarus. Saturn, we remember, began with the Greek Titan Kronos, who was sealed deep in the pit of Tartarus by Zeus in the wake of the Titanomachy, or battle between the gods and the Titans.[20] His emblematic scythe comes from his early association with agriculture, hence the Saturnalia festivals, but there is also the scythe wielded by the Grim Reaper of Christian folklore, this sort of Greco-Christian merger a hallmark of Schiller's re-imagining of antiquity.[21] In this one terse work, Schiller, his youthful ambitions immense, takes on Time and Death and eternal punishment. 'Fear is the spirit of all worship', he once wrote, and this vision of tortured souls is fearsome indeed.[22] That Schubert was drawn to poems about death well before his own death-sentence from disease is part of the Viennese culture of the day,[23] and he had a special affinity for poems that tell of the moment of death and the transition to the afterlife (for example, 'Der Tod und das Mädchen', composed some six months earlier in February 1817).

This poem is a *ne plus ultra* specimen of rhythmic-metric intricacies and verbal sound deployed to heighten terror and awe. The former's complexities might give even the most experienced composer headaches, and was, one guesses, implicated in Schubert's abandonment of the earlier version. Each line of the first quatrain is rhythmically different, the poem beginning in the strongest possible way with a monosyllabic imperative, followed by the dash that indicates a break in the thought and the passage of a brief instant of time in which one draws breath for whatever comes after the command. Here, it is a twofold analogy that proceeds in reverse order: anthropomorphized comparatives first (like the murmuring of the angry sea, like a

---

[19]   John Milton, *Paradise Lost*, Book 2, in *The Riverside Milton*, ed. Roy Flannagan (Boston and New York: Houghton Mifflin, 1998), p. 398.

[20]   See Giuseppe Pucci, 'Roman Saturn: The Shady Side' in *Saturn: From Antiquity to the Renaissance*, ed. Massimo Ciavolella and Amilcare A. Iannucci (Ottawa, Canada: Dovehouse Editions, Inc., 1992), pp. 37–49.

[21]   See Kurt Berger, 'Schiller und die Mythologie. Zur Frage der Begegnung und Auseinandersetzung zwischen christlicher und antiker Tradition in der klassischen Dichtung' in *Deutsche Vierteljahrschrift*, vol. 26 (1952), pp. 178–224; Wolfgang Schadewaldt, 'Der Weg Schillers zu den Griechen' in *Jahrbuch der Deutschen Schiller-Gesellschaft*, vol. 4 (1960), pp. 90–97; and Gerhard Storz, 'Schiller und die Antike', *Jahrbuch der Deutschen Schiller-Gesellschaft*, vol. 10 (1966), pp. 189–204.

[22]   Friedrich Schiller, 'Über die ästhetische Erziehung des Menschen: Vierundzwanzigster Brief', in *Sämtliche Werke: Philosophische Schriften*, p. 389: 'Der Geist seiner Gottesverehrung ist also Furcht, die ihn erniedrigt, nicht Ehrfurcht, die ihn in seiner eigenen Schätzung erhebt'.

[23]   See Hilde Schmölzer, *A schöne Leich: Der Wiener und sein Tod* (Vienna: Verlag Kremayr & Scheriau, 1980).

brook weeping through hollow, rocky gullies), identification last (a heavy, toneless groan). The initial analogy is couched in iambic tetrameters (wie *Mur*-meln des em-*pör*-ten *Meer*-es), with the preposition 'des' less accented than the other strong beats and the alliterative 'm's a significant factor in Schiller's verbal music. The second analogy consumes the entire second line in trochaic hexameters that halt abruptly at the final accented syllable, 'Bach'; one notes as well the concentration of two-syllable words in mid-line (hohler Felsen Becken) surrounded by terse, monosyllabic words on either side. The third and fourth lines are one statement but are disposed across two lines, I would guess in order to divide line three into two different sound-worlds and to bring us up short on the exclamation 'Ach!' in line four.[24] The enjambment from line three to line four is brilliant poetic ingenuity at work; if music cancels out such enjambed effects dependent on the *sight* of a poetic structure, Schubert makes his awareness of it apparent when he rises up the scale for the first two adjectives and then sustains the third ('*Qual*-erpreßtes') longer – and one notes as well the assonance of 'Qual-' and 'Ach'. The first sound-world in line three is a mouthful of percussive, obstructive 't's and 'd's, with dark vowels and diphthongs but ending with a piercingly bright 'ie': 'Stöhnt dort dumpfigtief'. The second sound-world is one both of liquefaction (the 's's and 'l' sounds) and panting, gasping panic, the end of the line fragmented as the rhyming adjectives 'schweres, leeres'. We instinctively emphasize the first syllable of each of those words when we declaim the poem, as I like to think Schubert must have done before setting to work on both versions.

And the rhythmic intricacies and attention to the sonic properties of words continue into the middle verse, a sestet that begins with a chopped-short line of trochaic dimeters enjambed with the second line; in one short poem in fourteen lines (a sonnet with a difference), we reel in horror between dimeters, hexameters, and almost everything in between. The percussive sizzle of the consonants 's' and 'z' in 'Schmerz verzerret / Ihr Gesicht, Verzweiflung sperret' punctuates the agony invoked here, and the doubled mournfulness of 'thränend' and 'Trauerlauf' in the final line of stanza 2 displays yet the poetic effect of alliteration. Nor do I find it coincidental that throughout the final quatrain, the diphthong 'ei' resounds over and over: 'einander', 'leise', 'sei', '[Ewig-]keit', 'Kreise', 'entzwei'. The final sound is 'ei'. One thinks of the ending of *Die schöne Müllerin* – 'Und der Himmel da oben, wie ist er so weit!' – and realizes that the same signification of opening out to infinity is at work here … but not as consolation. Quite the opposite.

[24]   Those scholars who examine Lieder are becoming newly aware of the sonic properties of poetry and how they interact with music. The theorist Stephen Rodgers, for example, is working on a book entitled *Song and the Music of Poetry* (in English-language verse), and Lorraine Byrne Bodley, in 'Reception and Transformation in "Der Musensohn"', in *Rethinking Schubert*, ed. Lorraine Byrne Bodley and Julian Horton (Oxford: Oxford University Press, 2016), p. 445, invokes Goethe's *Sprachmusik*: 'The poet's [she is speaking of Goethe] continual involvement with music manifests itself not only in the *Sprachmusik* or euphony of his verse, but also in the figures he portrays, Goethe's *Musensohn* and Harper being key examples'.

Schubert and 'Hell Music'

By the final version, Schubert was capable of responding to these verbal sonorities and rhythms with virtuosity from his own realm of music. The sound of the first word, 'Horch', beginning with an exhaled '-h' and ending with a whoosh, is an open invitation to composers to create music we *must hear*, and Schubert responds by placing that first pitch (D in the lower register) on the downbeat and sustaining it for half a bar of 12/8 metre; we hear the grating dissonance with the E♭ of the rising chromatic scale as the expelled breath lingers. Hypnotic chanting on that same pitch D for the first two of four iambs that follow the directive ('wie Murmeln des em-[pörten Meeres]') bespeaks the horrified fixed gaze, the persona frozen on the spot in order to listen more attentively. To tell us just how angry the metaphorical ocean waters are, Schubert 'gooses' the adjective 'em-PÖR-ten' so that it rises abruptly on the off-beat (a perfect example of *saltus duriusculus*, or 'harsh leap', of which more to come shortly), followed by a smaller appoggiatura 'heave' for 'Meeres', with similar gestures for 'weint' and 'Bach' in the next line of the stanza. At the third line, Schubert clearly saw that 'Stöhnt' and 'dort' command equal weight as two monosyllables dominated by the alliterative consonants 't' and 'd', and dark vowels; notice the crotchet rest that separates 'dort' from 'dumpfigtief', making both the final 't' of 'dort' and the initial 'd' of 'dumpfigtief' more emphatic. That the composer magnifies the rhyming, alliterative adjectives 'schweres, leeres' by directing the singer to take breaths (crotchet rests) after each one, imitative of gasping in fear, is another example of musical prosody as a brilliant interpretive reaction to the poet's linguistic derring-do (Example 8.2). Other instances of marvellous responses to Schiller's sounds and rhythms are discussed later in connection with the chromatic gestures one finds everywhere in Schubert's setting.

Both this setting and the 1816 draft, like earlier passages in his ballads 'Leichenfantasie' (to a poem by Schiller) and 'Der Vatermörder', are essays in what is called *ombra* music: music of the dark shadows where demons, furies, and malevolent deities lurk; music 'of an eerie, gothic cast', in John Gingerich's words.[25] Given the Viennese love for such scenes in opera and ballet, *ombra* style is everywhere in the late eighteenth and early nineteenth centuries. When you hear dark and brooding minor keys, angular melodic lines, incessant dotted rhythms, abundant use of dissonance, tonal indeterminacy, pervasive chromaticism, pedal

---

[25]   John M. Gingerich, *Schubert's Beethoven Project* (Cambridge: Cambridge University Press, 2014), p. 165 (in reference to the Andante of Schubert's Octet, D. 803). See also Clive McClelland, *Ombra: Supernatural Music in the Eighteenth Century* (Lanham, MD: Lexington Books, 2012); Birgitte Moyer, 'Ombra and fantasia in late eighteenth-century theory and practice', in *Convention in Eighteenth- and Nineteenth-Century Music: Essays in Honor of Leonard G. Ratner*, ed. Wye Allanbrook and Janet M. Levy (New York: Pendragon Press, 1992), pp. 283–306; and Michael Spitzer, 'Mapping the Human Heart: A Holistic Analysis of Fear in Schubert', in *Music Analysis* 28 (2010), pp. 149–213.

Example 8.2   Schubert, final version of 'Gruppe aus dem Tartarus', D. 583 (1817),
                     bars 7–21, vocal line

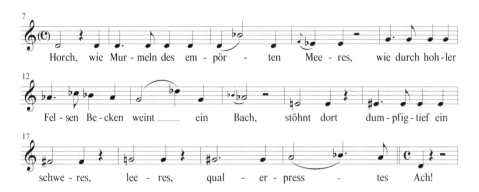

points and ostinatos, tremolos galore, and disjunct harmonies and bass lines, you
are probably in Hell, and the most famous example by far is the title character's
damnation in the Act II finale of Mozart's *Don Giovanni*. That Schubert revered
Mozart we know from his 14 June 1816 encomium in his diary after hearing one
of the great string quintets:[26] 'O Mozart, immortal Mozart, how many, oh how
endlessly many such comforting perceptions of a brighter and better life hast thou
brought to our souls!', he wrote, but he also availed himself of Mozart's *power*.[27]
That power is always there, beneath the most elegant and enchanting of Mozart's
surfaces, but at times, this most graceful of composers allows violent forces to roar
out into the open and overwhelm us – although, as Joe Davies has pointed out,
Mozart seeks eventual resolution whereas Schubert's violence is transgressive,
breaking all boundaries.[28] The Don and the damned beings impelled to their eternal
doom in Schiller's poem are all making a 'harsh passage' against their will; perhaps
this is why both Mozart and Schubert resort to their own versions of what earlier
composition treatises called the *passus duriusculus*, that is, a string of ascending or
descending semitones; 'duriusculus' means 'hard' or 'harsh', while 'passus' means

[26]   For a supremely thoughtful approach to the Schubert-Mozart nexus, see Susan
Wollenberg, *Schubert's Fingerprints: Studies in the Instrumental Works* (Farnham: Ashgate,
2011), Chapter 5, 'Schubert and Mozart', pp. 133–59.

[27]   Otto Erich Deutsch, *Schubert. Die Dokumente seines Lebens*, p. 43.

[28]   My thanks to Joe Davies for this insight in a personal communication. Scott Burnham, in
his enchanting book *Mozart's Grace* (Princeton and Oxford: Princeton University Press, 2013),
makes this same point in his second chapter, 'Thresholds: Summoning the Supernatural and
the Sacred'. He starts by examining the Commendatore's death in Act I, invoking as contrast
the very beginning of the opera's overture; bars 1–4 are, he rightly observes, 'one of the great
shockers of the Viennese Classical era' (p. 40).

'step' or 'passage'. This is not a term from rhetoric but a descriptive name for a musical device designed to stir the listener's emotions.[29] The Thuringian theorist, astronomer and composer Sethus Calvisius (originally Seth Kalwitz, 1556–1615) wrote in 1592 that chromatic scales are most apt 'wann man eine traurig Music machen will' ('when one wishes to create sad music').[30] Sixty years later, Christoph Bernhard (1628–1692), a pupil of the great Heinrich Schütz, invented the term *passus duriusculus* for such 'traurig Musik' in his *Tractatus compositionis augmentatus* of 1657, discussed in tandem with the *saltus duriusculus*, or 'harsh leap' (the tritone leap G–D♭ we hear at the verb 'weint' in bar 13 of 'Gruppe' and thereafter is a perfect example) and the *cadentia duriuscula*.[31] Anyone who listens to the Don's Damnation and 'Gruppe aus dem Tartarus' can hear that both are rife with chromatic scalar passages, especially rising scales, and the manner of their usage is breathtaking in Mozart and Schubert alike.

I doubt that Schubert ever came across a copy of Bernhard's treatise, and my delight in the appropriateness of Bernhard's term 'harsh steps' or 'harsh passage' – possibly his own invention, not taken from prior books on rhetoric – to Schubert's mammoth Schiller song is therefore ahistorical (if still enjoyable). But Schubert had musical antecedents, in addition to Mozart's Damnation Scene, to provide him with models we can be assured he knew, models that provided a challenge: that of devising original treatments of this traditional figure. For example, the 'Dance of the Furies' in Gluck's ballet *Don Juan, ou Le festin de pierre*, Wq. 52, recycled in the 1774 opera *Orfeo ed Euridice* and reappearing in the Viennese version performed in 1762, ends with a brilliant instance of the sort of chromaticism-upon or within-chromaticism that is my particular interest in this chapter, the effect all the more 'frightful' because of the alternating weak-beat *forte* accents and the succeeding *piano* dynamics; those *piano–forte* dynamics project the F♯ and E diminished seventh chords in bars 106–107 which serve the harmonic sequence (Example 8.3).[32] As this excerpt shows, the descending chromaticism in the bass is even echoed at the intervals of the diminished third and minor third (Schubert

[29]   Dietrich Bartel makes this point in *Musica Poetica: Musical-Rhetorical Figures in German Baroque Music* (Lincoln and London: University of Nebraska Press, 1997), the discussion of the *passus duriusculus* on pp. 357–8.

[30]   Sethus Calvisius, *Melopoiia sive melodiae condendae ratio* (Erfurt, 1592 and 1630).

[31]   Christoph Bernhard, *Tractatus compositionis augmentatus* (c. 1657), p. 77: 'Passus duriusculus, einer Stimmen gegen sich selbst, ist, wenn eine Stimme ein Semitonium minus steiget oder fället. Welcherley Gänge einige für chromatische Art Sätze gehalften, mit was vor Gründe aber, solches mögen sie ausfechten' ['Passus duriusculus within one voice occurs when a voice rises or falls a minor semitone. These progressions some have held as chromatic ones, the reasons for which they can fight out among themselves'].

[32]   See Christoph Willibald Gluck, *Orfeo ed Euridice (Wiener Fassung von 1762). Azione teatrale per musica in drei Akten von Raniero de' Calzabigi*, ed. Anna Amalie Abert and Ludwig Finscher (Kassel and Basel: Bärenreiter, 1963), p. 66.

Example 8.3   Christoph Willibald Gluck, *Orfeo ed Euridice* (Viennese version, 1762), bars 100–110, strings only

Note: This example is based with permission on Christoph Willibald Gluck: *Orfeo ed Euridice* (*Orpheus und Eurydike*), Azione teatrale per musica in drei Akten (Wiener Fassung von 1762), ed. Anna Amalie Abert and Ludwig Finscher – BA 2294 © Bärenreiter-Verlag Karl Vötterle GmbH & Co. KG, Kassel, p. 66.

will do something similar in 'Gruppe'). One notes as well the bracketed ascending minor seconds emphasized loudly within that bass line.

What a vivid passage this is! In addition to all that descending linear chromaticism (bracketed in the violin parts), we hear a sequence of major triads in bars 106–109 (Ab–G–F–Eb) and a bassline that descends an evocative diminished seventh (Ab–G–F–Eb–D–C–B♮). Hell, eternal pain, lords of the Underworld or Satan: it was all readily to hand when Schubert put the ascending and descending *passus duriusculus* to work in 'Gruppe', and he would never forget this tradition, never cease putting it to use in new contexts. More than a decade later, when he bade the piano hammer the ascending line A–A♯–B–C–C♯–C×–D♯ as the singer confronts his ghostly double in 'Der Doppelgänger' ('… meine eig'ne Gestalt. / Du Doppelgänger, du bleicher Geselle! / was äffst du nach mein Liebesleid'), I wonder whether he might not have recalled the earlier hellish suffering wrought to the young Schiller's words.[33]

[33] Peter Williams, in his superb study of *The Chromatic Fourth during Four Centuries of Music* (Oxford: Clarendon Press, 1997), p. 172, takes note of this massive instance of what I have called a *passus duriusculus*. He also points to Bach's frequent recourse to this device, including the sixth movement from Cantata BWV 40, *Darzu ist erschienen der Sohn Gottes*, with its evocation of the old serpent ['Satan'] (p. 78), and to 'ornamental' and 'essential' tracing of the chromatic fourth in bars 51–55 of Haydn's 'Vorstellung des Chaos' from *Die Schöpfung* (pp. 124–5).

In Schubert's 1817 final setting of 'Gruppe', *ombra* characteristics are everywhere regnant. At the upper level of both the left and right-hand parts, there is a bone-rattling ostinato on C – the herald of 'Ewigkeit' ('Eternity'), symbolized by C – while the lower level is an incomplete chromatic scale leading to prolonged emphasis on the dominant seventh of D♭ (or, potentially at least, Schubert's favourite German sixth chord) in bar 3. We expect resolution to D♭, but instead, we have the start of yet another chromatic ascent beginning on C♯. That enharmonic respelling and change of direction from the flat side to the sharp side on display here is, although we cannot know it as yet, a first foreshadowing of what happens in the final section; that it belongs to Schubert's musical symbolism of Life and Death as contained within one another, two sides of existence's coin, is on display eight years later in 'Todtengräbers Heimwehe', D. 842, from April 1825, whose gravedigger stands on the brink of the grave and can already see into the afterlife. 'Gruppe aus dem Tartarus' thus begins an almost prototypical, textbook specimen of a chromatically ascending 5–6 sequence, one we can hear in this context as an almost physical manifestation of rising angst and terror. Repeating the same asymmetrical three-bar pattern[34] – and we remember that in every cosmology, Hell is endless repetition of pain, or perhaps a pain/pleasure dialectic, evident in music that disturbs and entices in equal measure[35]– we rise to V⁷ of D in bar 6, and the next segment (yet another transposed repetition) brings us the singer, who has been listening to these sounds all the while – the obsessive accompaniment foreshadows another *Schauerlied*, 'Der Zwerg' – and who enters *in medias res*. Utmost pattern, rigid architecture, combines with utmost instability in Dante-esque fashion (Example 8.4).

Yet another chromatic ascent brings us to V⁷ of E♭ at bar 9, and here, things change, with a full resolution to E♭ major – the first triad, the first major chord – in the following bar. The subsequent E♭ pedal lasts for five bars, filled out by E♭ minor ninth chords and second-inversion A♭ minor harmonies; given the emphasis on D provided by the singer's entrance on that pitch, pointing to D minor as an eventual tonic, we can hear the E♭ as another Schubertian signature hallmark: the Neapolitan (Example 8.5) (and know that the D minor of Mozart's Requiem is associated with death in Schubert's mind: he uses it for 'Der Tod und das Mädchen',

---

[34] The vocal ending of the third three-bar passage in these ascending sequences (bar 10) is elided with the beginning of a new phrase in the piano; the singer joins it *in medias res* at bar 12 (the musical analogy to one structure forced inside another?). Not until bar 15 ('Stöhnt dort') do the voice and piano 'line up' with one another for an extended, also asymmetrical seven-bar phrase. Only with the Allegro second section of this song is there any quadratic phrasing to be found (bars 22–25, over piano figuration that began on the downbeat of bar 21 … more layering), with asymmetry returning almost immediately: the words 'Verzweiflung sperret ihren Rachen fluchend auf' (bars 26–30) extend the agony over five bars. Tartarus is where everything is distorted by torment.

[35] My thanks to Joe Davies for the latter suggestion in a personal communication.

Example 8.4   Schubert, 'Gruppe aus dem Tartarus', D. 583, bars 1–10

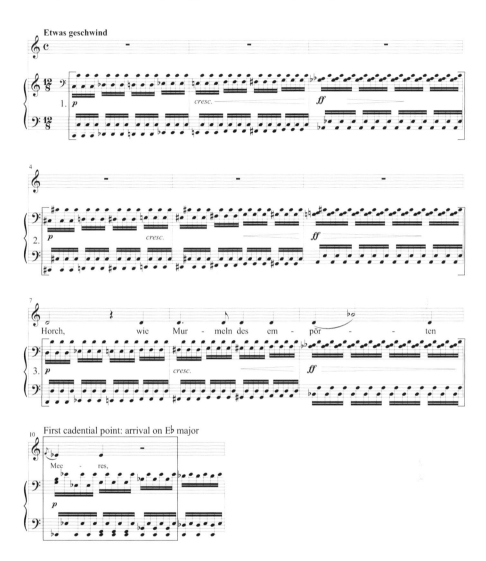

'Fahrt zum Hades', 'Freiwilliges Versinken', and 'Der König in Thule', among others). For the duration of the E♭ pedal, instead of the *passus duriusculus*, we now traverse different, often incomplete versions of these chords in the same pseudo-tremolo rhythmic disposition. Not until we are past the poet's 'wie' clauses (an analogy that diminishes, we note, from oceanic immensity to a narrower brook) does the *passus duriusculus* invade the vocal line and the harmonic rhythm quicken ominously. From the previous sustained E♭, the enharmonic respelling of A♭ as

Example 8.5   Schubert, 'Gruppe aus dem Tartarus', D. 583, bars 10–14

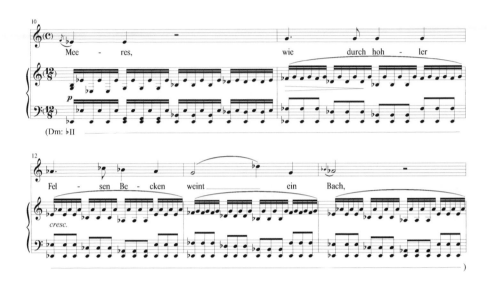

G♯ and C♭ as B♮, along with the semitone shift upward in the bass, bring us to an E major chord for one bar, followed by the bass continuing to climb upward chromatically: E♯ for one bar (harmonized as a diminished seventh chord on E♯), F♯ (B minor six-four chord), G♮ (G major chord in root position), G♯ (augmented sixth chord), and onward toward D minor. The B♭ seventh in bar 9 that earlier led to what we understand in retrospect as the Neapolitan to D minor, E♭ major, is now enharmonically respelled as a German sixth in D minor in bar 19, resolving to the dominant before confirmation of that key (Example 8.6).

Throughout these first twenty bars, multiple smaller chromatic scales rise within a larger chromatic pattern that ascends from C in bar 1 to the pitch B♭ in the first twenty bars; this layered effect is one source of drama in a passage that generally bespeaks *multum in parvo*. Forced inside Hell's passageway, there moves a massed crowd of terrified shades: one could hardly ask for a better demonstration of Schubert's ability to take a concept, an image, a picture, an idea from a poem and translate it into musical processes. And what could provide a composer with greater dramaturgical properties than Hell (or poets and artists, who have always been immoderately interested in what lies below)? The phrase compression and distortion; the claustrophobia induced by the unceasing, ominous tumult (pandemonium indeed); the musical indices of great power devoid of pity or mercy: Schubert deploys them all.

When we arrive at the Allegro section, the *passus duriusculus* becomes a doom-laden mid-bar chiming bell in the right hand, its leaping minor sixths reminiscent of the voice leaping the same distance in bar 9. The tolling bell rises from F to G♭,

Example 8.6   Schubert, 'Gruppe aus dem Tartarus', D. 583, bars 15–20

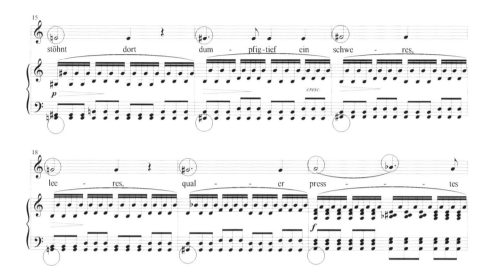

G♮, A♭, and A♮ in the piano, while the singer continues the rolling third motion: A–F, B♭–G♭, B♮–G♮, C–A♭, C♯–A♮, leading to D, doubling the *passus duriusculus* and lurching back and forth in a way that emphasizes Schiller's multiple 'z' sounds. The semitone motion doubled at the tenth in the inner voices creates a harmonic alternation between a major triad (B♭ major) and an augmented triad (A–C♯–F) in bars 22–26; I automatically think of Schubert's 'Der Atlas', D. 957, No. 7, composed eleven years later, and realize that the same indices of Titanic power are at work in both songs. We also realize that the apparent V–VI harmonic progression is a later result of the 5–6 sequence from the song's beginning, implemented differently but related nonetheless (Example 8.7).

But the sequence breaks at bar 30, and very dramatically, *fortissimo* – perhaps to save F♯ for later, and in its wake, we have another sequence, another version of multiple simultaneous incarnations of the *passus duriusculus* for the hollow eyes that gaze back at the bridge over the Cocytus River. The octave-doubled inner voices in bars 33–39 *descend* sequentially (D–D♭–C♭–B♭ / D♯–D–C–B / E–E♭–D♭–C / E♯–E♮–D–C♯) each consisting of semitones on either side of a whole tone in the middle, as a *rising* sequential progression traces an ascent from E♭ to F♯. Other voices, both outer and inner lines doubled at the sixth, as well as the singer, trace the same chromatic ascent. The harmonic emphasis is on first inversion dominant-seventh sonorities, with a raised seventh sounding as part of each first-inversion sonority, resolving to minor harmonies that rise by chromatic semitones the length of a tritone (one is tempted to say, 'of course') from F♯ minor to the dominant of B minor. The next step would be C, but we stall there, short of that goal, postponing

Example 8.7   Schubert, 'Gruppe aus dem Tartarus', D. 583, bars 21–30

the inevitability of Eternity's power. Cocytus is the group's last hope for either escape or rescue from impending damnation (Example 8.8).

The familiar figures from the start of the Allegro – the semitone figures and the outlined thirds (here interlocking) – now appear in new guise for the tearful pause on F♯ minor, Schubert's spirit-world key, the key of 'Schwestergruss', D. 762 of November 1822. This seven-bar passage (bars 40–46) is remarkable for the stark diatonicism of its first four bars, consisting harmonically of nothing more than repeated elemental tonic and dominant triads, and for the semitone neighbour notes – scraps of the *passus duriusculus* – moving, sighing, weeping, both ascending and descending on either side of the dominant pitch in the interior of the chords.

As the fearful shades ask over and over again if the end is nigh (Example 8.8), Schubert enacts both another doubled *passus duriusculus* (A–C♯, B♭–D, C♭–E♭, C–E, D♭–F, E♭–G) in the left hand of bars 48–63 as the singer doubles the downbeat bass tones in anti-lyrical chanting, almost in the manner of a ghostly Doppelgänger (all the more eerie for the *pianissimo* marking in bar 48); the dissonances on the word 'leise' – yet another semitone sighing figure excerpted from the *passus duriusculus* – send an electric charge through the parade of triads.

At bar 48 ('Fragen sich einander leise'), the thrumming repeated notes drive forward unimpeded, and yet another 5–6 sequence has an added twist, a chilling one. In bar 59, the ascending sequence *should*, according to the chromatic logic established elsewhere, go to F♯, but it does not. Shockingly, surprisingly, the sequence instead rises a tone, and the violation of what we have come to expect heightens the intensity of an already intense passage even more. Even more, it tells

Example 8.8   Schubert, 'Gruppe aus dem Tartarus', D. 583, bars 31–39

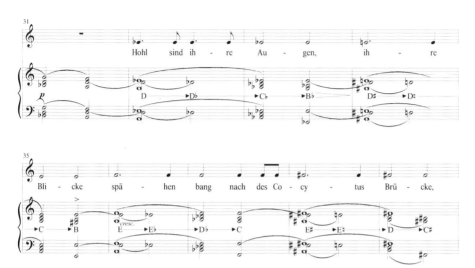

us that the spirits' mixture of sorrow and hope in the ghostly key of F♯ minor is no longer available. And yet, if we understand the emphatic C♯ major in bar 48 as a Neapolitan relationship to Eternity's C, then F♯ minor as a key area can be heard as a prolongation of C♯ major … which must, and does, lead to C major. Damnation is inevitable.

In the final section, Eternity arrives, putting an end to mortal time forever, and Schubert remembers Haydn's 'Und es ward LICHT' moment of blazing light in *Die Schöpfung*. How to interpret the massive advent of C major and the obvious allusion to Haydn's first day of creation is a fraught question, and other views certainly are possible, but I tend to hear it as an equally powerful moment of fiery clarity, the instant when chaos or terror is replaced by illumination – triumphal and overwhelming in Haydn, horrific and overwhelming in Schubert.[36] Throughout this astonishingly powerful ending, Schubert alternates between two different musical ideas: one is wheeling circles in music, rising and falling over hollow fifths and octaves (Example 8.10), and another is the breaking of Saturn's scythe.

How is one to enact the metamorphosis into music of such a vividly pictorial image? In Schubert's brilliant conception, the verb 'bricht' impels sudden musical violence, a jolt to the Neapolitan D♭, confirmed by a cadence and followed by a

[36]   Another possible reading can be found in Brian Newbould, *Schubert: The Music and the Man* (Berkeley: University of California Press, 1999), p. 155; Newbould interprets major mode as a sign of what is 'good', with Schubert's use of it therefore ironic.

Example 8.9   Schubert, 'Gruppe aus dem Tartarus', D. 583, bars 48–64

descending tetrachord that leads away from D♭ to four bars of F minor harmonies – we are on the flat side of C (Example 8.11).

   The elemental triads of the prior F♯ minor passage in bars 40–43 come back in bars 75–78, made savagely *martellato* on F minor (F♯ minor and F minor in a Neapolitan relationship to one another). There is something palpably Beethovenian about all those *forzando* accents. A *rising* tetrachord in the piano in bar 78 (C–D–E♭–E♮) then leads to enharmonic transformation (Schubert is making use of the

Example 8.10   Schubert, 'Gruppe aus dem Tartarus', D. 583, bars 64–70

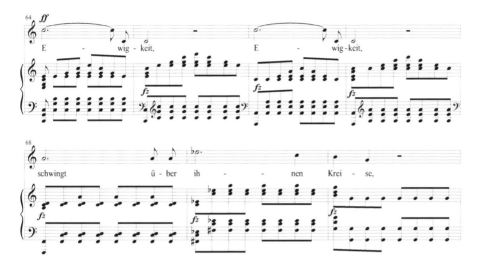

Example 8.11   Schubert, 'Gruppe aus dem Tartarus', D. 583, bars 71–76

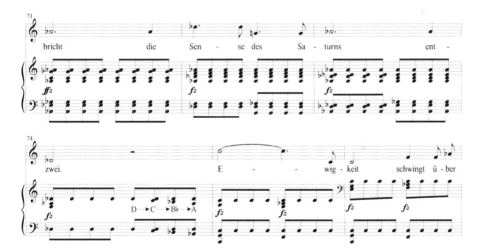

enharmonic relationship between the German sixth and the dominant seventh from earlier in the song), a blaze of sharps, and a mere two bars of F♯ minor, the spirit-key – a tritone distant from the C of Eternity. In other words, Schubert's scythe breaks on both sides of the tonal system; if the sharp side is emphasized by repetition, it is now harnessed to a progression that seals C minor as tonic now and forevermore (Example 8.12).

After all these variations on rising chromatic scales throughout the song, the postlude (bars 82–93) gives us *descending* motion through four octaves on an antique natural minor scale against the familiar repeated pitch ostinato, the scale sinking lower and lower, then emptying out; this is a reversal of the song's beginning and confirmation of its inevitability: the triumph of C, of Eternity, which never relinquishes power. Everything between the beginning and the ending on C, in one sense, is parenthetical, so overwhelming is the power of Ewigkeit (Eternity). The final rolled C minor chord – a last sigh of the damned – is enough to chill anyone's blood.[37]

Mozart and *Don Giovanni*

When I hear this song, I hear, superimposed on it, the Damnation music that follows the trio 'L'ultima prova dell' amor mio', in B♭ major for Don Giovanni, Leporello, and Donna Elvira in the Act II finale of *Don Giovanni*. Even in the trio, Leporello's chromatic crawl upwards in the bass at the words 'Se non si muove del suo dolore, di sasso ha il core, o cor non ha!' ('If her sorrow does not move him, he must have a heart of stone or no heart at all') prefigures an all-out outbreak of more intense rising chromaticism to follow shortly (Example 8.13).

His words in the trio are, of course, ironic, in keeping with so much that emanates from the realm of irony in this opera: the 'stone guest' is about to appear and damn the man with the heart of stone, after multiple injunctions to repent that his soul might be saved – an insistent but futile effort on the Commendatore's part. If Leporello's voice foreshadows the 'stone guest' and the coming of Death, Don Giovanni's almost primitive tonic-dominant alternation in response at the words

[37]   I am indebted to previous writers who have been as fascinated by this song as I am. Marjorie Wing Hirsch, in *Schubert's Dramatic Lieder* (Cambridge: Cambridge University Press, 1993), p. 3, calls it 'one of the most bizarre songs in Schubert's oeuvre' and points to it as an example of this composer's 'departure from traditional Lieder'. More recently, Hirsch has observed a connection between Schubert's song and the Andantino of his Piano Sonata in A major, D. 959. 'The sonata's hard-driving chromatic lines (bars 114–119), ascending chromatic progressions and extreme intensity are foreshadowed in "Gruppe aus dem Tartarus", depicting torments suffered by damned souls in hell'. See Marjorie Hirsch, 'Schubert's Reconciliation of Gothic and Classical Influences', in *Schubert's Late Music: History, Theory, Style*, ed. Lorraine Byrne Bodley and Julian Horton (Cambridge: Cambridge University Press, 2016), p. 159. I am – we all are – especially grateful to the great pianist and Schubertian Graham Johnson, whose commentary on both versions of this song is found in his *Franz Schubert: The Complete Songs*, vol. 1 (New Haven and London: Yale University Press, 2014), pp. 809–13; on p. 811, he memorably writes, 'The song even looks extraordinary on paper, the introduction a cut-away map of the underworld'.

Example 8.12   Schubert, 'Gruppe aus dem Tartarus', D. 583, bars 79–84

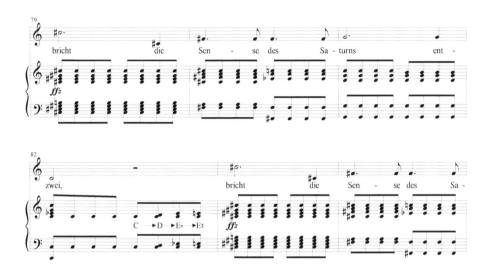

Example 8.13   Mozart, *Don Giovanni*, K. 527, Act II, No. 24, Finale, bars 296–302,
                    Leporello's vocal part

'Vivan le femmine, viva il buon vino!' denies any such possibility.[38] The diatonic-chromatic opposition is striking: death announces itself as a *passus duriusculus*, while Life (of the most sensual, willful variety) is set to basic chords of the key. One cannot help recalling the Don's so-called 'Champagne Aria', 'Finch'han dal vino', in Act I, also in Bb major and also featuring the contrast between descending

---

[38]   I am not the only person to hear echoes of *Don Giovanni* in Schubert; see Glenn Stanley, 'Schubert Hearing *Don Giovanni*: Mozartian Death Music in the "Unfinished" Symphony', in *Schubert's Late Music: History, Theory, Style*, ed. Lorraine Byrne Bodley and Julian Horton (Cambridge: Cambridge University Press, 2016), pp. 193–218.

chromatic lines ('Teco ancor quella cerca menar', when the Don is instructing Leporello to find girls in the piazza and bring them to the feast, and again when the Don is calling for different dances, 'ch'il menuetto … chi la follia … chi l'alemana') and un-subtle, primitive tonic-and-dominant harmonies in both the tonic and dominant keys (Example 8.14). If the Don does not realize that he is dancing with death well before the ultimate encounter with the statue, Mozart and his music do.

The instant the trio is over, an orchestral transitional passage consisting of a rising chromatic scale doubled both in major and minor thirds leads us to Elvira's scream on a diminished seventh horror chord and Don Giovanni's query about what has frightened her so and made her cry out. A rising chromatic bass line (B♭–B♮–C over eight bars, then G–A♭–A♮–B♭–B♮–C again over six bars) brings us first to C minor and then – after another iteration of the ascending chromatic scale doubled in thirds in the strings – to arrival at a half cadence of D minor (Example 8.15).

This too is an example of smaller chromatic scales in the upper voices of the orchestra within a larger chromatic design in the bass; that the bass pauses in place for the rising doubled thirds allows one to hear the dual planes on which this music operates, to our increasing horror. The terrified Leporello shuts the door on D minor doom temporarily and switches to his own key of F major for the plea to his employer, 'Ah! Signor! Per carità'; we first met him in that key at the beginning of Act I in 'Notte e giorno faticar'. But he cannot banish chromatic terror; in fact, it invades his vocal line at the start (Example 8.16).

The Don orders Leporello to open the door, this to knocking figures that also hark back to the opera's first number, and all hell ensues when he does so in Act II, Scene 15, the Commendatore making the grandest of grand entrances over a traditional *lamento* or chaconne bass line (D–C–B♭–A) of the sort Schubert would subsequently use early and often. Antiquity, grandeur, and most of all, *power*, are all attendant upon his arrival.

The marvellous Wye Allanbrook calls the scene from the Commendatore's entrance to his departure 'Armageddon forged into an operatic ensemble';[39]

---

[39]   Wye Allanbrook, *Rhythmic Gesture in Mozart: Le Nozze di Figaro & Don Giovanni* (Chicago and London: University of Chicago Press, 1986), p. 292. Much of my discussion of the Act II finale of *Don Giovanni* owes a transparent debt to this ground-breaking work. And it was only to be expected that Peter Williams, in *The Chromatic Fourth During Four Centuries of Music* (cited above), in particular pp. 139–45, would be drawn to the multiplying chromaticism in *Don Giovanni*, from the opening bars of the overture to its use in 'Fin ch'han dal vino' to the Damnation Scene. Here, Williams takes issue (p. 142) with Daniel Heartz for identifying ascending chromaticism as an erotic signifier and descending chromaticism as emblematic of pain, suffering, and death (in *Mozart's Operas*, ed. Thomas Bauman [Berkeley: University of California Press, 1990], pp. 210 and 215) and with Charles Rosen (in his review of Heartz in *New York Review of Books*, 19 December 1991, pp. 51–8) for his assertion that formulas such as the chromatic fourth were 'largely banal, conventional, and commonplace'. For me, eroticism, suffering, and death are fused signifiers in *Don Giovanni*,

Example 8.14   Mozart, *Don Giovanni*, K. 527, Act I, No. 11, Aria 'Finch'han dal vino', bars 21–28, Don Giovanni's vocal part

Example 8.15   Mozart, *Don Giovanni*, K. 527, Act II, No. 24, Finale, bars 359–370

Example 8.15 (continued)

Scott Burnham in turn notes that Don Giovanni 'is the lightning rod that both mesmerizes the other human characters and draws down the taboo energy of ageless terror', with the bolt striking in the second-act finale, after premonitions aplenty.[40] It is precisely Mozart's imposition of Russian-doll-like patterns in which rising chromaticism is doubled and trebled on chaos, the bonds of life dissolving in torment, that I would love to think inspired Schubert to invent his own chromaticism-within-chromaticism designs in 'Gruppe aus dem Tartarus'. The Commendatore's chromatic designs are show-stopping: as he tells the Don that those who partake of divine food have no need for mortal fare ('Non si pasce

---

'Der Doppelgänger', and – possibly – 'Gruppe'. We are not told why its massed souls are damned, but it is not difficult to imagine that erotic hells play their part.

[40]   Scott Burnham, *Mozart's Grace*, p. 48.

di cibo mortale, chi si pasce di cibo celeste!'), we hear the famous so-called eight-bar 'tone row' (the term is, of course, an obvious anachronism when applied to a late eighteenth-century passage), including every note except G and G♯, which are supplied in the bass – not a *passus duriusculus* but a re-scrambling of the chromatic scale into one *saltus duriusculus* after another (Example 8.17).[41] It is no wonder that Luigi Dallapiccola insisted on the Commendatore's centrality to the drama: Don Giovanni is damned from the moment he kills the older man, while the spirit of the Commendatore in Act II must, and does, express itself in utterly extraordinary music.[42]

Example 8.16   Mozart, *Don Giovanni*, K. 527, Act II, No. 24, Finale, bars 379–384

Example 8.17   Mozart, *Don Giovanni*, K. 527, Act II, No. 24, Finale, bars 354–361,
                Commendatore's vocal part, with violoncellos and double basses

[41]   See Wye Allanbrook, *Rhythmic Gesture in Mozart*, p. 303. Allanbrook does not cite any sources for the designation as a 'tone row', although she is clearly alluding to something already named as such. Hans Keller, in his article 'Strict Serial Techique in Classical Music' in *Tempo* 37 (Autumn 1955), p. 16, criticizes none other than Luigi Dallapiccola for supposedly making this proposition in 'Notes on the Statue Scene in *Don Giovanni*' from *Music Survey*, vol. 3 (1950), pp. 89–97; however, Dallapiccola does not designate this passage (cited on p. 96) as a tone row, but as a specimen of the Commendatore's near-Expressionistic manner.

[42]   Luigi Dallapiccola, 'Notes on the Statue Scene', p. 93.

When he tells the Don that he has come to earth for something far more grave than a dinner party ('Altre cure, più gravi di queste, altra brama quaggiù mi guidò'), we hear the first invocation of what I somewhat irreverently call the 'slithering scales' motif: this is one of the eeriest of all Mozart's inventions in this most terrifying of *ombra* denouements, and, I believe, demonstrates that we can arrive in Hell by many different pathways. The bass moves with ominous slowness upwards by step while the first violins (plus flutes doubling an octave above) delineate a variety of different scale patterns that go up and down by (what else?) rising semitones:

> bar 462, first half – A melodic minor with the raised sixth and seventh degrees ascending;
> bar 462, second half – A Aeolian descending, over the dominant of doom (A minor in first inversion);
> bar 463, first half – an ascending B♭ major scale over a D minor triad;
> bar 463, second half – B Locrian;
> bar 464, first half – C major;
> bar 464, second half – C♯ Super-Locrian;
> bar 465, first half – D melodic minor;
> bar 465, second half – D Aeolian;
> bar 466 – D Phrygian within the context of a B♭ major harmony;
> bar 467 – E♭ Lydian in the context of V/B♭;
> bar 468–469 – E Mixolydian (Example 8.18).

This is a brief history of scales from antiquity to the present compressed into a few bars; we not only travel to Hell by many passageways ('Many are the paths to Hades') but over many eons. This is a *passus duriusculus* whose every member on the way up is a scale rising and falling in a way that extends the instability of

Example 8.18   Mozart, *Don Giovanni*, K. 527, Act II, No. 24, Finale, bars 462–469

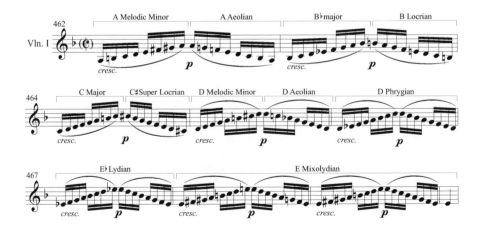

such chromaticism horribly. How to draw out the terror of death and damnation by extending the cliché of rising chromaticism, doubling and trebling it at every level: *this* was Mozart's mission.

As Leporello quakes in fear and the Don demands answers ('La terzana d'avere mi sembra / Parla dunque! Che chiedi?'), a rising tetrachord in the bass leads to the Commendatore's peremptory statement, 'Parlo; ascolta! Più tempo non ho', to a fragment of rising chromaticism (D♯–E–F), once again reinforcing the identification of supernatural agency with the *passus duriusculus* and the still living with a more diatonic order. As the Commendatore repeats his command and Leporello continues to quake in fear, a shorter passage of the slithering scales (three bars rather than eight) comes back, beginning on D rather than A this time and leading to the Commendatore's extended demand for a response ('Tu m'invitasti a cena, il tuo dover or sai'). Here, the *passus duriusculus* is not cloaked in those endlessly eerie scales but doubled and made massive (Example 8.19).

Example 8.19   Mozart, *Don Giovanni*, K. 527, Act II, No. 24, Finale, bars 487–501, Don Giovanni's, Commendatore's, and Leporello's parts, with strings

Example 8.20   Mozart, *Don Giovanni*, K. 527, Act II, No. 24, Finale, bars 582–588, Don
Giovanni's, Leporello's, and offstage chorus parts, with violoncellos' and
double basses' parts

Once again, we encounter rising chromaticism layered on rising chromaticism
in elided and overlapping fashion. In the bass, we rise chromatically for sixteen
bars from the starting point on A to G♭, where the motion is temporarily
arrested for the servant's ages-old excuse of no time; there, as Leporello circles
in semitones around his pitch F (F–G♭–F–E♮–F), we hear both a few seconds
of comedy counterpoised against the swelling tsunami of terror and pausing the
relentless movement for a brief instant. In the orchestral interstices between the
'Tu m'invitasti a cena' passage, we hear small fragments of rising chromaticism
beginning a tritone higher (bracketed in the example). As the Don is well and truly
damned and the Infernal Chorus breaks into song at the final Allegro ('Da qual
tremor insolito / Tutto a tue colpe è poco'), Mozart begins with a chromatically
embellished version of the chaconne pattern from the Commendatore's first
appearance (D–C♯–B–B♭–A) and then twice rises from A to D by semitones in
the bass and in poor Leporello's part (Example 8.20), also from D to A at the

Example 8.21   Mozart, *Don Giovanni*, K. 527, Act II, No. 24, Finale, bars 594–598,
                      woodwind parts

very end, with the Picardy third cadence slamming the doors of Hell down on the disappearing Don. Only as the flames engulf the Don does the chromaticism turn downward in the inner voice of the orchestra, against iron-clad D ostinato on either side and a D major Picardy third cadence to announce the triumph of damnation over the sinner (Example 8.21). Schubert too, we remember, bids the music descend as his damned souls disappear from sight and sound.

***

Is more chromatic saturation than this final scene of *Don Giovanni* even *possible*? Schubert, I believe, decided to try. After all, who would not be marked for life by music this powerful, this intricately constructed, this marvellous? Schubert must have longed for some excuse to put the antique *passus duriusculus* and the conventions of *ombra* music through a wringer of his own devising. If he does nothing so literal as to quote the Don's end directly in his song, he *does*, I believe, accept the dare extended to all nineteenth-century composers in Mozart's Damnation Scene. 'I too', I imagine him saying, 'can create smaller chromatic patterns within larger chromatic patterns, can make semitone scales raise the hair on the back of every listener's neck'. Most, if not all, music is both a conversation with the past and a challenge to the present; Schubert knew it and gave us a magnificent specimen of the phenomenon in his final version of 'Gruppe aus dem Tartarus'.

PART III

INSTRUMENTAL MUSIC

9

'Zumsteeg Ballads without Words': Inter-Generic Dialogue and Schubert's Projection of Drama through Form

Anne M. Hyland

> Form is not exclusively a property of the individual piece.
>
> – James Hepokoski[1]

Introduction

This chapter serves two concomitant ends: to revive engagement with Schubert's earliest chamber music for strings, a body of work which merits greater attention than it has hitherto received, and to explore the methodological implications of this repertoire's particular generic profile, specifically the dramatic potential of what I refer to as 'inter-generic dialogue': the merging or interaction of features characteristic of disparate genres within a single form.[2] It does this by analysing Schubert's earliest surviving chamber-music composition, the Overture for String Quintet in C minor, D. 8, written in June 1811 for his brother Ferdinand and reworked for string quartet later that year as D. 8A. This work's formal outline, I argue, is shaped by two discrete contemporary influences: the orchestral overture to Luigi Cherubini's rescue opera *Faniska* (a connection first proposed by Martin Chusid), and Schubert's first surviving vocal composition, 'Hagars Klage' (Hagar's Lament), D. 5, composed on 30 March 1811 and modelled on the ballad of the same title by Johann Rudolf Zumsteeg. In considering the significance of this intertextuality, this chapter explores the idea – mooted by the opening quotation – that the form of Schubert's earliest chamber music is not the sum of its internal

1   Quoted in William E. Caplin, James Hepokosi and James Webster, *Musical Form, Forms and Formenlehre: Three Methodological Reflections*, ed. Pieter Bergé (Leuven: Leuven University Press, 2009), p. 72.

2   The term has a long usage in literary criticism; see Andrew Baruch Wachtel, *An Obsession with History: Russian Writers Confront the Past* (Stanford: Stanford University Press, 1994). On the dramatic effect of inter-generic dialogue in Mozart's Piano Concertos, see Simon P. Keefe, *Mozart's Piano Concertos: Dramatic Dialogue in the Age of Enlightenment* (Woodbridge: Boydell Press, 2001).

parts but a product of its engagement with external forces such as diverse forms of musical drama and lyricism. Ultimately, by reflecting on methodology, the conclusion offers suggestions for how an analytical approach emphasizing dialogue between genres might provide an appropriate lens through which to view this repertoire while encouraging a meaningful interaction between music history and analysis.

Schubert's Lyric-Epic-*Dramatic* Sonata Style

The sonata has long been upheld as a fundamentally dramatic form which enacts a musical drama through the establishment of a network of generic expectations that are variously deferred, manipulated, or thwarted in individual works; Edward T. Cone memorably referred to this as the form's 'interplay of the anticipated and the actual'.[3] Although the question of what is expected from a given sonata is not a straightforward matter (listener expectation depends on a multitude of factors, such as experience, knowledge of the repertoire as well as familiarity with formal theories), on the most fundamental level, the sonata's dramatic narrative might be characterized as the playing out of a conflict or dialectical opposition between two agents, either key areas or themes. The sonata strives teleologically towards a pre-destined moment of resolution of this conflict in the recapitulation (sonata theory's essential structural closure is paradigmatic of this), and, optionally, a reflection on that process, or a delayed arrival of tonal closure, in a coda.[4]

Although this dramatic narrative can be (and frequently is) relayed in a myriad of diverse ways, early nineteenth-century theories of the form by Heinrich Christoph Koch, Carl Czerny, and Adolph Bernhard Marx were all heavily informed by Beethoven's compositional practice, in particular his 'heroic' middle-period works. The specific class of drama articulated by these works came to be understood as synonymous with the sonata's dramatic profile. Thus, as Gordon Sly rightly posits, our understanding of the form 'aligns itself with Beethoven's dramatic practice' of development via thematic fragmentation and tonal designs which are fundamentally fifth-based, and hence goal-directed.[5]

---

[3]   Edward T. Cone, 'The Uses of Convention: Stravinsky and his Models', *The Musical Quarterly* 48/3 (1962), pp. 287–99, at p. 291.

[4]   James Hepokoski and Warren Darcy, *Elements of Sonata Theory: Norms, Types, and Deformations in the Late-Eighteenth-Century Sonata* (New York and Oxford: Oxford University Press, 2006).

[5]   Gordon Sly, 'Design and Structure in Schubert's Sonata Forms: An Evolution Toward Integration', in *Keys to the Drama: Nine Perspectives on Sonata Forms*, ed. Gordon Sly (Farnham: Ashgate, 2009), pp. 129–55; at p. 131. See also Scott Burnham, *Beethoven Hero* (Princeton: Princeton University Press, 2000).

Schubert's sonata forms are routinely placed in opposition to this archetype since the subjectivity of their lyrical idiom does not give rise to the same dramatic designs. Early detractors of his style asserted that, 'energy is certainly not his strong point ... any attempt of his at a heroic style rings a false note of empty bombast'.[6] Marking the distinction between the two composers in his essay on Schubert's G major String Quartet, D. 887, Carl Dahlhaus writes that, 'the teleological energy characteristic of Beethoven's contrasting derivation is surely not absent from Schubert, but is perceptibly weaker', and he distinguishes Schubert's 'lyric-epic' sonata style from Beethoven's 'dramatic-dialectic'.[7] He holds that Schubert's lengthy lyrical themes do not lend themselves easily to the same thematic fragmentation characteristic of Beethoven's dramatic themes, and instead of driving forward, they are relaxed and retrospective – reminiscent, rather than goal-directed.[8] Theodor Adorno, writing in 1928, similarly urges us to hear Schubert's sonata forms as non-teleological: for him, Schubert's lyrical themes are closed forms that can be repeated but not broken up or combined with other ideas to create something entirely new; in short, they eschew the 'thematic, dialectical development' of Beethoven's sonatas.[9] Consequently, Schubert's sonata form is a 'potpourri' of lyrical moments – a static, repetitive metaphorical 'landscape', rather than a dramatic organic process.[10] This equation of drama with teleology has left Schubert wanting.

Yet, Schubert's lyric-epic style does not shun the dramatic. When listening to the instrumental chamber works he wrote in the first part of his career (1811–1816), as is my focus, one cannot help but be struck by their acute sense of drama. This dramatic narrative functions on multiple levels, incorporating harmonic, thematic, and textural elements. Moreover, Schubert is prone – especially, though not exclusively, in his early works – to begin the recapitulation away from the tonic in order to arrive there at a later point in the movement. This postponement of the final tonic – until an extended coda, for instance – was just one of Schubert's

[6]   Eric Blom, 'The Middle-Classical Schubert', *The Musical Times* 69 (1928), pp. 980–83, at p. 980.

[7]   Carl Dahlhaus, 'Sonata Form in Schubert: The First Movement of the G-Major String Quartet, Op. 161 (D. 887)', trans. Thilo Reinhard, in *Schubert: Critical and Analytical Studies*, ed. Walter Frisch (Lincoln, NE: University of Nebraska Press, 1986 [1978]), pp. 1–12, especially p. 8.

[8]   For an analytical critique of this idea, see Anne M. Hyland, 'In Search of Liberated Time, or Schubert's Quartet in G Major, D. 887: Once More Between Sonata and Variation', *Music Theory Spectrum* 38/1 (2016), pp. 85–108; Suzannah Clark, *Analyzing Schubert* (Cambridge: Cambridge University Press, 2011), Chapter 3; and Poundie L. Burstein, 'Lyricism, Structure, and Gender in Schubert's G Major String Quartet', *The Musical Quarterly* 81/1 (1997), pp. 51–63.

[9]   Theodor W. Adorno, 'Schubert (1928)', trans. Beate Perrey and Jonathan Dunsby, *19th-Century Music* 29/1 (Summer 2005), pp. 3–14, at p. 11.

[10]   Adorno, 'Schubert (1928)', pp. 9 and 3 respectively.

deviations from the above model which serves a dramatic purpose. That said, drama in these early works is not necessarily tied to a teleological trajectory, nor indeed only to the generic expectations of sonata form itself – in many cases, these are wilfully ignored. Instead, it is created by the composer's daring juxtaposition of lyrical and dramatic passages in strikingly original ways, his idiosyncratic tonal schemes, monothematic designs, lack of transitional or connective material between tonal centres, and by the expansion of the form to include more tonal areas than expected: elements which, taken individually, might not speak to a coherent whole, but when explored in tandem, reveal a logical and purposeful journey and an undeniable articulation of dramatic form.

Underlying and motivating this is a strong sense of generic cross-fertilization, or inter-generic dialogue, which functions on two levels: stylistic idiom and formal construction. The symphonic style of some of the writing in Schubert's early quartets is immediately palpable; I think, for instance, of the texturally dense passage (reaching triple *forte*) during the final forty-seven bars of the Finale of the Quartet in B♭, D. 36, or the slow introduction to the first movement of the Quartet in C major, D. 46.[11] Moreover, Schubert's use of octave doublings, repetition of material in the inner parts, and extensive tremolos in the early quartets belies a symphonic, rather than a chamber-music idiom. Indeed, pre-echoes of his own first symphony are to be found in the slow movement and Finale of his Quartet in D major, D. 74, suggesting that the quartet served as a kind of training ground for the larger form.[12]

On a formal level, a number of these early works are modelled on specific orchestral precursors: Chusid perceives in the Finale of the String Quartet in C major, D. 32, for instance, a modelling of the first movement of Haydn's Symphony No. 78 in C minor. Moreover, both he and Brian Newbould read the end of the development section of the B♭ Quartet's first movement, D. 36, in relation to the similar trumpet-like fanfare at the parallel moment in Beethoven's *Leonore* Overture, No. 3.[13] Working from models in this way at once reveals Schubert's familiarity with this repertoire, and his deviation from its practices.

The influence of vocal genres on these early chamber works is a more contentious issue. On the one hand, Schubert is well known for repurposing material from his own vocal compositions in later instrumental works, such as his use of 'Die Forelle' in the Piano Quintet in A major, D. 667-iv, 'Trockne-Blumen'

[11]   On this feature of the early chamber music, see Martin Chusid, 'Das "Orchestermässige" in Schuberts früher Streicherkammermusik', in *Zur Aufführungspraxis der Werke Franz Schuberts*, ed. Vera Schwarz (Munich and Salzburg: Musikverlag Emil Katzbichler, 1981), pp. 77–86.

[12]   See Martin Chusid, 'Schubert's Chamber Music: Before and After Beethoven', in *The Cambridge Companion to Schubert*, ed. Christopher H. Gibbs (Cambridge: Cambridge University Press, 1997), pp. 174–92, at p. 175.

[13]   See Chusid, 'Schubert's Chamber Music', pp. 175–6, and Brian Newbould, *Schubert: The Music and the Man* (London: Gollancz, 1997), p. 112.

in the Introduction and Variations for flute and piano, D. 802, 'Die Götter Griechenlands' and the incidental music to *Rosamunde* in the String Quartet in A minor, D. 804-ii, and 'Der Tod und das Mädchen' in the String Quartet in D minor, D. 810-ii. Finding inspiration in vocal music was therefore quite natural for him. On the other, the critical reception of these vocal influences has tended to focus on their adverse effect on form, and this aspect of the early quartets has fuelled some disparaging judgements. Donald Francis Tovey, for instance, writes:

> [Schubert's] earliest pieces, including the earliest string quartets, are fantasies of such ubiquitous rambling that the catalogue-maker cannot specify their keys. Some of them may possibly be regarded as Zumsteeg ballads without words; but why should we allow the young Schubert no child's-play at all?[14]

Tovey's passing remark that Schubert's earliest quartets resemble 'Zumsteeg ballads without words' rewards deeper reflection not least because of the dramatic associations of the ballad tradition. Marjorie Wing Hirsch, writing on Schubert's dramatic Lieder, tells us that 'the "Ballade" presents its narrative in stark dramatic terms'.[15] It is distinct from the Lied in its direct representation of action (usually through a protagonist's monologue or a dialogue between two personae), rather than the narration of a story. This aspect of Zumsteeg's ballads, which usually gives rise to dramatic juxtaposition of styles rather than seamless integration, had, as we shall explore, a particularly strong influence on the young composer of string quartets and quintets.

Thus D. 8 displays both orchestral and vocal influences in its style and formal outline, and employs them to dramatic end: formally and texturally, it is modelled on an orchestral overture, but its slow introduction and dramatic sectional design bespeak the influence of a dramatic vocal tradition through their allusion to Schubert's own work, 'Hagars Klage'. As such, D. 8 reveals itself as the meeting ground of diverse generic models – those that were at the forefront of the composer's mind in 1811 – and as a progenitor for his acknowledged technical expansion of the sonata in his mature works.

Schubert's Models for the Overture in C minor, D. 8: From the Margins to the Centre

The generic title of Schubert's D. 8 immediately suggests dramatic or representational associations beyond the scope of the sonata. Chusid's suggestion that it is modelled

14   Donald Francis Tovey, 'Franz Schubert (1797–1828)', in *The Heritage of Music*, ed. Hubert J. Foss (Oxford: Oxford University Press, 1927–51), pp. 82–122, at p. 100.
15   Marjorie Wing Hirsch, *Schubert's Dramatic Lieder* (Cambridge: Cambridge University Press, 1993), p. 66.

on the orchestral Overture to *Faniska* further augments the work's dramatic profile and is clearly supported by the music. To place this in context: Cherubini wrote *Faniska* specifically for Vienna, and it was premiered there on 25 February 1806 at the Kärntnertortheater. It was well received and widely celebrated: Haydn and Beethoven reportedly attended the premiere, and it was performed thirty times in Vienna during its opening year.[16] There exists no documentary evidence to support the claim that Schubert knew this work, and indeed in 1806 Schubert was only nine years of age, making it unlikely that he attended these performances; despite this, the numerous textural, motivic and tonal connections between the two works suggest very strongly that he did know the work, and knew it intimately.

As Chusid observed, the two Overtures are remarkably similar in terms of formal structure and proportion: they both begin with an introductory Largo in triple metre followed by an Allegro sonata-form movement. Beyond this, he has convincingly traced the gamut of textural and motivic connections between the two works, revealing a high level of intertextuality. One especially clear instance of this is Schubert's transition leading from the first subject group to the second, bars 95–98, as illustrated by Example 9.1 (a and b).[17] Here, Schubert remains very close to Cherubini's original: a descending step-wise melody in octaves with the same rhythmic and dynamic profile leads to a registrally emphasized chromatic chord. Cherubini's augmented sixth chord resolves unusually to a first-inversion E♭ chord in preparation for the next section in that key. Schubert's apex, on the other hand, is a Neapolitan chord (♭II in first inversion), the dramatic potential of which he continued to exploit throughout his career, culminating in the String Quintet in C, D. 956 of 1828. Both transitions lead into an ostinato section which functions in D. 8 as the second theme of the B group in the remote key of F minor.

It is perhaps no surprise that Schubert's first chamber-music exercise should be an overture for string ensemble based on a well-known opera overture considering that his father regularly made string-quartet and -quintet arrangements of orchestral works by Haydn, Mozart, and Beethoven for use by the family ensemble.[18] The young composer would also have performed arrangements of overtures for quartet

---

[16]   On the reception of *Faniska* in Vienna, see David Wyn Jones, *Music in Vienna: 1700, 1800, 1900* (Woodbridge: Boydell Press, 2016), pp. 134–5.

[17]   See Martin Chusid, 'Schubert's Overture for String Quintet and Cherubini's Overture to *Faniska*', *Journal of the American Musicological Society* 15 (1962), pp. 78–84.

[18]   The practice of arranging orchestral overtures for string ensemble was extremely popular in the first half of the nineteenth century. In Marie Sumner-Lott's recent study of nineteenth-century chamber-music practice, for instance, she found that the Berlin-based publishing firm of Adolph Martin Schlesinger published ninety-six chamber-music items between 1810 (when it was founded) and the end of the century, almost forty per cent of which consisted of arrangements of operas and overtures for chamber ensembles. See Sumner-Lott, *The Social Worlds of Nineteenth-Century Chamber Music: Composers, Consumers, Communities* (Urbana, Chicago and Springfield: University of Illinois Press, 2015).

Example 9.1a   Cherubini, Overture to *Faniska*, bars 102–106

Example 9.1b   Schubert, Overture for String Quintet in C minor, D. 8, bars 95–98

by his teacher Antonio Salieri, some of which were found at the family home.[19] But, Schubert's D.8 is no slavish arrangement of an orchestral work for performance by the family ensemble: as my analysis shall demonstrate, Schubert completely restructures Cherubini's tonal plot in a way that prefigures his own mature practice of reimagining sonata form's tonal polarity. The work also exhibits familiar Schubertian fingerprints such as the predilection for parallel keys, modal mixture, thematic proliferation or extension, and the expansion of sonata-form space via a three-key exposition and recapitulation.[20] In exploring these formal innovations, my work builds on and moves beyond Chusid's observations of the surface correspondences between the two works.

The second intertextual connection comes from an equally important, albeit less immediately obvious, source of inspiration: 'Hagars Klage', D. 5, which was completed three months prior to the composition of D. 8.[21] Based on a text by Clemens August Schücking concerning the story of Hagar and Ishmael (Genesis 21), the poem is a dramatic monologue delivered by Hagar, who clutches her son as she relays her story of banishment. The poem had been set to music by Zumsteeg

[19]   Chusid, 'Schubert's Chamber Music', p. 175.

[20]   For a comprehensive exploration of Schubert's stylistic traits, see Susan Wollenberg, *Schubert's Fingerprints: Studies in the Instrumental Works* (Farnham: Ashgate, 2011).

[21]   The manuscript copy is inscribed: 'Schubert's first song composition, written in the Konvikt at the age of fourteen, 30 March 1811'. See Newbould, *Schubert*, p. 30.

and published in 1797, and this setting acted as the model from which Schubert worked on his version, which is best described as a series of dramatic scenes, owing to its direct representation of the action.[22]

Zumsteeg was a German conductor and prolific composer of ballads and Lieder; his accomplishments in the realm of the ballad are aptly summarized thus:

> Zumsteeg's achievement was to find a means of freely alternating between recitative and melody so as to heighten the dramatic narrative (often with cunning tempo and key changes) at the same time as giving the conception a sweep and unity that kept the listener's attention over a relatively long time span.[23]

Although he has been relegated to a footnote in music history, Zumsteeg was incredibly important to the young Schubert, who developed a keen interest in his ballads while at the Stadtkonvikt, as his close friend, Joseph von Spaun, here recalls:

> I went to see [Schubert] in the music room where he was given an hour for practice. He had several of Zumsteeg's songs in front of him and told me that these songs moved him profoundly ... He said he could revel in these songs for days on end. And to this youthful predilection of his we probably owe the direction Schubert took, and yet how little of an imitator he was and how independent the path he followed.[24]

Schubert's immersion in Zumsteeg's ballads at a young age was to leave a lasting impression, perceptible not only in his vocal compositions – many of which modernize Zumsteeg's form – but also in the early instrumental music, a point which has been lamented in the secondary literature. Gerald Abraham, for instance, dismayed at Schubert's interest in the ballad form, arguing that 'his profound but misguided admiration for Zumsteeg's confused and piecemeal constructions led him down a number of blind alleys'.[25] Importantly, those blind alleys were apparently to be found in the instrumental music, rather than in the songs: Schubert's preference for paratactic structures was linked to Zumsteeg's 'piecemeal constructions', and his early instrumental music was criticized for its diffuseness and lack of hypotactic formal organization.

---

[22]   Hirsch has helpfully disentangled the genres of the Ballad and the 'dramatic scene': a dramatic scene has no single narrative perspective; instead, 'the words are ostensibly spoken by one or more usually identifiable personae who act out a particular episode'. Following this rationale, she classifies Schubert's 'Hagars Klage' as one of his dramatic scenes rather than as a ballad. See Hirsch, *Schubert's Dramatic Lieder*, p. 17.

[23]   Graham Johnson (with Eric Sams), 'Ballad' entry, *Oxford Music Online*, accessed 18 May 2017.

[24]   Joseph von Spaun, quoted in Marjorie Wing Hirsch, *Schubert's Dramatic Lieder*, p. 170.

[25]   Gerald Abraham, ed., *The New Oxford History of Music, Vol. 8: The Age of Beethoven, 1790– 1830* (Oxford: Oxford University Press, 1982), p. 563.

Clear allusions to 'Hagars Klage' are heard in D. 8. Schubert used its first nine bars – in the same key and tempo – as the opening bars of D. 8's slow introduction, now preceded by a unison chord. Indeed, the bars appear again, this time altered to G minor, in the Fantasie for Piano Duet in G minor, D. 9 of the same year. Example 9.2 (a, b, and c) reproduces the respective passages from the three works.

The outward correspondences between these works are symptomatic of an underlying concern of much of Schubert's early instrumental music: how to incorporate the inherent drama and intensity of the ballad tradition, or dramatic scene, into his instrumental forms. In drawing attention to these influences and their interaction, the ensuing analysis seeks to clarify the ways by which Schubert dramatizes sonata form.

The analytical approach I adopt to this end finds a middle ground between William Caplin's theory of formal functions and James Hepokoski's and Warren Darcy's Sonata Theory.[26] The use of terms such as the medial caesura (MC) and nonresolving recapitulation from the latter are useful here as they allow me to highlight the ways by which Schubert deviates from a more 'normative' model, and facilitates an explanation of how Schubert downplays the preparation of a new key. Additionally, the attention granted to localized syntax and intra-thematic functions, and their interactions with larger grouping structures and inter-thematic concerns in Caplin's theory makes it an apt framework for a study of D. 8, a work which actively expands traditional sentential and periodic phrasing.

My engagement with D. 8 follows a three-fold structure, offering respectively: (1) a form-functional analysis of the movement's thematic and tonal configuration; (2) a (re)positioning of the work in relation to Cherubini's overture and 'Hagars Klage', D. 5; and (3) a reflection on methodology. In so doing, this chapter proposes a new conception of the relationship between lyricism, development and dramatic form in Schubert's instrumental music, one which moves beyond the basic dualisms that currently define it. It thereby sets in motion a rehabilitation process, bringing works such as D. 8 from the margins into a more central position in the critical discourse surrounding Schubert's music and his development of form and syntax.

Modelling the Ballad: Thematic Extension, Parataxis and Tonal Form

D. 8 comprises a slow introduction of thirty-nine bars followed by an ambitious 274-bar Type 1 sonata form in C minor: a bi-rotational sonata without development section and with a recapitulation beginning in the tonic.[27] As Chusid notes, the Type 1 or bipartite sonata form was by far the most usual sonata type for

---

[26]   William E. Caplin, *Classical Form: A Theory of Formal Functions for the Instrumental Music of Haydn, Mozart, and Beethoven* (Oxford: Oxford University Press, 1998).

[27]   Type 1 sonata refers to the categories of sonata types proposed by James Hepokoski and Warren Darcy in *Elements of Sonata Theory*.

Example 9.2a   Schubert, 'Hagars Klage', D. 5, bars 1–9

Example 9.2b   Schubert, Overture for String Quintet in C minor, D. 8, bars 1–10

Example 9.2b (continued)

Example 9.2c   Schubert, Fantasie for Piano Duet, D. 9, bars 1–15, primo part

opera overtures at the time, although he does not class D. 8 as bipartite.[28] I believe, however, that Schubert reveals his familiarity with this tradition precisely through this choice. Despite the lack of a development section proper, D. 8 is a substantial work spanning 313 bars in total, longer than any of his earliest quartet first movements, and just one bar shy of Cherubini's 314-bar overture. Schubert expands and dramatizes the form of this movement by four main means: first, via thematic proliferation in the first-subject group (A) which extends the normal period model by means of deferred cadence and an internal transition; second, by the lack of a cadential medial caesura (MC) as preparation for the second tonal area (VI) and the establishment of a third, and unexpected key (iv, then IV) which is thematically stable and cadentially established; third, by the use of a nonresolving recapitulation, which closes in the subdominant minor; and finally, owing to this, by dramatically delaying the work's tonal resolution until the coda (bars 277–313).[29]

D. 8's first expositional group comprises two themes, A1 and A2, the first of which is greatly extended, spanning bars 40–68. As Example 9.3 illustrates, A1 comprises a six-bar sentence which acts as the antecedent of a large sentential period: a two-bar basic idea, followed by a two-bar repetition and two-bar continuation, ending on an active dominant seventh. This sets up the expectation of an answering sentence, or sentential consequent, which seems to begin during the upbeat to bar 46. The continuation phrase is, however, extended and instead of producing the expected cadence in the tonic, leads to a first-inversion chord of F minor in bar 52, and a weakly articulated Imperfect Authentic Cadence (IAC) in that key in bars 52–53 (the function of this as a true IAC is compromised because the dominant chord is given in second inversion, meaning that the bass line descends by step rather than from root-position dominant to tonic). F minor is then prolonged via two four-bar phrases each of which emphasize a recurring ♭6-5 motion from D♭ to C that gains in significance throughout the movement.[30] The second phrase incorporates this chromatic dyad into the articulation of a Half Cadence (HC) in F minor at bars 60–61. Given that the first phrase ends on a chord of F minor in second inversion (bar 57), and the second phrase on its dominant (bar 61), it is as though a greatly expanded cadential 6-4 in F minor is

---

[28]   My reading of this movement as a sonata without development differs from Chusid's, which reads a development section at bars 145–69. See Chusid, 'Schubert's Overture for String Quintet', p. 82.

[29]   James Hepokoski defines the nonresolving recapitulation thus: 'In a *nonresolving* recapitulation the composer has crafted this rhetorical recapitulatory revisiting, or new *rotation*, of previously ordered expositional materials to convey the impression that it "fails" to accomplish its additional generic mission of tonal closure'. See his 'Back and Forth from Egmont: Beethoven, Mozart, and the Nonresolving Recapitulation', *19th-Century Music* 25/2–3 (2001–2002), pp. 127–54, at p. 128, emphasis in original.

[30]   On the harmonic significance of this dyad, see Brian Black, *Schubert's Apprenticeship in Sonata Form: The Early String Quartets* (PhD dissertation, McGill University, 1996), p. 89.

Example 9.3   Schubert, Overture for String Quintet in C minor, D. 8, bars 40–68,
                   analysis of A1 theme

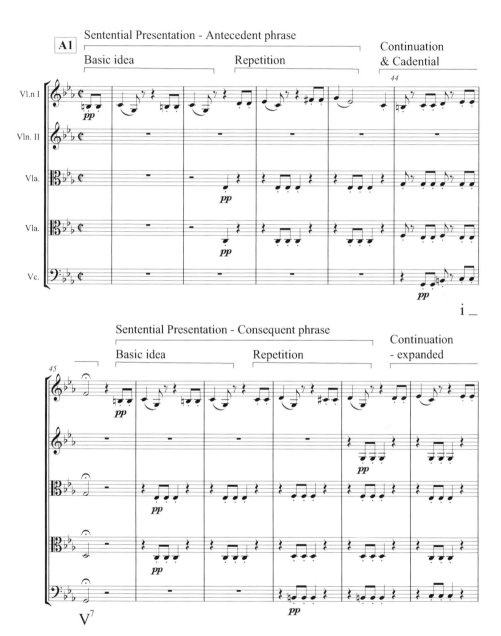

Example 9.3 (continued)

Modulating TR - returning to C minor

C minor: V^7

cadential function | **i : IAC elided with A2** | **A2** Presentation being set up. A variation on this phrase then leads into a modulating transition (TR) which brings the music back into the realm of the home tonic, and to a Perfect Authentic Cadence (PAC) in C minor at bars 67–68, which is elided with the presentation phase of A2.

This treatment of the A1 group serves not only to expand the form, but also to problematize the tonic key: even in this first group, the tonic is displaced by F minor. The preparatory treatment of the second key is similarly unorthodox. As shown in Figure 9.1, which provides a form-functional analysis of the exposition, the brief transition in bars 79–85 leads to a chord of Ab major, the submediant. This VI chord does not produce a cadential medial caesura, nor does it prepare the next section harmonically: without transition, it is simply reinterpreted as the key of the lyrical B1 theme in the next bar. Indeed, not only that, but also the arrival on I in Ab major at the end of B1 is itself elided with a second dramatic transition (bars 95–99), thereby significantly downplaying the moment of cadential arrival.

This tendency to undermine important structural cadences is a feature of Zumsteeg's ballad and Schubert's 'Hagars Klage': in both, tonal areas are starkly juxtaposed, often marked by a change in key signature, and with little by way of preparation for a new key. In D. 8, the lack of preparation for the move to Ab in the exposition, as well as the aforementioned elisions and the deceptive cadence leading from the Neapolitan chord into the F minor section (bar 98) are typical of the same tendency towards striking juxtaposition rather than integration. This procedure betrays the influence of parataxis on the construction of formal units, whereby one idea follows *upon* another, rather than following *from* another.[31]

The tonal plan itself, initially moving from C minor to a lyrical Ab major, is a small-scale replica of the directional tonality in 'Hagars Klage', which begins in C minor and ends in Ab major. This suggests that Schubert was exploring the possibilities of this tonal relationship at the time, and strengthens the link between the two works. The tonal scheme is also, as Brian Black has noted, prophetic of the *Quartettsatz* of 1820, a movement widely acknowledged as a watershed in Schubert's compositional development.[32] But, unlike the *Quartettsatz*, the exposition of D. 8

---

[31] I owe this succinct formulation of parataxis to Nicholas Marston. On the paratactic underpinnings of Schubertian lyricism, see Su Yin Mak, 'Schubert's Sonata Forms and the Poetics of the Lyric', *Journal of Musicology* 23/2 (2006), pp. 263–306.

[32] See Black, *Schubert's Apprenticeship in Sonata Form: The Early String Quartets*, p. 84. On the *Quartettsatz*, see Hali Fieldman, 'Schubert's *Quartettsatz* and Sonata Form's New Way', *Journal of Musicological Research* 21 (2002), pp. 99–146; Su Yin Mak, 'Et in Arcadia Ego: The Elegiac Structure of Schubert's Quartettsatz in C minor (D. 703)', in *The Unknown Schubert*, ed. Barbara M. Reul and Lorraine Byrne Bodley (Aldershot: Ashgate, 2008), pp. 145–53; and Anne M. Hyland, 'In What Respect Monumental? Schubert's *Quartettsatz* and the Dialectics of Private and Public', in *The String Quartet from the Private to the Public Sphere*, ed. Christian Speck (Turnhout: Brepols, 2016), pp. 141–64.

Bars	40–156										
Large-scale function	Exposition										
Interthematic function	40–79¹ A group				79–85 TR	86–152 B group					153–56 C
Intrathematic function	40–53 A1 — Extended period		54–61, 62–68 A1 extension ⇒ modulating TR	68–79¹ A2 — 11-bar sentence		86–95 B1 — 10-bar sentence	95–99 TR	100–123 B2 — Ostinato	124–44 B2 — Ostinato	145–52 B1 — 8-bar sentence	Based on B1 continuation
	40–45 — 6-bar sentential antecedent	46–53 — 8-bar sentential consequent									
Tonal plot	i	iv	i	i	–	VI	–	iv		IV	
Structural cadence	on V⁷/i — weak iv: IAC		60–61 — iv: HC — weak i: IAC elided with A2	i: PAC	on VI (no MC)	VI: PAC elided with TR	–	on V/F min.	iv: HC	IV: PAC	IV: PAC

IAC: Imperfect Authentic Cadence   PAC: Perfect Authentic Cadence   HC: Half Cadence   MC: Medial Caesura

TR: Transition

Figure 9.1   Schubert, Overture for String Quintet in C minor, D. 8, exposition, form-functional analysis

Example 9.4   Schubert, Overture for String Quintet in C minor, D. 8, bars 144–156

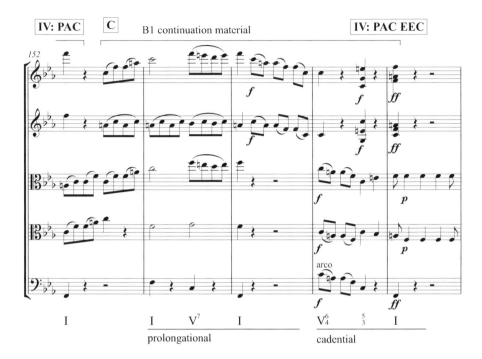

closes in the unexpected key of F major, the subdominant.[33] And this is no mere nod to F major via a cadential gesture as Schubert is sometimes prone to do with the dominant at the end of a three-key exposition: as Example 9.4 demonstrates, the lyrical B1 theme is stated fully in F major, followed by a brief closing section (C) based on B1 continuation material cadencing again in F major, meaning that the tonality is afforded prolonged thematic stability.

The use of the subdominant as the tonal goal of this sonata-form exposition is unorthodox, and distinct from Schubert's later three-key expositions, the majority of which end in the dominant, even those in minor keys.[34] Moreover, in a study on sources of the three-key exposition in sonata-form movements of the major composers between 1770 and 1820, Rey M. Longyear and Kate R. Covington found only one minor-mode sonata that does not move ultimately to v in the exposition (most move from i to III and finally to v).[35] The one exception, the

[33]   This is followed by a linking section that serves as a retransition to establish the dominant of the home key in preparation for the double return of A1 in C minor (bar 170).

[34]   Two exceptions to this are the first movements of two Violin Sonatas in D major, D. 385 and D. 408, the expositions of which end in the submediant.

[35]   Rey M. Longyear and Kate R. Covington, 'Sources of the Three-Key Exposition', *Journal of Musicology* 6/4 (1988), pp. 448–70.

first movement of J. Benda's Sonata No. 9, has an expositional close in III, having traversed the unorthodox path: i–III–V–♭I–III. None end in the subdominant. Equally, the three categories of three-key exposition identified by Graham Hunt (2009 and 2014) are unable to account for the tonal structure of D. 8, which moves from an initial tonic minor to VI and thence to IV.[36] D. 8 would possibly occupy an envisaged fourth category for Hunt, wherein both the second and third keys of the exposition are classed as 'deformational', the 'normative' keys in a minor-key exposition being either III or v.[37]

To my knowledge, Schubert employs this specific expositional tonal scheme in only one other work: the fourth movement of the Violin Sonata in A minor, D. 385 (Op. 137, No. 2) dating from 1816, the tonal scheme of which can be summarized as: i(A)–VI(B)–iv(C).[38] Indeed, the move to the *minor* subdominant in D. 385 also resonates with D. 8: of the overture exposition's 117 bars, approximately fifty-seven are spent on the dominant of F minor, or in the key of F minor itself. That is, almost half of D. 8's exposition points towards F minor, rather than either A♭ or F major. There are two significant moments where this is the case, both of which appear in Figure 9.1: the first is the consequent phrase of the A1 theme, discussed above in relation to the expansion of the group, and the other is the B2 theme from bar 100, which is an ostinato section borrowed from Cherubini. Here again, although F minor is denied a PAC, the phrase endings on C major in bars 123 and 144, as well as the constant juxtaposition of tonic and dominant harmonies of F minor in the intervening passages make the suggestion of the key strongly felt. Given this emphasis, it is plausible that F (minor/major), rather than A♭, provides the tonal 'other' to the tonic in this exposition, and that it alone requires resolution or balancing in the latter half of the work.

The unusual tonal relationships are rendered dramatic by the specific manner of their articulation, mirroring the sectional construction of 'Hagars Klage'. D. 5's dramatic, declamatory design is heightened by its alternation of different vocal forms such as recitative, arioso and passages of Lied-like lyricism. The result is a dramatic, if rather *ad hoc* form that begins and ends in different keys. This same paratactic impulse underlies Schubert's sonata forms in the early quartets, many of which alternate between the presentation of lyrical themes and highly charged, developmental passages with little or no transition. In D. 8, the lyricism of the second theme (B1) – indicated by the *dolce* marking, its clear sentential structure and setting in the subdominant major – is dramatically interrupted by the forceful interpolation, marked *fz*, discussed earlier as a reference to *Faniska*, at bars 95–99

---

[36]   See Graham Hunt, 'When Structure and Design Collide: The Three-Key Exposition Revisited', *Music Theory Spectrum* 36/2 (2014), pp. 247–69, at p. 251.

[37]   D. 8 does not feature in either of Hunt's in-depth examinations of this technique in Schubert's oeuvre. See Hunt (2014) and 'The Three-Key Trimodular Block and its Classical Precedents: Sonata Expositions of Schubert and Brahms, *Intégral* 23 (2009), pp. 65–119.

[38]   The recapitulation of this movement is a normative i–III–i.

	170–75	176–83	184–91	192–98	198–209¹	209–16	217–26	226–30	231–51	252–76	277–313
Bars	170–313										
Large-scale function	170–276 Recapitulation										277–313 Coda
Interthematic function	170–209¹ A group					209–16 TR	217–76 B group				
Intrathematic function	170–83 A1		184–91, 192–98 A1 extension ⇒ modulating TR		198–209¹ A2		217–26 B1	226–30 TR	231–51 B2	252–76 B2	
	Extended period				11-bar sentence		10-bar sentence		Ostinato	Ostinato	
	170–75 6-bar sentential antecedent	176–83 8-bar sentential consequent									
Tonal plot	i	iv	i		i	–	V	–	v	iv	i
Structural cadence	on V⁷/i	weak iv: IAC	90–91 iv: HC	weak i: IAC elided with A2	i: PAC	on V (no MC)	V: PAC elided with TR	–	on V/G min.	iv: PAC	i: PAC

IAC: Imperfect Authentic Cadence   PAC: Perfect Authentic Cadence   HC: Half Cadence   MC: Medial Caesura   TR: Transition

Figure 9.2   Schubert, Overture for String Quintet in C minor, D. 8, recapitulation, form-functional analysis

(shown above in Example 9.1b). Schubert heightens the disruptive effect of this passage by eliding its beginning with the arrival of the A♭ cadence, thus bringing the allusion to *Faniska* into dialogue with the parataxis of the ballad. As I have argued elsewhere, these dramatic interpolations sometimes develop the expositional ideas, as well as serving a transitional function.[39] Indeed, this was the central complaint Tovey held against these sonatas: that '[Schubert's] expositions digress into developments'.[40] Here, there is no development of thematic material, but instead a repurposing of Cherubini's material to serve a dramatic end.

Of course, with Schubert, it is never simply the case of oxymoronic juxtaposition of extremes without purpose; this usually functions alongside a high degree of musical organization. Thus, in D. 8, the lyrical sections are grounded in the major keys of A♭, F and G major while the dramatic passages (transitions and the ostinato) are rooted in the work's two opposing poles: C and F minor. What's more, the shifting between subdominant major and minor that dramatizes the work is enacted via the semitonal motion from C to D♭ foregrounded on the musical surface throughout.

Symmetrical Tonal Design and the Nonresolving Recapitulation: The Overture as Model

The recapitulation answers the exposition with a tonal plot that, as Figure 9.2 illustrates, moves from A1 and A2 in C minor to the first – and only – iteration of B1 in G major, and then to B2 in the keys of G minor and, surprisingly, F minor.

I read the recapitulation as ending with the PAC in F minor in bars 272–276 because – given that B1 is not repeated after B2 as it is in the exposition – this is the point at which the recapitulation's rotation of expositional material (the rhetorical recapitulation) ends.[41] Since this recapitulation does not resolve the exposition's B1 and B2 themes into the tonic key, two questions become of utmost importance: first, how might we understand Schubert's unusual harmonic scheme in relation to both his own subsequent output and the models with which he is engaging, and second, what are the dramatic implications of reading this as a so-called nonresolving recapitulation?

---

[39]   On the juxtaposition of the dramatic and lyric in the early quartets, see Anne M. Hyland, 'The "Tightened Bow": Analysing the Juxtaposition of Drama and Lyricism in Schubert's Paratactic Sonata-Form Movements', in *Irish Musical Analysis: Irish Musical Studies* 11, ed. Julian Horton and Gareth Cox (Dublin: Four Courts Press, 2014), pp. 17–40.

[40]   Donald Francis Tovey, *The Forms of Music* (Oxford: Oxford University Press, 1967), p. 231.

[41]   The 'rhetorical recapitulation' refers to the return of the thematic elements of the exposition in the recapitulation. See Hepokoski, 'Back and Forth from Egmont', p. 28.

Example 9.5a   Schubert, Overture for String Quintet in C minor, D. 8, reduction showing symmetrical tonal plot

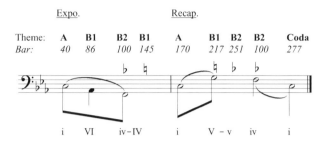

Example 9.5b   Schubert, String Quartet in C minor, D. 32, first movement, reduction showing symmetrical tonal plot

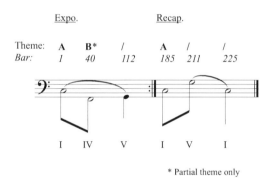

* Partial theme only

One response to the former is to read D. 8 as an early example of Schubert's characteristic use of tonal pairing or symmetry across exposition and recapitulation.[42] The expositional subdominant (minor then major) acts as the tonic's lower fifth, and is answered in the recapitulation with an upper-fifth move to G major (then minor). The tonic-dominant relationship therefore appears in the recapitulation as a means of balancing the lower fifth of the exposition. Schubert employed a similar tonal scheme in 1812 in the first movement of his String Quartet in C

---

[42]   Schubert's propensity for symmetrical tonal designs in his sonatas has been outlined by Sly (2009) and Clark (2011). Although I share Clark's acknowledgement of an underlying symmetry between the exposition and recapitulation in this work (see pp. 208–12), our readings of the recapitulation differ in two respects. For Clark, the material from bar 289 acts as a closing group within the recapitulation, while I read it as a post-cadential coda; thus,

major, D. 32, which also moves from tonic to subdominant in the exposition, and from tonic to dominant in the recapitulation. In the later work, however, Schubert ends the exposition with a cadential passage in the dominant, as a kind of last-minute gesture to the formal dictates: there is no theme actually heard in G major. The correspondences between these works are shown by the thick beams in Examples 9.5a and 9.5b.

Along similar lines, one might also emphasize that D. 8's design is prescient of the *Trout Quintet*, D. 667, the first and last movements of which are structured around similarly symmetrical tonal schemes: I–V / IV–I (in the first movement) and I–IV / V–I (in the Finale).

Lending support to this reading is the fact that the tonal plot of Cherubini's overture is also structured around an unusually placed fifth relationship within a three-key exposition, as illustrated by Example 9.6. Cherubini's exposition moves initially from the tonic, F major, via an MC in C major to Eb major (bVII!) for the statement of the B theme (the ostinato idea modelled by Schubert). The exposition ends in the dominant, C major, as expected.[43] The recapitulation answers this remarkable tonal scheme by moving down a fifth: the Eb passage is heard in Ab major, and the recapitulation ends in F major. Thus, Cherubini's scheme is structured symmetrically *around* the dominant, whereas Schubert's is symmetrical *from* the tonic; both offer a radical rethinking of the fifth-based relationship in sonata form, shifting it to the relationship between second-subject groups.

Example 9.6   Cherubini, Overture to *Faniska*, reduction showing symmetrical tonal plot

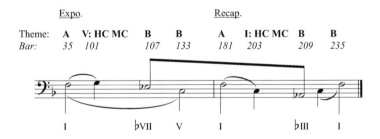

whereas in Clark's reading the recapitulation closes unproblematically in the tonic, I read a nonresolving recapitulation ending in F minor. Second, her analysis makes no reference to the return to F minor in the recapitulation, which I understand as being central to the dramatic narrative of the work.

43   For an alternative reading, see Clark's analysis of this exposition as moving 'from F major to Ab major for its first and second themes'. Clark, *Analyzing Schubert*, p. 232.

Of course, Schubert's nonresolving recapitulation reverts to F minor for its final cadence, thus complicating the symmetry achieved by the move to G. The motivation for this is surely dramatic. In returning to the key of the expositional second group, Schubert reverses the work's expected tonal path: rather than realizing the promise of G major to act as the dominant of the home key, Schubert's move to F minor for the recapitulation's final cadence is an example of how, as Dahlhaus put it, his music processes 'from later events back to earlier ones, and not by goal-consciousness, which presses from earlier to later'.[44] The recapitulation ends with B2 material in a pronounced PAC in F minor: the very cadence that was twice denied this theme in the exposition. Far from lacking a sense of goal, the dramatic effect of this move is created precisely by its realization of an earlier promise: the sudden *déjà entendu* experienced by the listener is accompanied by a sense of retrospective resolution at the cadence point. This is an unexpected turn in an already unorthodox plot.

After this point, there is an extended coda that derives motivically from the retransitional material (found in bars 156–159) and whose role it is to bring the movement back into the tonic key. In the process, Schubert introduces a new cadential melody which intensifies the drama in the final bars of the work (bars 299–304 and bars 306–311). It is here that the music is purged of the chromatic D♭s which signalled the move to F minor earlier in the work, such as in bar 60 leading to an HC in F minor (see again Example 9.3), and during the dramatic use of the Neapolitan at bar 98. As the asterisks in Example 9.7 illustrate, in the coda, this D♭ inflection is intensified dynamically and accentuated rhythmically in the lower parts until it is eventually subsumed within a cadence into C minor (bars 277–289).

Schubert's dramatic use of the coda to bring about tonal closure in the tonic is not to be found in Cherubini's overture, but in the *locus classicus* of the nonresolving recapitulation: Beethoven's *Egmont* Overture, Op. 84 of 1810, a work that shares its generic title with D. 8, and was performed in Vienna on 15 June of that year. In *Egmont*, the coda famously acts not only as a tonal resolution, but also as a dramatic telos for the work, the triumphant *Siegessymphonie* in F major.[45] Might this suggest that Schubert knew this work and wished to summon a similarly dramatic effect? Might he also have known Beethoven's *Coriolan* overture and Gluck's *Alceste* – both of which contain three-key expositions? One cannot say for certain. Nonetheless, it seems likely that, in composing his first overture, Schubert was engaging with this tradition wherein the tonal and thematic layout of the sonata tends to be comparatively free, and tonally mobile recapitulations are more frequently found. This is a feature of this repertoire that had a lasting impact on Schubert's chamber music.

[44] Dahlhaus, 'Sonata Form in Schubert', p. 8.
[45] On the hermeneutic implications of this reading, see Hepokoski, 'Back and Forth from Egmont', pp. 134–6.

Example 9.7   Schubert, Overture for String Quintet in C minor, D. 8, bars 276–289

Conclusion: Towards a Methodology

Despite its early composition date and the composer's relative inexperience, D. 8 is not a tentative exercise in form: there is a perceptible confidence here, one that arguably comes from working with existing models, but also one bolstered by a personal response to musical form, and particularly to the dramatic possibilities of inter-generic dialogue. The work's complex generic constitution is indicative of the fluid approach to form characteristic of much of Schubert's instrumental work. In bringing together diverse models in the service of the string quintet (and quartet), Schubert invites the listener to experience D. 8 as an interactive dialogue between traditions. This necessitates an understanding of musical form that emphasizes intertextuality and dialogue, and cannot easily be accommodated by the otherwise helpful 'conformational' or 'generative' approaches outlined by Mark Evan Bonds.[46] The foundation for such a dialogic approach is laid out in Sonata Theory's guiding principle that musical form is, at base, a product of a work's dialogue with a set of 'generic norms, guidelines, possibilities, expectations, and limits'.[47] This principle holds that in order to grasp the form of a piece of music, it is necessary to understand the generic conventions with which it is most clearly in dialogue; genre is thus 'the decoder of an otherwise unintelligible or free-floating musical message', and form is the product of our engaged understanding of the work's dialogue with it.[48]

As my reading of D. 8 demonstrates, however, the identification of a set of generic 'norms' against which to explore a given work is never a straightforward matter. Neither dialogue nor dialogic form is generically circumscribed: a work may place itself into dialogue with several genres simultaneously, and its compositional problematic is likely to be informed by this multi-way conversation to varying degrees. Moreover, some of these generic markers may take place at the level of what Caplin calls formal functions, rather than formal type, thereby complicating the identification of a single overarching generic norm, even rendering it redundant.[49] These reservations are not insuperable. The concept of dialogic form provides a suitable lens through which to view the dramatic formal strategies of Schubert's early chamber music if attention to small-scale phrase structures and intra-thematic functions (those within a given subject group) remains at the fore.[50]

[46]   Mark Evan Bonds, *Wordless Rhetoric: Musical Form and the Metaphor of the Oration* (Cambridge, MA: Harvard University Press, 1991).

[47]   Hepokoski, 'Sonata Theory and Dialogic Form', in *Musical Form, Forms and Formenlehre*, pp. 71–99, at p. 71.

[48]   Hepokoski and Darcy, *Elements of Sonata Theory*, p. 606.

[49]   On this point, see Caplin's response to Hepokoski in *Musical Form, Forms, and Formenlehre*, pp. 90–95.

[50]   Progress has been made on this front by analytical approaches informed by both Caplin's theory of formal functions and Sonata Theory. See Anne M. Hyland, *Tautology or Teleology?*

In the young Schubert's hands the sonata was an adaptable form, influenced by his study of dramatic song and operatic overture, as well as his part in the school orchestra, his study of the Classical masters, and his interest in contemporaneous compositional trends. The tendency to understand his sonata-form practices in terms of a strict definition of sonata types, and against an exclusively Beethovenian model to the exclusion of these other influences has stifled our engagement with Schubert's juvenilia. In recognizing the diverse, often competing influences that these works bring together, we might begin to acknowledge them as the work of a composer whose individual response to form was already quite apparent, if not yet developed. Moreover, it might encourage a more meaningful engagement with those aspects of form that are not exclusively a property of the individual piece.

❧

Towards an Understanding of Repetition in Franz Schubert's Instrumental Chamber Music (PhD dissertation, University of Cambridge, 2010); and Hyland, 'Rhetorical Closure in the First Movement of Schubert's Quartet in C major, D. 46: A Dialogue with Deformation', *Music Analysis* 28/1 (2009), pp. 111–42.

10

Lyricism and the Dramatic Unity of Schubert's Instrumental Music: The Impromptu in C Minor, D. 899/1 *

Brian Black

Introduction

Lyricism and drama do not sit well together in discussions of Schubert's instrumental music. Today it is widely accepted that the main impulse in his writing is 'lyrical' – a term that usually is set in opposition to 'dramatic', implying a looser, more relaxed approach to the way the music progresses and a privileging of the self-contained lyrical moment over the broader sweep of the work.[1] Yet Schubert's finest instrumental music is also animated by a compelling dramatic process that seizes the imagination of its listeners from the very first bar of the piece and does not relent until all issues and conflicts have been resolved. By 'dramatic' I mean that the music projects the continuity of a coherent chain of events moving irresistibly to a final denouement, much like the unfolding of a well-crafted play. Its hold on the listener depends upon consistency in the music's plan and a progressive development of its material in which the implications of initial actions are realized later in the form.[2] I would thus propose that in such instances, rather

* I would like to thank the editors, James Sobaskie and Joe Davies, for their very helpful comments and suggestions during the development of this chapter.

[1] This opposition implicitly stands behind two of the most important studies of Schubert's instrumental music from the early twentieth century: Felix Salzer's 'Die Sonatenform bei Franz Schubert', *Studien zur Musikwissenschaft* 15 (1928), pp. 86–125; and Donald Francis Tovey's 'Franz Schubert (1797–1828)', in *The Heritage of Music*, ed. H. J. Foss (Oxford: Oxford University Press, 1927) vol. 1, pp. 82–122. It is explicitly stated by Carl Dahlhaus in his differentiation between Beethoven's 'dramatic-dialectic form' and Schubert's 'lyric-epic' form. See his 'Sonata Form in Schubert: The First Movement of the G-Major String Quartet, Op. 161 (D. 887)', trans. Thilo Reinhardt, in *Schubert: Critical and Analytical Studies*, ed. Walter Frisch (Lincoln, NE: University of Nebraska Press, 1986), pp. 1–12. For more on these articles, see the discussion below.

[2] Such a concentrated approach can be found from the beginning of Schubert's compositional career, especially in his early string quartets. The sonata-form movements of these works are focused intensely on their opening material, which in the earliest quartets

than being diametrically opposed, drama and lyricism work together effectively to create a unified and engaging whole. Here the overall disposition and relationship of the parts of the form create a powerful dramatic shape or scenario within which lyricism plays a crucial role.

The principal features of lyricism in Schubert's instrumental music include motivic and melodic repetition, the use of variation as opposed to motivic development, and the presence of 'closed song forms' within the overall structure. These features have been cast as a brake on the forward drive of Schubert's music and thus deficient in producing a truly dramatic structure. As shall be demonstrated, however, they are not in themselves impediments to the realization of the music's potential as drama, but instead often contribute effectively to that realization. A prime example of how lyricism works within an essentially dramatic conception of form is provided by the Impromptu in C minor, D. 899/1, which shall be the exclusive focus of the discussion that follows here. Before dealing with it in some depth, though, it is necessary first to examine those attitudes towards lyricism and drama in Schubert's instrumental music that have shaped its critical reception.

Lyricism and Drama in the Critical Reception of Schubert's Instrumental Music

There are two important influences on the reception history of Schubert's instrumental music: (1) his stature as a composer of Lieder and (2) the Beethovenian yardstick, by which the special characteristics of Beethoven's instrumental music became the critical standard for the treatment of form in the nineteenth century. Concerning the first of these, Schubert's success in the Lied and his melodic gifts encouraged many commentators to look upon Schubert's instrumental forms as predominantly lyrical in nature.[3] Here the main focus fell on the beauty and expressive character of individual melodies without taking into account their wider role in the unfolding of the form. Such an approach led, in turn, to accusations of diffuseness of construction. This can be seen as early as the first substantial biography of the composer by Heinrich Kreissle von Hellborn published in 1864,

---

permeates the whole structure. Gradually from 1810 to 1813, however, the composer comes to admit motivic contrast into the form, yet he also continues to develop the initial harmonic idea of the main theme as a crucial unifying force in the unfolding of the form. See Brian Black, *Schubert's Apprenticeship in Sonata Form: The Early String Quartets* (PhD dissertation, McGill University, 1996), for a detailed discussion of this strategy.

[3]   The roots of this idea may be traced to the composer's own circle of friends. Joseph von Spaun, for instance, considered Schubert's instrumental music to be of secondary importance to the Lieder, although his opinion changed later in the century. See the quote from a letter of 1829 to Eduard Bauernfeld in Otto Erich Deutsch, *Schubert: A Documentary Biography*, trans. Eric Blom (London: Dent, 1946), pp. 895–6.

in which Schubert's instrumental works are characterized as presenting 'a series of exquisitely wrought-out fancies … yet lack[ing] that compactness of form and condensation of power which … seem the special heritage of other composers'.[4] Thus early in its reception history, an implicit dichotomy was set up between the lyrical qualities of Schubert's instrumental music and the requirements of a unified, dramatic structure.

Kreissle von Hellborn's mention of 'other composers' brings us to the Beethovenian standard. From the nineteenth to the mid-twentieth century, Beethoven's 'heroic style' was taken as the model of the dramatic in music.[5] The elemental character of his initial idea was considered crucial as a starting point for subsequent motivic development which at times seems to generate the piece itself.[6] Fundamental to this process is the forward-driving dynamic of the music in which the momentum of fragmentation and harmonic intensification prepares the arrival of important climactic points.[7] These aspects of Beethoven's music were long deemed essential in projecting a cohesive dramatic whole. In contrast, Schubert's lyricism was cast as something problematic, since his initial ideas were seen to be too distinctive and thus closed to further development. Such a view underpins much of the criticism of Schubert's supposedly lyrical, as opposed to dramatic, conception of form.

The definitive statement of this position is found in Felix Salzer's 1928 study of Schubert's sonata forms. Salzer considered their chief weakness to be Schubert's failure to check the lyrical impulse of repeating the same group of motives across a wide expanse, thereby creating a self-contained unit that blocked the necessary flow of the music. For Salzer, it was the improvisatory element that was fundamental to the form, providing a driving force that arises in moving from one small group of motives to the next without over-elaboration – and this basic principle he located

---

[4] Heinrich Kreissle von Hellborn, *Franz Schubert*, 2 vols, trans. Arthur Duke Coleridge (London: Longmans, Green & Co., 1869), vol. 2, pp. 204–5.

[5] For a discussion of Beethoven's heroic style and its influence on musical thinking in the nineteenth and twentieth centuries, see Scott Burnham, *Beethoven Hero* (Princeton: Princeton University Press, 1995). See also Carl Dahlhaus, *Ludwig van Beethoven: Approaches to his Music*, trans. Mary Whittall (Oxford: Clarendon Press, 1993), especially Chapter 4, 'The Symphonic Style'.

[6] See Carl Dahlhaus, *Ludwig van Beethoven: Approaches to his Music*, pp. 89–90, for a discussion of the significance of the rudimentary nature of the opening material of Beethoven's instrumental forms and a comparison of this process with the different temporal approach engendered by richer melodic material in Schubert's instrumental music.

[7] Fragmentation is a term taken from William Caplin's theory of formal functions. It refers to the successive reduction in the lengths of phrase or sub-phrase units. See *Classical Form: A Theory of Formal Functions for the Music of Haydn, Mozart, and Beethoven* (New York: Oxford University Press, 1998), p. 41 and Glossary, p. 255.

in the tradition from C. P. E. Bach through Haydn and Mozart to Beethoven, with Schubert lying irrevocably outside it.[8]

Other criticism, tacitly based upon the Beethovenian model, targeted Schubert's use of variation for consecutive or later statements of ideas, phrases, or themes. Here his practice was seen as something essentially ornamental, a poor substitute for the generative power of true motivic development and thus also an impediment to the dramatic unfolding of his forms.[9] Finally, Schubert's tonal schemes and the colouring of constituent keys by tonal excursions were attacked for their lack of logic or consistency, supposedly resulting in forms that are episodic in construction and thus lacking in dramatic urgency or drive.[10]

Recently a more positive attitude has emerged towards lyricism and its features in Schubert's instrumental music. (Although centred on his sonata forms, many of the statements about Schubert's style can be applied more broadly to other forms.) A watershed for this reassessment is Carl Dahlhaus's essay on the G major String Quartet, D. 887, in which Schubert's approach to sonata form, termed 'lyric-epic', is accepted as a distinct, but equally valid alternative to Beethoven's 'dramatic-dialectic' approach. Of particular importance is Dahlhaus's conclusion that the two linked characteristics of Beethoven's musical process, the logic of its 'motivic/thematic derivation' and the pathos of a 'development pressing constantly forward' are separable, thus allowing a distinctive logic for Schubert's treatment of the form in which a web of motives exists without the need for an unrelenting propulsive energy.

---

[8]   See Su Yin Mak, 'Felix Salzer's "Sonata Form in Franz Schubert" (1928): An English Translation and Edition with Critical Commentary', *Theory and Practice* 40 (2015), pp. 1–121. Mak also provides an excellent discussion of Salzer's argument in her article 'Schubert's Sonata Forms and the Poetics of the Lyric', *Journal of Musicology* 23/2 (Spring 2006), pp. 263–306.

[9]   Carl Dahlhaus confronts such attitudes with particular reference to the Schubert's use of variation in sonata form in 'Sonata Form in Schubert: The First Movement of the G-Major String Quartet, Op. 161 (D. 887)'. A very fine review of the theoretical treatment of variation, especially in relation to sonata form, can be found in Anne M. Hyland's recent article 'In Search of Liberated Time, or Schubert's Quartet in in G Major, D. 887: Once More Between Sonata and Variation', *Music Theory Spectrum* 38/1 (2016), pp. 85–108, specifically pp. 87–9.

[10]   Here once again Schubert's sonata forms are the main object of attack. Salzer focuses on the three-key exposition and condemns it as an illogical expansion of the form where two keys now compete against the tonic ('Die Sonatenform bei Franz Schubert', p. 102). Tovey also criticizes Schubert's handling of the subordinate theme group. He compares the more efficient practice of Mozart and Beethoven to that of Schubert where in the former, 'the admixture of a remote key within [the second subject's] own single phrase … instantly serves the purpose of Schubert's widest digressions'. See 'Franz Schubert (1797–1828)', pp. 106–7. James Webster's objection is broader in that he lists Schubert's inhibition 'against placing an entire large section in a single key' as one of the causes for his failure at times to achieve a subtle and artistic realization of sonata form. See 'Schubert's Sonata Form and Brahms's First Maturity, Part I', *19th-Century Music* 2 (1978), pp. 18–35, specifically p. 35.

The elimination of dramatic urgency as a formal requirement has cleared a way for new, more appreciative lines of inquiry into Schubert's instrumental lyricism. Some scholars have addressed lyricism's special qualities, for instance its suggestion of the workings of memory.[11] Others have explored the formal effect of lyricism, as in Anne M. Hyland's investigation of multiple layers of time and function in Schubert's sonata forms or William Kinderman's discussion of the composer's tragic projection of inner dreams against outer reality.[12] Many of these ideas are well accommodated in Su Yin Mak's argument for considering Schubert's sonata forms as essentially lyrical.[13] Here she draws on the distinction in rhetoric between hypotaxis (the clear, hierarchical arrangement of clauses in a sentence of prose) and parataxis (the looser, associative arrangement of clauses or ideas of equal status, best exemplified by lyric verse). Mak characterizes the normative Classical sonata style as hypotactic and Schubert's lyrical practice as paratactic. She sees lyricism in this sense as applicable to even the highest structural level of Schubert's sonata forms in such a work as the *Quartettsatz*, D. 703, where 'the formal design as a whole alternates between forward-driving sections and static ones, thereby suggesting parataxis on a large scale'.[14]

Thus what was once condemned as failed Beethovenian drama is now prized as successful Schubertian lyricism. Mak's argument provides a solid theoretical foundation for the understanding of the lyrical aspects of Schubert's instrumental music. The question arises, however, of how a looser, paratactic arrangement of the parts of the form can lead to a closely unified whole. Here she appeals to Schenkerian analysis and the presence of foreground motives at deeper structural levels, as in, again, the *Quartettsatz*, D. 703, where the 'descending tetrachord, appearing at the background level as an expanded repetition of the movement's principal motive, unifies the work both structurally and affectively'.[15]

I would argue that such unity also resides in the foreground events of Schubert's instrumental works, which in their arrangement and motivic associations project a powerful dramatic scenario. And in this scenario lyricism plays an extremely

[11]   Especially evocative is Scott Burnham's discussion of the lyrical moment's representation of the act of memory wherein the listener is lost in rapt attention. See his 'Schubert and the Sound of Memory', *Musical Quarterly* 84/4 (2000), pp. 655–63. Dahlhaus again is a pioneer in this approach as seen in his comments about Schubert's circular development process. See *Ludwig van Beethoven: Approaches to his Music*, pp. 89–90.

[12]   See Hyland, 'In Search of Liberated Time, or Schubert's Quartet in in G Major, D. 887: Once More Between Sonata and Variation'; and Kinderman, 'Schubert's Tragic Perspective', in *Schubert: Critical and Analytical Perspectives*, ed. Walter Frisch (Lincoln, NE: University of Nebraska Press, 1996), pp. 65–83.

[13]   See Su Yin Mak, 'Schubert's Sonata Forms and the Poetics of the Lyric'.

[14]   Mak, 'Schubert's Sonata Forms and the Poetics of the Lyric', p. 302.

[15]   This idea is advanced in Su Yin Mak's doctoral thesis, *Schubert's Lyricism Reconsidered: Structure, Design and Rhetoric* (Saarbrücken: Lambert, 2010), p. 112.

important, highly original role. Drama itself rarely consists of incessant action. Even in a driven work like *Macbeth*, the frozen horror of Lady Macbeth's mad scene contributes something crucial to the dramatic shape and meaning of the play. Thus the lyrical moments of Schubert's music should not be seen as static and self-sufficient, but must be understood in their relationship with the more dynamic passages and what that relationship contributes to the effect of the larger whole.[16] Furthermore, the procedures associated with Schubert's lyricism – his use of widespread motivic repetition, variation, tonal excursions, and 'closed' song forms – often generate forces that animate the music on the broadest level as a unified dramatic entity. To understand this we will now turn to the Impromptu in C minor, D. 899/1.

The General Form of the Impromptu

The Impromptu is the epitome of lyricism in that it essentially consists of the alternation of two highly profiled and cadentially closed themes, A and B, with the A theme grounded in the tonic (C minor in the first two statements and C major in the third, serving as a coda), and the B theme appearing first in A♭ major, then in G minor. The most obvious form this layout suggests is a peculiar rondo structure, ABABA, as found in a number of slow movements across Schubert's career, but especially in such late works as the String Quartet in G major, D. 887 and the Piano Sonatas in G major, D. 894, and C minor, D. 958. There are certain features of the Impromptu, however, that set it apart from these movements. Its B sections are extremely lyrical and tonally closed, unlike the highly unstable, fantasy-like B sections of the examples mentioned above.[17] There is also a pervasive reliance on variation at all levels of the form. These differences point to the influence

---

[16]   Anne M. Hyland discusses the synthesis of lyrical and dramatic elements within a paratactic structure in 'The "Tightened Bow": Analysing the Juxtaposition of Drama and Lyricism in Schubert's Paratactic Sonata-Form Movements', in *Irish Musical Analysis*, ed. Gareth Cox and Julian Horton, *Irish Musical Studies* 11, pp. 17–40 (Dublin: Four Courts Press, 2015).

[17]   The B sections of the G major String Quartet's slow movement have the highly unsettled character of a development, including large-scale sequential repetition. Those of the slow movement of the C minor Piano Sonata are truncated interior themes and thus cadentially open. For a discussion of such themes, see William Caplin, *Classical Form: A Theory for the Instrumental Music of Haydn, Mozart, and Beethoven*, pp. 212–13 and pp. 233–5 for the use of interior themes in the five-part rondo. The B sections of the G major Piano Sonata are also quite unstable and fantasy-like in character, although they are closed off cadentially. Consequently the B sections of all three movements project the character of a certain type of interior theme, rather than subordinate themes, and thus reinforce the rondo element of the music.

of two further formal types: an anomalous sonata form without development (sometimes referred to as a slow-movement form) and a set of double or alternating variations *à la* Haydn, in which the two themes are similar in their opening ideas, but contrasting in mode and affect.[18] Each of these two formal types brings with it its own dramatic implications and processes which affect the character of the Impromptu (see Figure 10.1).

With respect to the sonata-form paradigm, the initial modulation to Ab major for the B theme and that theme's intensely lyrical character and full cadential closure create the impression of a subordinate theme with the expectation that it will be recapitulated later in the tonic.[19] The recapitulation of the theme in G minor is thus a marked departure that generates, rather than resolves, structural tensions and demands interpretation (as shall be seen below, that resolution does occur, but in an unusual way and by thematic proxy). With respect to the double variation set, the alteration of each theme on its return has its own dramatic potential. First, the pervasive presence of variation helps to create a sense of constant forward momentum through an intensification of the thematic material, and this momentum overrides the simple alternation of the two themes and leads the listener to a precise moment of climax in the Impromptu. Second, the themes are not static in character, but in their transformations seem to react to events as they unfold. The B theme is the most radically changed when it is restated in G minor: its original vision-like quality with its flowing triplet quaver accompaniment (Example 10.1a) is replaced by an anxious feeling expressed in a nervous semiquaver accompaniment and syncopated quaver bass (Example 10.1b). And this anxiety erupts into the aggressive *forte* restatement of the theme in bars 139–148 (not shown).[20]

The Dramatization of Tonal Relationships

As the general key scheme and the transformation of the B theme suggest, the Impromptu presents a powerful dramatization of its tonal relationships, centred

[18] On Haydn's double variation sets, see Elaine Sisman's authoritative study *Haydn and the Classical Variation* (Cambridge, MA: Harvard University Press, 1993), pp. 150–62.

[19] The choice of key (the submediant in C minor), the unusual modulation to that key and the intense, lyrical character of the new theme are all shared with the *Quartettsatz*, D. 703, itself an anomalous sonata form. A full synthesis of the five-part ABABA rondo structure and sonata form can be found in the slow movement of the Symphony in C major 'The Great', D. 944. For a discussion of its structure, see A. Peter Brown, *The Symphonic Repertoire, Vol. 2 – The First Golden Age of the Viennese Symphony: Haydn, Mozart, Beethoven, and Schubert* (Bloomington: Indiana University Press, 2002), pp. 636–7.

[20] The strong change in character in the variation of the B theme is a departure from the style of Haydn double variations and represents a distinctly Romantic element in the Impromptu's form.

bb. 1–33	34–41	42–74	74–82	83–95	96–119	120–24	125–52	153–60	160–68	169–204
C minor		A♭ major			C minor		G minor	G major		C major

Sonata form without development:

bb. 1–33	34–41	42–74	74–82	83–95	96–119	120–24	125–52	153–60	160–68	169–204
Exposition					Recapitulation (anomalous)					Coda
Main theme		Subordinate theme			Main theme		Subordinate theme			
A	transition	B	closing section	retransition	A¹	transition	B¹	closing section	retransition	A²

Double variations:

bb. 1–33	34–41	42–74	74–82	83–95	96–119	120–24	125–52	153–60	160–68	169–204
Theme 1		Theme 2			Variation 1 of Theme 1		Variation 1 of Theme 2			Variation 2 of Theme 1

Figure 10.1 Formal Implications in the Structure of the Impromptu in C minor, D. 899/1

Example 10.1   Schubert, Impromptu in C minor, D. 899/1, transformation of B theme

a) B theme (bars 41–46)

b) B theme transformed in B¹ section (bars 124–129)

upon the initial contrast between C minor and A♭ major and expressed first through the difference in character and structure of the two themes A and B, and second through the projected substance of the keys they inhabit. In the latter case, the projection of the substance or stability of a key depends upon how that key is approached and how it behaves. In Schubert's mature instrumental music the use of a tonal feint or sudden deflection into an unexpected key can suggest that the new key is something insubstantial, akin to a vision or dream-like state, and this suggestion has a significance for the overall dramatic scenario of the movement, where a distinction is made between a key that has been carefully prepared and fully established and one that has arisen in an unusual way. Furthermore Schubert's 'unprepared' keys are often coloured by tonal digressions which undercut the solidity of the key while giving it a vulnerable, searching quality. The C minor Impromptu provides an excellent example of both of these processes, which we will discuss in more detail later. For the moment, however, it will suffice to provide a brief sketch of the tonal relations in the Impromptu and their dramatic implications.

While C minor is firmly established by repeated, emphatic PACs in the A section, the B section's A♭ major is presented as something less stable: it is entered through a sudden cadential deflection (bars 38–41, see Example 10.4 and discussion on pp. 245–6 including footnote 25) and is subsequently coloured by two digressions from its parallel minor to C♭ major (bars 47–51 and bars 66–70). Furthermore it returns immediately and directly to C minor in the ensuing retransition.[21] The rest of the piece pursues the dramatic implications of this instability by displacing the submediant for the minor dominant (G minor) in the B[1] section while at the same time completely altering that theme's character. B[1]'s closing section shifts to G major (bars 152–160), another unstable tonality which, reduced ultimately to the harmonic status of the home dominant, prepares for the return of the tonic in the retransition (bars 160–167) that leads to the coda (A[2]).[22]

These events are highly suggestive of a dramatic scenario, as can be seen in the similar interpretations of the Impromptu presented separately by Charles Fisk and Susan McClary.[23] Each considers the work to represent an interior journey, which Fisk situates within the figure of the wanderer in early Romanticism. For both, the germ of the music's drama lies in the contrast between the A theme (which conveys a feeling of confinement and frustration in its narrow melodic compass and repeatedly emphatic cadential closure in C minor) and the B theme (which, upon its sudden release into A♭ major, suggests the freedom of a dream with its flowing triplet accompaniment and expanding melodic range). It is the return of the B theme in G minor that represents the moment of reversal in their interpretative scheme, for in its now agitated, even agonized character it seems to be reacting to some catastrophe that has obliterated the hope of its earlier incarnation, and this shadow hangs over the concluding statement of the A theme in the coda, where its C major transformation is still haunted by reminiscences of C minor.[24]

---

[21]   Here the A♭ falls melodically to the G over a VI–I$^6_4$ in C minor (bars 83–84). Susan McClary deals with the instability of the submediant in the minor mode and the resulting character and significance of this key region in the C minor Impromptu. For McClary, much of the dream-like nature and tragic overtones of the modulation to A♭ major arise from the tension between the stable A♭ triad and contrapuntal tendency of degree 6̂ to fall to degree 5̂, as it does explicitly in the retransition to the A[1] section. See 'Pitches, Expression, Ideology: An Exercise in Mediation', *Enclitic* 7 (1983), pp. 76–86, specifically 77–8.

[22]   It is perhaps due to its instability arising from its natural tendency to assume the harmonic function of the home dominant that the major dominant key is rarely if ever used as the subordinate tonality in a Classical minor-mode sonata-form exposition.

[23]   Fisk, *Returning Cycles: Contexts for the Interpretation of Schubert's Impromptus and Last Sonatas* (Berkeley: University of California Press, 2001), pp. 25–7 and 123–36; McClary, 'Pitches, Expression, Ideology: An Exercise in Mediation'. A third, more recent interpretation of the dramatic scenario behind the Impromptu is provided by David Damschroder in his commentary on Fisk's discussion. See *Harmony in Schubert* (Cambridge: Cambridge University Press, 2010), pp. 201–11.

[24]   Although McClary and Fisk are quite close in their interpretations, they part company in what they see as the engine of the drama. According to McClary, it resides in the fatalistic

Dramatic Unity, Variation, and the Process
of Intensification across the Impromptu

That the music can support such interpretations convincingly is evidence of its successful construction as a *dramatic* unity, a topic which we will now pursue in more detail. Here we are mainly concerned with those processes animating the whole structure of the Impromptu and serving to dramatize the tonal relationships outlined above. Let us begin by looking more closely at the Impromptu's pervasive use of variation. This technique works in two ways in the piece. Concerning the B theme, variation transforms the affective character of the theme upon its return, and this transformation has a profound dramatic significance, as discussed above. Concerning the A theme, the variations applied to it bring into play a process of intensification that, in building to a central climax (bars 111–119), creates a clearly defined dramatic shape for the whole piece. Such a process is already a dominant feature of the opening A section, which consists of two statements of what will be referred to as a 'double period', meaning two melodically similar periods that work together as a unit (Example 10.2). Within the individual periods of the double period there is a textural intensification with the antecedents of each consisting of a single melodic line answered by the four-part harmony of their consequents (Example 10.2a, bars 1–4 compared to 5–8). Between the periods of the double period there is a harmonic intensification: while period 1 remains exclusively in C minor, both the antecedent and consequent of period 2 begin as if in E♭ major but settle back into C minor for their cadences (Example 10.2b, bars 9–13). This harmonic chiaroscuro increases the power of the C minor cadences, as the bright E♭ excursions darken into the tonic return. Finally the repetition of the full double period in bars 18–33 represents a more powerful statement of what has gone before: the antecedents thicken in texture to four-part harmony featuring a new distinctive bass; the consequents project an amplified chordal texture with bass octaves which reach a new low register for the dominant-to-tonic gesture of the concluding PACs (Example 10.2c, bars 17–25). Thus the A section is marked by a crescendo in intensity which emerges above all in the increasingly emphatic effect of its PACs (compare bars 8–9 to bars 32–33).

On the broader level, the A¹ section (bars 96–119) represents an intensified variation of the original A section (Example 10.3). It is now dominated by an agitated triplet quaver accompaniment and a new interior countermelody, while its consequents have become even more assertive with their powerful descending bass lines and fierce concluding PACs (bars 100–103 and 108–111). What is more, these alterations form part of a steady rhythmic progression across the piece

nature of the submediant key which initially projects a stable tonality, but must inevitably sink down to the dominant of the home key. For Fisk, on the other hand, it lies in the power of the dominant, which is set in motion with the opening G octave and continues throughout the piece, eventually denying any hope of escape from the wanderer's alienated condition.

Example 10.2   Schubert, Impromptu in C minor, D. 899/1, process of intensification across the A section

a) Textural intensification within the periods of the double period (bars 1–8)

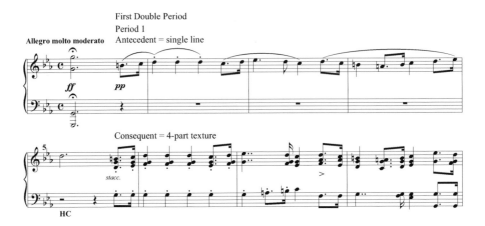

b) Harmonic intensification between the periods (bars 9–16)

connecting the A¹ section to the previous B section: the triplet rhythm originates in the new arpeggiated accompaniment of the B theme (bars 41–73), becoming a gentle murmur of repeated chords in the theme's closing section (bars 74–82). The repeated chords in turn are transformed into something more disturbed and aggressive in the powerful return to C minor of the retransition (bars 83–95) (here the low octave at the beginning of each bar helps to create the darker, more urgent effect). And the insistent triplet rhythm, now reduced to the pulsation of a single

c) Intensification between the double periods (bars 17–33)

G, electrifies the beginning of the A¹ section (bars 96–111) with an unsettling energy, which is released in the descending bass that drives that section's cadential progressions (bars 111–119).

The sense of a continuous unfolding of events is carried further in the climactic final cadences of the A¹ section (bars 111–119) in which the register is expanded simultaneously to both its highest and lowest limits, in the most rhetorically powerful cadences of the whole piece. This represents a transformation of the transition to A♭ major at the end of the A section and serves as the turning point of the drama, which consequently transforms the character of the ensuing B¹ section (Example 10.4). Here we turn to the dramatic significance of how a key is approached or prepared, a topic touched on earlier.

The original passage (Example 10.4a, bars 34–41) modulates to A♭ major for the B theme. It does so through two parallel cadences: the first in C minor, the second beginning in C minor but diverted into A♭ major with the introduction of the Db in bar 39. This unexpected tonal shift relieves the mounting tensions of the A section, evident in the section's increasingly emphatic PACs, and imbues the new key (Ab major) and its theme with the feeling of an escape into another world.[25] In contrast the cadential passage at the end of the A[1] section offers no magical escape through the Db (Example 10.4c, bars 111–119); this note now functions squarely as the root of the Neapolitan six chord, with both cadences ending powerfully in C minor (cadence 1 in bar 115 and cadence 2 in bar 119). The ensuing move to G minor (bars 119–124) is accomplished by another PAC (bars 122–124). The effect here is a complete reversal of the sudden dream-like release into Ab that initiated the B section back in bars 39–41. The cadence is focused on its destination from the beginning, resignedly sinking down into the new tonic; and this emotional atmosphere colours the anxious restatement of the B theme.

The marked contrast between the cadence in Ab major and the one in G minor reveals the importance of Schubert's modulatory ploys in the construction of his music as convincing drama. The unusual modulation to Ab is not merely a local colouristic effect but a crucial part of a carefully worked out and effective dramatic scenario in which – to turn to an analogy developed by William Kinderman[26] – the suggestion of an escape into an interior dream-like state in the modulation to Ab major is answered by the bitter return to reality in the modulation to G minor. The difference in the two modulations also illustrates Su Yin Mak's distinction between paratactic and hypotactic musical relations. The unusual entrance into Ab major is paratactic in that it seems to abandon the normal procedures of a carefully prepared modulation, while the G minor modulation is hypotactic in that it follows those procedures. Here, though, the paratactic does not function as the predominant method of organization in the piece, but rather as something out of the ordinary, a marked event that draws its dramatic significance from its contrast with the more normative, hypotactic modulation to G minor. Thus, as with lyricism itself, the paratactic plays a specific, carefully highlighted role in the unfolding of the musical drama.

---

[25] This 'deflected cadence' strategy is one of Schubert's most effective innovations in modulation and can be found in works across his career. See Brian Black, 'Schubert's "Deflected Cadence" Transitions and the Classical Style', in *Formal Functions in Perspective: Essays on Musical Form from Haydn to Adorno*, ed. Steven Vande Moortele, Julie Pedneault-Deslauriers and Nathan John Martin (Rochester, NY: University of Rochester Press, 2015), pp. 165–97. For a broader discussion of Schubert's unusual transition strategies and their effects, see Susan Wollenberg, 'Schubert's Transitions', in *Schubert Studies*, ed. Brian Newbould (Aldershot: Ashgate, 1998), pp. 16–61; and Wollenberg, *Schubert's Fingerprints: Studies in the Instrumental Works* (Farnham: Ashgate, 2011), pp. 47–99.

[26] See his 'Schubert's Tragic Perspective'.

The Dramatic/Motivic Role of the PAC

As can be seen in the cadences in A♭ major and G minor, the PAC carries substantial weight as a marker of the stages of the drama, and in this capacity is developed motivically throughout the piece. Of particular importance is the deflected-cadence modulation to A♭ major (Example 10.4a). The magical effect of this modulation depends upon the sudden transformation of the pitch content

Example 10.3   Schubert, Impromptu in C minor, D. 899/1, bars 95–111, rhythmic and textural intensification of A¹ section

Example 10.4   Schubert, Impromptu in C minor, D. 899/1, comparison of the
                  modulation to the B and the B¹ section

a) Modulation to B section (bars 33–41)

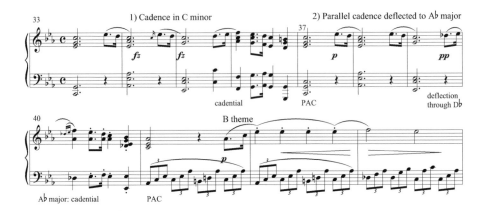

b) Modulation to B section, parallel cadences

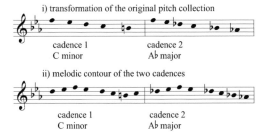

of the initial C minor cadence (bars 36–37) in the deflected cadence to A♭ major
(upbeat to bar 40 and bar 41, summary in Example 10.4b).[27] This transformation
seems to hang on the introduction of the foreign pitch D♭. A similar cadential
deflection then colours the new B theme in two excursions to C♭ major
(Example 10.5, bars 47–51 and bars 66–70, not shown). Here the plan depends
on two parallel phrases, the first cadencing in A♭ major, the second beginning
in A♭ major, suddenly darkening to A♭ minor and emerging unexpectedly into a

---

[27]   I have discussed the mechanics and effects of such deflected-cadence modulations in
'Remembering a Dream: The Tragedy of Romantic Memory in the Modulatory Processes of
Schubert's Sonata Forms', *Intersections* 25/1–2 (2005), pp. 202–28 and 'Schubert's "Deflected-
Cadence" Transitions and the Classical Style'.

c) Modulation to the B¹ section (bars 111–126)

cadence in C♭ major. Once again the pitch content of the original cadence (in A♭ major) is transformed in the subsequent cadence (in C♭ major), which here hangs on the introduction of the F♭ (Example 10.5b).[28] Although the B section is firmly grounded cadentially in A♭ major, the interior shifts to C♭ major become a defining element of the theme's character: they add a certain yearning quality to it that subtly undermines the solidity of A♭ major, as can be seen in a comparison

---

[28]   In both the modulation to A♭ major to initiate the B section and the B theme's internal modulations to C♭ we have an affecting interior transformation of the sound space, rather than a forceful, striving modulation. The effect is still profoundly dramatic, but more in the sense of a sudden revelation within a soliloquy rather than an energetic action on stage.

with theme A.[29] While theme A's E♭ excursions are still anchored by cadences in C minor, theme B's C♭ excursions culminate in cadences in C♭, thus generating a competing tonality locally. Consequently the character of the B theme stands in stark contrast to that of the A theme and its insistent cadences in C minor: from unflinching tonal certainty the music passes to a less stable identity; and the B theme's vulnerable character seems to have some relationship with the collapse of its dream in the theme's later G minor incarnation. To understand this more fully we must look at the motivic relationship of the A and B themes in some detail.

The Close Motivic Relationship of Theme A and Theme B

Despite their differences, the A and B themes are actually closely related in their initial ideas (Example 10.6): both share the same opening dotted rhythm, repeated-note figure and general profile, specifically their prominent neighbour-tone motion. The modulation to A♭ major in bar 41 only shifts this profile up a semitone from D to E♭, yet the sense of liberation is immediately felt in the unusual character of the modulation that colours the new theme. The B theme thus begins as a transfiguration of the A theme.[30] Why the return of the B theme in G minor has such a catastrophic sense to it is due in part to the fact that, in this key, the head of the B theme shifts back to the same pitches as the head of the A theme. Here the latent similarities between the heads of the two themes, which were obscured in the liberating effect of the modulation to A♭ major, now come into focus in the B theme's exact replication of the D–E♭ motion of the head of the A theme, as if the separate identity of the B theme has now been obliterated and along with it its bright promise.

The Dramatic Process and the Resolution of its Conflicts

Stepping back to view the Impromptu from a broader perspective, we can see the details just discussed come together to form a compelling dramatic plot. And the unique shape of this plot grows out of the ramifications of a striking interruption. Theme A builds in intensity from a subdued *pianissimo* beginning to *fortissimo*

[29]   These shifts also loosen up the tonal space of theme B. The beginning of the theme is similar to the A theme in that it occupies a restricted range (in this case a sixth from A♭ up to F). The range, however, expands radically following the cadence in C♭ at bar 51. This expansion contributes to the theme's yearning character mentioned above.

[30]   A similar point is made by Charles Fisk who refers to theme B as a variation of theme A. See his *Returning Cycles: Contexts for the Interpretation of Schubert's Impromptus and Last Sonatas*, p. 126.

Example 10.5   Schubert, Impromptu in C minor, D. 899/1, internal shift to C♭ major in the B section

a) Shift to C♭ major (bars 41–51)

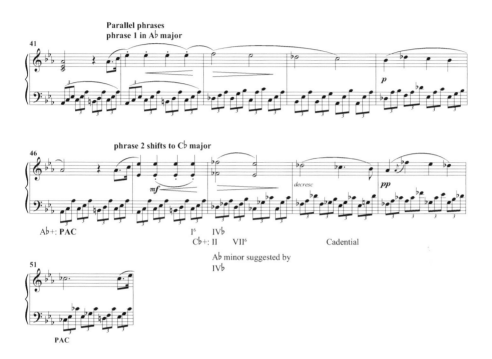

b) Summary of shift to C♭ major

i) transformation of the original pitch collection

cadence 1
A♭ major

cadence 2
C♭ major

ii) contour of B theme phrase 1 contour of B theme phrase 2

cadence 1
A♭ major

cadence 2
C♭ major

Example 10.6   Schubert, Impromptu in C minor, D. 899/1, comparison of the heads of
                    theme A and B

cadences in C minor which, at their most intense moment, are suddenly diverted
to A♭ major and the dream-like lyricism of Theme B. This vision, however, proves
unstable in its internal tonal excursions and disappears in the ensuing retransition
to C minor (bars 83–84). Now the process of intensification revives, reaching its
climax in the final overpowering cadences of the A¹ section. These cadences are
answered by a retreat into G minor. Here the B¹ theme is robbed of its original
vision-like quality as its opening phrases are confined within the melodic compass
of the A theme and clothed in an anxious subdued accompaniment. The shift to
G major in the B¹ theme's closing section prepares the retransition to C minor, but
at the last minute the music unexpectedly brightens into C major for the entrance
of the A² theme and the final reconciliation of the main conflicts in the drama
(Example 10.7).

The sudden modal transformation of the A² theme recalls the surprise of the
modulation to A♭ major that initiated the B section. Like A♭ major, the C major
of this incarnation of the A theme is complex. As the theme progresses it recapitulates
the tonal relationships of the B theme – the tonic major (bars 169–176), tonic minor
(bars 177–180) and relative of the tonic minor (bars 181–182). It then resolves the
conflict between E♭ and E♮ in favour of the latter in the final extended cadence in
C major (bars 185–193). In this respect, the A² theme assumes the function of
recapitulation in place of the failed B¹ theme in G minor (see Figure 10.1 above)
and the convincing resolution of the B theme's tonal relationships in the tonic
sphere is made possible by the audible similarities between the A and the B themes.

The most touching resolution, though, is reserved for the coda's final cadences.
All of the previous incarnations of the A theme have ended fatalistically in C minor
with cadences marked by an inexorable descent to the tonic. In the theme's
concluding statement, now in C major, the pattern threatens to reassert itself as the
consequent phrase is extended by repetitions of this descending motion of despair,
the last of which darkens to minor (bars 185–190). But at the last moment the
cadential 6/4 is quietly transfigured by a return to the major mode and a reversal of
the cadential motion, with the melody ascending to the tonic in a gesture of infinite
tenderness (bars 191–193). And this gesture is echoed in the coda's closing section,
each time answering the recall of those events that marked the very beginning of

Example 10.7   Schubert, Impromptu in C minor, D. 899/1, bars 164–204, retransition and A² section (coda)

Example 10.7 (continued)

the Impromptu – the stern G octave, now in counterpoint with the lonely first bars of the A theme. Thus, like a dramatic epilogue, the Impromptu's final cadential closure reflects on and brings a bittersweet solace to the whole work.

Lyricism and Innovation in the Impromptu's Dramatic Structure

Let us now return to the lyrical character of the C minor Impromptu. As mentioned earlier, this piece represents the essence of Schubert's lyricism. Its two themes are strongly profiled, intense entities. Each is a stable structure, as is evident in the balanced periodic construction of the A theme and the full cadential closure of the B theme, reinforced by a closing section.[31] These themes, however, are not self-sufficient or shut off from each other, with the dynamic of the form consisting of the static contemplation of one theme, then the other. As we have seen, there is a feeling of momentum that drives across the alternation of the themes to create an overarching and convincing whole.

Schubert achieves this momentum without relying on Beethovenian techniques. Instead of motivic development to drive the music, the focus falls on the thematic level and the drama inherent in the changes in a theme's character. Instead of fragmentation to power the build-up to the main climaxes, a steady four-bar rhythm is maintained which gives the music a monumental and irresistible power, as in the cadential closure of the A and A^1 sections.[32] Other processes, not usually associated with drama in music, also assume a dramatic significance in the Impromptu. Variation, for instance, is of central importance in the unfolding of the sequence of events, and it is neither static nor merely ornamental in character, but possesses a compelling energy in the process of intensification that animates it, as in the progression of the A theme up to the midpoint of the form. The course of this energy, once released, may be traced in the powerful rhythmic progression of the plot, which passes from the measured tread of the opening A theme through the increasingly anguished transformations of the B theme's triplet motion to the collapse of that theme in the nervous semiquaver accompaniment of the B^1 section. Modulation also comes to the fore in the dramatic meaning of the Impromptu, defining the role of a theme and its key in the overall scenario. Here the unusual way in which a key is approached and entered takes on specific affective qualities that colour the modulation's tonal and thematic goal, as in the contrast between the move to A♭ major in the B section and to G minor in the B^1 section.

Taken together these developments in the Impromptu define something new as far as the dramatic conception of music is concerned. In the changed character of the B^1 section we have a telling example of thematic transformation, a technique that plays a crucial role across the nineteenth century, especially in the overtly dramatic music of Hector Berlioz and Franz Liszt. In the striking modulation to A♭ major, with its suggestion of an escape into an interior state of being, we have the forerunner of similar modulations that explore an inner realm of experience, as in the famous shift to D♭ major for the lovers' theme in Tchaikovsky's *Romeo and Juliet Overture*. And in the immense build up to climaxes, where a steady phrase

---

[31]   Here, however, a distinction must be made between the structural stability of the theme and the tonal instability of its key of A♭ major, suggested by the theme's interior excursions to C♭ major (see Example 10.5 and discussion on pp. 248–50).

[32]   In the B theme, the phrase length actually increases to five bars. Poundie Burstein has proposed that the lack of fragmentation and even in some cases the expansion of units in Schubert's development process is an important mark of the lyrical nature of his writing. See 'Lyricism, Structure, and Gender in Schubert's G Major String Quartet', *The Musical Quarterly* 18/1 (1997), p. 53.

length is maintained we have a suggestion of the overwhelming power of the sublime in nature, a major preoccupation of the early Romantics.[33] Thus Schubert's Impromptu in C minor not only reveals the qualities of music as engaging drama, but also stands as an innovative art work pointing ahead to later developments in the nineteenth century.

※

---

[33]   Here I am referring to the psychological effect of the sublime as proposed in Edmund Burke's famous essay *A Philosophical Enquiry into the Origin of our Ideas of the Sublime and Beautiful* and pursued in early Romantic landscape painting. This, however, is a topic for another study. For a modern edition of the essay, see Edmund Burke, *A Philosophical Enquiry into the Origin of our Ideas of the Sublime and Beautiful*, ed. J. T. Boulton (London: Routledge and Kegan Paul, 1958).

11

Music as Poetry: An Analysis of the First Movement of Schubert's Piano Sonata in A Major, D. 959*

Xavier Hascher

Introducing the Poetic

Schubert's music abounds in extraordinary passages, and his mature instrumental works no less so than the rest of his oeuvre. One such passage, which bears his mark unmistakably, occurs in the exposition of the second theme in the first movement of the Piano Sonata in A major, D. 959. After a lengthy dominant preparation in E major that started in bar 39, the theme is introduced by a rising triplet motif in the right hand alone, which serves as a particularly florid lead-in to it, prolonging the dominant chord. As the left hand joins in and the texture thickens again while the rhythm slows down to quavers, the theme finally enters in bar 55, with a soft *pianissimo* dynamic. At a superficial hearing, its design seems quite straightforward: a first phrase member, *a*, starting on the tonic and coming to rest on the dominant, is repeated with a contrasting harmonic ending – this repetition forming what appears to be an answering phrase member of corresponding length, *a'*. These are followed by a continuation phrase, *b*, of a length approximately twice that of the initial phrase member, which rounds out the theme. However, its conclusion does not bring about the expected perfect cadence: instead, the dominant is extended, immediately allowing for a return of the triplets (Example 11.1).[1]

* My gratitude goes to Susan Wollenberg, of Oxford University, for her invitation to give the paper in which this chapter originates; to Christine Martin and the late Walther Dürr, of the *Neue Schubert Ausgabe*, for their warm welcome on my visit to Tübingen while I was preparing the material for it; to Michael Mahin, of Washington, DC, and Richard Hermann, of the University of New Mexico, for many stimulating exchanges; to Lorraine Byrne Bodley, of Maynooth University, for her scrupulous reading of my draft and invaluable suggestions.
[1] For a recent (and captivating) analysis of this movement, see Julian Horton, 'The First Movement of Schubert's Piano Sonata D. 959 and the Performance of Analysis', in *Schubert's Late Music: History, Theory, Style*, ed. Lorraine Byrne Bodley and Julian Horton (Cambridge: Cambridge University Press, 2016), pp. 171–90. Inevitably, my own analysis intersects in places with Horton's.

Example 11.1   Schubert, Piano Sonata in A major, D. 959, first movement, bars 39–76, end of transition and second theme

Details are important, and this is especially true of Schubert's music, where they are often revealing. It is interesting to note that both opening phrase members *a* and *a'* are five bars long, yet not because of the purported irregularity that this might entail. Though infrequent, five-bar groupings can be found in classical music.[2] This is not what happens here since each phrase member in fact presents a written fermata over its last chord so that, by eliminating this fermata, it could be rewritten to fit in exactly four bars (Example 11.2). What Schubert achieves is a subtle dissociation between the successive clauses. Moreover, the second phrase member, which we had first interpreted as an 'answer' out of an external resemblance of the whole with a classic 'sentence' structure, reveals itself as a variant of the first phrase member,[3] a

---

[2]   The most strikingly deliberate example being the opening theme of Mozart's String Quintet in C major K. 515, first movement.

[3]   I use the term 'sentence' here in the sense introduced by Arnold Schoenberg, *Fundamentals of Musical Composition* (London: Faber & Faber, 1967), p. 20.

rewriting of it, of which the last part is deflected towards V of G major, the relative key of E minor, in place of closing on I of E major. The harmony does not return to the tonic chord as it would with a proper 'answer'; it does not modulate to some other, substitutive tonic either, but comes to rest again on a dominant, at a minor third's distance from the actual one. The relation between the two phrase members is thus one of parallelism rather than complementarity.

The pause introduced by the fermata interrupts the action as if for a moment of reflection before the next gesture is undertaken. It is as though music was listening into itself for something other than what it is saying, something of which it is reminded and which it tries to recall. The harmonic deflection in the second phrase member is the result of this reflection: it renounces the expected harmonic symmetry in search of some lost thought – hidden as it were in the depths of music's own memory – which it seeks to recapture, and of which it has been reminded at the very same time that the theme is articulated.

Due to the new pause that ensues, the continuation phrase *b* is delayed and somewhat detached from what precedes. It enters as a reminiscence, as the result of an association of thoughts with the rhythm of the first two bars of the original phrase member, which was also facilitated by the change of key. It is not so much a

Example 11.2   Schubert, Piano Sonata in A major, D. 959, first movement, hypothetical
                 rewriting of second theme

continuation, in fact, than a theme in itself, a theme-stemming-from-the-theme like
some unexpected fluorescence, with a two-bar clause immediately repeated almost
literally, and giving way to its own continuation. Not only is G major a relatively
'darker', more muted key than E major, but the transposition of the second phrase
member in the higher register and its octave doublings give it a timbric richness
which, by comparison, makes the new phrase, with its compact distribution of notes
in the medium and low registers, sound more subdued. This effect is reinforced
by the use of inverted chords (I^6 and V_3^4, bars 65–69) which prevent the harmony
from resonating fully. The contrast between the two keys is even more perceptible
because of the sustained effervescence leading up to the theme, which saturates the
ear with the dominant of E major.

The tonal retrogression back three sharps translates aurally into temporal
distance and a move into some undefined past. Such an extraordinary impression
is dependent for its existence on the addition of an extra bar to each of the initial
phrase members, as well as on the quiet dynamics. It would be entirely ineffective
otherwise. The fermatas act as successive thresholds, as hesitations that bring
back the reminiscence step by step, isolating this particular moment from the rest
and setting it in relief. The return to E major in bar 70 reinstates the present in a
gradual, seamless way, as if by catching up with the normal course of the music.

If this moment is a reminiscence, it can only be of something that was there
before, i.e. before the sonata even started to unfold.[4] It belongs outside the frame

---

[4]   Memory has become a prominent trope in approaches to Schubert's instrumental music
over the last two decades, especially since the publication of *The Musical Quarterly* 84/4
(2000), a special issue dedicated to that topic with essays by Walter Frisch, John Daverio,
John Gingerich, Charles Fisk, and Scott Burnham. Reliance on memory, in relation to
notions of pastness, nostalgia, and reminiscence, is considered in a number of ways to

of the sonata – indeed, it may be said that it does not even belong in the sonata, or only associatively, since it is substituted for what should have been the proper continuation of the second theme. Schubert creates temporal depth by means of distinct tonal layers: as the music still moves on, though tentatively, we feel paradoxically taken back. Mozart's virtuosity may reside in his swift changes of moods whereby one topic glides into another effortlessly as though moving through an emotional kaleidoscope. Schubert is generally less mobile, but with him music becomes layered: there is an outside, and an inside; a without, and a within. Or, in Freud's words, a manifest and a latent.[5]

---

describe the singularity of Schubert's compositional technique and the manner in which his music is perceived by the listener. More recently, Benedict Taylor, in 'Schubert and the Construction of Memory: The String Quartet in A minor D. 804 ("Rosamunde")', *Journal of the Royal Musical Association* 139/1 (2014), pp. 41–88, has analysed how music can metaphorically embody the workings of memory, also in connection with nostalgia. Although nostalgia is a characteristic of Schubert's music, yearning is another and I do not share the view that his music is exclusively oriented towards the past or even retentive (although both aspects clearly account for some of the complexity of the passing of time one experiences in listening to it). As the present chapter endeavours to show, Schubert's music also gazes forward into the ideal, the two directions opposing and complementing each other. It is indeed possible to hear nostalgia in the passage discussed here, but the effect achieved by Schubert is far subtler than mere nostalgic evocation; this passage adds a new, fascinating take on the memory trope. It tackles the question asked by Taylor 'of how music, without alluding to anything which can be shown to have been heard prior to it, may already sound like a memory' ('Schubert and the Construction of Memory', p. 44). However, the present case is distinct since it is music itself that 'remembers', not the listener who is reminded. The metaphoric, poetic essence of the passage relies on this subtle distinction.

As to reminiscences, citations of, or allusions to Schubert's own or other composers' works, I find it more useful to address those through the early romantic concept of 'rewriting' which I refer to in the conclusion of this essay, and which also helps to deal more sanely with the inevitable issue of Beethoven's influence. Memory, particularly long-term, has a deep bearing on how we cognize music in general and Schubert's music calls upon memory in a very specific way. In a recent essay, 'Narrative Dislocations in the First Movement of Schubert's "Unfinished" Symphony', in *Rethinking Schubert*, ed. Lorraine Byrne Bodley and Julian Horton (New York: Oxford University Press), pp. 127–46, I have highlighted the role of memory in association with crossing from one structural level to another and the opposition between figure and ground. The present movement equally exploits these characteristics.

5   See Sigmund Freud, *On Dreams*, trans. James Strachey (London: The Hogarth Press, 1952), p. 12. The reluctant reader need not 'buy' psychoanalysis since these ideas can be understood from a purely descriptive perspective. I mean here that the essential elements of musical discourse are not always those that are given salience either by their function,

Put differently, the 'theme' is really the metaphor of a theme. It has the contour of one, but its content is replaced by an allusion to something other, to which it relates by analogy. By disrupting the continuity of the theme, Schubert makes its metric balance more difficult to apprehend. The immediate appreciation of proportions, which is so essential to the aesthetic understanding of a classical work, is weakened and rendered secondary. A sense of vagueness is introduced that separates this theme-within-the-theme from its context. When time is withheld, it cannot be measured. External, clock time recedes, while the pauses mark a progressive immersion into the self. Music becomes introspective; it becomes its own focus. The process is deeply and intrinsically poetic.

If drama can be understood as the handling of events in the unfolding of a piece, then this passage provides an arresting example of Schubert's conception of it. Yet, as this example suggests and as the remainder of this essay will confirm, the model for Schubert's economy of form does not lie in theatrical dramaturgy. In order to grasp its nature, however, we need to go beyond the opposition of the dramatic and the lyrical as it is usually made apropos of Schubert, but include these aspects within a larger, encompassing frame. In this exploration, poetry – especially in the wider romantic sense of the term – should provide a necessary lead.

Motivic Saturation

The alternation between the first inversion of the tonic chord and the last inversion of the dominant seventh chord in G major in bars 65–66 and 67–68 creates a minor second oscillation between B and C♮ in the bass, subsequently contradicted by the restoration of C♯ in bar 71 with the return to the key of E major. This would go unnoticed if it were not such a ubiquitous motif in the whole movement.[6] Originating in the first theme, this motif – which I shall label *x* – comes forcefully to the fore in the transition as E–F♮ in the bass (bar 28) before being submitted to various transpositions in the same passage; it then reappears, with equal force, in an even lower register, as a B–C♮ neighbour-note figure underlying the dominant preparation in the secondary key, first ascending (bars 39–43), then inverted to a descending C♮–B. As the dominant is further prolonged (bars 43–49), the descending version of the motif is repeated and alternates with the ascending fourth F♯–B. This new combination is later used by Schubert to close the exposition (bars 123–127), transposed to F♮–E–B–E and preceded by the same anapaestic stamping

---

position, or presentation (themes, melodies, etc.), but can often be those that remain out of focus without necessarily being hidden. It is the role of analysis to bring them into light.

[6]   See Horton's analysis of this passage in 'The First Movement of Schubert's Piano Sonata D. 959 and the Performance of Analysis', p. 184.

Example 11.3   Schubert, Piano Sonata in A major, D. 959, first movement, bars 27–36
                    (episode 1) and 82–94 (episode 2)

as in bar 82. Equally highlighting motif *x* on E–F♮, the latter initiates the second tonally perturbed episode (after that in bars 28–34 and strongly reminiscent of it) which occupies the central position in the second half of the exposition (bars 82–94). This episode is literally saturated with motif *x* (Example 11.3).

So far, motif *x* has been predominantly in the bass, but at the end of the first ending of the exposition it is heard as F♮, a minor dominant ninth, resolving to the octave of an E dominant seventh to bring back the beginning of the exposition (bars 131a–132a). This time, it is placed in the top part of the harmony.[7] As this interval is transposed to A–B♭ in the recapitulation (while B–C♮ itself becomes E–F♮), it induces the very last gesture of the movement (bars 349–352): after the final cadence of the coda, the tonic chord of A major is followed by a Neapolitan B♭ major chord in root position, which changes into an augmented sixth chord of the dominant before finally returning to the tonic (bars 353–357).

Most importantly, the semitonal motif x is elevated to a middleground oscillation between the keys of C major and B major in the first part of the development (bars 131–149). This passage, with its playful and ethereal atmosphere, is the most magical moment in the whole movement. Despite the fact that the motif belongs originally in the bass, there is no actual bass here and the music seems to hang in mid-air, oblivious to gravity. C and B major may be very distant keys on the circle of fifths, yet they are the closest possible pitch-wise; Schubert is keen to exploit that singularity by creating a delightful game of repetition and variation, or permanence and change.[8] Which key, however, is auxiliary to which? To analyse C major as the submediant of E minor, and B major as its dominant, merely rationalizes their harmonic connection from a textbook perspective; it fails to account for the impalpability of our experience.[9] Each chord is tonicized in turn, though over a pedal point, and yields an impression of enchanting immobility before becoming unstable and resolving into the other. The ear is wonderfully teased each time by the delicate ambiguity of this bistable equilibrium, where time seems suspended, caught as it were in the circularity of repetition and new beginnings.

The semitonal motif crops up again at the end of the development, during the dominant pedal that precedes the recapitulation (bars 180–184). It is associated here with the semiquaver rhythm that appeared with the conclusive phrase of the exposition (bars 121–122), based on the second theme. At first presented as a scale fragment to form what I shall call motif y, this rhythm pervades the development, ending in a repeated neighbour-note figure (bars 165 and 167, 177 and 179). First in the bass, then in the treble, and giving rise to a downward sequence, the descending interval F♮–E is subsequently elongated to the length of a whole bar, and superimposed at a beat's distance on its ascending inversion two octaves below,

---

[7]   This motif, with this particular harmony, has particular resonances with Schubert. It is the crucial motif introduced by the horns in bars 20–21 of the first movement of the 'Unfinished' Symphony D. 759 and, before that, it is the heart-rending wrench (A–B♭) in the top part of the piano, under the words 'sein Kuss!', in 'Gretchen am Spinnrade', D. 118 (bar 68).

[8]   See Charles Rosen, *Sonata Forms*, 2nd edn (New York: Norton, 1988), pp. 360–61, where this moment is described as a 'stasis'; and Rosen, 'Schubert's Inflections of Classical Form', in *The Cambridge Companion to Schubert*, ed. Christopher Gibbs (Cambridge: Cambridge University Press, 1997), pp. 89–92.

[9]   The E minor chords in bars 138 and 148 sound in fact plagal, rather than as tonic chords.

Example 11.4   Schubert, Piano Sonata in A major, D. 959, first movement,
                  bars 161–192, end of development and retransition

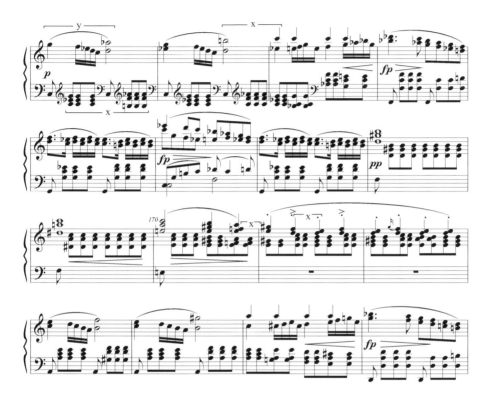

D♯–E (bars 184–186). The quaver/quaver-rest punctuation across the registers prepares for the return of the main theme (Example 11.4).[10]

Lastly, although motif *x* seems absent from the first two phrase members *a* and *a'* of the second theme, it nevertheless underlies them as is made apparent when, considering only the topmost pitches in both hands, C♯ (bars 57–58), the whole-tone neighbour note to B, is replaced by C♮ (bars 62–63) – a transformation, as we have seen, later to be cancelled by the bass (bar 71).[11]

---

[10]   Schubert rewrites the rhythm of the bass at the opening of the recapitulation (bars 198–200), using quavers followed by quaver rests instead of staccato crotchets as at the start of the exposition (bars 1–3). Compare with the orthography of bars bars 23–28.

[11]   The exchange between (one-lined) C and (small) B in the left hand, in the medium register, in bars 103–104, and the key of C major also relate to the development. Conversely, in the cadence that immediately ensues, the aborted veering of the harmony towards G major (bars 107–109) recalls the events of the second theme.

Example 11.4 (continued)

Organicism: Goethe and Novalis

Though superficially resemblant, the means employed by Schubert in this movement depart substantially from the classical technique of 'motivic economy' by which different, even contrasting themes and motifs are assembled from the same basic cells.[12] Instead, the name for the principle at work here is 'organicism'. In musicological, especially music-analytical milieus, this word is often understood as the principle whereby all themes and motifs of a piece are thought of as originating in a single, usually melodic cell; or, in the Schenkerian tradition, as the way in which the real structure of the piece is deemed to lie beneath its apparent surface and derive from the expansion of the tonic triad by virtue of the latter's composing-out. Thus every single note is connected, directly or indirectly, with either the

[12]   See for instance, the first movement of Mozart's Piano Sonata in B♭ major, K. 333, where the second theme is constructed from elements belonging to the first. This is rendered even more explicit in the recapitulation.

fundamental arpeggiation, the fundamental line, their middleground recursions, or their authorized prolongations.

Organicism, in that sense, is an intrinsic quality which can only be identified by those who are able to hear 'structurally' and perceive the hidden, long-range counterpoint that ensures the strict coherence of the work – and indeed, for Schenker, its status as a masterwork. It is revealed only by the analyst, whose science of music allows him or her to disclose the intentions of the composer in compliance with nature's superior commands and the immanent 'will of the tone', to use Schenker's own expression.[13] Structural hearing is an analytical scalpel that strips music of its flesh to reveal its bare bones.

This view of organicism originates in the growth of the plant from its germ as described by Goethe in his influential essay of 1790, *Versuch die Metamorphose der Pflanzen zu erklären*.[14] But while Goethe is keen to show how each part of the plant relates morphologically to all the others, he is not content with reducing everything to a single, original *Urphänomenon*. It is the elevation process that interests him, the successive transformation of one part into another whereby differences in shape and also in function are introduced, rather than the extolment of the mere reproduction of the same. Diversity is as essential to this process as is unity. It is also directed, ascending from root to pistil. Goethe's approach, in his own description, is *Genetisch* – 'genetic' – we might now say 'generative'.[15] By this, one should not merely observe nature as something that is fixed and has already become, but should also intuit its creative process as something that is changing and becoming.[16] And while nature remains 'mysterious in broad daylight' to our feeble eyes, she in fact conceals nothing so that she should not be forced to reveal her secrets; instead, it is up to us to let our imagination assist our vision. In relation to music, this may be seen to contradict the arcane character of the Schenkerian and other analytical methods.

After Goethe, whose work he had generously served up to then, Novalis represented for Schubert, according to Michael Kohlhäufl, a 'literarisches Neuland' – a fertile, new literary land.[17] Schubert discovered Novalis's *Hymnen an die Nacht*

[13]   *Der Tonwille* is of course the title of Heinrich Schenker's collection of essays and analyses published in the form of a periodical between 1921 and 1924. See *Der Tonwille: Pamphlets/ Quarterly Publication in Witness of the Immutable Laws of Music, Offered to a New Generation of Youth*, ed. William Drabkin, 2 vols (New York: Oxford University Press, 2004–2005).

[14]   Johann Wolfgang von Goethe, *The Metamorphosis of Plants*, ed. G. L. Miller, trans. D. Miller (Cambridge, MA: MIT Press, 2009).

[15]   See Goethe, 'Studies for a Physiology of Plants', in *Scientific Studies*, ed. and trans. D. Miller (New York: Suhrkamp, 1988), pp. 73–5.

[16]   For a study of the idea of 'becoming' though with a different perspective, see Janet Schmalfeldt, *In the Process of Becoming: Analytical and Philosophical Perspectives on Form in Early Nineteenth-Century Music* (Oxford: Oxford University Press, 2011).

[17]   See Michael Kohlhäufl, *Poetisches Vaterland. Dichtung und politisches Denken im Freundeskreis Franz Schuberts* (Kassel, Bärenreiter, 1999), p. 218. Mayrhofer's admiration

through Johann Mayrhofer, and the two friends would have been able to discuss the work as they lived together in the years 1818–1821. There is no doubt that within the cultivated circle to which Schubert belonged and that had so many writers, poets and artists as its members, the aesthetic, literary and philosophical ideas of the Romantics were discussed, and were even crucial to them.[18]

The Early Romantics admired Goethe and attempted to carry his ideas further, to a point where he would no longer recognize them. To Moritz, Schelling, August and Friedrich Schlegel, Tieck, and Novalis, art is an autonomous, self-referential system, which is neither bound to the imitation of nature, nor to the expression of feelings.[19] What is imitated is the genetic principle of nature, her creative power. Organicism is the way the artwork grows out of its own necessities to create a world of its own. The aloofness of romantic music from the external world is revealed by its paucity of referential, transitive 'topics' with which classical music was replete, and which are replaced by intransitive symbols. Just as, according to Novalis, philosophy explains itself rather than explain nature, poetry – and music as a form of poetry – is also exclusively concerned with itself. Hence, to Novalis but also to Wackenroder, Herder, Tieck, Hoffman and others, instrumental music is the superior, purest form of that art.

Organicism is not a goal to be attained, but a foundation on which to build – a means for the imagination to play at leisure with its own freely chosen motifs. The organic germ does not replicate itself everywhere in a self-similar way out of

---

for Novalis is a documented fact. Novalis's possible influence on Schubert is suggested by Deutsch in reference to *Mein Traum*: see Otto Erich Deutsch, *Schubert: Die Dokumente seines Lebens* (Wiesbaden: Breitkopf & Härtel, 1996), p. 159. See also Ilija Dürhammer, 'Zu Schuberts Literaturaesthetik', *Schubert durch die Brille* 14 (1995), pp. 5–99, and Richard Douglas Bruce, *Schubert's Mature Operas: An Analytical Study* (PhD dissertation, Durham University, 2003); that Schubert learnt of Novalis through Mayrhofer is suggested by Brigitte Massin in her *Schubert* (Paris: Fayard, 1994), p. 167.

[18]   Franz von Bruchmann, whose father hosted several Schubertiads, went to Erlangen to attend Schelling's lecture at the university from January to April 1821 and again in 1823, while Johann Senn had already been able to hear Schelling before 1820 (see Deutsch, *Dokumente*, pp. 134 and 198). In addition to Goethe and Schelling, Bruchmann was also an admirer of August and Friedrich Schlegel and was acquainted with the latter, whose *Lucinde* Bruchmann's sister Justina regarded highly. Vogl also admired both brothers and may have prompted Schubert to set some of their poems to music. Other members of Schubert's circle also knew the Schlegels personally. For a more detailed and recent assessment, see John M. Gingerich, 'Those of Us Who Found our Life in Art', in *Franz Schubert and His World*, ed. Christopher Gibbs and Morten Solvik (Princeton: Princeton University Press, 2014), pp. 67–114.

[19]   See for instance Margaret Mahony Stoljar's Introduction to her edition of Novalis's *Philosophical Writings* (Albany, NY: State University of New York Press, 1997), p. 10.

some independent will, but yields an ever-changing foliage as the inventiveness of the composer is stimulated. It is akin to the common element that Freud perceives behind the variegated and seemingly unrelated formations of the dream.[20] And indeed the dream, together with the fairy tale, is a model and an ideal for the romantic artist. Freedom and imagination define romanticism: the organic germ, in Novalis's words, is 'an idea rich in ideas'.[21] It undergoes unforeseeable metamorphoses that confer a poetic character on the whole as well as the parts. It is this very poeticality – in Schellingian terms, the representation of the infinite (alluded to in Schubert's development by immobility and absence of gravity) through the finite – which the composer, like every romantic artist, endeavours to achieve primarily.[22]

Thus, there is no predicting, from the occurrences of motif x between pitches C and B or F and E in the exposition, the role that this motif will take in the development. The latter 'combines freely' (to quote from Novalis once more)[23] from the material of the exposition to create something new. Although the melodic material of the development is obviously based on the variant of the second theme introduced in bars 121–122, it is important to note that the register is also similar to that of those bars (and of the second theme's a' phrase member, bars 60–64), which nevertheless bring the cadence of the exposition. But the cadence does not 'announce' the development in any identifiable way, not even through its abnormal register, and no analytic rationale can make the latter derive from it or any other event as if by some process of deduction. There is a gap between the two moments that cannot be bridged by logical or rhetorical means. The relationship is both an expression of wit and a leap into dream and fantasy. Organicism proceeds associatively; it overrides coherence and allows form to appear disjointed. Even more, it favours it (Example 11.5).[24]

When the second theme variant, y, appears at the end of the exposition, it is as a mere ornamental diminution of the conclusive return of the theme. Although timbrally striking, it seems paradoxically weightless and counts for very little in the exposition. It bears no apparent consequences: that the development should be based on it therefore comes as a surprise. The two-bar question and answer is

---

[20]   Freud, *On Dreams*, p. 23.

[21]   Novalis, *Philosophical Writings*, p. 78.

[22]   See Friedrich Wilhelm Joseph Schelling, *System des transscendentalen Idealismus* (Tübingen: Cotta, 1800), p. 465: 'das Unendliche endlich dargestellt ist Schönheit'.

[23]   Novalis, *Philosophical Writings*, p. 77.

[24]   See my discussion of Schubert's reordering of Heine's poems in Xavier Hascher, '"In dunklen Träumen": Schubert's Heine-Lieder through the Psychoanalytical Prism', *Nineteenth-Century Music Review* 5/2 (2008), pp. 43–70. See also the notion of 'parataxis' as introduced by Su Yin Mak in *Schubert's Lyricism Reconsidered: Structure, Design and Rhetoric* (Saarbrücken: Lambert, 2010), p. 31.

Example 11.5   Schubert, Piano Sonata in A major, D. 959, first movement,
bars 113–144, end of exposition and beginning of development

expanded to a five-bar phrase member (as per *a* and *a'* in the second theme) which
is repeated four times, including its varied presentation, before being transferred
to the bass for the following part of the development. But this second part, from
bars 150 to 159, is still made of two five-bar phrase members and still oscillates
between C and B before returning to C, although the character of the music is
changed and no longer owes anything to the exposition's cadential moment. As
the two hands exchange their material, the atmosphere is transformed and no
longer displays the playfulness of the first section. Technically, the C–B oscillation
is prolonged and recedes further towards the background since these notes are no
longer heard throughout (Example 11.6).

The third part of the development proposes a further metamorphosis of its
elements, at first in the contrasting shades of C minor (bars 161–167) then in the
intermediate ones of A minor (bars 173–179). While the passage relies essentially
on motif *y*, motif *x* is still present as evidenced in the second half of bar 162, where
the original minor third in the right hand is inverted to a major sixth so as to project
the B–C semitone in the top part. A previous occurrence of the same motif, in the

same register as at the beginning of the development, takes place in the left hand accompaniment of the previous bar, over the pedal C in the bass. Repetitions of F–E in the right hand serve to connect the two key areas (bars 171–172), before the return of the same interval in the retransition.

The narrative of the development is thus created out of the combination of *y* and the structural amplification of *x*, which is enlarged from the level of a punctual event within a phrase to that of container for a whole, modulating phrase, which itself articulates *y* as its contained event. This enlargement and the multiple repetitions of *y*, wound up around itself, lift both elements above their original function and elevate them 'to the power of themselves', to use both Novalis's and Friedrich Schlegel's expression. The development instances in music the romantic principle of 'poeticization': it grows out of the metamorphosis of previous material which is used without constraints to create from it a story that emancipates itself from its surroundings and becomes almost self-contained. Such an episode, of course, releases the tight hierarchical architecture of classic form. It also frees itself from the strictures of tonality by refusing to articulate a clear cadential progression. Moreover, it is characteristic of Schubert that *x*, the semitonal motif, circulates between structural levels and also from figure to ground, sometimes being propelled to the fore, at other times remaining out of focus.

Example 11.6   Schubert, Piano Sonata in A major, D. 959, first movement,
                bars 145–160, development (continued)

Flowering and Metamorphosis

The beginning of the sonata possesses little of the character with which we usually associate with Schubert. It is severe and resolute; the placement of the chords in the lower register, the percussive, unadorned piano writing with its stark, repeated rhythms impart on it a kind of idealized Beethovenian wilfulness. The harsh, mineral quality of the opening is probably intensified by the relentless repetition of the same note A in the top part over the first five bars against the step-by-step rise of the bass and inner parts.[25] Two features, however, counterbalance this first impression: the plagal orientation of the harmony, which makes the ascent terminate with E and G♮ returning to D and F♯ (bars 3–4); and the final yielding of the right hand in the sixth bar with the embellished resolution to G♯ of the suspended A when the dominant is finally reached. Despite the pianism of its octave doubling, the figure introduces a religious connotation (though more in a pantheistic sense than a Christian one) while retrospectively conferring a hymn-like resonance on the homophonic chords of the preceding bar.[26]

For all its peremptoriness, it is striking that the initial phrase of the movement disappears as soon as it has been uttered. It is not heard again before the recapitulation, and then again in the coda (bars 331–349) where it receives two successive statements of ten bars each, the last bar being fused with the beginning of the next phrase.[27] Each of these statements is subdivided into two five-bar clauses and ends in a perfect cadence (bars 339–340 and 348–349) to replace the half cadence in bar 6. The character of the theme is considerably transformed by the *pianissimo* dynamic and the harmonic deflections in the intermediate cadences (bars 335 and 344). The first of these brings about D major to complete the plagal leaning mentioned above, while the second substitutes the minor subdominant with its relative major, F – a key which also plays an important role in the recapitulation.[28] The repetition of the embellished resolution of the suspension at each cadence gives salience to this motive so that it flavours the whole passage, now tenderly rather than imposingly; and the qualitative transformation of the top F♯ from third of D major to octave of the root of an F♯ dominant seventh in bars 335–336, paralleled by that of A from third of F major to root of an inverted A

[25] See Charles Fisk, *Returning Cycles: Contexts for the Interpretation of Schubert's Impromptus and Last Sonatas* (Berkeley: University of California Press, 2001), p. 207, who already underlines the presence of the repeated As above the ascending bass line.

[26] Some of that hymn-like quality can be seen to be transferred to the beginning of the second theme. It would be beyond the scope of this essay to follow the transformations and metamorphoses of all topics, motifs, and especially rhythms throughout the movement.

[27] I leave aside here the symbolically potent return of the initial chords in retrograde order at the end of the Sonata's fourth movement. I likewise do not address connections between movements of this work: useful insights into these aspects can be found in both Robert Hatten, 'Schubert the Progressive: The Role of Resonance and Gesture in the Piano Sonata in A, D. 959', *Intégral* 7 (1993), pp. 38–81 (French translation by Xavier Hascher in *Cahiers F. Schubert* 9 [1996], pp. 9–48), and Fisk, *Returning Cycles*, pp. 204–16. For discussion of the expressive qualities of the work's slow movement, see Chapter 13 in this volume, 'Stylistic Disjuncture as a Source of Drama in Schubert's Late Instrumental Works' by Joe Davies.

[28] The harmonic shunt into F major in bars 221–231 (end of the first theme and beginning of the transition) is one of the most interesting features in the rewriting afforded by the recapitulation.

major chord in bars 344–445, creates variation and metamorphosis even on a small scale with typical Schubertian harmonic delicacy. This transformation accompanies the unexpected, magical changes in harmonic lighting resulting from the chromatic chord transformations in the same bars (Example 11.7).[29]

The care lavished by Schubert on such a rewriting of the initial material is significant as to its importance, emphasized as this rewriting is by the fermata over a one-bar rest (bar 330) that precedes its entry. It is a moment highly charged with symbolic value; and if symbols in romanticism allude to a higher, ideal world, then this passage acts as a musical 'Wegweiser' to the Infinite and to the Absolute. Its modulations point to an elsewhere that is situated outside the boundaries of the sonata as well as beyond the here-and-now experience of the listener or the pianist. It alludes to a loftier spiritual realm after which we yearn, a transcendental world. In Goethean terms, the coda allows the theme to flower as the highest and richest point attained so far, the movement's most beautiful and expressive culmination. The theme is not merely varied: it undergoes a profound metamorphosis, an ennoblement. The new formulation raises the first theme above its earlier earthbound character, deeply 'rooted' as it were in the lower register. It is now at once sensuous and incorporeal. For Goethe, 'Steigerung' ('elevation') and 'Polarität' ('polarity') characterize nature's process of organic development; the theme displays both.

The coda thus achieves a poetic transfiguration of the theme, a 'romanticization' of it in the Novalisian sense, a further elevation that takes it beyond Goethe's own concept of elevation, from the natural into the supernatural, the purely spiritual. And yet this moment is again a case of reminiscing: in a typically Schubertian paradox, the flowering of the theme coincides with its return as a recollection, a dream-like apparition.[30] This reaching above is balanced by a downwards motion with each perfect cadence as the coda's formal function is to regain the initial register of the movement by bringing the second phrase of the theme down an octave in order to sound again the left-hand contra A of the opening. Once more in the recapitulation the final cadence has taken place in the wrong register, sounding the one-lined A as its lowest note; the ensuing codetta (bars 324–329) only manages to lower it one octave, into the small register. Changes of register echo each other throughout the movement, also acquiring semiotic and symbolic value.

---

[29]   My use of the term 'magical' here refers both to Susan Wollenberg's perceptive qualification of some of Schubert's procedures in his sonata-form transitions and to the importance of magic in relation to poetry in Novalis's philosophical writings. See Susan Wollenberg, 'Schubert's Transitions', in *Schubert Studies*, ed. Brian Newbould (Aldershot: Ashgate, 1998), p. 16.

[30]   I am grateful to Malcolm Bilson, of Cornell University, for reminding me in conversation of the character of this particular moment in the movement as a memory. Yet, even embellished memories are fainter than the events they recall, while they are also less complete. This one is considerably richer, pointing as it is in several directions, and it is also more complete.

Example 11.7   Schubert, Piano Sonata in A major, D. 959, first movement,
                    bars 323–357, end of recapitulation and coda

Drama and the Novel

Summing up recent literature, Horton opposes the sense of teleology expected from classical forms with the episodic character of Schubert's music, also identifying a 'dichotomy' between its vaunted lyricism and the developmental nature of Beethovenian classicism.[31] A third contrast is that between the temporal and the spatial: instead of making an economical and dramatic use of time, Schubert's music seems instead to wander as if through a landscape.[32] Despite the validity of this observation – and in the light of early German literary romanticism which I have attempted to project – to consider Schubert's mature instrumental music through such oppositions as have just been recapitulated is, nevertheless, to put the question the wrong way.

In a famous passage from part V of *Wilhelm Meisters Lehrjahre*, Goethe differentiates the drama from the novel:

> In the novel it is predominantly sentiments and events that are to be presented; in drama, characters and deeds. The novel must move slowly and the sentiments of the main personage must, in some way or another, hold up the progression of the whole toward its resolution. But drama must move quickly and the character of the main personage must move toward the end, not himself holding up this progression, but being held up by it. The hero of a novel must be passive, or at least not active to a high degree; from the hero of a play we demand effective action and deeds.[33]

Goethe establishes a dichotomy too, but of a different kind, by observing the existence of two essentially diverging forms of narrative. Yet Goethe refuses to rank one above the other, declaring instead that 'each could be excellent in its own way'. Goethe's statement is performative as much as constative since it describes in the first place

---

[31]   See Horton, 'The First Movement of Schubert's Piano Sonata D. 959 and the Performance of Analysis', pp. 171–5.

[32]   The image of the landscape comes up naturally in relation to the character of the wanderer popularized by Schubert's songs and the seeming 'roving' quality of some of the harmonic progressions in his music. Adorno makes a well-known case of it in his essay on Schubert. See Theodor W. Adorno, 'Schubert (1928)', trans. Jonathan Dunsby and Beate Perry, *19th-Century Music* 29/1 (2005), pp. 3–14. I have explored from a music-theoretical perspective the relation of the 'Wanderschaft' and Schubert's harmony with the idea of the landscape as a subtext in 'Sur les pas du "Wanderer": pour une cartographie de l'errance schubertienne', in *Le style instrumental de Schubert: Sources, analyse, évolution*, ed. Xavier Hascher (Paris: Publications de la Sorbonne, 2007), pp. 181–211. See also Scott Burnham's 'Landscape as Music, Landscape as Truth: Schubert and the Burden of Repetition' in the same issue of *19th-Century Music* mentioned above, pp. 31–41.

[33]   Johann Wolfgang von Goethe, *Wilhelm Meister's Apprenticeship*, trans. Eric A. Blackall and Victor Lange (Princeton: Princeton University Press, 1989), pp. 185–6.

what he set out to achieve in his own novel, which is in the making as he writes those lines. The genre of the novel is also a novel genre whose dignity is affirmed, on a par with the older literary forms derived from ancient or French models.

To the cultivated minds in Schubert's circle and to Schubert himself, this conception of the novel must have corresponded to a new form of expression which they could embrace, one which could allow them as a generation to break away from their elders. Rather than consider Schubert from the perspective of his filiation to Beethoven, therefore taking a backward glance at the cost of reinforcing prejudices about his dependence on his elder, it may prove more fruitful to glance forward by envisaging Schubert in the context of the artistic aspirations of his age and what could have been his own aims. Goethe's distinction can provide us with a useful paradigm for interpreting Schubert's music independently of the dichotomies recalled above, even challenging their individual terms, such as – particularly – the lyrical and the teleological. Moreover, to adopt the vantage point of the novel may allow us to approach the traditional pitting of the 'passive' Schubert against the 'active' Beethoven in a fresh way.

For Novalis and his contemporaries, the prototype of the novel was *Wilhelm Meisters Lehrjahre*, and the novel was equated with natural poetry. Yet Novalis sought to bring the poetic element even further. To him,

> A novel must be poetry through and through. For poetry … must be a harmonious mood of our mind, where everything is made beautiful, where everything finds its proper aspect – everything finds an *accompaniment* and *surroundings* that suit it. Everything in a truly poetic book seems so *natural* – and yet so marvellous. We think it could not be otherwise, as if we had only been asleep in the world before now – and now for the first time the right meaning for the world dawns on us.[34]

In this combination of the natural and the marvellous as well as the seeming tangibility granted to dreamlike apparitions, we recognize some of the characteristics of Schubert's mature music in this work as well as others.

Lyricism may be a sub-category of poetry, but not all poetry is lyrical. Neither is all romanticism about expression of the self, nor sentiments centred about the self. Like the poet, the musician is a visionary who can penetrate magic truths and reveal the veritable, symbolic meaning of the world. Thus, Schubert's music may not merely be the sentimental or elegiac confession which we too readily perceive in it. More often than not, it is objective but the objects to which it relates are immaterial and the world with which it is connected is ideal. It is impersonal rather than individual, universal rather than personal. It aims at giving us a glimpse of the superior world which music instances poetically. As often in Schubert's mature style, it reverses our common categories of 'subjective' and 'objective', transforming one into the other.

---

[34] Novalis, *Philosophical Writings*, p. 153.

Schubert's forms may not be teleological in the sense attributed to Beethoven's, but they are nonetheless directed, following the same pattern of elevation as the Goethean plant. The variants and variations to which his material is subjected are metamorphoses culminating in its flowering. The material does therefore develop, but it does so through a process of variation and enrichment, polarization and ennoblement, and eventually poeticization.[35] If Schubert's music possesses the spatial quality which has been attributed to it, then it does not progress on a plane surface, but on one that rises gradually in spite of its possible unevenness, the presence of local traps or sudden eruptions (such as those represented in the exposition of the first movement of D. 959 by the two 'dramatic' episodes of bars 28–39 and 82–94). Finally, the paratactic structure of the music may agree with its poetic nature as parataxis may indeed be a characteristic of poetic discourse, but this should not lead us to overlook the organic elements at work, which transform parataxis – or disparate juxtaposition – into analogy. Contiguity is always underlain by similarity, and sections of the work echo each other despite, at times, the absence of proper cadential or functional coordination (see for instance, in this movement, bars 1–6 and 16–20, or bars 7–11 and 22–26, 12–13 and 29–30, etc., in addition to all the occurrences already mentioned).

The return of the initial phrase in the movement's coda therefore goes beyond the notion of completing the 'unfinished business' left by the half cadence of bar 6 through giving the phrase a perfect cadence. As we have seen, the opening's incompleteness and rudimentary aspect finds its accomplishment through its ultimate elevation and flowering. Yet the first phrase is more than a failed attempt at some Beethovenian grandeur which Schubert proves unable to sustain. The connection to the next phrase (bars 7–15) is a good example of parataxis, since some logical transition seems missing and the two phrases appear at first unrelated. They are in fact related both melodically and rhythmically, as every detail reveals while the rising A–B–C♯ diatonic sequence of the bass transforms into a chromatic one, starting from E. The two phrases are thus essentially similar, including, as Fisk observes, the presence of a static top D against which the bass ascends in bars 7–13 in place of the top A in bars 1–6, although the registers differ (Example 11.8).[36]

Contrary to Fisk, however, I do not view the opposition between the two phrases as that between objective and subjective – unless it is in the reversed sense which I have mentioned above – but rather as a wonderful instantiation of romantic irony. The second phrase questions the affirmative character of the first and its pretension to accomplishing a gesture in the real world; it reveals the hollowness of the first phrase and points instead to the otherworldliness and ideality of 'true'

---

[35] The importance of variations in some of Schubert's sonata-form movements has been highlighted on several occasions, the last being in Anne Hyland's article 'In Search of Liberated Time, or Schubert's Quartet in G Major, D. 887: Once More Between Sonata and Variation', *Music Theory Spectrum* 38/1 (2016), pp. 85–108.

[36] Fisk, *Returning Cycles*, p. 207.

Example 11.8   Schubert, Piano Sonata in A major, D. 959, first movement, bars 1–26,
                    first theme and beginning of transition

reality. The second phrase is like a mirror which is presented to the first: it is a
reflection *of* it as well as a reflection *on* it. By virtue of this gesture, the theme is
raised 'to the power of itself' and romanticized.[37] This mirroring process originates
in Goethean polarization but outgrows it to achieve a quintessential romantic move.

The opposition between the diatonic and the chromatic versions of the bass
ascent is a key to the whole dialectic of the movement: the diatonic version
reappears under the second theme (bars 56–58) and the chromatic in the cadential

---

[37]   Novalis, *Philosophical Writings*, p. 6.

phrase of bars 95–100, completing the episode in bars 82–94.[38] The latter amplifies the previous episode in bars 28–39, which gives rise to motif *x*, contradicting the quiet diatonic neighbour note motion of bars 23 and 25 where the motif is given in the inner parts. In the first episode, the contrast between the repeated note and the ascending minor second becomes sharply dissonant, sounding almost like a stab. This biting dissonance will reappear in the final part of the development (bars 170–172) and in the retransition (bars 180–186).

Although evoked several times, the two dramatic outbursts in bars 28–39 and 82–94 have not been discussed so far. They have an oppressive, obsessional quality that sets them apart from the rest of the movement. They also stand alone in refusing to articulate the authentic division of the octave by the fifth through proceeding instead by steps of major thirds. They are not 'developmental', however, in that they do not actually modulate but end in E where they began.[39] The drama that they express is, as so often in Schubert, unexpected and unprepared in relation to what precedes them. Like the central phrase of the second theme, they refer to something outside the sonata, an event that took place even before it began, albeit of a different kind. Drama in Schubert is something that happened before, and of which music is the aftermath.[40] Although from a strictly formal and harmonic point of view both passages could be left out, their omission would immediately deprive the movement of an essential element of contrast. In the growth process towards flowering, they represent the opposite drive, a '*retrogressive* metamorphosis' of which Goethe evokes the possibility.[41]

The Romantic Sonata as Rewriting

Schubert's music is always alluding to something other than itself; it points elsewhere both in space and in time. It does not merely happen here and now,

---

[38] Repeated notes in the top part also crop up in the codetta, bars 126–129.

[39] Contrary to a phrase in the exposition (apart from the transition), a phrase in the development normally ends in a different key to that in which it started.

[40] This notion is very potent when looking at works from the 'Unfinished' Symphony onwards: see my essay 'Narrative Dislocations in the First Movement of Schubert's "Unfinished" Symphony' for the particular 'dramatic'-narrative economy of that work. It has to be remembered that etymologically, 'drama' (τό δρᾶμα) refers to an action, and more specifically to a misdeed. In 'Der Atlas', D. 957, No. 8 from *Schwanengesang*, the poet makes it clear that his estrangement from his home city and his current unhappiness are consequences of an event that occurred before the start of his wanders yet which remains unexplained. A similar situation is reflected in *Winterreise*, where the character experiences his solitude as a punishment for a deed that he himself cannot explain. This is also consistent with the theme of Schubert's literary composition of 1822, *Mein Traum*.

[41] Goethe, *The Metamorphosis of Plants*, p. 6.

but recalls distant memories and creates ideal visions of a world that is not of the present world. But the ideal which is offered by music is also and ultimately a musical one. What Schubert's music celebrates is the power of art not only to elevate and transfigure reality, but even to create a higher, harmonious reality; as in Mayrhofer's *Heliopolis*, where the City of the Sun – in which art is the real origin of light, warmth and life – is substituted for the legendary Sais of Plato's *Timaeus*, art is substituted for the dreamed Orient of wisdom and for perfect love; despite Goethe's own disapproval of the Early Romantics' extreme conceptions, the cultivation of art becomes the principal aim of individual *Bildung*, conceived as the human equivalent to metamorphosis and flowering. As Freud would later theorize, such flight from reality could only be compensated through a complex balance between artistic sublimation and neurosis, the medical name for the profound Viennese malaise that prompted the same Mayrhofer to take his own life in 1836.

The image of Schubert that I wish to convey here is not that of an isolated artist – even though surrounded with friends – but instead of one who shared and upheld the ideals of a whole generation. Not only did Schubert know about the philosophy and aesthetics of his age, but he was also able to understand them deeply and respond to them through the medium of his own art.[42] In the same sense that, for Friedrich Schlegel, 'All the classical poems of the ancients … form an organic whole',[43] so are the sonatas of Haydn, Mozart, Beethoven, and Schubert organically related. If Schubert's own sonatas refer to those of his predecessors, it is not a sign of Schubert's dependency on his elders but a clue to the nature of his artistic conception. As, for the Early Romantics, each new work offers a critique of previous works in their own medium and elevates them to a higher power, Schubert's sonatas are sonatas *about* sonatas; they are sonatas squared, or best, 'elevated to the power of themselves': they rewrite the genre. The Sonata in A major, D. 959, provides a wonderful illustration of such a poetic rewriting.

---

[42]   Interestingly, John Daverio, in his *19th-Century Music and the German Romantic Ideology* (New York: Schirmer Books, 1993), does not consider Schubert.

[43]   Friedrich Schlegel, *Ideen*, fragment 95, in *Athenaeum* 3/1 (1800), p. 21.

12

Virtual Protagonist and Musical Narration in the Slow Movements of Schubert's Piano Sonatas D. 958 and D. 960

Lauri Suurpää

Introduction

Those philosophers or philosophically oriented musical scholars who have addressed the relationship between music and emotions have often asked the following perplexing question: whose emotions are we talking about when we associate music with emotions? Although there is a wide variety of opinion, recent contributions to the debate can be divided into two main categories. On the one hand, there are scholars who argue that when we discuss music in emotive terms, we are essentially referring to emotional abstractions that are not felt by anyone. Stephen Davies, for example, speaks of 'emotion characteristics in appearances' that refer to publicly displayed emotional signs that we can recognize without associating them with anyone's real, felt emotions.[1]

In contrast to such views, there are scholars who argue that the emotions we associate with music are those felt by a 'virtual musical persona', a kind of implicit protagonist who traverses through a musical work, experiencing the emotions that the work is said to display. Edward T. Cone asserts that 'a dramatic impersonation underlies all poetry, all fiction, indeed all literature worth the name',[2] and then avers that an analogous persona can be established in music. Jenefer Robinson emphasizes that through references to this kind of a 'virtual musical persona' we can discuss emotions so finely nuanced that their recognition through appearances only would be impossible. In this way, 'cognitively complex emotions can be expressed by instrumental music without words'.[3] Robinson and Robert Hatten, in turn, note that 'one of the appealing features of the persona theory of musical expressiveness is

[1]   Stephen Davies, *Musical Meaning and Expression* (Ithaca, NY: Cornell University Press, 1994), pp. 221–8.
[2]   Edward T. Cone, 'Some Thoughts on "Erlkönig"', in *The Composer's Voice* (Berkeley: University of California Press, 1974), p. 2.
[3]   Jenefer Robinson, *Deeper than Reason: Emotion and its Role in Literature, Music, and Art* (Oxford: Clarendon Press, 2005), p. 327.

that it allows for emotions … to be represented in music by musical processes'.[4] That is, they argue that persona theory may provide a foundation for musical narration.

This essay is a case study in musical narrativity in the slow movements of Schubert's Piano Sonatas in C minor, D. 958, and B♭ major, D. 960 (1828). I will examine the interplay between two virtual musical personae. On the one hand, central to both movements' narration is a 'protagonist', a positive musical agent.[5] The listener sympathizes with the protagonist. On the other hand, both movements feature an antagonist, a negative musical agent.[6]

In D. 958-ii and D. 960-ii, tensions between the protagonist and the antagonist provide the foundation for the music's dramatic narrative. At the core of the movements' musical plots are conflicts between positive aspects represented by the protagonist and negative aspects represented by the antagonist. In both movements, which show related yet different and unique narrative arches, I follow how the antagonist attempts to lead the protagonist astray from the hoped-for path. In other words, the antagonist attempts to prevent the protagonist from reaching the goal he or she would like to attain.[7] The antagonist's attempts and the protagonist's reactions to them underlie the movements' expressive drama.[8]

My interpretation of the musical narrative and expression will be based primarily on analysis of musical structure. That is, structural features such as tensions, their resolutions, or postponements of resolutions are understood to underlie conflicts between the two primary virtual personae, the protagonist and the antagonist. Accordingly, I argue that the music's expressive level, its dramatic course, is not

---

[4]   Jenefer Robinson and Robert S. Hatten, 'Emotions in Music', *Music Theory Spectrum* 34/2 (2012), p. 78.

[5]   In the theory of literary narrative, a counterpart for the 'protagonist' can be found, for example, in the 'hero' in Vladimir Propp's groundbreaking study of the Russian folktales, or in the actant 'subject' in A. J. Greimas's actantial model of narrative; see Vladimir Propp, *Morphology of the Folktale*, trans. Laurence Scott (Austin: University of Texas Press, 1968; Russian original 1928), p. 80; and A. J. Greimas, *Structural Semantics: An Attempt at a Method*, trans. Daniele McDowell, Ronald Schleifer, and Alan Velie (Lincoln, NE: University of Nebraska Press, 1983; French original 1966), pp. 202–3.

[6]   The antagonist finds its counterpart in Propp's 'villain' and in Greimas's actant 'opponent'; see Propp, *Morphology of the Folktale*, p. 79, and Greimas, *Structural Semantics*, pp. 205–6.

[7]   The hoped-for state finds its counterpart in Propp's 'princess (a sought-for person) and her father' and in Greimas the actant 'object'; see Propp, *Morphology of the Folktale*, p. 79; and Greimas, *Structural Semantics*, pp. 202–3.

[8]   Although not suggesting the presence of a musical persona quite in the way I have discussed above, Charles Fisk, too, interprets Schubert's late piano music (the last three sonatas and the impromptus) from the perspective of a kind of protagonist. He argues that this music may be mirrored against the idea of a 'wanderer', an outsider. See *Returning Cycles: Contexts for the Interpretation of Schubert's Impromptus and Last Sonatas* (Berkeley: University of California Press, 2001).

independent of its structure but is rather constituted, to a great extent, by it. I will discuss the movements' harmony and voice leading from the Schenkerian perspective, complementing the harmonic picture through references to formal functions as clarified by William Caplin.[9]

Victory over Threat: D. 958

In the narrative of the C minor Sonata's slow movement, the antagonist challenges the protagonist's stable state of mind, but ultimately the protagonist is able to overcome the antagonist's threat. In this movement, the antagonist appears quite concretely, assuming a guise of a musical gesture that interferes with the continuity of the music. Because this gesture becomes more emphatic as the movement unfolds, it functions in the manner of a 'thematic gesture' as defined by Robert Hatten: 'Thematic gestures are those that play a significant role in the drama of a work, as subjects for musical discourse ... By contributing their particular expressive meaning to the ongoing thematic discourse, gestural motives can help shape the *expressive genre*, or the dramatic trajectory of a movement or work'.[10] The movement thus thematizes the antagonist.

Figure 12.1 provides an outline of the movement's form and its primary key areas. The antagonist's gesture appears towards the end of each A section. Example 12.1 clarifies the A¹ section's phrase structure and voice leading. The opening phrase-structural unit (bars 1–8) is straightforward from the formal perspective (Caplinian 'hybrid 3' consisting of a compound basic idea and a continuation),[11] as well as from the harmonic perspective (motion from the tonic to a tonicized dominant). Thus, the

Bars	1–18	19–42	43–61	62–93	94–115
Section	A¹	B¹	A²	B²	A³
Key	Ab	db → ab: V	Ab → A	d → a: V? No, Ab: V	Ab → A? No, Ab

Figure 12.1   Schubert, Piano Sonata in C minor, D. 958, second movement, chart of form

[9]   The formal terminology applied in this study is clarified in William Caplin, *Classical Form: A Theory of Formal Functions for the Instrumental Music of Haydn, Mozart, and Beethoven* (New York: Oxford University Press, 1998).

[10]   Robert S. Hatten, *Interpreting Musical Gestures, Topics, and Tropes: Mozart, Beethoven, Schubert* (Bloomington: Indiana University Press, 2004), p. 177 (italics in the original).

[11]   For more on these concepts, see Caplin, *Classical Form*, pp. 59–63, 'Hybrid Themes and Compound Themes'.

Example 12.1   Schubert, Piano Sonata in C minor, D. 958, second movement,
bars 1–18, A¹ section, analytical sketch

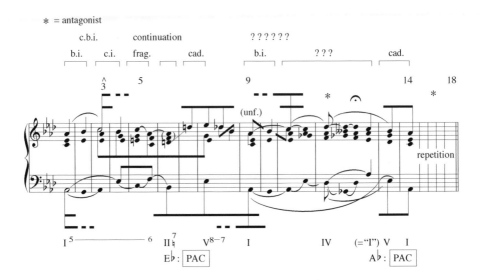

movement's opening suggests stability, enhanced by the somewhat pious quality of the chorale texture – the protagonist experiences an untroubled nontragic expression.

The ensuing phrase-structural unit (bars 9–18) challenges the stability. The gesture of bar 12 seems to stop the music's steady course: the phrase-structural function of bars 11–12 is uncertain and the fermata of bar 12 halts the flow of music. In addition, the G♭ minor chord on the second quaver of bar 12 casts a fleeting tragic shadow over the nontragic expression that has governed so far. In spite of these troubling features, the underlying harmonic structure remains clear, and bar 12 prolongs the IV leading to the cadence of bars 13–14. The ensuing bars 15–18 repeat the music just heard; the interfering gesture is therefore also repeated. The gesture of bar 12, and its repetition in bar 16, can be understood as a sign of the antagonist – an emblem of threat – that attempts to shake the protagonist's steady state of affairs. Yet the untroubled harmonic structure of bars 9–14 (I–IV–V–I) suggests that the protagonist is fundamentally unaffected by the threat.

The B¹ section begins, with almost no preparation, in a tragic minor key (the minor subdominant). The tonal structure now becomes very complex; the antagonist's unsteady gesture is able to undermine the protagonist's self-assurance. From the B section's initial D♭ minor the music moves to E major (bar 26), which is then transformed into minor (bar 28). After bar 32 the sense of a clearly governing key disappears, and roving harmonies appear until the arrival at the dominant of A♭ minor, the minor-mode tonic, in bar 42. Also the underlying voice leading seems to lose the steady path (Example 12.2). At the deep middleground, the D♭ minor triad of bar 19 functions as a modally inflected IV that is regained in bar 41, one

Example 12.2   Schubert, Piano Sonata in C minor, D. 958, second movement,
bars 1–43, B¹ section, analytical sketch

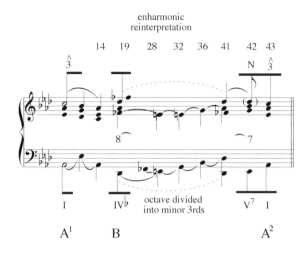

bar before the arrival at the B section's tonal goal, the dominant. The way in which
the IV♭ is prolonged challenges the principles of tonal voice leading. The D♭s in the
bass (bars 19 and 41) are connected through an arpeggiation that divides the octave
equally into minor thirds. Thus the prolongation does not grow out of the tonic-
dominant axis, and there is an enharmonic reinterpretation.[12] In all, the B section's
tonal framework gradually becomes more unstable, while the increasing dynamic
and rhythmic activity intensifies the musical rhetoric. Both of these qualities may be
interpreted as reflecting the protagonist's growing concern about the consequences
of the antagonist's interference with the music's bliss in bars 12 and 16.

The reaching of the dominant in bar 42 brings the protagonist back to the
original path, and the onset of the A² section regains, at least apparently, the
peace that governed at the movement's beginning. Yet the triplet figuration of the
accompaniment in bars 43–50, derived from the triplets of the B¹ section, suggests
that the threat has not been left behind. Indeed, in the A² section the antagonist's

---

[12] The equal subdivision of the octave is clarified by the surface design, where a change of
figuration signals the arrival of each new bass pitch. The equal division of the octave as such
has been understood in the literature either as a phenomenon expanding the boundaries of
tonal voice leading (e.g. Edward Aldwell and Carl Schachter, *Harmony and Voice Leading*,
2nd edn [San Diego: Harcourt Brace Jovanovich, 1979], pp. 542–51) or as a technique
transcending the boundaries of tonality (e.g. Richard Cohn, 'Maximally Smooth Cycles,
Hexatonic Systems, and the Analysis of Late-Romantic Triadic Progressions', *Music Analysis*
15/1 [1996], pp. 9–11).

Example 12.3   Schubert, Piano Sonata in C minor, D. 958, second movement,
bars 51–62, A² section, analytical sketch

gesture has tonally far-reaching consequences (Example 12.3): it resurfaces first in bar 54 at the original pitch level and in the ensuing bar (and again in bar 59) a semitone higher. The transposition is important; the repetition in bar 55 leads to a cadential closure a semitone above the tonic, in A major (bars 56–57, repeated in bars 60–61). As a result, the repetition shakes the tonal stability through ending the A² section in the remote A major.

In the global tonal structure, the A major chord of bar 57 should be understood enharmonically as B♭♭; that is, as a Neapolitan, ♭II. Thus, its dominant in bar 56 is an F♭ major chord, which is connected to the opening tonic through a 5–♭6 progression (Example 12.3a). Unlike in the A¹ section, the antagonist is now able to misguide the protagonist from his or her stable tonal path. The outwardly calm quality of the cadential closure – in the 'wrong' key of B♭ major – might suggest, in addition, that the protagonist is not yet aware of the misguided step. When the B² section begins, the music tonicizes E♭♭ minor, the minor-mode lowered dominant, a chord very rarely tonicized in tonal repertory (Example 12.3).[13] The false step that the antagonist's gesture initiates thus leads the harmonic structure to a remote and strange path.

As in the B¹ section, an equal division of the octave into minor thirds in the bass underlies much of the structure of the B² section (Example 12.4). But now the tonal excursions are even more remote than in the B¹ section and the surface rhetoric even more violent, qualities that together create a sense of horror; the music refers to *ombra* and *tempesta* topics that can be associated with the awe raised by something supernatural.[14] It is as if the protagonist were horrified of the consequences of the innocent false step, brought forth by the repetition of the antagonist's gesture in bar 55. Only the passing major-mode colouration within the prolonged F triad in bars 70–82 attempts to introduce a more optimistic expression.

The lower harmonic analysis of Example 12.4b shows that up to bar 92 the music follows the false path taken in the A² section; the prolongation of an E♭♭ minor chord, an apparent IV♭ of B♭ major, seems to lead, in bar 92, to a dominant of B♭ minor. Thus the music is at the threshold of confirming, in a very strong manner, the false step that the repetition of the antagonist's gesture in bar 55 initiated. At the last minute, the protagonist opposes the antagonist's false step. In bar 92 the music enharmonically reinterprets the apparent dominant of B♭ as a German augmented

---

[13]   When ♭V is tonicized, its bass usually forms a goal of an arpeggiation consisting of two consecutive minor thirds: in the minor-mode environment, such a procedure can be found, for example, in bars 1–16 of the third movement of Beethoven's Piano Sonata, Op. 26 (for an analysis, see Heinrich Schenker, *Free Composition*, ed. and trans. Ernst Oster [New York: Longman, 1979; German original 1935], Fig., 40/6), and in the major-mode environment in bars 34–44 of the second movement of Haydn's String Quartet, Op. 54, No. 1 (for an analysis, see Aldwell and Schachter, *Harmony and Voice Leading*, pp. 570–71). A relatively unmediated I–♭V motion, without the arpeggiation of minor thirds, occurs in another late slow movement by Schubert, that of the piano sonata D. 959, in which ♭V is tonicized in bar 85.

[14]   For a thorough discussion of the *ombra* and *tempesta* topics, see Clive McClelland, 'Ombra and Tempesta', in *The Oxford Handbook of Topic Theory*, ed. Danuta Mirka (New York: Oxford University Press, 2014), pp. 279–300. A more general aesthetic context for the sense of horror can be sought from the concept of 'sublime', which referred, in Schubert's time, to awe and terror one senses in front of the limitless – something too vast, obscure, and indeterminate to be fully grasped; for a thorough discussion of the relationships between sublime and music in the late eighteenth and early nineteenth centuries, see Kiene Brillenburg Wurth, *Musically Sublime: Indeterminacy, Infinity, Irresolvability* (New York: Fordham University Press, 2009). For a discussion of the *tempesta* topic in Schubert's Lieder, see Clive McClelland's chapter in this volume.

Example 12.4   Schubert, Piano Sonata, D. 958 in C minor, second movement, bars 43–94, B² section, analytical sketch

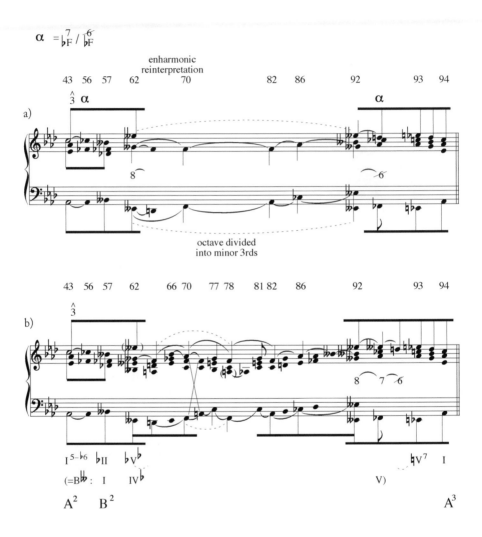

sixth chord. As a result, the chord that first sounded as an element about to establish the remote B♭♭ minor turns out to function as an element that leads the music to the home-key dominant, thus correcting, so to speak, the A² section's false step. Symbol α in Example 12.4a shows the enharmonic equivalence of the F♭ major sonority (bar 56) and the augmented sixth chord leading to the home-key dominant (bar 92), thus indicating that the right path is found at the end of the B² section through a revaluation of the element that led the music astray at the end of the A² section. The revaluation can be understood as an active deed of the protagonist, who now refuses to accept the antagonist's false step by cancelling the element that initially confirmed the remote B♭♭ major.

The closing A³ section again begins as if all threat had been left behind, but the section's second phrase (bars 102–111) shows that this is not the case. Now the antagonist is more active than earlier. Immediately in bar 102, played in the triple *piano* dynamic not heard elsewhere in the movement, the inner-voice neighbour-note above E♭ is not the diatonic F, but rather the important F♭ that earlier functioned as the bass of the α chord. This chromatic alteration leads to a brief motion into A♭ minor, with the *Kopfton* transformed in bar 104 into C♭ (Example 12.5). The tonal path seems to be lost after this: the top-voice C♭ is immediately transformed into a B♮, and in bar 105 we have the first of the antagonist's gestures heard three times in a row.[15] The gestures appear around C major, D♭ major, and E♭♭ major triads,

Example 12.5   Schubert, Piano Sonata in C minor, D. 958, second movement, bars 1–18, A³ section, analytical sketch

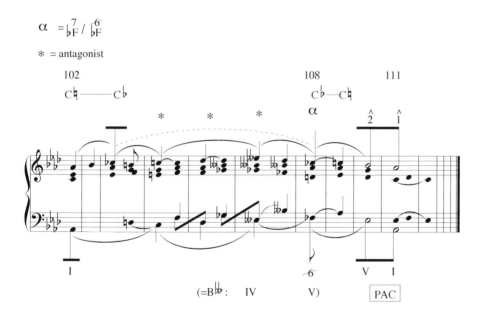

15   In spite of their enharmonic equality, the C♭ and B♮ in bar 104 structurally represent two different, chromatically inflected scale degrees (C♭ is ♭3̂ while B♮ is ♮2̂); thus, B♮ is shown as a neighbour note in Example 12.5, its enharmonic equality with the C♭ notwithstanding. In Schubert's music, one can occasionally find such situations where repetitions of the same pitch represent two different scale degree functions. At the local levels this occurs, for example, in bars 124–129 of the song 'Aufenhalt' (*Schwanengesang*), where E♭ functions as

respectively, each sounded a semitone higher that the preceding one. This chromatic motion locally hides all sense of tonal centre. As bar 108 sounds the dominant of B♭ major, the last gesture's E♭ major chord retrospectively seems to be a IV in this key (Example 12.5). That is, the antagonist again attempts to lead the music to B♭ major. But the protagonist is by now familiar with this trick, and now he or she immediately reinterprets the α chord as a German augmented sixth chord. Thus the protagonist disarms the antagonist, as it were, which means overcoming the threat. Now that the danger has been left behind, the music's background structure can reach its closure. The final seal to the protagonist's victory occurs in bars 111–112, right after the completion of the *Urlinie*, when an inner voice sounds a neighbouring E♭–F–E♭ motion, in which the diatonic F corrects the neighbouring F♭ of bar 102, a pitch that initiated the antagonist's last attempt to lead the protagonist astray. At the movement's end, the threat has been fully eradicated.

From Agony to Transcendence: D. 960

The Andante sostenuto of the B♭ major Sonata avoids the kinds of rhetorically underlined culminations that we have encountered in the slow movement of the C minor Sonata. The dynamic level is quiet most of the time, and even the few *forte* passages are not like the almost violent outbursts heard in the B sections of D. 958. The movement is in a ternary form (see Figure 12.2). The framing A sections of the C♯ minor movement are contemplative, whereas the central B section in A major is more extrovert and active. Thematically, the two A sections repeat fundamentally the same material, but from the perspective of harmony they are different; most importantly, while the A¹ section ends, as expected, in the tonic minor, the A² closes in an otherworldly C♯ major, sounded throughout in the soft triple *piano* dynamic. Yet the expressive quality of the movement's major-mode ending does not suggest a victory following an active struggle – a narrative archetype common in nineteenth-century music at least since Beethoven's Fifth Symphony – but rather a transcendent sense of peace. The narrative path leading to this resigned conclusion can be elucidated through tensions between a musical protagonist and a musical antagonist.

The A¹ section consists of three phases, the first two of which sound the same thematic material, mostly even at the same pitch level: (1) bars 1–17 move from the tonic C♯ minor to the mediant E major; (2) bars 18–33 lead the music from E major back to the tonic; (3) bars 34–42 form a cadential unit that includes both

---

♭1̂ while D♯ functions as ♯7̂. At deeper levels, in the slow movement of the String Quintet, D. 956, the *Kopfton* G♯ (3̂) that is established at the movement's opening section moves, at the beginning of the middle section, to an A♭ (neighbouring ♭4̂), which is later corrected into the diatonic A♮ (for an analysis of the Quintet, see Lauri Suurpää, 'The Path from Tonic to Dominant in the Second Movement of Schubert's String Quintet and in Chopin's Fourth Ballade', *Journal of Music Theory* 44/2 [2000], pp. 460–61).

Bars	1–42	43–89	90–138
Section	A¹	B	A²
Key	c♯	A → c♯: V	c♯ → C♯

Figure 12.2   Schubert, Piano Sonata in B♭ major, D. 960, second movement, chart of form

an imperfect authentic cadence (bars 36–37) and a perfect authentic cadence (bars 40–41). The first of these phases, which introduces important elements for the movement's narrative, invites further examination (Example 12.6a). The harmonic structure is relatively uncomplicated. The opening tonic is prolonged in bars 1–8 after which the music reaches the dominant, a chord prolonged in bars 9–13. In bar 14 the music's harmonic colour changes drastically. The dominant of bars 9–13 is transformed, through a chromaticized 5–6 progression, into an E major six-three chord, and this sonority begins a cadential progression. A firm E major five-three tonic is then reached in bar 17 through a perfect authentic cadence, the first cadence in the movement.

But the formal organization lends the music an aura of uncertainty. As Example 12.6a indicates, the underlying formal functions create a somewhat inconsistent trajectory. Bars 1–8 consist of a 'compound basic idea' and its repetition; thus, they suggest an initiating function and imply, most likely, the onset of a 'sixteen-bar sentence'. However, the dominant chord that arrives in bar 9 challenges these expectations. This V is sounded at the moment one expects the 'eight-bar continuation' to begin. But the chord's arrival signals no clearly recognizable formal function; as it is preceded by an initiating function only, the chord does not constitute a half cadence and thus has no cadential function, and as it suggests no fragmentation or sequential activity, it does not seem to represent the medial function, either. In other words, even though the dominant is a powerful gesture, one does not know if it suggests an initiation of a new formal unit, a closure of the preceding unit, or the medial phase in an ongoing unit.

This functional ambiguity is enhanced by the prolongation of the dominant, a 'standing on the dominant' that usually, but not here, signals a post-cadential, framing function.[16] In bars 14–17 the situation is further obscured by an expanded cadential progression, which suggests, on the one hand, the beginning of a new formal unit in E major, and, on the other, the ending of the preceding unit in a concluding, cadential function.

---

[16] William Caplin (*Classical Form*, pp. 75 and 113–15) has noted that not all standing on the dominants represent the post-cadential function, even though this is by far the normative function. Here the situation is further complicated by the fact that the movement has just started, and we have only heard the opening initiating function.

Example 12.6   Schubert, Piano Sonata in B♭ major, D. 960, second movement, bars 1–42, A¹ section, analytical sketch

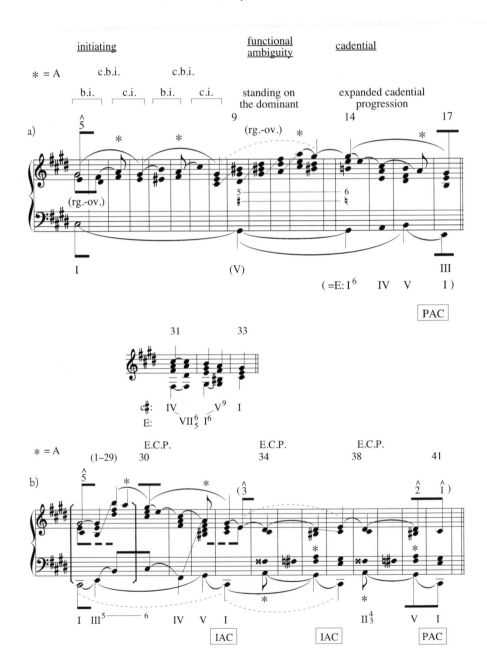

These events can be interpreted from the perspective of the two musical personae, the protagonist and the antagonist. The first eight bars establish a deeply tragic expression, which is enhanced by the repeated, age-old symbol of agony, the semitone between scale degrees 6 and 5 (see the asterisks in Example 12.6a). But significantly for the narrative, bars 1–8 only signal a functional initiation and they feature no dominant, thus medial and cadential functions are anticipated to follow and to seal the initial tragic expression. But as we have seen, the non-cadential dominant of bars 9–13 complicates the situation, and the transformation of this dominant into an E major chord in bar 14 changes the tonal goal from the minor-mode tonic into a more positive major key.

The movement's first cadential arrival is in a nontragic major key in bar 17, that of E major, and this cadence completes a process, which shifts the music from a possibility of confirming a minor key (the dominant of C♯ minor in bars 9–13) into a cadential confirmation of a major key (the expanded cadential progression in E major in bars 14–17). It is as if the protagonist consciously denied the confirmation of the tragic expression and confirmed the nontragic instead. As we will see, this is the first step in a series in which the music refuses to confirm the tragic expression. From a narrative perspective, we can understand the gloomy emotion as the antagonist, and the avoidance of confirmation of tragic expression as the protagonist's attempt to resist the antagonist.

The ensuing music shows that in spite of this initial success, the protagonist is not able to escape the power of the antagonist and the tragic expression. The thematic material of the opening of the movement is repeated in bars 18–33, and now the music starts by moving from the tonic of E major to its dominant (bars 18–29). Like in bars 9–13, the dominant is not an element confirming the preceding key, but rather it unexpectedly leads to a new tonal centre, this time back to the tonic in bar 30. The C♯ minor chord of bar 30 suggests multiple functions. If we elucidate it in the context of the preceding music, it seems to be a VI in E major, whereas when examined from the perspective of the ensuing music, it is the tonic of C♯ minor that begins an expanded cadential progression.

In the middleground, I do not take the chord of bar 30 as a structural tonic (Example 12.6b); as it has not been prepared in any way, it does not sound like a goal of motion. Rather, I read its bass note C♯ as an unfolded upper sixth above the E of bar 17. As a result, I interpret in bars 17–32 a stepwise E–F♯–G♯ bass progression. This progression has an impact on the function of the E major chord; the chord occurs within a unified tonic-prolonging harmonic progression (I–III$^{5-6}$–IV–V–I). Thus the E major triad, an element that attempts to avoid confirmation of the minor-mode tonic, is, at deep levels, part of the tragic C♯ minor diatony.

The multi-layered function of the C♯ minor chord in bar 30 is important for the protagonist's aspirations. As we have seen, earlier the tonicized E major helped the protagonist to escape the tragic minor-tonic. But now it seems that the gloomy expression is unavoidable, and the tonic minor gradually breaks forth from the nontragic E major environment, first in bar 30 as a non-structural element and in bar 33 unavoidably as the structural tonic (Example 12.6b). At deep levels the tonic sonority has governed throughout, and the E major chord functions as a contrapuntal sonority within the I–V progression of bars 1–32, so the protagonist's efforts have had no effect on the global structure. Yet the protagonist tries to stick to the E major; as the stave above Example 12.6b shows, the IV and V of C♯ minor, chords that secure at deep levels the return of the tragic tonic, recall, very locally, the nontragic E major. It is as if the protagonist attempted in vain to resist the return of the tragic tonic. But the tonic is now unavoidable, and the A¹ section's final third phase (bars 34–42) consists of two concluding and confirming expanded cadential progressions, the first one of which ends in an imperfect and the second in a perfect authentic cadence.

Even though it may now seem that the protagonist's attempts to resist the tragic tonic had no lasting effect, this is not quite the case. The recurring A in the top voice has kept $\hat{5}$ active until the return of the structural tonic in bar 33 (see the asterisks in Example 12.6), and the final descent toward the concluding $\hat{1}$, to be reached in bar 41, begins in this bar. But significantly, on the second crotchet of bar 33, the concluding descent begins from $\hat{3}$, which is, at deep levels, an inner-voice pitch. Thus the A¹ section's middleground voice leading leaves the situation open, as it were, as there is no $\hat{4}$ to lead the music in a stepwise manner from the opening $\hat{5}$ to the concluding $\hat{1}$. One might go as far as to suggest, programmatically, that the avoidance of a full closure in the tragic tonic is an outcome of the protagonist resisting the governing agony.[17]

The B section immediately tonicizes A major, at the same time increasing the music's rhythmic activity. The nontragic major key suggests that now the protagonist is actively challenging the antagonist and the tragic expression of the A section. However, in spite of the character and texture that differ greatly from the A¹ section, the remotest levels recall two factors familiar from the preceding C♯ minor section (Example 12.7a): first, neighbouring A governs both the top voice and the bass; second, the inner-voice $\hat{3}$ begins an active linear motion. One might argue that elements of reality in the A section thus provide the global framework for the B section's attempts to escape from the tragic emotion. It is as if the B section tried to deny the tragic expression of the preceding A section, but

[17]   In his fascinating study of this movement, Eric Wen reads the structure in a slightly different way. The main difference concerns the reading of the B major chord (bars 26–29). While I read it as subordinate to the preceding E major triad, Wen takes it as a sonority built on the lower neighbour of the tonic (VII). As a result, he also takes the C♯ minor chord of bar 30 as the regained structural tonic, rather than as a contrapuntal sonority prolonging III as I do. In addition, owing to the emphasis he gives to VII, Wen reads a $\hat{4}$ as its top voice, thus interpreting a stepwise fifth progression underlying the entire A¹ section. See Eric Wen, 'Schubert's *Wiegenlied*: The Andante Sostenuto from the Piano Sonata in B♭, D. 960', in *Schubert's Late Style: History, Theory, Style*, ed. Lorraine Byrne Bodley and Julian Horton (Cambridge: Cambridge University Press, 2016), pp. 134–48.

Example 12.7   Schubert, Piano Sonata in B♭ major, D. 960, second movement, bars 43–90, B section, analytical sketch

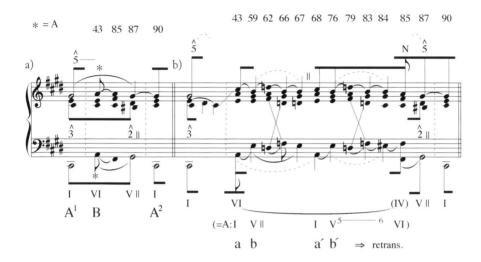

the shared structural elements indicate that the A section's material intrudes, in a rather hidden way, into the nontragic B section as well.

The B section consists of four phrases, which are labelled in Example 12.7b as *a*, *b*, *a'*, and *b'*. The opening *a* phrase (bars 43–58) consists of a repeated parallel period prolonging the A major tonic. Thus it provides the B section with a stable opening, confirming the protagonist's attempt to establish a nontragic major key. The ensuing *b* phrase (bars 59–67) is more complex. It opens with a dominant chord, which I have interpreted – owing to the onset of a new formal segment as well as the thematic and registral association between bars 43 and 59 – as a back-relating dominant. But because a D major chord is strongly tonicized in bar 62, the high structural status of the dominant in bar 59 is by no means unequivocal – indeed, David Beach and Eric Wen give priority for the D major chord over the dominant in bar 59.[18] It is not vital here to opt for one reading over the other, however. The main musical issue that is important for us is the air of uncertainty concerning the music's structural course – the antagonist may be now understood to cast a shadow of doubt over the clarity of the protagonist's non-tragic expression.

This antagonist's shadow can be seen to appear more strongly in the ensuing *a'* and *b'* phrases. To begin with, the *a'* phrase (bars 68–75) is invested with

---

[18]   David Beach, 'The Submediant as Third Divider: Its Representation at Different Structural Levels', in *Music Theory in Concept and Practice*, ed. James M. Baker, David W. Beach, and Jonathan W. Bernard (Rochester, NY: University of Rochester Press, 1997), p. 323; Eric Wen, 'Schubert's *Wiegenlied*', examples 9 and 10, and personal communication.

minor-mode colouration, so the protagonist senses threat, so to speak. But more significantly, the *b'* phrase (bars 76–89) undergoes a functional reinterpretation, which transforms it into a retransition; that is, its musical process does not conclude in A major but rather leads the music back to the tragic tonic key, ending with the home-key dominant concluding the first branch of the movement's interrupted deep-level structure (Example 12.7b).[19] The transformation is an outcome of an enharmonic reinterpretation of an element already heard in the *b* phrase: the F♮ of bar 66 is reinterpreted in the corresponding bars 83–84 as an E♯, which is a chromatic alteration of the dominant of bar 76 (Example 12.7b). In other words, the music now takes, in a concrete manner, a path different from the *b* phrase. The route here followed leads to agony; the protagonist must now abandon the hope of establishing a nontragic expression, and thus concede the antagonist's tragic power.

The protagonist's frustrated attempts to resist the antagonist in the B section may be seen to affect the course of the closing A^2 section. Until the onset of the concluding tonic major in bar 123, the thematic material and the alteration between tonic minor and non-tonic major keys correspond to the A^1 section. But now the tonal structure is far more complex: in bar 103 the music tonicizes a remote C major, and when E major occurs (bar 111), it is only represented by an E major six-four chord and by a dominant.

Example 12.8b clarifies the voice leading: the C major chord is built on a chromatic passing tone C♮, which is itself an enharmonic reinterpretation of the leading tone B♯. E major, in turn, is an apparent key only, built around a neighbouring VII. The weak or apparent tonics of the major keys show that the protagonist is no longer able or willing to oppose the antagonist as strongly as in the A^1 section. Yet the protagonist is not yet ready to accept a closure, symbolized by a deep-level stepwise progression descending from $\hat{5}$: even though both the top voice's chromatic passing-tone G♯ (bar 103) and the contrapuntal six-four chord of bars 111–114 drive the top voice towards $\hat{4}$, a reaching over once more brings in bar 119 the $\hat{5}$ back to the top voice (Example 12.8b). Indeed, the middleground progression of the top voice in bar 90–119 can be understood as an expansion of bars 1–4 that initiated the avoidance of a $\hat{4}$–$\hat{3}$ progression (cf. Examples 12.6a and 12.8a).[20]

---

[19] The phenomenon of formal transformation, where a section begins in one function and ends in another, has been thoroughly discussed by Janet Schmalfeldt; see *In the Process of Becoming: Analytic and Philosophical Perspectives on Form in Early Nineteenth-Century Music* (New York: Oxford University Press, 2011). She uses the term 'becoming' to describe this factor, and shows it with a double-lined arrow.

[20] Unlike the corresponding chord in bar 30, I read the C♯ minor triad of bar 119 as a structural tonic. The reason for interpreting apparently similar chords in two different ways lies in the preceding music: while the chord of bar 30 is preceded by a firmly tonicized III, whose upper fifth B leads to C♯, the chord of bar 119 is, by contrast, only preceded by unstable contrapuntal sonorities. Thus a weaker C♯ minor triad suffices to bring the structural tonic back in the A^2 section than in the A^1.

Example 12.8   Schubert, Piano Sonata in B♭ major, D. 960, second movement,
                      bars 90–142, A2 section, analytical sketch

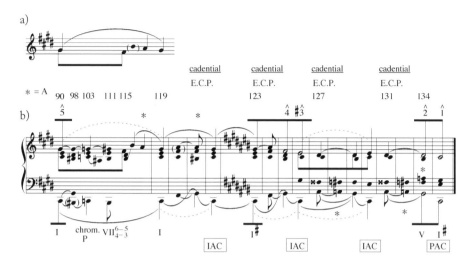

With the reaching of the major-mode tonic in bar 123, the top voice finally starts to descend: in bars 125–126 we hear a $\hat{4}$–$\hat{3}$ motion, with $\hat{3}$, significantly, in the raised, major-mode form (Example 12.8b). After the arrival at $\hat{3}$, all that remains to be heard, from the structural perspective, is the completion of the *Urlinie* that occurs in bar 135. The motivically significant A♮ is still heard (see asterisks in Example 12.8b), but it sounds like a recollection of the preceding drama rather than an element keeping it alive.

The musical expression at the movement's end signals the air of peace and relief, which can be elucidated through Robert Hatten's notion of 'abnegation', a term referring to 'willed resignation as a spiritual acceptance of a (tragic) situation that leads to a positive inner state, implying transcendence'. The knowledge that there is no longer need to struggle brings along a positive, transcendent state, an emotion close to Aristotelian catharsis. The protagonist accepts the unavoidable state of affairs and stops opposing the powerful antagonist.[21]

---

[21]   Robert S. Hatten clarifies the term 'abnegation' in *Musical Meaning in Beethoven: Markedness, Correlation, and Interpretation* (Bloomington: Indiana University Press, 1994), 287. In an essay discussing Schubert's self-elegies – pieces that can be understood to mourn the composer's own anticipated death – James Sobaskie has also applied the term abnegation when describing the affective quality at the end of the B♭ major Sonata's slow movement, suggesting that the end 'conveys no sense of triumph or success, but release and relief'; see 'Schubert's Self-Elegies', *Nineteenth-Century Music Review* 5/2, pp. 98–102. As a background for the ending's abnegation, Sobaskie traces the function of the tonic major's

Epilogue

The narratives in the two slow movements discussed here include both common features and differences. Of the similarities, the one primary for our concerns is the view that the movements' overall structural courses forge narrative arches, kinds of musical plots. This kind of narrative quality in Schubert's music was already noted in 1838 by Robert Schumann who wrote, significantly in an essay also examining the last three piano sonatas, that Schubert's music tells the listeners, in particular the younger ones, 'about the things that most appeal to them – romantic stories, knights, maidens and adventures'.[22] An additional similarity between the two movements is formed by their narratives, which can both be interpreted as growing out of an opposition of the protagonist and an antagonist, the latter representing something unpleasant or unwanted. Both movements end, furthermore, in a nontragic expression signifying that the protagonist reaches, at the end of both movements, a positive state. The movements' musical plots thus move from tension to release.

The positive states and the paths leading to them are very different, however. The slow movement of the C minor Sonata can be located in a common narrative archetype moving from struggle to victory. But even here the overall narrative clearly differs from the standard mode as it appears in Beethoven's Fifth Symphony, for example, where the music moves from a tragic state (the first movement's restless C minor) into a nontragic one (the finale's heroic C major). In the slow movement of Schubert's C minor Sonata, in contrast, the music opens in a nontragic and serene state, and it is only the antagonist's brief one-bar gesture that challenges the positive expression – first fleetingly interfering with the local flow of music, but ultimately, through its harmonic consequences, threatening to destroy the movement's entire tonal framework. Thus, the movement's narrative, as well as the protagonist's experiences, are nuanced and multilayered, considerably elaborating and deepening the framework of moving from struggle to victory.

In the second movement of the B♭ major sonata the global narrative course follows the framework of moving from a tragic to a transcendent expression, a framework discussed in detail by Robert Hatten in his analysis of the slow movement of Beethoven's *Hammerklavier* Sonata.[23] But again, Schubert elaborates

---

third E♯ in the movement (moving from an embellishing pitch, displacing the minor mode's E♮, to a firm chordal third), as well as the juxtapositions of major and minor keys.

[22] Robert Schumann, *Schumann on Music: A Selection from the Writings*, ed. and trans. Henry Pleasants (New York: Dover, 1988), p. 141. Schumann was, of course, by no means the only nineteenth-century writer who used the metaphor of narrative (or a novel or a story) when describing music. For further discussion on narrative as a metaphor of music in the nineteenth century, see, for example, Thomas Grey, 'Metaphorical Modes in Nineteenth-Century Music Criticism: Image, Narrative, and Idea', in *Music and Text: Critical Inquiries*, ed. Steven Paul Scher (Cambridge: Cambridge University Press, 1992), pp. 93–117.

[23] Hatten, *Musical Meaning in Beethoven*, pp. 9–28.

this underlying schema. Throughout the movement, the protagonist attempts to avoid confirming the tragic expression, as is shown by the music's avoidance of complete confirmations of the tragic tonic key. Only towards the end of the movement, after the protagonist's attempts to resist the tragic expression have become weaker, does the transcendent emotion emerge. The closing expression grants relief for the protagonist, signalling that there is no longer need to resist the unavoidable.

In both movements, then, Schubert follows a narrative archetype that is familiar from earlier musical repertory, a model that one can also find in Beethoven's music that Schubert deeply admired. Yet he elaborates these schemes in unique and touching ways that make the listener follow with sympathy – indeed, with empathy – the protagonist's experiences as he or she faces the threats, horrors, and reliefs of the music.

13

Stylistic Disjuncture as a Source of Drama in Schubert's Late Instrumental Works*

Joe Davies

Setting the Scene: Schubertian Strangeness

Schubert's late instrumental works are replete with strange, disjunctive moments.[1] Prominent examples include the abrupt modal shifts in the opening bars of the String Quartet in G major, D. 887, the sudden intrusion of the distorted march-like theme in the opening movement of the Piano Duet Fantasy in F minor, D. 940, and the eerie trill in low register that interrupts the lyrical primary theme in the first movement of the Piano Sonata in B♭ major, D. 960. Markers of disjuncture in these examples range from underlying structural fractures, through harmonic dislocations, to rhetorical figures that leave a disruptive imprint on the musical surface. Such features create a mode of drama that resides not in the smooth unfolding of a linear narrative, but rather in the pivotal shifts between expressive scenes, in moments of suspended silence, or in gestural intrusions from elsewhere.

In this chapter I undertake a comparative reading of two extreme instances of stylistic disjuncture in Schubert's oeuvre: the Adagio from the String Quintet in C major, D. 956, and the Andantino of the Piano Sonata in A major, D. 959, both composed in the final months of his life, 1828.[2] My exegesis is constructed

* I express gratitude to James Sobaskie and Susan Wollenberg for their insightful comments on earlier versions of this chapter; and to Robin Hagues for his efficiency and professionalism in processing the music examples that appear within its pages.

[1] For a general discussion of expressive contrast in Schubert's late instrumental works, see Benjamin Korstvedt, '"The Prerogative of Late Style": Thoughts on the Expressive World of Schubert's Late Works', in *Schubert's Late Music: History, Theory, Style*, ed. Lorraine Byrne Bodley and Julian Horton (Cambridge: Cambridge University Press, 2016), pp. 404–25.

[2] In exploring these movements from an intertextual perspective, I offer a response to John Gingerich's suggestion that 'in spite of the very different works to which these slow movements form the core, the very extremity of the need for expression of which they are the miraculous result seems to demand that they be heard together'. See John Gingerich, *Schubert's Beethoven Project* (Cambridge: Cambridge University Press, 2014), p. 308.

within a 'hermeneutical theatre',[3] a framework in which semiotic analysis of the dramaturgical properties of these movements is followed by hermeneutic reflection on their shared aesthetic qualities.[4] In regard to the latter, I propose that the category of the grotesque provides a lens through which to re-evaluate the strangeness of this music and to situate it within its broader cultural context.[5]

From Dream to Nightmare: Schubert's Adagio (D. 956)

What can be detected in the ternary framework of the Adagio of Schubert's String Quintet, D. 956, is a distinctive structural trope involving the dramatization of irreconcilable contrasts.[6] Table 13.1 provides an overview of the movement's expressive topography.[7]

---

[3] The term 'hermeneutical theatre' is taken from Richard Kramer, 'Against the Grain: The Sonata in G (D. 894) and a Hermeneutics of Late Style', in *Schubert's Late Music*, pp. 111–33: here Kramer explores the ways in which the first movement of the G major Piano Sonata, D. 894, and Schubert's setting of Franz Bruchmann's 'Schwestergruß', D. 762, might be said 'to speak to one another' through a 'shared lexicon of tropes and figures'. The present chapter adopts a similar intertextual approach to the expressive vocabulary of Schubert's Adagio (D. 956) and Andantino (D. 959).

[4] My interpretation draws on terminology used in Robert Hatten, *Interpreting Musical Gestures, Topics, and Tropes: Mozart, Beethoven, and Schubert* (Bloomington: Indiana University Press, 2004), particularly his notion of 'shifts in the level of discourse' (pp. 268–9). For wider discussion of topical hermeneutics, see Danuta Mirka, ed., *The Oxford Handbook of Topic Theory* (Oxford and New York: Oxford University Press, 2014); and Kofi Agawu, *Music as Discourse: Semiotic Adventures in Romantic Music* (Oxford and New York: Oxford University Press, 2008), esp. Chapter 2.

[5] While references to the grotesque can be found within the discourse on Schubert's Lieder, to my knowledge his late instrumental music has not previously been read in connection with this aesthetic category. On the former, see Susan Youens, 'Of Dwarves, Perversion, and Patriotism: Schubert's "Der Zwerg", D. 771', *19th-Century Music* 21/2 (1997), pp. 177–207.

[6] For more on 'structural tropes', see Lawrence Kramer, *Music as Cultural Practice, 1800–1900* (Berkeley: University of California Press, 1990), Chapter 1.

[7] On the harmonic and structural properties of the movement, see James William Sobaskie, 'The "Problem" of Schubert's String Quintet', *Nineteenth-Century Music Review* 2/1 (2005), pp. 57–92, esp. pp. 76–9; and Lauri Suurpää, 'The Path from Tonic to Dominant in the Second Movement of Schubert's String Quintet and in Chopin's Fourth Ballade', *Journal of Music Theory* 44/2 (2000), pp. 451–85, esp. pp. 455–65. For recent analytical approaches to the Quintet more broadly, see the essays by Scott Burnham, Julian Horton, John Koslovsky, and Nathan John Martin and Steven Vande Moortele in the special issue of *Music Analysis*, ed. William Drabkin, 'Schubert's String Quintet in C major, D. 956', 33/2 (2014).

Table 13.1   Schubert, String Quintet in C major, D. 956, second movement, overview

Bars	Section	Tonal regions	Topical zones
1–28	A	E major with forays into F♯ major (bar 5) and A major (bar 13), returning subsequently to E major	Lyrical dreamworld
(28)		E major $\Rightarrow$ F minor	*Durchbruch*; distorted trilled gesture
29–63	B	In flux; C minor breakthrough (bar 38)	Nightmarish music
64–91	A'	E major, F♯ major (bar 69), and A major (bar 76), E major	Disturbed dreamworld: original 'A' material resurfaces in dislocated guise with ghostly voices in first violin and second cello
91–94	Coda	Neapolitan (f) intrusion, followed by a final cadence in E major	Remnant of the initial *Durchbruch*

In the 'A' section the music withdraws from a sense of the present reality into a space suffused with transience,[8] evoking, in John Gingerich's words, a 'static dream tableau',[9] while simultaneously pointing to an infinite realm beyond its reach. Its thematic profile is comprised of an intricately layered texture – a characteristic Schubertian configuration – with each part injecting a distinctive element into the musical frame. As Example 13.1 illustrates, the second violin, viola, and first cello present a spacious mode of lyricism that negates an overtly teleological trajectory and draws attention inward to the sensuous surface. Beneath the inner trio, the second cello provides a plucked harmonic backdrop, its fragile utterances lacking firm grounding, while at the top of the layered texture the first violin speaks in a recitative-like style, suggesting a lyrical voice in the process of formation.[10] At

[8]   An earlier example of this fusion of dream-like fragility with visionary breadth is found in the 'A' sections of Schubert's Notturno in E♭ major for piano trio, D. 897 – a piece that distils the essence of Schubertian beauty within its compact framework.

[9]   Gingerich, *Schubert's Beethoven Project*, p. 318; see also Gingerich, 'Remembrance and Consciousness in Schubert's C-Major String Quintet, D. 956', *Musical Quarterly* 84/4 (2000), pp. 619–34.

[10]   For alternative readings of the 'A' material, see Susan Wollenberg, *Schubert's Fingerprints: Studies in the Instrumental Works* (Farnham: Ashgate, 2011), pp. 168–70; Xavier Hascher, 'Eine "traumhafte" *barcarola funebre*': Fragmente zu einer Deutung des langsamen Satzes des Streichquintetts D 956', in *Schubert und das Biedermeier, Beiträge zur Musik des frühen 19. Jahrhunderts: Festschrift für Walther Dürr zum 70. Geburtstag*, ed. Michael Kube (Kassel:

times the music assumes greater urgency, notably in bar 7 with the expansion in register and dynamic gradation; at other moments, such as bar 15, it appears increasingly transient, conveyed in part through the contraction to triple *piano*. These subtle shifts suggest perspectival fluctuations in the dreamworld, hinting at disruptive undercurrents beneath its beguiling surface.

If the 'A' section appears 'too good, too pure, to be true', the musical events that follow in its pathway cast a shadow over its idyllic aura.[11] At bar 28, which

Example 13.1   Schubert, String Quintet in C major, D. 956, second movement, bars 1–4

Note: The excerpts from D. 956-ii are based with permission on *Franz Schubert: Streichquintett in C, D 956*, Urtext der Neuen Schubert-Ausgabe, TP 287 © Bärenreiter-Verlag Karl Vötterle GmbH & Co. KG, Kassel.

Bärenreiter, 2002), pp. 127–38; and Peter Gülke, 'In what Respect a Quintet? On the Disposition of Instruments in the String Quintet D 956', in *Schubert Studies: Problems of Style and Chronology*, ed. Eva Badura-Skoda and Peter Branscombe (Cambridge: Cambridge University Press, 1982), pp. 173–85.

11   The phrase quoted is from Benedict Taylor's characterization of the similarly tranquil opening theme of Schubert's Piano Sonata in G major, D. 894. Benedict Taylor, 'Schubert

establishes a dialectical tension between sectional closure and narrative disruption, the peaceful cadential confirmation of E major is undermined by an abrupt shift to the Neapolitan (F) minor,[12] triggered by trilled unisons in all parts (see Example 13.2). Forgoing syntactical connections with the surrounding scenery, these trilled notes shatter the prevailing stillness with an outburst of harsh instrumental sonority. A sudden surge of rhythmic motion is combined with extreme dynamic and textural intensification, the peaceful tonic becoming a tension-filled leading note within the space of one beat. In this context, divorced from its usual function as a marker of graceful embellishment, the trill represents a strategy of disjuncture, serving to collapse the boundaries of the 'A' material into the onset of the 'B' section.[13]

Imbued with multiple layers of meaning, the disruptive content of bar 28 invites a range of hermeneutic readings. In Scott Burnham's view, it functions as a 'threshold', one that represents 'an astonishing transformation' of thematic material rather than 'a willed process of development',[14] while Lorraine Byrne Bodley detects the 'rapid oscillation between Paradise and Inferno [that] is central to Schubert's vision, whereby the irreconcilable opposites are deliberately collapsed into each other, threatening absolute tranquillity'.[15] In light of its forceful entry and lasting impact, the passage might also be interpreted as an instance of *Durchbruch* – an explosive intrusion that ruptures the music's flow and determines its subsequent course of action.[16] That all aspects of the music (rhythm, dynamics, texture, style, and tonality) are implicated in the procedure emphasizes its shocking impact. Beyond its effect at the local level of fracturing the musical surface, the

---

and the Construction of Memory: The String Quartet in A Minor, D. 804 ("Rosamunde")', *Journal of the Royal Musical Association* 139/1 (2014), pp. 41–80, here p. 60.

[12] F minor represents Schubert's subversive choice as alternative to the major Neapolitan.

[13] The 'B' section retains a recurrent memory of the initial rupture (see for example the lingering leading notes in the second cello part at bars 29 and 38).

[14] Burnham, 'Thresholds Between, Worlds Apart', *Music Analysis* 33/2, special issue: 'Schubert's String Quintet in C major, D. 956' (2014), p. 159.

[15] Lorraine Byrne Bodley, 'A Place at the Edge: Reflections on Schubert's Late Style', *Oxford German Studies* 44/1 (2015), pp. 18–29, here p. 28.

[16] To my knowledge there has not been sustained critical discussion of the aesthetic category of *Durchbruch* in Anglophone scholarship on Schubert's music. For an introduction to Schubertian breakthroughs, see Peter Gülke, 'Zum Bilde des späten Schubert: Vorwiegend analytische Betrachtungen zum Streichquintett, Op. 163', in *Musik-Konzepte Sonderband: Franz Schubert*, ed. Heinz-Klaus Metzger and Rainer Riehm (Munich: Edition Text+Kritik, 1979), pp. 107–66. For wider discussion of the concept, see Theodor W. Adorno, *Mahler: A Musical Physiognomy*, trans. Edmund Jephcott (Chicago: The University of Chicago Press, 1992), esp. Chapter 3.

Example 13.2   Schubert, String Quintet in C major, D. 956, second movement,
                bars 28–31

breakthrough triggers a prominent shift in the level of discourse,[17] deconstructing the foundations of the lyrical dreamworld and giving voice to a nightmarish reality.

Further stylistic dislocations together with expressive use of *Durchbruch* are foregrounded within the movement's 'B' section, notably in bar 30 where the music breaks out into a dramatic duet between the first violin and first cello, underpinned by restless utterances in the second cello and angular, intensely physical interjections

[17]   Robert Hatten observed apropos such writing that 'if the disruption involves sufficient contrast in style, or sufficient differentiation along other dimensions, it may suggest not only a shift in temporal experiencing, but also a shift in the discourse itself, generally to a higher level that comments on or reacts to the ongoing, unmarked discourse of piece time'; Hatten, *Interpreting Musical Gestures, Topics, and Tropes*, p. 269.

Example 13.3   Schubert, String Quintet in C major, D. 956, second movement,
                    bars 35–38

in the second violin and viola (Example 13.2).[18] As the strange proceedings of
the 'B' section unfold, there are a number of flashbacks to earlier parts of the
movement: the boundaries between the music's distinct scenes become increasingly
blurred. One such example can be seen in bar 35 (Example 13.3). Here the
dynamic marking drops suddenly to *piano*, and a series of trilled notes transpires
in the upper registers of the first violin and first cello. The emphasis on the trill as
a rhetorical gesture, recalling the disruptive *Durchbruch* of bar 28, creates the effect

[18] The dramatic nature of the 'B' section – an instrumental equivalent to a climactic vocal
ensemble – reminds us that Schubert had deeply rooted aspirations as a composer for the stage.

of an internal time warp.[19] Rising in pitch and volume, the trilled notes lead to
a secondary breakthrough in bar 38,[20] at which point the duet between the first
violin and first cello resumes its course, now in C minor. From bar 38 onwards the
music follows an increasingly digressive pathway, incorporating another flashback
in bars 51–54 (not shown), the climactic high point of the 'B' section, where the
first violin and first cello present what Burnham calls 'a shuddering *Zerrbild*' of the
turn-like contour of the material from the movement's opening bars.[21] Whereas
the gesture is initially quiet and virtually motionless, in this later manifestation
it is surrounded by forceful rhythmic agitation – a thematic transformation that
intensifies the sense of disjuncture between the 'A' and 'B' material; the visionary
qualities of the dreamworld recede further into the distance, as if constituting only
a fading memory.

While the 'B' section is initiated disruptively, its closing bars (shown in
Example 13.4a) are imbued with the quality of suspended time, presenting a
weightless profile. The dynamic marking drops to triple *piano*; the intense rhythmic
agitation from the preceding material subsides; and all parts inject fragile sigh-
like figurations into the texture. Underpinning this passage is a process of gradual
disintegration, implied not only through the suspension of motion, but also through
the dissolving nature of the discourse: each thematic fragment is punctuated by
silence. Against this backdrop, the varied return of the 'A' material introduces
further displacement, here in the form of a disturbed reprise: see Example 13.4b.[22]
Stripped of its original expressive connotations, the opening material resurfaces
with a reconfigured profile, the dreamworld now tinged with a distorted reality.
Strangely, the outer parts creep around the lyrical contours of the main theme;
their ghostly scaled-based interjections subvert the original (albeit rather fragile)
tranquillity. In particular, the demisemiquaver figuration in the second cello
part (which retains a memory of the semitonal transition in bar 28) suggests an

[19]   While moments of recollection and reminiscence in Schubert's late music have been
much discussed as elements that stand apart from the unfolding action, the central section
of D. 956-ii demonstrates an alternative compositional approach. Here dramatic effect
is conveyed through the way in which evocations of the past appear within a disruptive
context. For an overview of recent critical approaches to Schubertian memory, see the essays
by Walter Frisch, John Daverio, John Gingerich, Charles Fisk, and Scott Burnham in the
special issue 'Music and Culture' of *The Musical Quarterly* 84/4 (2000).

[20]   Beneath the trilled notes, the second cello part carries traces (with octave dislocation)
of an inverted version of the chromatic line that, when descending, evokes lament and death
(the pattern is presented as follows: F♯ in bar 35; G followed by G♯ in bar 36; A, B♭, and B in
bar 37, leading to C in bar 38).

[21]   Burnham, 'Thresholds Apart, Worlds Between', p. 159.

[22]   The notion of a 'disturbed' reprise is discussed in Lawrence Kramer, 'Romantic Meaning
in Chopin's Prelude in A Minor', *19th-Century Music* 9/2 (1985), pp. 145–55.

obsessive subdivision of time, clouding the theme with an aura of restlessness. The impression left by this final section is that of 'brokenness';[23] the music is unable to sustain its original identity.

Further subversion of the 'A' material occurs just moments before the end of the movement when the disturbed dreamworld comes into direct contact with the gestural language of the central section. As shown in Example 13.5, at bar 91 a remnant of the initial *Durchbruch* of bar 28 resurfaces in the first violin, leading to a similarly forceful Neapolitan-inflected interjection. The dramatic implications of this gesture are two-fold: it not only reinforces the sense of a disturbed reprise, but also portrays resistance to closure, undermining the possibility of overt reconciliation between the opposing expressive styles of the movement. Although cadential confirmation of E major is provided in the final two bars, the flashback

Example 13.4a   Schubert, String Quintet in C major, D. 956, second movement,
                 bars 57–62

23 For wider discussion of brokenness in nineteenth-century music, see Laura Tunbridge, *Schumann's Late Style* (Cambridge: Cambridge University Press, 2007), pp. 135–87.

Example 13.4b   Schubert, String Quintet in C major, D. 956, second movement, bars 64–67

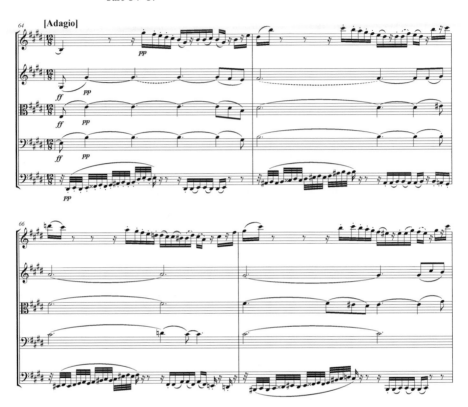

to the moment of transition to the central disruption infuses the ending with a disjunctive tone:[24] the possibility of complete rapprochement is negated and an image of unresolved conflict prevails.[25]

[24] That the closing bars of the finale recall the disruptive ending of the second movement – injecting, in Taylor's words, a 'dark Neapolitan twist that spreads an uncanny shadow over the conclusion of [the] work' – further substantiates the view that D. 956 is an essay in irreconcilable contrasts. Taylor, 'Schubert and the Construction of Memory', p. 56.

[25] In a private communication Susan Wollenberg noted that 'an alternative or maybe somehow compatible view is that the horrors of the central section are recalled at a distance and come to terms with finally, now understood in the context of the E major material (whereby V^7/f becomes an augmented sixth of E, a recognizable cadential preparation) – peaceful tonic closure is achieved successfully thereafter'. These two readings pay testament to the way in which Schubert's late instrumental works continually invite contrasting modes of emotional and critical engagement.

Example 13.5   Schubert, String Quintet in C major, D. 956, second movement,
                      bars 89–94

From Eerie Lyricism to Distorted Fantasia: Schubert's Andantino (D. 959)

As with the Quintet's Adagio, so the Andantino of Schubert's A major Piano
Sonata, D. 959, embodies a structural trope premised on stylistic disjuncture,
though in the 'A' section of the latter movement there are no traces of an idealized
dreamworld; the music strikes a disturbed tone from the outset.[26] Table 13.2 offers
an overview of its structural and expressive properties.

[26] See Charles Fisk, *Returning Cycles: Contexts for the Interpretation of Schubert's Impromptus
and Last Sonatas* (Berkeley: University of California Press, 2001), Chapter 8; William
Kinderman, 'Wandering Archetypes in Schubert's Instrumental Music', *19th-Century Music*
21/2 (1997), pp. 208–22; Leon Plantinga, 'Schubert, Social Music and Melancholy', in
Rethinking Schubert, ed. Lorraine Byrne Bodley and Julian Horton (Oxford and New York:
Oxford University Press, 2016), pp. 237–50, esp. pp. 243–50; and Wollenberg, *Schubert's
Fingerprints*, Chapter 6.

Table 13.2   Schubert, Piano Sonata in A major, D. 959, second movement, overview

Bars	Section	Tonal regions	Topical zones
1–68	A	F♯ minor, with intimations of the relative major in bars 19–26 and 51–58	Eerie lyrical style, accompanied by a haunting pedal point (*idée fixe*)
69–84	Transition	⇒ C minor via a series of diminished sevenths	Fantasia
85–122	B	C minor, C♯ minor, E minor, F minor, F♯ minor, C♯ minor	Distorted fantasia
123–158	Retransition	C♯ minor/D major/ F♯ minor	Dialectic between recitative and fantasia
159–195	A′	F♯ minor/A major	'A' theme in dislocated guise with additional ghostly layers
196–202	Coda	F♯ minor	Disembodied spread chords sounding from the depths of the keyboard

In contrast to the familiar lyricism in Schubert's oeuvre that exudes wholeness and illusory beauty (such as we find in the 'A' section of D. 956-ii), the 'A' theme of D. 959-ii shown in Example 13.6a is distinguished by its eerie character. Its contours rise and fall within restricted parameters, looping around the interval of a fourth above and third below its starting point, while the accompanimental figure hovers on an isolated C♯ pedal point in the manner of an *idée fixe*: these features intensify the haunting materiality of the discourse.[27] Aside from occasional dynamic swells and *sforzando* outbursts foreshadowing the disruptions to come, the music is drained of life, its scenery barren and dejected.

---

[27] A parallel can be drawn here with the 'A' section of the slow movement of Schubert's Piano Sonata in B♭, D. 960, which similarly presents an eerie lyrical theme unfolding within confined melodic and harmonic parameters, its accompanimental backdrop (a C♯ pedal point split across four octaves) suggesting obsessive fixation on a lost object. See Lauri Suurpää's chapter in this volume: 'Virtual Protagonist and Musical Narration in the Slow Movements of Schubert's Piano Sonatas D. 958 and D. 960'; Eric Wen, 'Schubert's *Wiegenlied*: The Andante Sostenuto from the Piano Sonata in B♭, D. 960', in *Schubert's Late Music*, pp. 134–48; and James William Sobaskie, 'Schubert's Self-Elegies', *Nineteenth-Century Music Review* 5/2 (2008), pp. 71–105.

Thematic repetition (a characteristic feature of Schubert's late instrumental music in general)[28] is deployed to unprecedented extremes in this movement. In the 'A' section the main theme appears ten times in a paratactic manner, whereby syntactical connections are downplayed in favour of a chain-like unfolding of thematic material.[29] Time appears to be frozen in a void; the music constantly retraces its pathway. Adorno's commentary on the nature of late Schubertian landscapes is apposite here:

> The ex-centric construction of [the] landscape, in which every point is equally close to the centre, reveals itself to the wanderer walking around it with no actual progress. … [Schubert's] themes know of no history, but only shifts in perspective: the only way they change is through a change of light, and this explains Schubert's inclination to use the same theme two or three times in different works, and different ways.[30]

Rotating around a fixed point, and blurring the boundaries between the centre and the margins of the landscape, the 'A' section of D. 959-ii enters an exilic realm comparable to that of 'Der Leiermann' from *Winterreise*, D. 911.[31] With each repetition of the theme, the eerie atmosphere is intensified, creating a world in which the lyrical verges on the mechanical: the music, like that of 'Der Leiermann', simultaneously reveals and removes vestiges of human presence.[32]

While modal fluctuations in Schubert's music have been much discussed as representing contrasting expressive realms (with major tonality reserved for fantasies and dreams, minor for harsh reality),[33] in D. 959-ii they resist such

---

[28] See Scott Burnham, 'Landscape as Music, Landscape as Truth: Schubert and the Burden of Repetition', *19th-Century Music* 29/1, pp. 31–41; and Anne Hyland, 'In Search of Liberated Time, or Schubert's Quartet in G Major, D. 887: Once More Between Sonata and Variation', *Music Theory Spectrum* 38/1 (2016), pp. 85–108.

[29] On parataxis, see Su Yin Mak, 'Schubert's Sonata Forms and the Poetics of the Lyric', *Journal of Musicology* 23/2 (2006), pp. 263–306.

[30] Theodor Adorno, 'Schubert (1928)', trans. Jonathan Dunsby and Beate Perrey, *19th-Century Music* 2/1 (2005), p. 12.

[31] For discussion of the expressive qualities of 'Der Leiermann', see Lorraine Byrne Bodley, 'Music of the Orphaned Self? Schubert and the Concepts of Late Style', in *Schubert's Late Music*, pp. 331–56; and Susan Youens, *Retracing a Winter's Journey: Schubert's Winterreise* (Ithaca, NY: Cornell University Press, 1991), pp. 298–307.

[32] The music's quasi-mechanical qualities bring to mind the world of automata – a world in which the 'animate' cannot be clearly distinguished from the 'inanimate', as memorably depicted in the tales of E. T. A. Hoffmann. For discussion of musical automata, see *inter alia* Carolyn Abbate, 'Outside Ravel's Tomb', *Journal of the American Musicological Society* 52/3 (1999), pp. 465–530.

[33] Kinderman has noted apropos Schubert's late works that 'the contrast between major and minor may represent one aspect of a more profound thematic juxtaposition

categorization. The two forays into the relative major within the 'A' section do little to dispel the prevailing eeriness, appearing entwined in the expressive fabric of the tonic minor. As Example 13.6b shows, the first glimpse of A major enters in a tentative manner, an impression that is heightened by the lack of cadential affirmation of this key: a possible modulation to A major is withdrawn and the phrase moves gradually back to F♯ minor, confined to the tonic key. Similarly, the final statement of the theme in bars 51–58 (not shown) opens with a suggestion of A major before returning to the tonic minor. In the words of Charles Fisk, 'the key of A major comes as a memory: not as a goal achieved but … as a source lost and suddenly remembered'.[34] That these phrases are marked *pianissimo* (the quietest level of the 'A' section) further highlights the transience of the relative major: both its appearances here represent distant visions in the landscape. As the opening section draws to a close, with alternating tonic and subdominant chords sounding in low register – a ghostly reference to the chordal progression that opened the whole work – the lyrical theme moves further into the distance.

Set apart from the 'A' section, the ensuing transitional passage (bars 69–84) initiates a process of topical metamorphosis (Example 13.7a). Here the lyrical voice gives way initially to a monophonic arabesque-like figuration before dissolving into the language of fantasia, evoking the spirit of C. P. E. Bach, an echo of the distant past intruding into the present.[35] The term fantasia is used to refer not only to a topical configuration[36] – implied through the improvisatory right-hand figurations and the profusion of diminished-seventh harmonies – but also to a broader aesthetic that, as Annette Richards has demonstrated, functions as an agent of destabilization.[37] In this context, the restless rhythmic activity of the right-hand material disturbs the prevailing impression of stasis; and its chromatic language

suggesting the dichotomy of inward imagination and external perception'. In D. 959-ii the situation is less clearly defined: 'inward imagination and external perception' are presented simultaneously, creating the impression of multiple layers in the discourse. See Kinderman, 'Schubert's Tragic Perspective', in *Schubert: Critical and Analytical Studies*, ed. Walter Frisch (Lincoln and London: University of Nebraska Press, 1986), pp. 65–83, here p. 75.

[34] Fisk, *Returning Cycles*, p. 221.

[35] The harmonic progression underpinning this passage resonates with C. P. E. Bach's observation that 'as a means of reaching the most distant keys more quickly and with agreeable suddenness, no chord is more convenient and fruitful than the seventh chord with a diminished seventh and fifth'. Quoted in Susan Wollenberg, "'Es lebe die Ordnung und Betriebsamkeit! Was hilft das beste Herz ohne jene!'": A New Look at Fantasia Elements in the Keyboard Sonatas of C. P. E. Bach', *Eighteenth-Century Music* 4/1 (2007), pp. 119–28, here p. 124.

[36] See Matthew Head, 'Fantasia and Sensibility', in *The Oxford Handbook of Topic Theory*, ed. Danuta Mirka (Oxford and New York: Oxford University Press, 2014), pp. 259–78.

[37] See Annette Richards, *The Free Fantasia and the Musical Picturesque* (Cambridge: Cambridge University Press, 2001), esp. Chapter 1.

Example 13.6a   Schubert, Piano Sonata in A major, D. 959, second movement, bars 1–8

Example 13.6b   Schubert, Piano Sonata in A major, D. 959, second movement,
bars 19–27

Note: The excerpts from D. 959-ii are based with permission on the G. Henle Verlag Urtext edition. Copyright (1961/89) G. Henle Verlag, Munich.

undermines the music's tonal centre, creating a sense of entering the unknown. In other words, the transition introduces marked duality into the music. While at first the threshold between fantasy and lyricism is quite clearly delineated, the relationship between these two stylistic zones becomes increasingly antagonistic as the movement unfolds.

What is unleashed in the central part of the movement (Example 13.7b) is a bizarre compositional idiom. Its thematic profile constantly changes, with one idea merging into another, the impression of ordered discourse slipping out of reach. Derailing the confined tonal trajectory of the preceding section, the music progresses through a remote harmonic labyrinth in which clearly articulated cadential progressions are avoided – areas of C minor (bar 85), C♯ minor (bar 92), E minor (bar 94), F minor (bar 100), and F♯ minor (bar 103) are juxtaposed in quick succession. This digressive tonal language underpins an equally disruptive stylistic vocabulary, in a synchronous relationship between topical mode and harmonic structure. Improvisatory rhetoric takes centre stage,[38] suggesting an intertextual

---

[38]   I borrow the concept of 'improvisatory rhetoric' from James Webster, 'The Rhetoric of Improvisation in Haydn's Keyboard Music', in *Haydn and the Performance of Rhetoric*, ed. Tom Beghin and Sander M. Goldberg (Chicago: University of Chicago Press, 2007), pp. 172–212, here p. 176. Webster notes that improvisatory rhetoric encompasses 'the

connection with the slow movement of the 'Wanderer' Fantasy in C major, D. 760: the music spirals out of control as it roams the fantastical landscape.[39]

Part of the strangeness of the 'B' section stems from the way in which familiar compositional styles are transplanted to new contexts, detached from their usual expressive associations. If, as Marjorie Hirsch has pointed out, the imitative scale-based entries in bars 85–98 of Example 13.7b recall a style associated with eighteenth-century keyboard inventions, then the material's disjointed phrase structure and abrupt tonal shifts serve to defamiliarize this topical frame of reference.[40] The long stretches of trills, which also are employed beyond their conventional usage, add to the music's strangeness, functioning not in an indexical manner to highlight syntactical elements but rather as sonic oscillations that distort the musical surface. Collectively these features convey an image of topical displacement, a grotesque representation of an archaic contrapuntal style.

Just as musical topics and ornamental devices are placed in strange contexts, so too is thematic material from the 'A' section, thus accentuating all the more the extreme dissonance between the expressive scenes of the movement. A key element in this transformation is the pedal point figure which is fixated from the start on the note C♯. Originally an element that conjures eerie stasis, it returns obsessively in the midst of the central section with a disfigured rhythmic identity, reinforcing while distorting its status as the movement's *idée fixe*. Examples include the semiquaver reiterations of G♯ in bars 92–93, split between an upper and lower octave; the C♯ oscillations in bars 103–105, leading to the first highpoint in the form of a four-octave scalar descent;[41] and the demisemiquaver pedal point that emerges in low register at bar 116, propelling the section to a dramatic climax in bar 122. Despite being closely related to the movement's overall tonic, the climactic C♯ minor chords

impression of excessive freedom, unmotivated contrast, or insufficient coherence; seeming to "lose one's way"; [and] the unexpected subversion of an apparently stable formal type'.

[39] This intertextual association is suggested through the use of a shared stylistic vocabulary involving frenzied passagework. On the stylistic idiom of D. 760-ii, see Jonathan Dunsby, 'Adorno's Image of Schubert's "Wanderer" Fantasy Multiplied by Ten', *19th-Century Music* 29/1 (2005), pp. 209–36.

[40] Marjorie Hirsch detects an allusion to the 'archaic severity of a two-part invention' but does not discuss the process of expressive distortion. Hirsch, 'Schubert's Reconciliation of Classical and Gothic Influences', in *Schubert's Late Music*, p. 157. The theme of topical displacement (where the usual expressive associations of topics are distorted) has broader resonance in Schubert's late works, with further examples found in the first movement of the G major String Quartet, D. 887, and the slow movement of the F minor Fantasy, D. 940, both of which present a misshapen version of a French overture topic.

[41] A remnant of this scalar passage resurfaces in bars 34–36 of the ensuing Scherzo movement; its disruptive presence continues to haunt the music's expressive trajectory. For further discussion of these inter-movement connections, see Fisk, *Returning Cycles*, Chapter 8, esp. pp. 225–7.

Example 13.7a   Schubert, Piano Sonata in A major, D. 959, second movement, bars 69–84

Example 13.7b   Schubert, Piano Sonata in A major, D. 959, second movement, bars 85–122

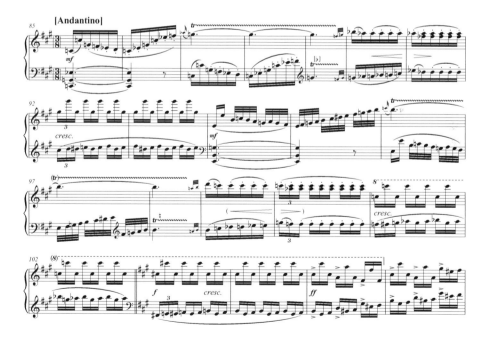

Example 13.7b (continued)

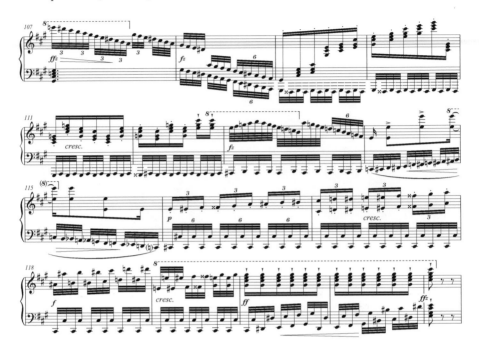

sound remote in light of the preceding harmonic eccentricities:[42] the music reaches an expressive apex that is dissociated from its surroundings, subsequently falling away into eerie silence that hints at complete dissolution of the musical discourse.

Commentators have, not surprisingly, pointed to the central section of D. 959-ii as something of an anomaly in Schubert's late music. Robert Winter views the material as 'an episode which comes as close to a nervous breakdown as anything in Schubert's output';[43] in William Kinderman's words, it 'unleashes not just turbulence and foreboding, but chaotic violence';[44] and Marjorie Hirsch asserts that the music 'seems caught up in an unexpected emotional maelstrom,

---

[42]   Charles Fisk has noted that Schubert often dramatizes the key of C♯ minor, the 'Wanderer key', in alienating ways in his late instrumental works. An example of such tonal alienation can be heard in the slow movement of the 'Wanderer' Fantasy, D. 760, where the intrusion of C♯ minor in the context of C major conjures qualities of estrangement, while recalling the key of the song 'Der Wanderer', D. 489, whose thematic material and mood it also reflects. See Fisk, *Returning Cycles*, pp. 64–78.

[43]   Robert Winter, 'Schubert' in *The New Grove Dictionary of Music and Musicians*, p. 683.

[44]   Kinderman, 'Wandering Archetypes in Schubert's Instrumental Music', *19th-Century Music* 21/2 (1997), p. 218.

overwhelming any sense of predictability, stability or security'.[45] What differentiates this writing from other examples of Schubertian strangeness is its length and sheer extremity:[46] it moves beyond the remit of a temporary contrast and represents a significant structural disruption to the movement, projecting damaging implications for the material that follows.

In the aftermath of the central section, the retransitional passage shown in Example 13.8 presents a dramatic 'breaking of the voice'.[47] The process begins in bar 123 when a fragment of the opening theme (specifically its characteristic turn-like figure) emerges in a quasi-recitative guise. Prevented from developing into lyricism, the murmuring figure is shattered almost immediately by a chordal outburst (C♯ minor) that represents a remnant of the 'B' section's destructive climax. Two subsequent recitative fragments are similarly silenced by chordal interruptions: the second of these in bar 128 erupts from a scalar gesture reminiscent of the central fantasy, shifting to D major in an abrupt manner characteristic of Schubert's Neapolitan-inflected intrusions.[48] The way in which these contrasting styles are presented in a dialectical relationship plays out the return to the 'A' material in notably dramatic mode.[49] From a semiotic perspective, this fusion can be interpreted as an instance of topical troping, a process defined by Hatten as 'the synthesis of otherwise contradictory topics that are juxtaposed in a single functional location or rhetorical moment'.[50] Its effect is extremely disturbing: the lyrical acquires a 'broken' identity, unable to retain wholeness. If the music appears to find solace from bar 147 onwards, emerging with smoother contours in the parallel major, and banishing at this point the spectre of the frenzied 'B' material, the impression of a broken voice is not lost. In bar 152 a trill in low register fractures the musical surface once again,[51] setting an eerie scene for the varied return of the 'A' theme.

[45] Hirsch, 'Schubert's Reconciliation of Gothic and Classical Influences', p. 152.

[46] For broader reference, see Hugh Macdonald, 'Schubert's Volcanic Temper', *Musical Times* 119 (1978), pp. 949–52.

[47] See Julian Johnson, 'The Breaking of the Voice', *Nineteenth-Century Music Review* 8/2, special issue: 'Mahler: Centenary Commentaries on Musical Meaning' (2011), pp. 179–95.

[48] Examples elsewhere include the forceful entry of the Neapolitan (D♭) major in the opening bars of the *Quartettsatz*, D. 703, and the sudden intrusion of the Neapolitan (F) minor in the slow movement of the String Quintet, D. 956.

[49] Wollenberg has compared this material to the scene from Gluck's *Orfeo* where Orpheus pleads with the chorus of Furies, thereby drawing attention to its dramatic character. Wollenberg, *Schubert's Fingerprints*, p. 166.

[50] Hatten, *Interpreting Musical Gestures, Topics, and Tropes*, pp. 68–89.

[51] A parallel can be drawn here with the similarly disorientating effect of the trill that disrupts the flow of the opening theme in D. 960, first movement. On the latter, see Nicholas Marston, 'Schubert's Homecoming', *Journal of the Royal Musical Association* 125/2 (2000), pp. 248–70.

As in D. 956-ii, the final section (bars 159–202) of D. 959-ii subjects the original 'A' material to a disturbed reprise (see Example 13.9). Here the dynamic palette barely rises above *pianissimo*, suggesting physical suppression, while the thematic material resurfaces with a doubly fractured identity, haunted by recurrent C♯ iterations – a 'rhythmic shudder'[52] – in the upper voice, coupled with an additional inner voice in the accompanimental figuration. After conjuring eerie stasis in the opening section, then becoming implicated in the destructive central section, the repeated C♯ figure appears finally in the guise of a revenant.[53] In its newly

Example 13.8   Schubert, Piano Sonata in A major, D. 959, second movement,
                bars 123–158

52   Hirsch, 'Schubert's Reconciliation of Gothic and Classical Influences', p. 166.
53   Schubert demonstrated a fascination with ghostly music throughout his compositional career. In the realm of Lied, besides the case of 'Der Doppelgänger' from *Schwanengesang*, D. 957/13, memorable examples include his 'Geistertanz', D. 116, the two settings of Schiller's Thekla 'Eine Geisterstimme', D. 73 and D. 595, the closing lines of

Example 13.9   Schubert, Piano Sonata in A major, D. 959, second movement, bars 159–166

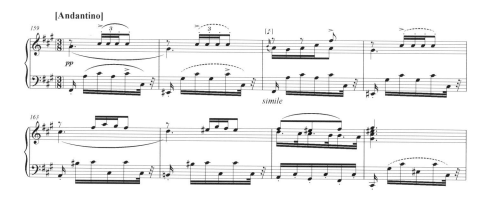

reconfigured guise, the theme strongly evokes a *Doppelgänger* of the original 'A' material, its multiple textural strands conveying the impression of a divided subject.

Negating the opportunity for stylistic reconciliation or redemptive transfiguration,[54] the coda (bars 196–202) completes the process of disintegration initiated throughout the movement's preceding sections.[55] The spread chords in the closing bars leave traces of a disembodied voice, their gradual descent into the registral depths suggesting withdrawal to a remote region of the musical landscape. In this way, the music closes in a space poised at the boundaries of presence and absence; its haunting sounds continue to reverberate beyond the movement's framework.

'Der Wanderer', D. 489, where a ghostly voice pronounces the wanderer's fate, and his setting of Franz Bruchmann's 'Schwestergruß', D. 762, a particularly spine-chilling essay in musical haunting.

[54] Its bleak ending differs significantly to that of the slow movement of D. 960, where there is, in Eric Wen's words, 'an incandescent metamorphosis' from minor to tonic major, representing a moment of transcendence. See Wen, 'Schubert's *Wiegenlied*', in *Schubert's Late Music*, p. 148.

[55] My reading of the closing section differs in critical orientation to two recent interpretations by Gingerich and Hirsch. For Gingerich the final section presents 'gestures of consolation', offering a form of 'gently redemptive benediction', while in Hirsch's view the movement presents an overarching 'reconciliation of diverse compositional influences', resolving the conflict between 'classical' and 'gothic' styles. See Gingerich, *Schubert's Beethoven Project*, pp. 308–13; and Hirsch, 'Schubert's Reconciliation of Gothic and Classical Influences', pp. 149–70. On the latter, see my review of *Schubert's Late Music, Nineteenth-Century Music Review* (forthcoming).

Shared Concerns: Schubert the Dramatist?

Examining D. 956-ii and D. 959-ii within the 'hermeneutical theatre' raises questions about the broader aesthetic implications of their intertextual connections. Put simply, how might we contextualize their shared strangeness?[56] In a welcome critique of Arthur Hutchings's view that Schubert 'gives us nothing but beauty',[57] Susan Wollenberg has suggested that:

> there are numerous instrumental movements in Schubert's oeuvre where beauty is allowed to flourish relatively untroubled: the slow movement of the B♭ Piano Trio, D. 898, is an example. Elsewhere, though, beauty is created alongside and in relation to those darker moods that colour it indelibly, thereby lending it an even greater profundity.[58]

To Wollenberg's observations I would add that the Adagio of D. 956 and the Andantino of D. 959 can be viewed as movements that shatter the boundaries of beauty entirely,[59] entering the distorted world of the grotesque, and exploring new contexts for musical drama.[60]

---

[56]   Not entirely *sui generis*, the strangeness of D. 959-ii and D. 956-ii is foreshadowed in the Andantes of the G major Piano Sonata, D. 894, and the G major String Quartet, D. 887, both of which unfold across a more expansive five-part framework, incorporating bizarre outbursts in their 'B' sections together with the destructive treatment of lyricism. For further discussion of these earlier movements, see Susan Wollenberg, *Schubert's Fingerprints*, pp. 195–201.

[57]   Framing his observation in terms of a comparison, Hutchings observed that 'whereas with Beethoven the quartet reached a mystical world, at once the farthest and the innermost region attained by any musician, Schubert gives us nothing but beauty'. A. J. B. Hutchings, *Schubert* (London: J. M. Dent, 1945, reprinted 1956), p. 110. For a critical reappraisal of Schubertian beauty – a topic that remains ripe for further hermeneutic exploration – see among others Scott Burnham, 'Schubert and the Sound of Memory', *Musical Quarterly* 84/4 (2000), pp. 655–63.

[58]   Wollenberg, *Schubert's Fingerprints*, p. 189.

[59]   Such an approach distinguishes Schubert's late works from the music of his predecessors, especially Mozart, where dramatic contrasts and disruptions (arising primarily through topical juxtaposition) are only temporary, ultimately giving way to reconciliation.

[60]   For further discussion of Schubertian grotesquerie, see Joe Davies, *Interpreting the Expressive Worlds of Schubert's Late Instrumental Works* (DPhil dissertation, University of Oxford, 2018), Chapter 4. For wider discussion of musical grotesquerie, see (among others) Elizabeth Le Guin, '"One Says That One Weeps, but One Does Not Weep": *Sensible, Grotesque, and Mechanical Embodiments in Boccherini's Chamber Music', *Journal of the American Musicological Society* 55/2 (2002), pp. 207–54; Patricia Pinson, *The Shattered Frame: A Study of the Grotesque in Nineteenth-Century Literature and Music* (PhD dissertation,

The grotesque occupied a central position in the late eighteenth- and early nineteenth-century European imagination.[61] Among the characterizations of the grotesque from this period,[62] we find revealing insights into its key features embedded within Friedrich Schlegel's writings, as demonstrated in the following excerpt from the 1798 *Athenaeum*: 'Just as the naïve plays with the contradictions between theory and practice, so the grotesque plays with the wonderful permutations of form and matter, loves the illusion of the random and the strange and, as it were, coquettes with infinite arbitrariness'.[63] In Schlegel's view, the French Revolution constituted the 'most frightful grotesque of the age', 'where the most profound prejudices and their most brutal punishments are mixed up in a fearful chaos and woven as bizarrely as possible into a monstrous human tragicomedy'.[64] What emerges from Schlegel's fragments is an image of the grotesque as an intrinsically paradoxical mode of expression that is premised on the fusion of stylistic opposites and an underlying incompatibility between form and content. It is above all an aesthetic category that transgresses the borders of everything that is familiar, slipping into the territory of the frightful and the monstrous.

Ohio University, 1971); and Annette Richards, 'Haydn's London Trios and the Rhetoric of the Grotesque', in *Haydn and the Performance of Rhetoric*, ed. Tom Beghin and Sander M. Goldberg (Chicago: University of Chicago Press, 2007), pp. 251–80.

[61]   For a general overview of the history of the grotesque, see Justin D. Edwards and Rune Graulund, *Grotesque: The New Critical Idiom* (New York: Routledge, 2013); and Karlheinz Barack et al., eds, 'Grotesk', in *Ästhetische Grundbegriffe: Band 2 Dekadent bis Grotesk* (Stuttgart: J. B. Metzler Verlag, 2001), pp. 880–98.

[62]   Influential German treatises on the grotesque include Justus Möser's *Harlekin, oder Vertheidigung des Groteske-Komischen* (1761); Karl Flögel's *Geschichte des Groteske-komischen* (1788); C. L. Stieglitz's *Über den Gebrauch des Grotesken und Arabesken* (1790); and J. D. Fiorillo's *Über die Groteske* (1791).

[63]   Fragment 305, quoted in Friedrich Schlegel, *Philosophical Fragments*, trans. Peter Firchow (Minneapolis: University of Minnesota Press, 1991), p. 60. For broader discussion of Schlegel's aesthetic theory, see Frederick Burwick, 'The Grotesque in the Romantic Movement', in *European Romanticism: Literary Cross-currents, Modes, and Models*, ed. Gerhart Hoffmeister (Detroit: Wayne State University Press, 1989), pp. 45–6; and Burwick, 'Grotesque "Bilderwitz": Friedrich Schlegel', in *The Haunted Eye: Perception and the Grotesque in English and German Romanticism* (Heidelberg: Carl Winter Universitätsverlag, 1987), pp. 72–92.

[64]   Fragment 424, quoted in *Philosophical Fragments*, p. 86. Jean Paul's discussion of 'die vernichtende Idee des Humors' ('the annihilating idea of humour') in his *Vorschule der Ästhetik* (1804) resonates with Schlegel's view of the grotesque as a 'monstrous human tragicomedy': here he described a kind of humour that is dark, terrible, painful and awe-inspiring – a product of 'inverse sublimity'. See Kathleen Wheeler, ed., 'Jean Paul Richter, From School for Aesthetics', in *German Aesthetic and Literary Criticism: The Romantic Ironists and Goethe* (Cambridge: Cambridge University Press, 1984), pp. 162–98.

Like Schlegel, E. T. A. Hoffmann contributed imaginative insights to the discourse surrounding the grotesque. One such example can be found in his short essay on the drawings and etchings of Jacques Callot:

> Why can I not see enough of your strange and fantastic pages, most daring of artists! Why can I not get your figures, often suggested merely by a few bold strokes, out of my mind? When I look long at your compositions which overflow with the most heterogeneous elements, then the thousands of figures come to life, and – often from the furthest background, where at first they are hard even to descry – each of them strides powerfully forth in the most natural colour.
>
> No master has known so well as Callot how to assemble together in a small space such an abundance of motifs, emerging beside each other, even within each other, yet without confusing the eye, so that individual elements are seen as such, but still blend with the whole. [...] His art really goes beyond the rules of painting; or rather his drawings are but reflexes of all the fantastic apparitions called up by the magic of his exuberant fantasy. [...] Callot's grotesque forms, created out of animal and man, reveal to the serious, deeper-seeing observer all the hidden meanings that lie beneath the cloak of absurdity.[65]

Here Hoffmann declared unrestrained enthusiasm for the strange, intricately conceived style of Callot's work, establishing a connection between grotesquerie and 'exuberant fantasy', a realm in which the defiance of 'rules' takes centre stage. The 'hidden meanings' of his artwork, like all grotesque images and objects, demand hermeneutic exegesis, overwhelming the eye with a profusion of strange figures and unrelated ideas.[66]

Scholarship on the grotesque has paid close attention to its awkward and transgressive nature. In Geoffrey Harpham's theoretical formulation, 'the perception of the grotesque is never a fixed or stable thing, but always a process, a progression':[67]

[65] *E. T. A. Hoffmann's Musical Writings: Kreisleriana, The Poet and the Composer, Music Criticism*, ed. David Charlton and trans. Martyn Clarke (Cambridge: Cambridge University Press, 1989), pp. 76–8.

[66] Grotesque imagery of the kind Hoffmann admired in Callot's work assumes an equally prominent position in his own novels and short tales. His essays in grotesquerie comprise such specimens as the *Fantasiestücke in Callots Manier* (1814), *Die Elixiere des Teufels* (1815), and his *Nachtstücke* (1817), the latter of which includes the eccentric *Der Sandmann*. On Hoffmann's literary style, see Birgit Röder, *A Study of the Major Novellas of E. T. A. Hoffmann* (Woodbridge: Camden House, 2003); and John MacAuslan, *Schumann's Music and E. T. A. Hoffmann's Fiction* (Cambridge: Cambridge University Press, 2016).

[67] Geoffrey G. Harpham, *On the Grotesque: Strategies of Contradiction in Art and Literature* (Princeton: Princeton University Press, 1982), p. 17.

All images split, assuming incongruous double functions, and everything is thrown into doubt. These designs are called grotesques not only because of certain formal characteristics, but because they throw the reader/viewer into that intertextual "interval". [...] The interval of the grotesque is the one in which, although we have recognized a number of different forms in the object, we have not yet developed a clear sense of the dominant principle that defines it and organizes its various elements. [...] Looking for unity between center and margin, the interpreter must, whether he finds it or not, pass through the grotesque.[68]

From this perspective, the grotesque represents a dynamic experience that demands visceral engagement; it actively draws the interpreter into its contradictory world.

The art historian Frances Connelly has offered further perspectives on the dynamic qualities of the grotesque. A key feature of its ontology, she argues, is the sense of its being constantly in flux: 'it always represents a state of change, breaking open what we know and merging it with the unknown'.[69] In this respect, the grotesque behaves in the manner of a 'boundary creature, existing only in the tension between distinct realities', or as a 'catalyst' that opens 'the boundaries of two disparate entities, and [sets] a reaction in motion'.[70] It forces the interpreter into 'an in-between, unresolved space',[71] eliciting 'contradictory and conflicting' responses. Central to all manifestations of the grotesque, Connelly suggests, is the notion of 'the image at play': 'whatever the rules or conventions, the grotesque subverts them, creating a *Spielraum* full of conflict and new possibilities'.[72]

***

While it would be a stretch to suggest that Schubert was well versed in contemporaneous theories of the grotesque, there is nevertheless a sense that he was aware of the expressive potential of its characteristic stylistic hybridity.[73] In a

---

[68]   Harpham, *On the Grotesque*, pp. 17–19.

[69]   Frances Connelly, *The Grotesque in Western Art and Culture: The Image at Play* (Cambridge: Cambridge University Press, 2012), p. 5.

[70]   Connelly, *The Grotesque in Western Art and Culture*, p. 8.

[71]   Connelly, *The Grotesque in Western Art and Culture*, p. 12.

[72]   Connelly, *The Grotesque in Western Art and Culture*, pp. 14–15.

[73]   It is not improbable that Schubert would have encountered notions of the grotesque (as part of a broader aesthetic *Zeitgeist*) within his circle of poets and visual artists. For discussion of Schubert's cultural milieu, see David Gramit, *The Intellectual and Aesthetic Tenets of Franz Schubert's Circle: Their Development and Their Influence on His Music* (PhD dissertation, Duke University, 1987); John Gingerich, '"Those of us who Found our Life in Art": The Second-Generation Romanticism of the Schubert-Schober Circle, 1820–25', in *Franz Schubert and his World*, ed. Christopher H. Gibbs and Morten Solvik (Princeton:

diary entry dated 16 June 1816, while under the influence of his teacher Antonio
Salieri, Schubert penned the following:

> It must be beautiful and refreshing for an artist [Salieri] to see all his students
> gathered around ... and to hear in [their] compositions the expression of mere nature,
> free from all the bizarre elements which are common among composers nowadays
> and owed almost entirely to one of our greatest German artists [Beethoven]; that
> eccentricity which joins and confuses the tragic with the comic, the agreeable with
> the repulsive, heroism with howlings and the holiest with harlequinades, without
> distinction, so as to goad people to madness.[74]

In Schubert's final years, the strange fusions that he decried there gradually became
absorbed into his compositional idiom, assuming a particularly prominent position
in the Adagio of D. 956 and Andantino of D. 959. Beyond their points of topical
overlap, these movements can be viewed as speaking to one another – and indeed
about each other – through their joint participation in the poetics of the grotesque:
distortion and contradiction are foregrounded as key features of their identity.

The grotesquerie of the Quintet's slow movement revolves around the fusion
of dreams and nightmares. While such contrasts feature prominently in Schubert's
late oeuvre,[75] the trope reaches a new level of extremity in D. 956-ii, involving
blurred ontological boundaries between the two worlds. In defining the grotesque,
Connelly suggested that its 'deeper workings' are revealed 'through its changes, in
the interstitial moments when the familiar turns strange or shifts unexpectedly into

Princeton University Press 2014), pp. 67–114; and Raymond Erickson, ed., *Schubert's Vienna*
(New Haven: Yale University Press, 1997).

[74] Otto Erich Deutsch, ed. and trans. Eric Blom, *The Schubert Reader: A Life of Franz
Schubert in Letters and Documents* (New York: W. W. Norton & Co., 1949), p. 64. I am not
the first to engage with this diary entry: Marjorie Hirsch and William Kinderman have used
the document as a point of departure for exploring Schubert's changing attitude towards the
music of Beethoven in his final years. See Hirsch, 'Schubert's Reconciliation of Gothic and
Classical Influences', pp. 167–8; and William Kinderman, 'Franz Schubert's "New Style"
and the Legacy of Beethoven', in *Rethinking Schubert*, pp. 43–4.

[75] A notable example among the vocal works is 'Frühlingstraum' from *Winterreise*,
D. 911/11, whose musical setting includes stylistic contrasts as striking as the psychological
twists and turns in the poetic text: here the initial dreamworld, depicted in a lyrical dancelike
idiom, is harshly juxtaposed with a fragmentary style of music in the minor mode when the
protagonist's thoughts are jerked back to reality. As Susan Youens put it, '"Frühlingstraum" is
a study in contrasts and disjunctions, the silences between sections dramatizing the shocking
changes of tempo, voicing, motion, tonal direction, and mood'. Youens, *Retracing a Winter's
Journey*, p. 211. Susan Wollenberg (in *Schubert's Fingerprints*, pp. 171–4) has suggested that
'Frühlingstraum' offers a poetic context in which to understand the expressive content of the
late instrumental movements cast in similarly episodic form.

something else'.[76] The trilled unisons in bar 28 provide compelling musical evidence of such a view. Appearing both embodied and disembodied, the gesture distorts the beauty of the opening section with music that exhibits registral, dynamic, and timbral extremity. In this moment, the dreamworld becomes directly entangled with nightmarish music that gazes into a void – a fusion that induces feelings of horror tinged with a sense of aesthetic pleasure.

In contrast to D. 956-ii, where drama is conveyed through the abrupt shift from the dreamlike and the nightmarish, the Andantino of D. 959 creates the effect of being gradually drawn into a world of grotesquerie. Central to this process is the way in which the transitional passage (Example 13.7a) opens up a gap in the narrative where the juncture between lyricism and fantasy is slowly ruptured. That the music of the transition bears no topical resemblance to its surrounding context serves to enhance its alienating effect.

If, as Burnham suggests, Schubert's late works convey 'subjectivized spaces', then the central sections of D. 956-ii and D. 959-ii profile grotesque spaces replete with contradictory features.[77] Of relevance here is Robert Schumann's observation that 'apart from Schubert's music, none exists that is so psychologically unusual in the course and connection of its ideas'.[78] There is a powerful sense of the discourse being in flux. In a manner akin to the prose style of Jean Paul and Friedrich Schlegel,[79] where linear narratives are disrupted by plot twists and extended parentheses, the music in the central parts of these movements digresses from one region to another, problematizing the distinction between what is central and what is marginal: all frames of topical reference are subjected to defamiliarization.

A further point of intersection between these movements is formed by the disturbed thematic reprises in their A' sections, both of which present eerie *Doppelgängers* of the original material. In his study of 'double visions' in German literary culture, Andrew Webber suggested that 'the *Doppelgänger* returns compulsively both within its host texts and intertextually from one to the other. Its performances repeat both its host subject and its own previous appearances'.[80] Viewed within this intertextual field, the *Doppelgänger* that emerges in the final section of D. 959-ii can be heard not only to displace its original identity, but also to portray echoes of the haunted return in the Adagio of D. 956. Because of the way in

---

[76]   Connelly, *The Grotesque in Western Art and Culture*, p. 3.

[77]   Burnham, 'Landscape as Music, Landscape as Truth', pp. 31–41, esp. p. 36.

[78]   Quoted from John Daverio, *Crossing Paths: Schubert, Schumann, and Brahms* (Oxford and New York: Oxford University Press, 2002), p. 14.

[79]   For an overview of the literary style of Jean Paul and Friedrich Schlegel, see Anthony Phelan, 'Prose Fiction of the German Romantics', in *The Cambridge Companion to German Romanticism*, ed. Nicholas Saul (Cambridge: Cambridge University Press, 2009), pp. 41–66.

[80]   Andrew J. Webber, *The Doppelgänger: Double Visions in German Literature* (Oxford: Oxford University Press, 1996), p. 5.

which the themes return in a fractured state, the overarching impression left by both movements is that of displacement; the music closes in a state of estrangement.[81]

Besides their intertextual engagement with the grotesque, these movements present variations on the theme of fractured subjectivity. The music's obsessional elements, its temporal dislocations between past and present, and the extreme stylistic distortion are all elements that conjure an image of a subject that is unable to return to a past state or to form a new mode of totality. In the end, we are left to find meaning in the music's internal psychological worlds. Therein lies the essence of late Schubertian dramaturgy.

⁂

[81]   Such qualities suggest a further intertextual connection with Schubert's Heine settings in D. 957, particularly 'Der Atlas' and 'Der Doppelgänger', both of which can be seen to give voice to the grotesque through the dark, abject subject matter of their poetic texts. For general discussion of these songs and their poetic sources, see Graham Johnson, *Franz Schubert: The Complete Songs*, vol. 3 (London and New Haven: Yale University Press, 2014), pp. 39–42 and 59–64; and Susan Youens, *Heinrich Heine and the Lied* (Cambridge: Cambridge University Press, 2007), Chapter 1.

Select Bibliography

Adorno, Theodor W. 'Schubert (1928)', trans. Jonathan Dunsby and Beate Perrey, *19th-Century Music* 29/1 (2005), pp. 3–14.

Agawu, Kofi. *Music as Discourse: Semiotic Adventures in Romantic Music* (New York: Oxford University Press, 2008).

Badura-Skoda, Eva and Peter Branscombe, eds. *Schubert Studies: Problems of Style and Chronology* (Cambridge: Cambridge University Press, 1982).

Barry, Barbara. 'A Shouting Silence: Further Thoughts about Schubert's "Unfinished"', *The Musical Times* 151 (2010), pp. 39–52.

———. 'Schubert's Quartettsatz: A Case Study in Confrontation', *The Musical Times* 155 (2014), pp. 31–49.

Beach, David. 'Schubert's Experiments with Sonata Form', *Music Theory Spectrum* 15/1 (1993), pp. 1–18.

———. *Schubert's Mature Instrumental Music: A Theorist's Perspective* (Rochester, NY: University of Rochester Press, 2017).

Black, Brian. *Schubert's Apprenticeship in Sonata Form: The Early String Quartets* (PhD dissertation, McGill University, 1996).

———. 'Remembering a Dream: The Tragedy of Romantic Memory in the Modulatory Processes of Schubert's Sonata Forms', *Intersections* 25/1–2 (2005), pp. 202–28.

Black, Leo. *Franz Schubert: Music and Belief* (Woodbridge: Boydell Press, 2003).

Branscombe, Peter. 'Schubert and the Melodrama', in *Schubert Studies: Problems of Style and Chronology*, ed. Eva Badura-Skoda and Peter Branscombe (Cambridge: Cambridge University Press, 1982), pp. 105–41.

Brett, Philip. 'Piano Four-Hands: Schubert and the Performance of Gay Male Desire', *19th-Century Music* 21/2 (1997), pp. 149–76.

Brown, Peter A. *The Symphonic Repertoire, Vol. 2 – The First Golden Age of the Viennese Symphony: Haydn, Mozart, Beethoven, and Schubert* (Bloomington: Indiana University Press, 2002).

Burnham, Scott. *Beethoven Hero* (Princeton: Princeton University Press, 1995).

———. 'Schubert and the Sound of Memory', *Musical Quarterly* 84/4 (2000), pp. 655–63.

———. 'Landscape as Music, Landscape as Truth: Schubert and the Burden of Repetition', *19th-Century Music* 29 (2005), pp. 31–41.

———. 'Thresholds Between, Worlds Apart', *Music Analysis* 33/2, special issue: 'Schubert's String Quintet in C major, D. 956', ed. William Drabkin (2014), pp. 156–67.

Burstein, Poundie. 'Lyricism, Structure, and Gender in Schubert's G Major String Quartet', *The Musical Quarterly* 18/1 (1997), pp. 51–63.

Byrne Bodley, Lorraine. *Schubert's Goethe Settings* (Aldershot: Ashgate, 2003).

———. 'Goethe and Schubert: *Claudine von Villa Bella* – Conflict and Reconciliation', in *The Unknown Schubert*, ed. Barbara Reul and Lorraine Byrne Bodley (Aldershot: Ashgate, 2008), pp. 119–36.

———. 'A Place at the Edge: Reflections on Schubert's Late Style', *Oxford German Studies* 44/1 (2015), pp. 18–29.

———. 'In Pursuit of a Single Flame? On Schubert's Settings of Goethe's Poems', *Nineteenth-Century Music Review* 13/2 (2016), pp. 11–33.

Byrne Bodley, Lorraine and Julian Horton, eds. *Rethinking Schubert* (New York: Oxford University Press, 2016).

———, eds. *Schubert's Late Music: History, Theory, Style* (Cambridge: Cambridge University Press, 2016).

Capell, Richard. *Schubert's Songs* (London: Ernest Benn, 1928).

Caplin, William. *Classical Form: A Theory of Formal Functions for the Music of Haydn, Mozart, and Beethoven* (New York: Oxford University Press, 1998).

Chusid, Martin. 'Schubert's Chamber Music: Before and After Beethoven', in *The Cambridge Companion to Schubert,* ed. Christopher H. Gibbs (Cambridge: Cambridge University Press, 1997), pp. 174–92.

Clark, Suzannah. *Analyzing Schubert* (Cambridge: Cambridge University Press, 2011).

———. 'Rossini and Beethoven in the Reception of Schubert', in *The Invention of Beethoven and Rossini: Historiography, Analysis, Criticism*, ed. Nicholas Mathew and Benjamin Walton (Cambridge: Cambridge University Press, 2013), pp. 96–120.

Clive, Peter. *Schubert and his World: A Biographical Dictionary* (Oxford: Clarendon Press, 1997).

Cohn, Richard L. 'As Wonderful as Star Clusters: Instruments for Gazing at Tonality in Schubert', *19th-Century Music* 22 (1999), pp. 213–32.

Cone, Edward T. *The Composer's Voice* (Berkeley, Los Angeles, and London: University of California Press, 1974).

———. 'Schubert's Promissory Note: An Exercise in Musical Hermeneutics', *19th-Century Music* 5/3 (1982), pp. 233–41.

Dahlhaus, Carl. 'Sonata Form in Schubert: The First Movement of the G-Major String Quartet, Op. 161 (D. 887)', trans. Thilo Reinhard, in *Schubert: Critical and Analytical* Studies, ed. Walter Frisch (Lincoln, NE: University of Nebraska Press, 1986), pp. 1–12.

Damschroder, David. *Harmony in Schubert* (Cambridge: Cambridge University Press, 2010).

Daverio, John. '"One More Beautiful Memory of Schubert": Schumann's Critique of the Impromptus, D. 935', *Musical Quarterly* 84/4 (2000), pp. 604–18.

———. *Crossing Paths: Schubert, Schumann, and Brahms* (New York and Oxford: Oxford University Press, 2002).

Davies, Joe. Review of *Schubert's Late Music: History, Theory, Style*, ed. Lorraine Byrne Bodley and Julian Horton (Cambridge: Cambridge University Press, 2016), *Nineteenth-Century Music Review* (2017; forthcoming in print).

———. *Interpreting the Expressive Worlds of Schubert's Late Instrumental Works* (DPhil dissertation, University of Oxford, 2018).

Davies, Stephen. *Musical Meaning and Expression* (Ithaca, NY: Cornell University Press, 1994).

Denny, Thomas A. 'The Years of Schubert's A-flat-Major Mass, First Version: Chronological and Biographical Issues, 1819–1822', *Acta Musicologica* 63/1 (1991), pp. 73–97.

———. 'Schubert's Operas: "The Judgment of History?"', in *The Cambridge Companion to Schubert*, ed. Christopher H. Gibbs (Cambridge: Cambridge University Press, 1997), pp. 224–40.

Deutsch, Otto Eric. *Schubert: A Documentary Biography*, trans. Eric Blom (London: J. M. Dent & Sons, 1946).

———. *The Schubert Reader: A Life of Franz Schubert in Letters and Documents*, trans. Eric Blom (New York: W. W. Norton & Co., 1949).

———, ed. *Schubert. Die Erinnerungen seiner Freunde* (Wiesbaden: Breitkopf & Härtel, 1957, repr. 1983).

———. *Schubert: Memoirs by his Friends*, trans. Rosamund Ley and John Nowell (London: Adam and Charles Black, 1958).

———. *Schubert: Die Dokumente seines Lebens* (Kassel: Bärenreiter Verlag, 1964, reprinted 1980 and 1996).

Donington, Robert. *Opera and its Symbols: The Unity of Words, Music and Staging* (New Haven and London: Yale University Press, 1990).

Dunsby, Jonathan. 'Adorno's Image of Schubert's "Wanderer" Fantasy Multiplied by Ten', *19th-Century Music* 29/1 (2005), pp. 209–36.

Dürr, Walter, Arnold Feil, Christa Landon et al., eds. *Franz Schubert: Neue Ausgabe sämtlicher Werke [NSA]* (Kassel: Bärenreiter, 1964–).

———. *Franz Schubert: Thematisches Verzeichnis seiner Werke in chronologischer Folge von Otto Erich Deutsch*, *NSA*, VIII/4 (Kassel: Bärenreiter, 1978).

Einstein, Alfred. *Schubert*, trans. David Ascoli (London: Panther Books, 1971 [1951]).

Erickson, Raymond, ed. *Schubert's Vienna* (New Haven: Yale University Press, 1997).

Feurzeig, Lisa, *Schubert's Lieder and the Philosophy of Early German Romanticism* (Farnham: Ashgate, 2014).

Fieldman, Hali. 'Schubert's Quartettsatz and Sonata Form's New Way', *Journal of Musicological Research* 12/1–2 (2002), pp. 99–146.

Fisk, Charles. 'Schubert Recollects Himself: The Piano Sonata in C Minor, D. 958', *Musical Quarterly* 84/4 (2000), pp. 635–54.

———. *Returning Cycles: Contexts for the Interpretation of Schubert's Impromptus and Last Sonatas* (Berkeley: University of California Press, 2001).

Frisch, Walter, ed. *Schubert: Critical and Analytical Studies* (Lincoln, NE: University of Nebraska Press, 1986).

————. "'You Must Remember This": Memory and Structure in Schubert's String Quartet in G Major, D. 887', *Musical Quarterly* 84/4 (2000), pp. 582–603.

Gibbs, Christopher H. "'Komm geh mit mir": Schubert's Uncanny "Erlkönig"', *19th-Century Music* 19/2 (1995), pp. 115–35.

————, ed. *The Cambridge Companion to Schubert* (Cambridge: Cambridge University Press, 1997).

Gibbs, Christopher H. and Morten Solvik, eds. *Franz Schubert and His World* (Princeton: Princeton University Press 2014).

Gingerich, John. "'To How Many Shameful Deeds must you Lend your Image": Schubert's Pattern of Telescoping and Excision in the Texts of His Latin Masses', *Current Musicology* 70 (2000), pp. 61–99.

————. 'Remembrance and Consciousness in Schubert's C-Major String Quintet, D. 956', *Musical Quarterly* 84/4 (2000), pp. 619–34.

————. "'Those of us who Found our Life in Art": The Second-Generation Romanticism of the Schubert-Schober Circle, 1820–25', in *Franz Schubert and his World*, ed. Christopher H. Gibbs and Morten Solvik (Princeton: Princeton University Press 2014), pp. 67–114.

————. *Schubert's Beethoven Project* (Cambridge: Cambridge University Press, 2014).

Gramit, David. *The Intellectual and Aesthetic Tenets of Franz Schubert's Circle* (PhD dissertation, Duke University, 1987).

————. "'The Passion for Friendship": Music, Cultivation, and Identity in Schubert's Circle', in *The Cambridge Companion to Schubert*, ed. Christopher H. Gibbs (Cambridge: Cambridge University Press, 1997), pp. 56–71.

Greimas, A. J. *Structural Semantics: An Attempt at a Method*, trans. Daniele McDowell, Ronald Schleifer, and Alan Velie (Lincoln, NE: University of Nebraska Press, 1983; French original 1966).

Gülke, Peter. 'In what Respect a Quintet? On the Disposition of Instruments in the String Quintet D 956', in *Schubert Studies: Problems of Style and Chronology*, ed. Eva Badura-Skoda and Peter Branscombe (Cambridge: Cambridge University Press, 1982), pp. 173–85.

————. *Schubert und seine Zeit* (Laaber: Laaber-Verlag, 1991).

Hallmark, Rufus. 'The Literary and Musical Rhetoric of Apostrophe in *Winterreise*', *19th-Century Music* 35/1 (2011), pp. 3–33.

Hascher, Xavier, ed. *Cahiers Franz Schubert: Revue de musique classique et romantique* 1–17 (1992–2009).

————. *Schubert, la forme sonate et son évolution* (Bern: Peter Lang, 1996).

————. 'Eine "traumhafte" *barcarola funebre*: Fragmente zu einer Deutung des langsamen Satzes des Streichquintetts D 956', in *Schubert und das Biedermeier, Beiträge zur Musik des frühen 19. Jahrhunderts* (*Festschrift für Walther Dürr zum 70. Geburtstag*), ed. Michael Kube (Kassel: Bärenreiter, 2002), pp. 127–38.

————, ed. *Le style instrumental de Schubert: Sources, analyse, évolution* (Paris: Publications de la Sorbonne, 2007).

————. "'In dunklen Traümen": Schubert's Heine-Lieder through the Psycho-analytical Prism', *Nineteenth-Century Music Review* 5/2 (2008), pp. 43–70.

Hatten, Robert S. *Interpreting Musical Gestures, Topics, and Tropes: Mozart, Beethoven, and Schubert* (Bloomington: Indiana University Press, 2004).

———. 'A Surfeit of Musics: What Goethe's Lyrics Concede When Set to Schubert's Music', *Nineteenth-Century Music Review* 5/2 (2008), pp. 7–18.

———. 'Reflections Inspired by a Response': *Nineteenth-Century Music Review* 13/2 (2016), pp. 35–8.

Hepokoski, James and Warren Darcy, *Elements of Sonata Theory: Norms, Types, and Deformations in the Late-Eighteenth-Century Sonata* (New York and Oxford: Oxford University Press, 2006).

Hilmar, Ernst. *Franz Schubert in seiner Zeit* (Vienna: Hermann Böhlaus Nachfolger, 1985), trans. Reinhard G. Pauly as *Franz Schubert in his Time* (Portland: Amadeus Press, 1988).

Hilmar, Ernst and Margaret Jestremski, eds. *Schubert Lexikon* (Graz: Akademische Druck- und Verlagsanstalt, 1997).

Hinrichsen, Hans-Joachim. *Untersuchungen zur Entwicklung der Sonatenform in der Instrumentalmusik Franz Schuberts* (Tutzing: Hans Schneider, 1994).

Hirsch, Marjorie Wing. *Schubert's Dramatic Lieder* (Cambridge: Cambridge University Press, 1993).

———. *Romantic Lieder and the Search for Lost Paradise* (Cambridge: Cambridge University Press, 2007).

Howe, Blake. 'The Allure of Dissolution: Bodies, Forces, and Cyclicity in Schubert's Final Mayrhofer Settings', *Journal of the American Musicological Society* 62/2 (2009), pp. 271–322.

———. 'Bounded Finitude and Boundless Infinitude: Schubert's Contradictions at the "Final Barrier"', in *Schubert's Late Music: History, Theory, Style,* ed. Lorraine Byrne Bodley and Julian Horton (Cambridge: Cambridge University Press, 2016), pp. 357–82.

Hunter, Mary. *The Culture of Opera Buffa in Mozart's Vienna: A Poetics of Entertainment* (Princeton: Princeton University Press, 1999).

Hunter, Mary and James Webster, eds. *Opera Buffa in Mozart's Vienna* (Cambridge: Cambridge University Press, 1997).

Huron, David. *Sweet Anticipation: Music and the Psychology of Expectation* (Cambridge, MA: MIT Press, 2006).

Hyland, Anne M. 'The "Tightened Bow": Analysing the Juxtaposition of Drama and Lyricism in Schubert's Paratactic Sonata-Form Movements', in *Irish Musical Studies, Vol. 11: Irish Musical Analysis*, ed. Gareth Cox and Julian Horton (Dublin: Four Courts Press, 2014), pp. 17–40.

———. 'In Search of Liberated Time, or Schubert's Quartet in G Major, D. 887: Once More Between Sonata and Variation', *Music Theory Spectrum* 38/1 (2016), pp. 85–108.

———. 'In What Respect Monumental? Schubert's *Quartettsatz* and the Dialectics of Private and Public', in *The String Quartet from the Private to the Public Sphere,* ed. Christian Speck (Turnhout: Brepols, 2016).

Johnson, Graham. *Franz Schubert: The Complete Songs*, 3 vols (New Haven and London: Yale University Press, 2014).

Jones, David Wyn. *Music in Vienna: 1700, 1800, 1900* (Woodbridge: Boydell Press, 2016).

Kerman, Joseph. *Opera as Drama*, new and revised edn (Berkeley and Los Angeles: University of California Press, 1988).

Kinderman, William. 'Schubert's Tragic Perspective', in *Schubert: Critical and Analytical Studies*, ed. Walter Frisch (Lincoln, NE: University of Nebraska Press, 1986), pp. 65–83.

———. 'Wandering Archetypes in Schubert's Instrumental Music', *19th-Century Music* 21/2 (1997), pp. 208–22.

———. 'Schubert's Piano Music: Probing the Human Condition', in *The Cambridge Companion to Schubert*, ed. Christopher H. Gibbs (Cambridge: Cambridge University Press, 1997), pp. 155–73.

Kramer, Lawrence. *Music as Cultural Practice, 1800–1900* (Berkeley: University of California Press, 1990).

———. *Franz Schubert: Sexuality, Subjectivity, Song* (Cambridge: Cambridge University Press, 1998).

Kramer, Richard. *Distant Cycles: Schubert and the Conceiving of Song* (Chicago: University of Chicago Press, 1994).

———. 'Against the Grain: The Sonata in G (D. 894) and a Hermeneutics of Late Style', in *Schubert's Late Music: History, Theory, Style*, ed. Lorraine Byrne Bodley and Julian Horton (Cambridge: Cambridge University Press, 2016), pp. 111–33.

Krause, Andreas. *Die Klaviersonaten Franz Schuberts: Form, Gattung, Ästhetik* (Kassel: Bärenreiter, 1992).

Kurth, Richard. 'On the Subject of Schubert's "Unfinished" Symphony: *Was bedeutet die Bewegung?*', *19th-Century Music* 23/1 (1999), pp. 3–32.

Leppert, Richard. 'On Reading Adorno Hearing Schubert', *19th-Century Music* 29/1 (2005), pp. 56–63.

Macdonald, Hugh. 'Schubert's Volcanic Temper', *The Musical Times* 119 (1978), pp. 949–52.

Mak, Su Yin. 'Schubert's Sonata Forms and the Poetics of the Lyric', *Journal of Musicology* 23/2 (2006), pp. 263–306.

———. 'Schubert as Schiller's Sentimental Poet', *Eighteenth-Century Music* 4/2 (2007), pp. 251–63.

———. 'Et in Arcadia Ego: The Elegiac Structure of Schubert's *Quartettsatz* in C Minor (D. 703)', in *The Unknown Schubert*, ed. Barbara Reul and Lorraine Byrne Bodley (Aldershot: Ashgate, 2008), pp. 145–53.

———. *Schubert's Lyricism Reconsidered: Structure, Design and Rhetoric* (Saarbrücken: Lambert, 2010).

Marston, Nicholas. 'Schubert's Homecoming', *Journal of the Royal Musical Association* 125/2 (2000), pp. 248–70.

Martin, Christine. 'Die Particell-Entwürfe zu Schuberts Fierabras und ihre Bedeutung für den Kompositionsprozess der Oper', *Schubert-Perspektiven* 8/1 (2008), pp. 1–16.

McClary, Susan. 'Constructions of Subjectivity in Schubert's Music', in *Queering the Pitch: The New Gay and Lesbian Musicology*, ed. Philip Brett, Gary Thomas, and Elizabeth Wood (New York and London: Routledge, 1994), pp. 205–33.

———. 'The Impromptu that Trod on a Loaf: Or How Music Tells Stories', *Narrative* 5/1 (1997), pp. 20–35.

McClelland, Clive. 'Death and the Composer: The Context of Schubert's Supernatural Lieder', in *Schubert the Progressive: History, Performance Practice, Analysis*, ed. Brian Newbould (Aldershot: Ashgate, 2003), pp. 21–35.

———. *Ombra: Supernatural Music in the Eighteenth Century* (Lanham, MD: Lexington Books, 2012).

———. *Tempesta: Stormy Music in the Eighteenth Century* (Lanham, MD: Lexington Books, 2017).

McKay, Elizabeth N. *Franz Schubert's Music for the Theatre* (Vienna: Hans Schneider, 1991).

———. *Franz Schubert: A Biography* (Oxford: Oxford University Press, 1996).

Messing, Scott. *Schubert in the European Imagination*, 2 vols (Woodbridge: Boydell Press, 2006, 2007).

Mirka, Danuta. *The Oxford Handbook of Topic Theory* (New York: Oxford University Press, 2014).

Muxfeldt, Kristina. 'Schubert's Songs: The Transformation of a Genre', in *The Cambridge Companion to Schubert*, ed. Christopher H. Gibbs (Cambridge: Cambridge University Press, 1997), pp. 121–37.

———. *Vanishing Sensibilities: Schubert, Beethoven, Schumann* (New York: Oxford University Press, 2011).

Newbould, Brian. *Schubert* (Berkeley and Los Angeles: University of California Press, 1997).

———, ed. *Schubert the Progressive: History, Performance Practice, Analysis* (Aldershot: Ashgate, 2003).

Perry, Beate. 'Exposed: Adorno and Schubert in 1928', *19th-Century Music* 29/1 (2005), pp. 15–24.

Perry, Jeffrey. 'The Wanderer's Many Returns: Schubert's Variations Reconsidered', *Journal of Musicology* 19/2 (2002), pp. 374–416.

Reed, John. *The Schubert Song Companion* (Manchester: Manchester University Press, 1985).

Reul, Barbara M. and Lorraine Byrne Bodley, eds. *The Unknown Schubert* (Aldershot: Ashgate, 2008).

Reynolds, Christopher A. *Motives for Allusion: Context and Content in Nineteenth-Century Music* (Cambridge, MA: Harvard University Press, 2003).

Samuels, Robert. 'Schubert's Instrumental Voice: Vocality in Melodic Construction in the Late Works', in *On Voice* [Word and Music Studies, vol. 13], ed. Walter Bernhart and Lawrence Kramer (Amsterdam: Rodopi, 2014), pp. 161–78.

Schmalfeldt, Janet. *In the Process of Becoming: Analytical and Philosophical Perspectives on Form in Early Nineteenth-Century Music* (Oxford: Oxford University Press, 2011).

Sly, Gordon, ed. *Keys to the Drama: Nine Perspectives on Sonata Forms* (Farnham and Burlington, VT: Ashgate, 2009).

Sobaskie, James William. 'Tonal Implication and the Gestural Dialectic in Schubert's A Minor String Quartet', in *Schubert the Progressive: History, Performance Practice, Analysis*, ed. Brian Newbould (Aldershot: Ashgate, 2003), pp. 53–79.

————. 'The "Problem" of Schubert's String Quintet', *Nineteenth-Century Music Review* 2/1 (2005), pp. 57–92.

————. 'A Balance Struck: Gesture, Form, and Drama in Schubert's E flat Major Piano Trio', in *Le style instrumental de Schubert: sources, analyse, évolution*, ed. Xavier Hascher (Paris: Publications de la Sorbonne, 2007), pp. 115–46.

————. 'Precursive Prolongation in the *Préludes* of Chopin', *Journal of the Society for Musicology in Ireland* 3 (2007–2008), pp. 25–61.

————. 'Schubert's Self-Elegies', *Nineteenth-Century Music Review* 5/2 (2008), pp. 71–105.

————. 'Conversations Within and Between Two Early Lieder of Schubert', *Nineteenth-Century Music Review* 13/1 (2016), pp. 83–102.

————. 'Contextual Processes in Schubert's Late Sacred Choral Music', in *Rethinking Schubert,* ed. Lorraine Byrne Bodley and Julian Horton (Oxford: Oxford University Press, 2016), pp. 295–332.

Solomon, Maynard. 'Franz Schubert and the Peacocks of Benvenuto Cellini', *19th-Century Music* 13/3 (1989), pp. 193–206.

Stanley, Glenn. 'Schubert's Religious and Choral Music: Toward a Statement of Faith', in *The Cambridge Companion to Schubert*, ed. Christopher H. Gibbs (Cambridge: Cambridge University Press, 1997), pp. 207–23.

Steblin, Rita. *Die Unsinnsgesellschaft: Franz Schubert, Leopold Kupelwieser und ihr Freundeskreis* (Vienna: Böhlau, 1998).

Sumner-Lott, Marie. *The Social Worlds of Nineteenth-Century Chamber Music: Composers, Consumers, Communities* (Urbana, Chicago, and Springfield: University of Illinois Press, 2015).

Suurpää, Lauri. 'The Path from Tonic to Dominant in the Second Movement of Schubert's String Quintet and in Chopin's Fourth Ballade', *Journal of Music Theory* 44/2 (2000), pp. 451–85.

————. *Death in Winterreise: Musico-Poetic Associations in Schubert's Song Cycle* (Bloomington: Indiana University Press, 2014).

Taylor, Benedict. 'Schubert and the Construction of Memory: The String Quartet in A Minor, D. 804 ("Rosamunde")', *Journal of the Royal Musical Association* 139/1 (2014), pp. 41–88.

Thomas, Walter. 'Bild und Aktion in *Fierabras*. Ein Beitrag zu Schuberts musikalischer Dramaturgie', in *Franz Schubert. Jahre der Krise 1818–1823. Arnold Feil zum 60. Geburtstag am 2. Oktober 1985*, ed. Werner Aderhold et al. (Kassel: Bärenreiter Verlag, 1985), pp. 85–112.

Till, Nicholas, 'Introduction: Opera Studies Today', in *The Cambridge Companion to Opera*, ed. Nicholas Till (Cambridge: Cambridge University Press, 2012), pp. 1–22.

Tunbridge, Laura. *Schumann's Late Style* (Cambridge: Cambridge University Press, 2007).

————. 'Saving Schubert: The Evasions of Late Style', in *Late Style and its Discontent: Essays in Art, Literature, and Music*, ed. Gordon McMullan and Sam Smiles (New York: Oxford University Press, 2016), pp. 120–30.

Waidelich, Till G. *Franz Schubert: Alfonso und Estrella. Eine frühe durchkomponierte deutsche Oper. Geschichte und Analyse* (Tutzing: Schneider, 1991).

Webster, James. 'Schubert's Sonata Form and Brahms's First Maturity, Part I', *19th-Century Music* 2 (1978), pp. 18–35.

Wen, Eric. 'Schubert's *Wiegenlied*: The Andante Sostenuto from the Piano Sonata in B flat, D. 960', in *Schubert's Late Style: History, Theory, Style*, ed. Lorraine Byrne Bodley and Julian Horton (Cambridge: Cambridge University Press, 2016), pp. 134–48.

Whitton, Kenneth S. *Goethe and Schubert: The Unseen Bond* (Portland: Amadeus Press, 1999).

Winter, Robert. 'Paper Studies and the Future of Schubert Research', in *Schubert Studies: Problems of Style and Chronology*, ed. Eva Badura-Skoda and Peter Branscombe (Cambridge: Cambridge University Press, 1982), pp. 209–76.

Wollenberg, Susan. 'Schubert and the Dream', *Studi musicali* 9 (1980), pp. 135–50.

————. 'Schubert's Transitions', in *Schubert Studies*, ed. Brian Newbould (Aldershot: Ashgate, 1998), pp. 16–61.

————. 'The C major String Quintet D 956: Schubert's "Dissonance" Quintet?', *Schubert durch die Brille* 28 (2002), pp. 45–55.

————. '"Dort, wo du nicht bist, dort ist das Glück": Reflections on Schubert's Second Themes', *Schubert durch die Brille* 30 (2003), pp. 91–100.

————. 'Schubert's Poetic Transitions', in *Le style instrumental de Schubert: Sources, analyse, évolution*, ed. Xavier Hascher (Paris: Publications de la Sorbonne, 2007), pp. 261–77.

————. *Schubert's Fingerprints: Studies in the Instrumental Works* (Farnham: Ashgate: 2011).

————. 'From Song to Instrumental Style: Some Schubert Fingerprints', in *Rethinking Schubert*, ed. Lorraine Byrne Bodley and Julian Horton (New York: Oxford University Press, 2016), pp. 61–76.

Youens, Susan. *Retracing a Winter's Journey: Schubert's Winterreise* (Ithaca, NY: Cornell University Press, 1991).

———. *Franz Schubert: Die schöne Müllerin* (Cambridge University Press, 1992).

———. *Schubert's Poets and the Making of Lieder* (Cambridge: Cambridge University Press, 1996).

———. *Schubert, Müller, and Die schöne Müllerin* (Cambridge: Cambridge University Press, 1997).

———. 'Schubert and his Poets: Issues and Conundrums', in *The Cambridge Companion to Schubert*, ed. Christopher H. Gibbs (Cambridge: Cambridge University Press, 1997), pp. 99–117.

———. *Schubert's Late Lieder: Beyond the Song Cycles* (Cambridge: Cambridge University Press, 2002).

———. *Heinrich Heine and the Lied* (Cambridge: Cambridge University Press, 2007).

———. 'Swan Songs: Schubert's "Auf dem Wasser zu singen"', *Nineteenth-Century Music Review* 5/2 (2008), pp. 19–42.

Index

Printed in the United States
By Bookmasters